# Beginner's Guide to Half Marathons: 12 Week Training Workbook

by Scott Oscar Morton

ll rights reserved. This book or parts thereof may not be reproduced in any form, stored in any retrieval system, or transmitted in any form by any means—electronic, mechanical, photocopy, recording, or otherwise—without the prior written consent of the publisher, except as provided by United States of America copyright law. For reproduction rights, write to the publisher, at "Attention: Reproduction Rights," at the address below.

© 2017 by LERK Publishing, LLC. All rights reserved.

LERK Publishing, LLC

Edited by Krystal Boots

Cover by LERK Publishing, LLC

ISBN **978-1-947010-34-5**

**Follow me on Facebook and Twitter:**

Twitter: @BeginR2FinishR

Facebook: facebook.com/BeginnerToFinisher/

Website: www.halfmarathonforbeginners.com

Email: scottmorton@halfmarathonforbeginners.com

To my kids Luke, Ella, and Ryker.

## Medical Disclaimer

The information in this book is meant to supplement, not replace, proper half marathon training. A sport involving speed, equipment, balance and environmental factors, and running, will involve some inherent risk. The authors and publisher advise readers to take full responsibility for their safety and know their limits. Before practicing the skills described in this book, be sure that your equipment is well maintained, and do not take risks beyond your level of experience, aptitude, training, and comfort level.

# *Other Books by Scott O. Morton*

## **Beginner to Finisher Series:**

**Book 1:** *Why New Runners Fail: 26 Ultimate Tips You Should Know Before You Start Running!*

**Book 2**: *5K Fury: 10 Proven Steps to Get You to the Finish Line in 9 weeks or less!*

**Book 3:** *10K Titan: Push Beyond the 5K in 6 Weeks or Less!*

**Book 4:** *Beginner's Guide to Half Marathons: A Simple Step-By-Step Solution to Get You to the Finish Line in 12 Weeks!*

**Book 5:** *Long Run Hacks: 20 Ultimate Tips to Help You Push Through Hard Runs!*

**Book 6:** *How to Avoid a Half Marathon Meltdown: 10 Things You Need to Know to Make Sure Your First Half Marathon Isn't Your Last!*

**Book 7:** *Marathon Machine - Breakthrough Your Running Barrier in 18 weeks and Conquer Your Dream! (COMING SOON)*

## **Supercharge Your Walking Life:**

**Book 1:** *42,000 Steps: 100 simple ways to maximize your daily step count!*

**Book 2:** *Supercharged Walking: 20 Simple Methods to Help You Level Up Your Stride!*

**Book 3:** *Walkathon - The Ultimate Guide to Walking a 5K, 10K, Half Marathon, or Marathon!*

## Why I Wrote This Book

I wrote this book for anyone with a burning desire to take their running distance to the next level. I truly want everyone that reads this book to complete a half marathon. If I can help at least one person achieve this goal, then all the time put into this book will be worthwhile.

This book is designed for anyone with a desire to complete a half marathon. If you follow the steps outlined in this book, you will achieve this goal. This book is not intended to be a guide for the experienced runner. Increasing your speed and decreasing your finish times are not covered in this book. Tons of other books and websites cover beating your personal best records and reducing your overall 5k, 10k, half marathon, and marathon run times.

Reasons for running:
- Most races are linked to some worthwhile cause.
- A terrific way to get in shape.
- Great way to feel a sense of accomplishment.

## *Safety*

My goal is for each runner to safely finish a half marathon. Do not attempt to skip the long run sessions, unless you are a seasoned runner or you plan on walking, not running, the half marathon. If you decide to walk the half marathon, make sure that you are in good enough shape to skip the long runs. If you get to race day and you haven't been training according to some long duration training schedule, you could injure your legs, knees, or feet. Running is an impact sport, and your body must get used to running long duration distances. Your legs must be built up to maintain your stamina for the duration of your half marathon race. Building stamina is the sole purpose of having a training cycle that lasts 12 weeks. For marathons, the minimum suggested training cycle is 18 weeks if you have never run a marathon before.

# Table of Contents

Training Pace Examples……………………………………………………………………...1
The Optional Races………………………………………………………………………..2
5K Finish Time = 20 minutes……………………………………………………………..3
5K Finish Time = 21 minutes……………………………………………………………...17
5K Finish Time = 22 minutes……………………………………………………………...31
5K Finish Time = 23 minutes……………………………………………………………...45
5K Finish Time = 24 minutes……………………………………………………………...59
5K Finish Time = 25 minutes……………………………………………………………...73
5K Finish Time = 26 minutes……………………………………………………………...87
5K Finish Time = 27 minutes……………………………………………………………..101
5K Finish Time = 28 minutes……………………………………………………………..115
5K Finish Time = 29 minutes……………………………………………………………..129
5K Finish Time = 30 minutes……………………………………………………………..143
5K Finish Time = 31 minutes……………………………………………………………..157
5K Finish Time = 32 minutes……………………………………………………………..171
5K Finish Time = 33 minutes……………………………………………………………..185
5K Finish Time = 34 minutes……………………………………………………………..199
5K Finish Time = 35 minutes……………………………………………………………..213
5K Finish Time = 36 minutes……………………………………………………………..227
5K Finish Time = 37 minutes……………………………………………………………..241
5K Finish Time = 38 minutes……………………………………………………………..255
5K Finish Time = 39 minutes……………………………………………………………..269
5K Finish Time = 40 minutes……………………………………………………………..283
5K Finish Time = 41 minutes……………………………………………………………..297
5K Finish Time = 42 minutes……………………………………………………………..311
5K Finish Time = 43 minutes……………………………………………………………..325
5K Finish Time = 44 minutes……………………………………………………………..339
5K Finish Time = 45 minutes……………………………………………………………..353
5K Finish Time = 46 minutes……………………………………………………………..367
5K Finish Time = 47 minutes……………………………………………………………..381
5K Finish Time = 48 minutes……………………………………………………………..395
5K Finish Time = 49 minutes……………………………………………………………..409
5K Finish Time = 50 minutes……………………………………………………………..423
5K Finish Time = 51 minutes……………………………………………………………..437
5K Finish Time = 52 minutes……………………………………………………………..451
5K Finish Time = 53 minutes……………………………………………………………..465
Training Logs……………………………………………………………………………..479
Training Schedules………………………………………………………………………..484

# Training Pace Examples

Described below are the different paces outlined in the following training schedules that will give you a pace to shoot for during your training runs.

In the first example below, let's assume your 5k overall runtime is at 33:00 minutes which is a pace of 11:00 minutes/mile:

    11:33 predicted half marathon pace
  2:31:00 predicted half marathon overall finish time

Training Paces will be:

| Slow Pace (Long Run) | 11:33 - 14:03 | 0 to 2 minutes 30 seconds slower than Half marathon pace |
|---|---|---|
| Easy Pace | 11:33 – 13:33 | 1 to 2 minutes slower than half marathon pace |
| Medium Pace | 11:33 - 12:33 | 0 to 1 minute slower than half marathon pace |
| Half marathon pace | 11:33 | |

In the second example below, let's assume your 5k overall runtime is at 30:00 minutes which is a pace of 10:00 minutes/mile:

    10:30 predicted half marathon pace
  2:18:00 predicted half marathon overall finish time

## All runs do the following:

- Get plenty of sleep the night before your long duration run.
- Try to run your long duration run early in the morning.
- After each of your runs, it's important to stretch out your muscles.

## If your walking:

Try to maintain a pace no slower than 20 minutes/mile.

## Day Before Long Runs:

Do as little activity as possible. Fridays are important rest days. For your muscles to grow stronger, they need rest. Do not drink alcohol the day before your long run.

## The Long Run:
Do not attempt to run these at your half marathon predicted pace. Run at a slower pace than your easy pace. This is somewhere between x and x.

# The optional races: 5K, 10K, Beta 13.1

These are all optional races. If the race doesn't fall on the weekend the training schedules, then simply readjust your schedule accordingly. The only thing I suggest is don't swap out a 5K race for an 11-mile (18 km) race. The most important part of your half marathon training is your long runs. Every other race that is optional is secondary in priority.

## PLEASE READ - IMPORTANT

If you're a brand new runner and you're attempting to run a half marathon please start with Week A, B, and C.

Runners starting at Week 1 should be able to complete the distance of a 5K (3.1 miles) by either walking or running. If you can complete this distance then skip over Week A, B, and C and start with Week 1.

## PLEASE READ – IF YOU ARE STILL HAVING PROBLEMS WITH WEEK A, B, AND C.

If week A, B, and C are still giving you trouble you need to take a few steps back and work on completing the distance of a 5K (3.1 miles). I have written two books that will help new runners jump start their running career at the absolute beginner level:

*Why New Runners Fail: 26 Ultimate Tips You Should Know Before You Start Running!*

*5K Fury: 10 Proven Steps to Get You to the Finish Line in 9 weeks or less!*

CLICK HERE TO BUY THESE BOOKS

Half Marathon Training Schedule for

runners with a 5K finish time of 20 minutes

and a pace of *6:30* minutes/mile.

# Predicted Half Marathon Finish Time:

## *1* hour(s) *35* minutes

# PACING TABLES

| Pace | Pace (minutes/miles) |
|---:|---|
| 5k | 6:30 |
| Half marathon | 7:15 |
| Medium | Between 7:15 - 8:15 |
| Easy | Between 7:15 - 9:15 |
| Slow | Between 7:15 - 9:45 |

| Race | Finish Times (predicted) |
|---:|---|
| 5k | 20 minutes |
| Half marathon | 1 hour(s) 35 minutes |

| \ | Determining your pace |
|---|---|
| Slow Pace | Extremely easy to hold a conversation. |
| Easy Pace | You can hold a conversation with someone. Your breathing might break up some of the flow of the conversation. |
| Medium | You can hold a conversation with someone, but it's broken up into smaller sentences and smaller responses. |
| Half Marathon Pace | Conversation is difficult. One and two word responses back and forth at best. |

## Definitions in the table below:

CT = Cross Training

S = Slow Pace (long run pace)

E = Easy Pace

M = Medium Pace

HM = Half Marathon Pace

# Training - Week A (Optional)

5K Pace: **6:30**  5k Finish Time: **20 minutes**

| Day | Dist. Mile | Dist. KM | Difficulty | Pace (Range) | Instructions |
|---|---|---|---|---|---|
| Monday | Rest | Rest | Rest | Rest | Take it easy. Don't run. If you need to exercise, I recommend a walk for no longer than 30 minutes. |
| Tuesday | 1 | 1.5 | E | 7:15 - 9:15 | walk/run at an easy pace. |
| Wednesday | 1 | 1.5 | HM | 7:15 | walk/run at your half marathon pace. |
| Thursday | 1 | 1.5 | M | 7:15 - 8:15 | walk/run at a medium pace. |
| Friday | Rest | Rest | Rest | Rest | Rest. |
| Saturday | 1.5 | 2.5 | S | 7:15 - 9:45 | walk/run at a slow pace. The most important piece of your long duration runs is finishing the run. |
| Sunday | Rest/CT | Rest/CT | Rest | Rest | Rest. If your body feels good, then go ahead and do some form of cross-training for 30 to 60 minutes. |

# Training - Week B (Optional)

| Day | Dist. Mile | Dist. KM | Difficulty | Pace (Range) | Instructions |
|---|---|---|---|---|---|
| Monday | Rest | Rest | Rest | Rest | Take it easy. Don't run. If you need to exercise, I recommend a walk for no longer than 30 minutes. |
| Tuesday | 1.5 | 2.5 | E | 7:15 - 9:15 | walk/run at an easy pace. |
| Wednesday | 1.5 | 2.5 | HM | 7:15 | walk/run at your half marathon pace. |
| Thursday | 1.5 | 2.5 | M | 7:15 - 8:15 | walk/run at a medium pace. |
| Friday | Rest | Rest | Rest | Rest | Rest. |
| Saturday | 2 | 3 | S | 7:15 - 9:45 | walk/run at a slow pace. The most important piece of your long duration runs is finishing the run. |
| Sunday | Rest/CT | Rest/CT | Rest | Rest | Rest. If your body feels good, then go ahead and do some form of cross-training for 30 to 60 minutes. |

# Training - Week C (Optional)

5K Pace: **6:30**  5k Finish Time: **20 minutes**

| Day | Dist. Mile | Dist. KM | Difficulty | Pace (Range) | Instructions |
|---|---|---|---|---|---|
| Monday | Rest | Rest | Rest | Rest | Take it easy. Don't run. If you need to exercise, I recommend a walk for no longer than 30 minutes. |
| Tuesday | 2 | 3 | E | 7:15 - 9:15 | walk/run at an easy pace. |
| Wednesday | 2 | 3 | HM | 7:15 | walk/run at your half marathon pace. |
| Thursday | 2 | 3 | M | 7:15 - 8:15 | walk/run at a medium pace. |
| Friday | Rest | Rest | Rest | Rest | Rest. |
| Saturday | 3 | 5 | S | 7:15 - 9:45 | walk/run at a slow pace. The most important piece of your long duration runs is finishing the run. |
| Sunday | Rest/CT | Rest/CT | Rest | Rest | Rest. If your body feels good, then go ahead and do some form of cross-training for 30 to 60 minutes. |

# Training - Week 1

5K Pace: **6:30**     5k Finish Time: **20 minutes**

| Day | Dist. Mile | Dist. KM | Difficulty | Pace (Range) | Instructions |
|---|---|---|---|---|---|
| Monday | Rest | Rest | Rest | Rest | Take it easy. Don't run. If you need to exercise, I recommend a walk for no longer than 30 minutes. |
| Tuesday | 3 | 5 | E | 7:15 - 9:15 | walk/run at an easy pace. |
| Wednesday | 3 | 5 | HM | 7:15 | walk/run at your half marathon pace. |
| Thursday | 3 | 5 | M | 7:15 - 8:15 | walk/run at a medium pace. |
| Friday | Rest | Rest | Rest | Rest | Rest. |
| Saturday | 4 | 6 | S | 7:15 - 9:45 | walk/run at a slow pace. The most important piece of your long duration runs is finishing the run. |
| Sunday | Rest/CT | Rest/CT | Rest | Rest | Rest. If your body feels good, then go ahead and do some form of cross-training for 30 to 60 minutes. |

# Training - Week 2

| Day | Dist. Mile | Dist. KM | Difficulty | Pace (Range) | Instructions |
|---|---|---|---|---|---|
| Monday | Rest | Rest | Rest | Rest | Take it easy. Don't run. If you need to exercise, I recommend a walk for no longer than 30 minutes. |
| Tuesday | 3 | 5 | E | 7:15 - 9:15 | walk/run at an easy pace. |
| Wednesday | 3 | 5 | HM | 7:15 | walk/run at your half marathon pace. |
| Thursday | 3 | 5 | M | 7:15 - 8:15 | walk/run at a medium pace. |
| Friday | Rest | Rest | Rest | Rest | Rest. |
| Saturday | 5 | 8 | S | 7:15 - 9:45 | walk/run at a slow pace. The most important piece of your long duration runs is finishing the run. |
| Sunday | Rest/CT | Rest/CT | Rest | Rest | Rest. If your body feels good, then go ahead and do some form of cross-training for 30 to 60 minutes. |

# Training - Week 3

5K Pace: **6:30**     5k Finish Time: **20 minutes**

| Day | Dist. Mile | Dist. KM | Difficulty | Pace (Range) | Instructions |
|---|---|---|---|---|---|
| Monday | Rest | Rest | Rest | Rest | Take it easy. Don't run. If you need to exercise, I recommend a walk for no longer than 30 minutes. |
| Tuesday | 3 | 5 | E | 7:15 - 9:15 | walk/run at an easy pace. |
| Wednesday | 4 | 6 | HM | 7:15 | walk/run at your half marathon pace. |
| Thursday | 3 | 5 | M | 7:15 - 8:15 | walk/run at a medium pace. |
| Friday | Rest | Rest | Rest | Rest | Rest. |
| Saturday | 6 | 10 | S | 7:15 - 9:45 | walk/run at a slow pace. The most important piece of your long duration runs is finishing the run. |
| Sunday | Rest/CT | Rest/CT | Rest | Rest | Rest. If your body feels good, then go ahead and do some form of cross-training for 30 to 60 minutes. |

# Training - Week 4 (5K Optional)

5K Pace: **6:30**     5k Finish Time: **20 minutes**

| Day | Dist. Mile | Dist. KM | Difficulty | Pace (Range) | Instructions |
|---|---|---|---|---|---|
| Monday | Rest | Rest | Rest | Rest | Take it easy. Don't run. If you need to exercise, I recommend a walk for no longer than 30 minutes. |
| Tuesday | 3 | 5 | E | 7:15 - 9:15 | walk/run at an easy pace. |
| Wednesday | 4 | 6 | HM | 7:15 | walk/run at your half marathon pace. |
| Thursday | 3 | 5 | M | 7:15 - 8:15 | walk/run at a medium pace. |
| Friday | Rest | Rest | Rest | Rest | Rest. |
| Saturday | 6.5 | 10.5 | S | 7:15 - 9:45 | walk/run at a slow pace. The most important piece of your long duration runs is finishing the run. |
| Sunday | Rest/CT | Rest/CT | Rest | Rest | Rest. If your body feels good, then go ahead and do some form of cross-training for 30 to 60 minutes. |

## 5K Optional

| Day | Dist. Mile | Dist. KM | Difficulty | Pace (Range) | Instructions |
|---|---|---|---|---|---|
| Saturday | 3.1 | 5 | - | 6:30 | Run a 5k race instead of your long run. This is completely your choice. I recommend running a 5k race to help you get used to running races. You should see a difference in your race time if you have kept to your training schedule. Don't try for a personal best, run the 5K at your 5K pace. |

# Training - Week 5

5K Pace: **6:30**      5k Finish Time: **20 minutes**

| Day | Dist. Mile | Dist. KM | Difficulty | Pace (Range) | Instructions |
|---|---|---|---|---|---|
| Monday | Rest | Rest | Rest | Rest | Take it easy. Don't run. If you need to exercise, I recommend a walk for no longer than 30 minutes. |
| Tuesday | 3 | 5 | E | 7:15 - 9:15 | walk/run at an easy pace. |
| Wednesday | 4 | 6 | HM | 7:15 | walk/run at your half marathon pace. |
| Thursday | 3 | 5 | M | 7:15 - 8:15 | walk/run at a medium pace. |
| Friday | Rest | Rest | Rest | Rest | Rest. |
| Saturday | 7 | 11 | S | 7:15 - 9:45 | walk/run at a slow pace. The most important piece of your long duration runs is finishing the run. |
| Sunday | Rest/CT | Rest/CT | Rest | Rest | Rest. If your body feels good, then go ahead and do some form of cross-training for 30 to 60 minutes. |

## NOTE:

- Your long duration runs will begin to become more difficult for week 5 and beyond.
- If you get tired during a long duration run, walk for 1/10 mile or 3-5 minutes.

# Training - Week 6

5K Pace: **6:30**     5k Finish Time: **20 minutes**

| Day | Dist. Mile | Dist. KM | Difficulty | Pace (Range) | Instructions |
|---|---|---|---|---|---|
| Monday | Rest | Rest | Rest | Rest | Take it easy. Don't run. If you need to exercise, I recommend a walk for no longer than 30 minutes. |
| Tuesday | 3 | 5 | E | 7:15 - 9:15 | walk/run at an easy pace. |
| Wednesday | 4 | 6 | HM | 7:15 | walk/run at your half marathon pace. |
| Thursday | 3 | 5 | M | 7:15 - 8:15 | walk/run at a medium pace. |
| Friday | Rest | Rest | Rest | Rest | Rest. |
| Saturday | 8 | 13 | S | 7:15 - 9:45 | walk/run at a slow pace. The most important piece of your long duration runs is finishing the run. |
| Sunday | Rest/CT | Rest/CT | Rest | Rest | Rest. If your body feels good, then go ahead and do some form of cross-training for 30 to 60 minutes. |

# Training - Week 7

5K Pace: **6:30**     5k Finish Time: **20 minutes**

| Day | Dist. Mile | Dist. KM | Difficulty | Pace (Range) | Instructions |
|---|---|---|---|---|---|
| Monday | Rest | Rest | Rest | Rest | Take it easy. Don't run. If you need to exercise, I recommend a walk for no longer than 30 minutes. |
| Tuesday | 3 | 5 | E | 7:15 - 9:15 | walk/run at an easy pace. |
| Wednesday | 5 | 8 | HM | 7:15 | walk/run at your half marathon pace. |
| Thursday | 3 | 5 | M | 7:15 - 8:15 | walk/run at a medium pace. |
| Friday | Rest | Rest | Rest | Rest | Rest. |
| Saturday | 8.5 | 13.5 | S | 7:15 - 9:45 | walk/run at a slow pace. The most important piece of your long duration runs is finishing the run. |
| Sunday | Rest/CT | Rest/CT | Rest | Rest | Rest. If your body feels good, then go ahead and do some form of cross-training for 30 to 60 minutes. |

## 10K Optional

| Day | Dist. Mile | Dist. KM | Difficulty | Pace (Range) | Instructions |
|---|---|---|---|---|---|
| Thursday | 2 | 3 | E | 7:15 - 9:15 | If you run the optional 10K, either completely rest today or run 2 miles (3 km). |
| Saturday | 6.2 | 10K | - | 6:30 | Run a 10k race instead of your long run. This is completely your choice. I recommend running a 10k race to help you get used to running races. You should see a difference in your race time if you have kept to your training schedule. Don't try for a personal best, run the 10K at your 5K pace. |

# Training - Week 8

5K Pace: **6:30**     5k Finish Time: **20 minutes**

| Day | Dist. Mile | Dist. KM | Difficulty | Pace (Range) | Instructions |
|---|---|---|---|---|---|
| Monday | Rest | Rest | Rest | Rest | Take it easy. Don't run. If you need to exercise, I recommend a walk for no longer than 30 minutes. |
| Tuesday | 3 | 5 | E | 7:15 - 9:15 | walk/run at an easy pace. |
| Wednesday | 5 | 8 | HM | 7:15 | walk/run at your half marathon pace. |
| Thursday | 3 | 5 | M | 7:15 - 8:15 | walk/run at a medium pace. |
| Friday | Rest | Rest | Rest | Rest | Rest. |
| Saturday | 9 | 14 | S | 7:15 - 9:45 | walk/run at a slow pace. The most important piece of your long duration runs is finishing the run. |
| Sunday | Rest/CT | Rest/CT | Rest | Rest | Rest. If your body feels good, then go ahead and do some form of cross-training for 30 to 60 minutes. |

# Training - Week 9

5K Pace: **6:30**     5k Finish Time: **20 minutes**

| Day | Dist. Mile | Dist. KM | Difficulty | Pace (Range) | Instructions |
|---|---|---|---|---|---|
| Monday | Rest | Rest | Rest | Rest | Take it easy. Don't run. If you need to exercise, I recommend a walk for no longer than 30 minutes. |
| Tuesday | 3 | 5 | E | 7:15 - 9:15 | walk/run at an easy pace. |
| Wednesday | 5 | 8 | HM | 7:15 | walk/run at your half marathon pace. |
| Thursday | 3 | 5 | M | 7:15 - 8:15 | walk/run at a medium pace. |
| Friday | Rest | Rest | Rest | Rest | Rest. |
| Saturday | 8.5 | 13.5 | S | 7:15 - 9:45 | walk/run at a slow pace. The most important piece of your long duration runs is finishing the run. |
| Sunday | Rest/CT | Rest/CT | Rest | Rest | Rest. If your body feels good, then go ahead and do some form of cross-training for 30 to 60 minutes. |

## 13.1 Beta/Test Run Optional

| Day | Dist. Mile | Dist. KM | Difficulty | Pace (Range) | Instructions |
|---|---|---|---|---|---|
| Thursday | Rest | Rest | Rest | Rest | This is a rest day – it simulates race week |
| Friday | Rest | Rest | Rest | Rest | This is a rest day – it simulates race week |
| Saturday | 13.1 | 21 | S | 6:30 | I recommend that you attempt to go the full 13.1 miles (21 km) for a half marathon test run. <u>Only walk/run the first 10 miles (16 km) then walk the last 3.1 miles (5 km)</u>. If you are successful, you will have a race ghost time to compete against. It will help energize and refocus your training on beating yourself in 3 weeks at the half marathon race. Also, it allows your mind to grasp the achievement of "completing the distance of a half marathon." |

# Training - Week 10

5K Pace: **6:30**    5k Finish Time: **20 minutes**

| Day | Dist. Mile | Dist. KM | Difficulty | Pace (Range) | Instructions |
|---|---|---|---|---|---|
| Monday | Rest | Rest | Rest | Rest | Take it easy. Don't run. If you need to exercise, I recommend a walk for no longer than 30 minutes. |
| Tuesday | 3 | 5 | E | 7:15 - 9:15 | walk/run at an easy pace. |
| Wednesday | 5 | 8 | HM | 7:15 | walk/run at your half marathon pace. |
| Thursday | 3 | 5 | M | 7:15 - 8:15 | walk/run at a medium pace. |
| Friday | Rest | Rest | Rest | Rest | Rest. |
| Saturday | 11 | 18 | S | 7:15 - 9:45 | walk/run at a slow pace. The most important piece of your long duration runs is finishing the run. |
| Sunday | Rest/CT | Rest/CT | Rest | Rest | Rest. If your body feels good, then go ahead and do some form of cross-training for 30 to 60 minutes. |

# Training - Week 11

| Day | Dist. Mile | Dist. KM | Difficulty | Pace (Range) | Instructions |
|---|---|---|---|---|---|
| Monday | Rest | Rest | Rest | Rest | Take it easy. Don't run. If you need to exercise, I recommend a walk for no longer than 30 minutes. |
| Tuesday | 3 | 5 | E | 7:15 - 9:15 | walk/run at an easy pace. |
| Wednesday | 5 | 8 | HM | 7:15 | walk/run at your half marathon pace. |
| Thursday | 3 | 5 | M | 7:15 - 8:15 | walk/run at a medium pace. |
| Friday | Rest | Rest | Rest | Rest | Rest. |
| Saturday | 12 | 20 | S | 7:15 - 9:45 | walk/run at a slow pace. The most important piece of your long duration runs is finishing the run. |
| Sunday | Rest/CT | Rest/CT | Rest | Rest | Rest. If your body feels good, then go ahead and do some form of cross-training for 30 to 60 minutes. |

# Training - Week 12

5K Pace: **6:30**     5k Finish Time: **20 minutes**

| Day | Dist. Mile | Dist. KM | Difficulty | Pace (Range) | Instructions |
|---|---|---|---|---|---|
| Monday | Rest | Rest | Rest | Rest | Take it easy. Don't run. If you need to exercise, I recommend a walk for no longer than 30 minutes. |
| Tuesday | 3 | 5 | E | 7:15 - 9:15 | walk/run at an easy pace. |
| Wednesday | 2 | 1.5 | HM | 7:15 | walk/run at your half marathon pace. |
| Thursday | Rest | Rest | Rest | Rest | Rest. |
| Friday | Rest | Rest | Rest | Rest | Rest. |
| Saturday | 13.1 | 21 | HM | 7:15 | RACE DAY! |
| Sunday | Rest | Rest | Rest | Rest | DRINK A VICTORY BEER! |

## NOTE:

- Get plenty of sleep the night before your long duration run.
- Try to run your long duration run early in the morning.
- After each run, it's important to stretch out your muscles.
- This week your body needs as much rest as possible.
- Don't run past Wednesday.

# BEGINNER TO FINISHER RUNNING

Half Marathon Training Schedule for

<u>runners with a 5K finish time of 21 minutes</u>

and a pace of *6:50* minutes/mile.

## Predicted Half Marathon Finish Time:

<u>*1*</u> hour(s) <u>*40*</u> minutes

# PACING TABLES

| Pace | Pace (minutes/miles) |
|---:|---|
| 5k | 6:50 |
| Half marathon | 7:40 |
| Medium | Between 7:40 - 8:40 |
| Easy | Between 7:40 - 9:40 |
| Slow | Between 7:40 - 10:10 |

| Race | Finish Times (predicted) |
|---:|---|
| 5k | 21 minutes |
| Half marathon | 1 hour(s) 40 minutes |

| Determining your pace | |
|---|---|
| Slow Pace | Extremely easy to hold a conversation. |
| Easy Pace | You can hold a conversation with someone. Your breathing might break up some of the flow of the conversation. |
| Medium | You can hold a conversation with someone, but it's broken up into smaller sentences and smaller responses. |
| Half Marathon Pace | Conversation is difficult. One and two word responses back and forth at best. |

## Definitions in the table below:

CT = Cross Training

S = Slow Pace (long run pace)

E = Easy Pace

M = Medium Pace

HM = Half Marathon Pace

## Training - Week A (Optional)

5K Pace: **6:50**  5k Finish Time: **21 minutes**

| Day | Dist. Mile | Dist. KM | Difficulty | Pace (Range) | Instructions |
|---|---|---|---|---|---|
| Monday | Rest | Rest | Rest | Rest | Take it easy. Don't run. If you need to exercise, I recommend a walk for no longer than 30 minutes. |
| Tuesday | 1 | 1.5 | E | 7:40 - 9:40 | walk/run at an easy pace. |
| Wednesday | 1 | 1.5 | HM | 7:40 | walk/run at your half marathon pace. |
| Thursday | 1 | 1.5 | M | 7:40 - 8:40 | walk/run at a medium pace. |
| Friday | Rest | Rest | Rest | Rest | Rest. |
| Saturday | 1.5 | 2.5 | S | 7:40 - 10:10 | walk/run at a slow pace. The most important piece of your long duration runs is finishing the run. |
| Sunday | Rest/CT | Rest/CT | Rest | Rest | Rest. If your body feels good, then go ahead and do some form of cross-training for 30 to 60 minutes. |

## Training - Week B (Optional)

| Day | Dist. Mile | Dist. KM | Difficulty | Pace (Range) | Instructions |
|---|---|---|---|---|---|
| Monday | Rest | Rest | Rest | Rest | Take it easy. Don't run. If you need to exercise, I recommend a walk for no longer than 30 minutes. |
| Tuesday | 1.5 | 2.5 | E | 7:40 - 9:40 | walk/run at an easy pace. |
| Wednesday | 1.5 | 2.5 | HM | 7:40 | walk/run at your half marathon pace. |
| Thursday | 1.5 | 2.5 | M | 7:40 - 8:40 | walk/run at a medium pace. |
| Friday | Rest | Rest | Rest | Rest | Rest. |
| Saturday | 2 | 3 | S | 7:40 - 10:10 | walk/run at a slow pace. The most important piece of your long duration runs is finishing the run. |
| Sunday | Rest/CT | Rest/CT | Rest | Rest | Rest. If your body feels good, then go ahead and do some form of cross-training for 30 to 60 minutes. |

# Training - Week C (Optional)

5K Pace: **6:50**     5k Finish Time: **21 minutes**

| Day | Dist. Mile | Dist. KM | Difficulty | Pace (Range) | Instructions |
|---|---|---|---|---|---|
| Monday | Rest | Rest | Rest | Rest | Take it easy. Don't run. If you need to exercise, I recommend a walk for no longer than 30 minutes. |
| Tuesday | 2 | 3 | E | 7:40 - 9:40 | walk/run at an easy pace. |
| Wednesday | 2 | 3 | HM | 7:40 | walk/run at your half marathon pace. |
| Thursday | 2 | 3 | M | 7:40 - 8:40 | walk/run at a medium pace. |
| Friday | Rest | Rest | Rest | Rest | Rest. |
| Saturday | 3 | 5 | S | 7:40 - 10:10 | walk/run at a slow pace. The most important piece of your long duration runs is finishing the run. |
| Sunday | Rest/CT | Rest/CT | Rest | Rest | Rest. If your body feels good, then go ahead and do some form of cross-training for 30 to 60 minutes. |

# Training - Week 1

5K Pace: **6:50**     5k Finish Time: **21 minutes**

| Day | Dist. Mile | Dist. KM | Difficulty | Pace (Range) | Instructions |
|---|---|---|---|---|---|
| Monday | Rest | Rest | Rest | Rest | Take it easy. Don't run. If you need to exercise, I recommend a walk for no longer than 30 minutes. |
| Tuesday | 3 | 5 | E | 7:40 - 9:40 | walk/run at an easy pace. |
| Wednesday | 3 | 5 | HM | 7:40 | walk/run at your half marathon pace. |
| Thursday | 3 | 5 | M | 7:40 - 8:40 | walk/run at a medium pace. |
| Friday | Rest | Rest | Rest | Rest | Rest. |
| Saturday | 4 | 6 | S | 7:40 - 10:10 | walk/run at a slow pace. The most important piece of your long duration runs is finishing the run. |
| Sunday | Rest/CT | Rest/CT | Rest | Rest | Rest. If your body feels good, then go ahead and do some form of cross-training for 30 to 60 minutes. |

# Training - Week 2

| Day | Dist. Mile | Dist. KM | Difficulty | Pace (Range) | Instructions |
|---|---|---|---|---|---|
| Monday | Rest | Rest | Rest | Rest | Take it easy. Don't run. If you need to exercise, I recommend a walk for no longer than 30 minutes. |
| Tuesday | 3 | 5 | E | 7:40 - 9:40 | walk/run at an easy pace. |
| Wednesday | 3 | 5 | HM | 7:40 | walk/run at your half marathon pace. |
| Thursday | 3 | 5 | M | 7:40 - 8:40 | walk/run at a medium pace. |
| Friday | Rest | Rest | Rest | Rest | Rest. |
| Saturday | 5 | 8 | S | 7:40 - 10:10 | walk/run at a slow pace. The most important piece of your long duration runs is finishing the run. |
| Sunday | Rest/CT | Rest/CT | Rest | Rest | Rest. If your body feels good, then go ahead and do some form of cross-training for 30 to 60 minutes. |

# Training - Week 3

5K Pace: **6:50**  5k Finish Time: **21 minutes**

| Day | Dist. Mile | Dist. KM | Difficulty | Pace (Range) | Instructions |
|---|---|---|---|---|---|
| Monday | Rest | Rest | Rest | Rest | Take it easy. Don't run. If you need to exercise, I recommend a walk for no longer than 30 minutes. |
| Tuesday | 3 | 5 | E | 7:40 - 9:40 | walk/run at an easy pace. |
| Wednesday | 4 | 6 | HM | 7:40 | walk/run at your half marathon pace. |
| Thursday | 3 | 5 | M | 7:40 - 8:40 | walk/run at a medium pace. |
| Friday | Rest | Rest | Rest | Rest | Rest. |
| Saturday | 6 | 10 | S | 7:40 - 10:10 | walk/run at a slow pace. The most important piece of your long duration runs is finishing the run. |
| Sunday | Rest/CT | Rest/CT | Rest | Rest | Rest. If your body feels good, then go ahead and do some form of cross-training for 30 to 60 minutes. |

# Training - Week 4 (5K Optional)

5K Pace: **6:50**     5k Finish Time: **21 minutes**

| Day | Dist. Mile | Dist. KM | Difficulty | Pace (Range) | Instructions |
|---|---|---|---|---|---|
| Monday | Rest | Rest | Rest | Rest | Take it easy. Don't run. If you need to exercise, I recommend a walk for no longer than 30 minutes. |
| Tuesday | 3 | 5 | E | 7:40 - 9:40 | walk/run at an easy pace. |
| Wednesday | 4 | 6 | HM | 7:40 | walk/run at your half marathon pace. |
| Thursday | 3 | 5 | M | 7:40 - 8:40 | walk/run at a medium pace. |
| Friday | Rest | Rest | Rest | Rest | Rest. |
| Saturday | 6.5 | 10.5 | S | 7:40 - 10:10 | walk/run at a slow pace. The most important piece of your long duration runs is finishing the run. |
| Sunday | Rest/CT | Rest/CT | Rest | Rest | Rest. If your body feels good, then go ahead and do some form of cross-training for 30 to 60 minutes. |

## 5K Optional

| Day | Dist. Mile | Dist. KM | Difficulty | Pace (Range) | Instructions |
|---|---|---|---|---|---|
| Saturday | 3.1 | 5 | - | **6:50** | Run a 5k race instead of your long run. This is completely your choice. I recommend running a 5k race to help you get used to running races. You should see a difference in your race time if you have kept to your training schedule. Don't try for a personal best, run the 5K at your 5K pace. |

# Training - Week 5

5K Pace: **6:50**     5k Finish Time: **21 minutes**

| Day | Dist. Mile | Dist. KM | Difficulty | Pace (Range) | Instructions |
|---|---|---|---|---|---|
| Monday | Rest | Rest | Rest | Rest | Take it easy. Don't run. If you need to exercise, I recommend a walk for no longer than 30 minutes. |
| Tuesday | 3 | 5 | E | 7:40 - 9:40 | walk/run at an easy pace. |
| Wednesday | 4 | 6 | HM | 7:40 | walk/run at your half marathon pace. |
| Thursday | 3 | 5 | M | 7:40 - 8:40 | walk/run at a medium pace. |
| Friday | Rest | Rest | Rest | Rest | Rest. |
| Saturday | 7 | 11 | S | 7:40 - 10:10 | walk/run at a slow pace. The most important piece of your long duration runs is finishing the run. |
| Sunday | Rest/CT | Rest/CT | Rest | Rest | Rest. If your body feels good, then go ahead and do some form of cross-training for 30 to 60 minutes. |

## NOTE:

- Your long duration runs will begin to become more difficult for week 5 and beyond.
- If you get tired during a long duration run, walk for 1/10 mile or 3-5 minutes.

# Training - Week 6

5K Pace: **6:50**     5k Finish Time: **21 minutes**

| Day | Dist. Mile | Dist. KM | Difficulty | Pace (Range) | Instructions |
|---|---|---|---|---|---|
| Monday | Rest | Rest | Rest | Rest | Take it easy. Don't run. If you need to exercise, I recommend a walk for no longer than 30 minutes. |
| Tuesday | 3 | 5 | E | 7:40 - 9:40 | walk/run at an easy pace. |
| Wednesday | 4 | 6 | HM | 7:40 | walk/run at your half marathon pace. |
| Thursday | 3 | 5 | M | 7:40 - 8:40 | walk/run at a medium pace. |
| Friday | Rest | Rest | Rest | Rest | Rest. |
| Saturday | 8 | 13 | S | 7:40 - 10:10 | walk/run at a slow pace. The most important piece of your long duration runs is finishing the run. |
| Sunday | Rest/CT | Rest/CT | Rest | Rest | Rest. If your body feels good, then go ahead and do some form of cross-training for 30 to 60 minutes. |

# Training - Week 7

5K Pace: **6:50**     5k Finish Time: **21 minutes**

| Day | Dist. Mile | Dist. KM | Difficulty | Pace (Range) | Instructions |
|---|---|---|---|---|---|
| Monday | Rest | Rest | Rest | Rest | Take it easy. Don't run. If you need to exercise, I recommend a walk for no longer than 30 minutes. |
| Tuesday | 3 | 5 | E | 7:40 - 9:40 | walk/run at an easy pace. |
| Wednesday | 5 | 8 | HM | 7:40 | walk/run at your half marathon pace. |
| Thursday | 3 | 5 | M | 7:40 - 8:40 | walk/run at a medium pace. |
| Friday | Rest | Rest | Rest | Rest | Rest. |
| Saturday | 8.5 | 13.5 | S | 7:40 - 10:10 | walk/run at a slow pace. The most important piece of your long duration runs is finishing the run. |
| Sunday | Rest/CT | Rest/CT | Rest | Rest | Rest. If your body feels good, then go ahead and do some form of cross-training for 30 to 60 minutes. |

## 10K Optional

| Day | Dist. Mile | Dist. KM | Difficulty | Pace (Range) | Instructions |
|---|---|---|---|---|---|
| Thursday | 2 | 3 | E | 7:40 - 9:40 | If you run the optional 10K, either completely rest today or run 2 miles (3 km). |
| Saturday | 6.2 | 10K | - | 6:50 | Run a 10k race instead of your long run. This is completely your choice. I recommend running a 10k race to help you get used to running races. You should see a difference in your race time if you have kept to your training schedule. Don't try for a personal best, run the 10K at your 5K pace. |

# Training - Week 8

5K Pace: **6:50**     5k Finish Time: **21 minutes**

| Day | Dist. Mile | Dist. KM | Difficulty | Pace (Range) | Instructions |
|---|---|---|---|---|---|
| Monday | Rest | Rest | Rest | Rest | Take it easy. Don't run. If you need to exercise, I recommend a walk for no longer than 30 minutes. |
| Tuesday | 3 | 5 | E | 7:40 - 9:40 | walk/run at an easy pace. |
| Wednesday | 5 | 8 | HM | 7:40 | walk/run at your half marathon pace. |
| Thursday | 3 | 5 | M | 7:40 - 8:40 | walk/run at a medium pace. |
| Friday | Rest | Rest | Rest | Rest | Rest. |
| Saturday | 9 | 14 | S | 7:40 - 10:10 | walk/run at a slow pace. The most important piece of your long duration runs is finishing the run. |
| Sunday | Rest/CT | Rest/CT | Rest | Rest | Rest. If your body feels good, then go ahead and do some form of cross-training for 30 to 60 minutes. |

# Training - Week 9

5K Pace: **6:50**    5k Finish Time: **21 minutes**

| Day | Dist. Mile | Dist. KM | Difficulty | Pace (Range) | Instructions |
|---|---|---|---|---|---|
| Monday | Rest | Rest | Rest | Rest | Take it easy. Don't run. If you need to exercise, I recommend a walk for no longer than 30 minutes. |
| Tuesday | 3 | 5 | E | 7:40 - 9:40 | walk/run at an easy pace. |
| Wednesday | 5 | 8 | HM | 7:40 | walk/run at your half marathon pace. |
| Thursday | 3 | 5 | M | 7:40 - 8:40 | walk/run at a medium pace. |
| Friday | Rest | Rest | Rest | Rest | Rest. |
| Saturday | 8.5 | 13.5 | S | 7:40 - 10:10 | walk/run at a slow pace. The most important piece of your long duration runs is finishing the run. |
| Sunday | Rest/CT | Rest/CT | Rest | Rest | Rest. If your body feels good, then go ahead and do some form of cross-training for 30 to 60 minutes. |

## 13.1 Beta/Test Run Optional

| Day | Dist. Mile | Dist. KM | Difficulty | Pace (Range) | Instructions |
|---|---|---|---|---|---|
| Thursday | Rest | Rest | Rest | Rest | This is a rest day – it simulates race week |
| Friday | Rest | Rest | Rest | Rest | This is a rest day – it simulates race week |
| Saturday | 13.1 | 21 | S | 6:50 | I recommend that you attempt to go the full 13.1 miles (21 km) for a half marathon test run. <u>Only walk/run the first 10 miles (16 km) then walk the last 3.1 miles (5 km).</u> If you are successful, you will have a race ghost time to compete against. It will help energize and refocus your training on beating yourself in 3 weeks at the half marathon race. Also, it allows your mind to grasp the achievement of "completing the distance of a half marathon." |

# Training - Week 10

5K Pace: **6:50**  5k Finish Time: **21 minutes**

| Day | Dist. Mile | Dist. KM | Difficulty | Pace (Range) | Instructions |
|---|---|---|---|---|---|
| Monday | Rest | Rest | Rest | Rest | Take it easy. Don't run. If you need to exercise, I recommend a walk for no longer than 30 minutes. |
| Tuesday | 3 | 5 | E | 7:40 - 9:40 | walk/run at an easy pace. |
| Wednesday | 5 | 8 | HM | 7:40 | walk/run at your half marathon pace. |
| Thursday | 3 | 5 | M | 7:40 - 8:40 | walk/run at a medium pace. |
| Friday | Rest | Rest | Rest | Rest | Rest. |
| Saturday | 11 | 18 | S | 7:40 - 10:10 | walk/run at a slow pace. The most important piece of your long duration runs is finishing the run. |
| Sunday | Rest/CT | Rest/CT | Rest | Rest | Rest. If your body feels good, then go ahead and do some form of cross-training for 30 to 60 minutes. |

# Training - Week 11

| Day | Dist. Mile | Dist. KM | Difficulty | Pace (Range) | Instructions |
|---|---|---|---|---|---|
| Monday | Rest | Rest | Rest | Rest | Take it easy. Don't run. If you need to exercise, I recommend a walk for no longer than 30 minutes. |
| Tuesday | 3 | 5 | E | 7:40 - 9:40 | walk/run at an easy pace. |
| Wednesday | 5 | 8 | HM | 7:40 | walk/run at your half marathon pace. |
| Thursday | 3 | 5 | M | 7:40 - 8:40 | walk/run at a medium pace. |
| Friday | Rest | Rest | Rest | Rest | Rest. |
| Saturday | 12 | 20 | S | 7:40 - 10:10 | walk/run at a slow pace. The most important piece of your long duration runs is finishing the run. |
| Sunday | Rest/CT | Rest/CT | Rest | Rest | Rest. If your body feels good, then go ahead and do some form of cross-training for 30 to 60 minutes. |

# Training - Week 12

5K Pace: **6:50**        5k Finish Time: **21 minutes**

| Day | Dist. Mile | Dist. KM | Difficulty | Pace (Range) | Instructions |
|---|---|---|---|---|---|
| Monday | Rest | Rest | Rest | Rest | Take it easy. Don't run. If you need to exercise, I recommend a walk for no longer than 30 minutes. |
| Tuesday | 3 | 5 | E | 7:40 - 9:40 | walk/run at an easy pace. |
| Wednesday | 2 | 1.5 | HM | 7:40 | walk/run at your half marathon pace. |
| Thursday | Rest | Rest | Rest | Rest | Rest. |
| Friday | Rest | Rest | Rest | Rest | Rest. |
| Saturday | 13.1 | 21 | HM | 7:40 | RACE DAY! |
| Sunday | Rest | Rest | Rest | Rest | DRINK A VICTORY BEER! |

# NOTE:

- Get plenty of sleep the night before your long duration run.
- Try to run your long duration run early in the morning.
- After each run, it's important to stretch out your muscles.
- This week your body needs as much rest as possible.
- Don't run past Wednesday.

# BEGINNER TO FINISHER RUNNING

Half Marathon Training Schedule for

runners with a 5K finish time of 22 minutes

and a pace of *7:10* minutes/mile.

# Predicted Half Marathon Finish Time:

# *1* hour(s) *45* minutes

# PACING TABLES

| Pace | Pace (minutes/miles) |
|---:|---|
| 5k | 7:10 |
| Half marathon | 8:00 |
| Medium | Between 8:00 - 9:00 |
| Easy | Between 8:00 - 10:00 |
| Slow | Between 8:00 - 10:30 |

| Race | Finish Times (predicted) |
|---:|---|
| 5k | 22 minutes |
| Half marathon | 1 hour(s) 45 minutes |

| \ | Determining your pace |
|---|---|
| Slow Pace | Extremely easy to hold a conversation. |
| Easy Pace | You can hold a conversation with someone. Your breathing might break up some of the flow of the conversation. |
| Medium | You can hold a conversation with someone, but it's broken up into smaller sentences and smaller responses. |
| Half Marathon Pace | Conversation is difficult. One and two word responses back and forth at best. |

## Definitions in the table below:

CT = Cross Training

S = Slow Pace (long run pace)

E = Easy Pace

M = Medium Pace

HM = Half Marathon Pace

# Training - Week A (Optional)

5K Pace: **7:10**     5k Finish Time: **22 minutes**

| Day | Dist. Mile | Dist. KM | Difficulty | Pace (Range) | Instructions |
|---|---|---|---|---|---|
| Monday | Rest | Rest | Rest | Rest | Take it easy. Don't run. If you need to exercise, I recommend a walk for no longer than 30 minutes. |
| Tuesday | 1 | 1.5 | E | 8:00 - 10:00 | walk/run at an easy pace. |
| Wednesday | 1 | 1.5 | HM | 8:00 | walk/run at your half marathon pace. |
| Thursday | 1 | 1.5 | M | 8:00 - 9:00 | walk/run at a medium pace. |
| Friday | Rest | Rest | Rest | Rest | Rest. |
| Saturday | 1.5 | 2.5 | S | 8:00 - 10:30 | walk/run at a slow pace. The most important piece of your long duration runs is finishing the run. |
| Sunday | Rest/CT | Rest/CT | Rest | Rest | Rest. If your body feels good, then go ahead and do some form of cross-training for 30 to 60 minutes. |

# Training - Week B (Optional)

| Day | Dist. Mile | Dist. KM | Difficulty | Pace (Range) | Instructions |
|---|---|---|---|---|---|
| Monday | Rest | Rest | Rest | Rest | Take it easy. Don't run. If you need to exercise, I recommend a walk for no longer than 30 minutes. |
| Tuesday | 1.5 | 2.5 | E | 8:00 - 10:00 | walk/run at an easy pace. |
| Wednesday | 1.5 | 2.5 | HM | 8:00 | walk/run at your half marathon pace. |
| Thursday | 1.5 | 2.5 | M | 8:00 - 9:00 | walk/run at a medium pace. |
| Friday | Rest | Rest | Rest | Rest | Rest. |
| Saturday | 2 | 3 | S | 8:00 - 10:30 | walk/run at a slow pace. The most important piece of your long duration runs is finishing the run. |
| Sunday | Rest/CT | Rest/CT | Rest | Rest | Rest. If your body feels good, then go ahead and do some form of cross-training for 30 to 60 minutes. |

# Training - Week C (Optional)

5K Pace: **7:10**     5k Finish Time: **22 minutes**

| Day | Dist. Mile | Dist. KM | Difficulty | Pace (Range) | Instructions |
|---|---|---|---|---|---|
| Monday | Rest | Rest | Rest | Rest | Take it easy. Don't run. If you need to exercise, I recommend a walk for no longer than 30 minutes. |
| Tuesday | 2 | 3 | E | 8:00 - 10:00 | walk/run at an easy pace. |
| Wednesday | 2 | 3 | HM | 8:00 | walk/run at your half marathon pace. |
| Thursday | 2 | 3 | M | 8:00 - 9:00 | walk/run at a medium pace. |
| Friday | Rest | Rest | Rest | Rest | Rest. |
| Saturday | 3 | 5 | S | 8:00 - 10:30 | walk/run at a slow pace. The most important piece of your long duration runs is finishing the run. |
| Sunday | Rest/CT | Rest/CT | Rest | Rest | Rest. If your body feels good, then go ahead and do some form of cross-training for 30 to 60 minutes. |

# Training - Week 1

5K Pace: **7:10**     5k Finish Time: **22 minutes**

| Day | Dist. Mile | Dist. KM | Difficulty | Pace (Range) | Instructions |
|---|---|---|---|---|---|
| Monday | Rest | Rest | Rest | Rest | Take it easy. Don't run. If you need to exercise, I recommend a walk for no longer than 30 minutes. |
| Tuesday | 3 | 5 | E | 8:00 - 10:00 | walk/run at an easy pace. |
| Wednesday | 3 | 5 | HM | 8:00 | walk/run at your half marathon pace. |
| Thursday | 3 | 5 | M | 8:00 - 9:00 | walk/run at a medium pace. |
| Friday | Rest | Rest | Rest | Rest | Rest. |
| Saturday | 4 | 6 | S | 8:00 - 10:30 | walk/run at a slow pace. The most important piece of your long duration runs is finishing the run. |
| Sunday | Rest/CT | Rest/CT | Rest | Rest | Rest. If your body feels good, then go ahead and do some form of cross-training for 30 to 60 minutes. |

# Training - Week 2

| Day | Dist. Mile | Dist. KM | Difficulty | Pace (Range) | Instructions |
|---|---|---|---|---|---|
| Monday | Rest | Rest | Rest | Rest | Take it easy. Don't run. If you need to exercise, I recommend a walk for no longer than 30 minutes. |
| Tuesday | 3 | 5 | E | 8:00 - 10:00 | walk/run at an easy pace. |
| Wednesday | 3 | 5 | HM | 8:00 | walk/run at your half marathon pace. |
| Thursday | 3 | 5 | M | 8:00 - 9:00 | walk/run at a medium pace. |
| Friday | Rest | Rest | Rest | Rest | Rest. |
| Saturday | 5 | 8 | S | 8:00 - 10:30 | walk/run at a slow pace. The most important piece of your long duration runs is finishing the run. |
| Sunday | Rest/CT | Rest/CT | Rest | Rest | Rest. If your body feels good, then go ahead and do some form of cross-training for 30 to 60 minutes. |

# Training - Week 3

5K Pace: **7:10**     5k Finish Time: **22 minutes**

| Day | Dist. Mile | Dist. KM | Difficulty | Pace (Range) | Instructions |
|---|---|---|---|---|---|
| Monday | Rest | Rest | Rest | Rest | Take it easy. Don't run. If you need to exercise, I recommend a walk for no longer than 30 minutes. |
| Tuesday | 3 | 5 | E | 8:00 - 10:00 | walk/run at an easy pace. |
| Wednesday | 4 | 6 | HM | 8:00 | walk/run at your half marathon pace. |
| Thursday | 3 | 5 | M | 8:00 - 9:00 | walk/run at a medium pace. |
| Friday | Rest | Rest | Rest | Rest | Rest. |
| Saturday | 6 | 10 | S | 8:00 - 10:30 | walk/run at a slow pace. The most important piece of your long duration runs is finishing the run. |
| Sunday | Rest/CT | Rest/CT | Rest | Rest | Rest. If your body feels good, then go ahead and do some form of cross-training for 30 to 60 minutes. |

# Training - Week 4 (5K Optional)

5K Pace: **7:10**     5k Finish Time: **22 minutes**

| Day | Dist. Mile | Dist. KM | Difficulty | Pace (Range) | Instructions |
|---|---|---|---|---|---|
| Monday | Rest | Rest | Rest | Rest | Take it easy. Don't run. If you need to exercise, I recommend a walk for no longer than 30 minutes. |
| Tuesday | 3 | 5 | E | 8:00 - 10:00 | walk/run at an easy pace. |
| Wednesday | 4 | 6 | HM | 8:00 | walk/run at your half marathon pace. |
| Thursday | 3 | 5 | M | 8:00 - 9:00 | walk/run at a medium pace. |
| Friday | Rest | Rest | Rest | Rest | Rest. |
| Saturday | 6.5 | 10.5 | S | 8:00 - 10:30 | walk/run at a slow pace. The most important piece of your long duration runs is finishing the run. |
| Sunday | Rest/CT | Rest/CT | Rest | Rest | Rest. If your body feels good, then go ahead and do some form of cross-training for 30 to 60 minutes. |

## 5K Optional

| Day | Dist. Mile | Dist. KM | Difficulty | Pace (Range) | Instructions |
|---|---|---|---|---|---|
| Saturday | 3.1 | 5 | - | **7:10** | Run a 5k race instead of your long run. This is completely your choice. I recommend running a 5k race to help you get used to running races. You should see a difference in your race time if you have kept to your training schedule. Don't try for a personal best, run the 5K at your 5K pace. |

# Training - Week 5

5K Pace: **7:10**     5k Finish Time: **22 minutes**

| Day | Dist. Mile | Dist. KM | Difficulty | Pace (Range) | Instructions |
|---|---|---|---|---|---|
| Monday | Rest | Rest | Rest | Rest | Take it easy. Don't run. If you need to exercise, I recommend a walk for no longer than 30 minutes. |
| Tuesday | 3 | 5 | E | 8:00 - 10:00 | walk/run at an easy pace. |
| Wednesday | 4 | 6 | HM | 8:00 | walk/run at your half marathon pace. |
| Thursday | 3 | 5 | M | 8:00 - 9:00 | walk/run at a medium pace. |
| Friday | Rest | Rest | Rest | Rest | Rest. |
| Saturday | 7 | 11 | S | 8:00 - 10:30 | walk/run at a slow pace. The most important piece of your long duration runs is finishing the run. |
| Sunday | Rest/CT | Rest/CT | Rest | Rest | Rest. If your body feels good, then go ahead and do some form of cross-training for 30 to 60 minutes. |

## NOTE:

- Your long duration runs will begin to become more difficult for week 5 and beyond.
- If you get tired during a long duration run, walk for 1/10 mile or 3-5 minutes.

# Training - Week 6

5K Pace: **7:10**     5k Finish Time: **22 minutes**

| Day | Dist. Mile | Dist. KM | Difficulty | Pace (Range) | Instructions |
|---|---|---|---|---|---|
| Monday | Rest | Rest | Rest | Rest | Take it easy. Don't run. If you need to exercise, I recommend a walk for no longer than 30 minutes. |
| Tuesday | 3 | 5 | E | 8:00 - 10:00 | walk/run at an easy pace. |
| Wednesday | 4 | 6 | HM | 8:00 | walk/run at your half marathon pace. |
| Thursday | 3 | 5 | M | 8:00 - 9:00 | walk/run at a medium pace. |
| Friday | Rest | Rest | Rest | Rest | Rest. |
| Saturday | 8 | 13 | S | 8:00 - 10:30 | walk/run at a slow pace. The most important piece of your long duration runs is finishing the run. |
| Sunday | Rest/CT | Rest/CT | Rest | Rest | Rest. If your body feels good, then go ahead and do some form of cross-training for 30 to 60 minutes. |

# Training - Week 7

5K Pace: **7:10**     5k Finish Time: **22 minutes**

| Day | Dist. Mile | Dist. KM | Difficulty | Pace (Range) | Instructions |
|---|---|---|---|---|---|
| Monday | Rest | Rest | Rest | Rest | Take it easy. Don't run. If you need to exercise, I recommend a walk for no longer than 30 minutes. |
| Tuesday | 3 | 5 | E | 8:00 - 10:00 | walk/run at an easy pace. |
| Wednesday | 5 | 8 | HM | 8:00 | walk/run at your half marathon pace. |
| Thursday | 3 | 5 | M | 8:00 - 9:00 | walk/run at a medium pace. |
| Friday | Rest | Rest | Rest | Rest | Rest. |
| Saturday | 8.5 | 13.5 | S | 8:00 - 10:30 | walk/run at a slow pace. The most important piece of your long duration runs is finishing the run. |
| Sunday | Rest/CT | Rest/CT | Rest | Rest | Rest. If your body feels good, then go ahead and do some form of cross-training for 30 to 60 minutes. |

## 10K Optional

| Day | Dist. Mile | Dist. KM | Difficulty | Pace (Range) | Instructions |
|---|---|---|---|---|---|
| Thursday | 2 | 3 | E | 8:00 - 10:00 | If you run the optional 10K, either completely rest today or run 2 miles ( 3 km). |
| Saturday | 6.2 | 10K | - | **7:10** | Run a 10k race instead of your long run. This is completely your choice. I recommend running a 10k race to help you get used to running races. You should see a difference in your race time if you have kept to your training schedule. Don't try for a personal best, run the 10K at your 5K pace. |

# Training - Week 8

5K Pace: **7:10**     5k Finish Time: **22 minutes**

| Day | Dist. Mile | Dist. KM | Difficulty | Pace (Range) | Instructions |
|---|---|---|---|---|---|
| Monday | Rest | Rest | Rest | Rest | Take it easy. Don't run. If you need to exercise, I recommend a walk for no longer than 30 minutes. |
| Tuesday | 3 | 5 | E | 8:00 - 10:00 | walk/run at an easy pace. |
| Wednesday | 5 | 8 | HM | 8:00 | walk/run at your half marathon pace. |
| Thursday | 3 | 5 | M | 8:00 - 9:00 | walk/run at a medium pace. |
| Friday | Rest | Rest | Rest | Rest | Rest. |
| Saturday | 9 | 14 | S | 8:00 - 10:30 | walk/run at a slow pace. The most important piece of your long duration runs is finishing the run. |
| Sunday | Rest/CT | Rest/CT | Rest | Rest | Rest. If your body feels good, then go ahead and do some form of cross-training for 30 to 60 minutes. |

# Training - Week 9

5K Pace: **7:10**  5k Finish Time: **22 minutes**

| Day | Dist. Mile | Dist. KM | Difficulty | Pace (Range) | Instructions |
|---|---|---|---|---|---|
| Monday | Rest | Rest | Rest | Rest | Take it easy. Don't run. If you need to exercise, I recommend a walk for no longer than 30 minutes. |
| Tuesday | 3 | 5 | E | 8:00 - 10:00 | walk/run at an easy pace. |
| Wednesday | 5 | 8 | HM | 8:00 | walk/run at your half marathon pace. |
| Thursday | 3 | 5 | M | 8:00 - 9:00 | walk/run at a medium pace. |
| Friday | Rest | Rest | Rest | Rest | Rest. |
| Saturday | 8.5 | 13.5 | S | 8:00 - 10:30 | walk/run at a slow pace. The most important piece of your long duration runs is finishing the run. |
| Sunday | Rest/CT | Rest/CT | Rest | Rest | Rest. If your body feels good, then go ahead and do some form of cross-training for 30 to 60 minutes. |

## 13.1 Beta/Test Run Optional

| Day | Dist. Mile | Dist. KM | Difficulty | Pace (Range) | Instructions |
|---|---|---|---|---|---|
| Thursday | Rest | Rest | Rest | Rest | This is a rest day – it simulates race week |
| Friday | Rest | Rest | Rest | Rest | This is a rest day – it simulates race week |
| Saturday | 13.1 | 21 | S | 7:10 | I recommend that you attempt to go the full 13.1 miles (21 km) for a half marathon test run. Only walk/run the first 10 miles (16 km) then walk the last 3.1 miles (5 km). If you are successful, you will have a race ghost time to compete against. It will help energize and refocus your training on beating yourself in 3 weeks at the half marathon race. Also, it allows your mind to grasp the achievement of "completing the distance of a half marathon." |

# Training - Week 10

5K Pace: **7:10**     5k Finish Time: **22 minutes**

| Day | Dist. Mile | Dist. KM | Difficulty | Pace (Range) | Instructions |
|---|---|---|---|---|---|
| Monday | Rest | Rest | Rest | Rest | Take it easy. Don't run. If you need to exercise, I recommend a walk for no longer than 30 minutes. |
| Tuesday | 3 | 5 | E | 8:00 - 10:00 | walk/run at an easy pace. |
| Wednesday | 5 | 8 | HM | 8:00 | walk/run at your half marathon pace. |
| Thursday | 3 | 5 | M | 8:00 - 9:00 | walk/run at a medium pace. |
| Friday | Rest | Rest | Rest | Rest | Rest. |
| Saturday | 11 | 18 | S | 8:00 - 10:30 | walk/run at a slow pace. The most important piece of your long duration runs is finishing the run. |
| Sunday | Rest/CT | Rest/CT | Rest | Rest | Rest. If your body feels good, then go ahead and do some form of cross-training for 30 to 60 minutes. |

# Training - Week 11

| Day | Dist. Mile | Dist. KM | Difficulty | Pace (Range) | Instructions |
|---|---|---|---|---|---|
| Monday | Rest | Rest | Rest | Rest | Take it easy. Don't run. If you need to exercise, I recommend a walk for no longer than 30 minutes. |
| Tuesday | 3 | 5 | E | 8:00 - 10:00 | walk/run at an easy pace. |
| Wednesday | 5 | 8 | HM | 8:00 | walk/run at your half marathon pace. |
| Thursday | 3 | 5 | M | 8:00 - 9:00 | walk/run at a medium pace. |
| Friday | Rest | Rest | Rest | Rest | Rest. |
| Saturday | 12 | 20 | S | 8:00 - 10:30 | walk/run at a slow pace. The most important piece of your long duration runs is finishing the run. |
| Sunday | Rest/CT | Rest/CT | Rest | Rest | Rest. If your body feels good, then go ahead and do some form of cross-training for 30 to 60 minutes. |

# Training - Week 12

5K Pace: **7:10**     5k Finish Time: **22 minutes**

| Day | Dist. Mile | Dist. KM | Difficulty | Pace (Range) | Instructions |
|---|---|---|---|---|---|
| Monday | Rest | Rest | Rest | Rest | Take it easy. Don't run. If you need to exercise, I recommend a walk for no longer than 30 minutes. |
| Tuesday | 3 | 5 | E | 8:00 - 10:00 | walk/run at an easy pace. |
| Wednesday | 2 | 1.5 | HM | 8:00 | walk/run at your half marathon pace. |
| Thursday | Rest | Rest | Rest | Rest | Rest. |
| Friday | Rest | Rest | Rest | Rest | Rest. |
| Saturday | 13.1 | 21 | HM | 8:00 | RACE DAY! |
| Sunday | Rest | Rest | Rest | Rest | DRINK A VICTORY BEER! |

## NOTE:

- Get plenty of sleep the night before your long duration run.
- Try to run your long duration run early in the morning.
- After each run, it's important to stretch out your muscles.
- This week your body needs as much rest as possible.
- Don't run past Wednesday.

Half Marathon Training Schedule for

<u>runners with a 5K finish time of 23 minutes</u>

and a pace of *7:30* minutes/mile.

## Predicted Half Marathon Finish Time:

<u>*1* hour(s) *50* minutes</u>

# PACING TABLES

| Pace | Pace (minutes/miles) |
|---:|:---|
| 5k | 7:30 |
| Half marathon | 8:25 |
| Medium | Between 8:25 - 9:25 |
| Easy | Between 8:25 - 10:25 |
| Slow | Between 8:25 - 10:55 |

| Race | Finish Times (predicted) |
|---:|:---|
| 5k | 23 minutes |
| Half marathon | 1 hour(s) 50 minutes |

| Determining your pace | |
|:---:|:---|
| Slow Pace | Extremely easy to hold a conversation. |
| Easy Pace | You can hold a conversation with someone. Your breathing might break up some of the flow of the conversation. |
| Medium | You can hold a conversation with someone, but it's broken up into smaller sentences and smaller responses. |
| Half Marathon Pace | Conversation is difficult. One and two word responses back and forth at best. |

## Definitions in the table below:

CT = Cross Training

S = Slow Pace (long run pace)

E = Easy Pace

M = Medium Pace

HM = Half Marathon Pace

## Training - Week A (Optional)

5K Pace: **7:30**     5k Finish Time: **23 minutes**

| Day | Dist. Mile | Dist. KM | Difficulty | Pace (Range) | Instructions |
|---|---|---|---|---|---|
| Monday | Rest | Rest | Rest | Rest | Take it easy. Don't run. If you need to exercise, I recommend a walk for no longer than 30 minutes. |
| Tuesday | 1 | 1.5 | E | 8:25 - 10:25 | walk/run at an easy pace. |
| Wednesday | 1 | 1.5 | HM | 8:25 | walk/run at your half marathon pace. |
| Thursday | 1 | 1.5 | M | 8:25 - 9:25 | walk/run at a medium pace. |
| Friday | Rest | Rest | Rest | Rest | Rest. |
| Saturday | 1.5 | 2.5 | S | 8:25 - 10:55 | walk/run at a slow pace. The most important piece of your long duration runs is finishing the run. |
| Sunday | Rest/CT | Rest/CT | Rest | Rest | Rest. If your body feels good, then go ahead and do some form of cross-training for 30 to 60 minutes. |

## Training - Week B (Optional)

| Day | Dist. Mile | Dist. KM | Difficulty | Pace (Range) | Instructions |
|---|---|---|---|---|---|
| Monday | Rest | Rest | Rest | Rest | Take it easy. Don't run. If you need to exercise, I recommend a walk for no longer than 30 minutes. |
| Tuesday | 1.5 | 2.5 | E | 8:25 - 10:25 | walk/run at an easy pace. |
| Wednesday | 1.5 | 2.5 | HM | 8:25 | walk/run at your half marathon pace. |
| Thursday | 1.5 | 2.5 | M | 8:25 - 9:25 | walk/run at a medium pace. |
| Friday | Rest | Rest | Rest | Rest | Rest. |
| Saturday | 2 | 3 | S | 8:25 - 10:55 | walk/run at a slow pace. The most important piece of your long duration runs is finishing the run. |
| Sunday | Rest/CT | Rest/CT | Rest | Rest | Rest. If your body feels good, then go ahead and do some form of cross-training for 30 to 60 minutes. |

# Training - Week C (Optional)

5K Pace: **7:30**    5k Finish Time: **23 minutes**

| Day | Dist. Mile | Dist. KM | Difficulty | Pace (Range) | Instructions |
|---|---|---|---|---|---|
| Monday | Rest | Rest | Rest | Rest | Take it easy. Don't run. If you need to exercise, I recommend a walk for no longer than 30 minutes. |
| Tuesday | 2 | 3 | E | 8:25 - 10:25 | walk/run at an easy pace. |
| Wednesday | 2 | 3 | HM | 8:25 | walk/run at your half marathon pace. |
| Thursday | 2 | 3 | M | 8:25 - 9:25 | walk/run at a medium pace. |
| Friday | Rest | Rest | Rest | Rest | Rest. |
| Saturday | 3 | 5 | S | 8:25 - 10:55 | walk/run at a slow pace. The most important piece of your long duration runs is finishing the run. |
| Sunday | Rest/CT | Rest/CT | Rest | Rest | Rest. If your body feels good, then go ahead and do some form of cross-training for 30 to 60 minutes. |

# Training - Week 1

5K Pace: **7:30**     5k Finish Time: **23 minutes**

| Day | Dist. Mile | Dist. KM | Difficulty | Pace (Range) | Instructions |
|---|---|---|---|---|---|
| Monday | Rest | Rest | Rest | Rest | Take it easy. Don't run. If you need to exercise, I recommend a walk for no longer than 30 minutes. |
| Tuesday | 3 | 5 | E | 8:25 - 10:25 | walk/run at an easy pace. |
| Wednesday | 3 | 5 | HM | 8:25 | walk/run at your half marathon pace. |
| Thursday | 3 | 5 | M | 8:25 - 9:25 | walk/run at a medium pace. |
| Friday | Rest | Rest | Rest | Rest | Rest. |
| Saturday | 4 | 6 | S | 8:25 - 10:55 | walk/run at a slow pace. The most important piece of your long duration runs is finishing the run. |
| Sunday | Rest/CT | Rest/CT | Rest | Rest | Rest. If your body feels good, then go ahead and do some form of cross-training for 30 to 60 minutes. |

# Training - Week 2

| Day | Dist. Mile | Dist. KM | Difficulty | Pace (Range) | Instructions |
|---|---|---|---|---|---|
| Monday | Rest | Rest | Rest | Rest | Take it easy. Don't run. If you need to exercise, I recommend a walk for no longer than 30 minutes. |
| Tuesday | 3 | 5 | E | 8:25 - 10:25 | walk/run at an easy pace. |
| Wednesday | 3 | 5 | HM | 8:25 | walk/run at your half marathon pace. |
| Thursday | 3 | 5 | M | 8:25 - 9:25 | walk/run at a medium pace. |
| Friday | Rest | Rest | Rest | Rest | Rest. |
| Saturday | 5 | 8 | S | 8:25 - 10:55 | walk/run at a slow pace. The most important piece of your long duration runs is finishing the run. |
| Sunday | Rest/CT | Rest/CT | Rest | Rest | Rest. If your body feels good, then go ahead and do some form of cross-training for 30 to 60 minutes. |

# Training - Week 3

5K Pace: **7:30**     5k Finish Time: **23 minutes**

| Day | Dist. Mile | Dist. KM | Difficulty | Pace (Range) | Instructions |
|---|---|---|---|---|---|
| Monday | Rest | Rest | Rest | Rest | Take it easy. Don't run. If you need to exercise, I recommend a walk for no longer than 30 minutes. |
| Tuesday | 3 | 5 | E | 8:25 - 10:25 | walk/run at an easy pace. |
| Wednesday | 4 | 6 | HM | 8:25 | walk/run at your half marathon pace. |
| Thursday | 3 | 5 | M | 8:25 - 9:25 | walk/run at a medium pace. |
| Friday | Rest | Rest | Rest | Rest | Rest. |
| Saturday | 6 | 10 | S | 8:25 - 10:55 | walk/run at a slow pace. The most important piece of your long duration runs is finishing the run. |
| Sunday | Rest/CT | Rest/CT | Rest | Rest | Rest. If your body feels good, then go ahead and do some form of cross-training for 30 to 60 minutes. |

# Training - Week 4 (5K Optional)

5K Pace: **7:30**     5k Finish Time: **23 minutes**

| Day | Dist. Mile | Dist. KM | Difficulty | Pace (Range) | Instructions |
|---|---|---|---|---|---|
| Monday | Rest | Rest | Rest | Rest | Take it easy. Don't run. If you need to exercise, I recommend a walk for no longer than 30 minutes. |
| Tuesday | 3 | 5 | E | 8:25 - 10:25 | walk/run at an easy pace. |
| Wednesday | 4 | 6 | HM | 8:25 | walk/run at your half marathon pace. |
| Thursday | 3 | 5 | M | 8:25 - 9:25 | walk/run at a medium pace. |
| Friday | Rest | Rest | Rest | Rest | Rest. |
| Saturday | 6.5 | 10.5 | S | 8:25 - 10:55 | walk/run at a slow pace. The most important piece of your long duration runs is finishing the run. |
| Sunday | Rest/CT | Rest/CT | Rest | Rest | Rest. If your body feels good, then go ahead and do some form of cross-training for 30 to 60 minutes. |

## 5K Optional

| Day | Dist. Mile | Dist. KM | Difficulty | Pace (Range) | Instructions |
|---|---|---|---|---|---|
| Saturday | 3.1 | 5 | - | 7:30 | Run a 5k race instead of your long run. This is completely your choice. I recommend running a 5k race to help you get used to running races. You should see a difference in your race time if you have kept to your training schedule. Don't try for a personal best, run the 5K at your 5K pace. |

# Training - Week 5

5K Pace: **7:30**     5k Finish Time: **23 minutes**

| Day | Dist. Mile | Dist. KM | Difficulty | Pace (Range) | Instructions |
|---|---|---|---|---|---|
| Monday | Rest | Rest | Rest | Rest | Take it easy. Don't run. If you need to exercise, I recommend a walk for no longer than 30 minutes. |
| Tuesday | 3 | 5 | E | 8:25 - 10:25 | walk/run at an easy pace. |
| Wednesday | 4 | 6 | HM | 8:25 | walk/run at your half marathon pace. |
| Thursday | 3 | 5 | M | 8:25 - 9:25 | walk/run at a medium pace. |
| Friday | Rest | Rest | Rest | Rest | Rest. |
| Saturday | 7 | 11 | S | 8:25 - 10:55 | walk/run at a slow pace. The most important piece of your long duration runs is finishing the run. |
| Sunday | Rest/CT | Rest/CT | Rest | Rest | Rest. If your body feels good, then go ahead and do some form of cross-training for 30 to 60 minutes. |

## NOTE:

- Your long duration runs will begin to become more difficult for week 5 and beyond.
- If you get tired during a long duration run, walk for 1/10 mile or 3-5 minutes.

# Training - Week 6

5K Pace: **7:30**     5k Finish Time: **23 minutes**

| Day | Dist. Mile | Dist. KM | Difficulty | Pace (Range) | Instructions |
|---|---|---|---|---|---|
| Monday | Rest | Rest | Rest | Rest | Take it easy. Don't run. If you need to exercise, I recommend a walk for no longer than 30 minutes. |
| Tuesday | 3 | 5 | E | 8:25 - 10:25 | walk/run at an easy pace. |
| Wednesday | 4 | 6 | HM | 8:25 | walk/run at your half marathon pace. |
| Thursday | 3 | 5 | M | 8:25 - 9:25 | walk/run at a medium pace. |
| Friday | Rest | Rest | Rest | Rest | Rest. |
| Saturday | 8 | 13 | S | 8:25 - 10:55 | walk/run at a slow pace. The most important piece of your long duration runs is finishing the run. |
| Sunday | Rest/CT | Rest/CT | Rest | Rest | Rest. If your body feels good, then go ahead and do some form of cross-training for 30 to 60 minutes. |

# Training - Week 7

5K Pace: **7:30**     5k Finish Time: **23 minutes**

| Day | Dist. Mile | Dist. KM | Difficulty | Pace (Range) | Instructions |
|---|---|---|---|---|---|
| Monday | Rest | Rest | Rest | Rest | Take it easy. Don't run. If you need to exercise, I recommend a walk for no longer than 30 minutes. |
| Tuesday | 3 | 5 | E | 8:25 - 10:25 | walk/run at an easy pace. |
| Wednesday | 5 | 8 | HM | 8:25 | walk/run at your half marathon pace. |
| Thursday | 3 | 5 | M | 8:25 - 9:25 | walk/run at a medium pace. |
| Friday | Rest | Rest | Rest | Rest | Rest. |
| Saturday | 8.5 | 13.5 | S | 8:25 - 10:55 | walk/run at a slow pace. The most important piece of your long duration runs is finishing the run. |
| Sunday | Rest/CT | Rest/CT | Rest | Rest | Rest. If your body feels good, then go ahead and do some form of cross-training for 30 to 60 minutes. |

## 10K Optional

| Day | Dist. Mile | Dist. KM | Difficulty | Pace (Range) | Instructions |
|---|---|---|---|---|---|
| Thursday | 2 | 3 | E | 8:25 - 10:25 | If you run the optional 10K, either completely rest today or run 2 miles ( 3 km). |
| Saturday | 6.2 | 10K | - | 7:30 | Run a 10k race instead of your long run. This is completely your choice. I recommend running a 10k race to help you get used to running races. You should see a difference in your race time if you have kept to your training schedule. Don't try for a personal best, run the 10K at your 5K pace. |

# Training - Week 8

5K Pace: **7:30**     5k Finish Time: **23 minutes**

| Day | Dist. Mile | Dist. KM | Difficulty | Pace (Range) | Instructions |
|---|---|---|---|---|---|
| Monday | Rest | Rest | Rest | Rest | Take it easy. Don't run. If you need to exercise, I recommend a walk for no longer than 30 minutes. |
| Tuesday | 3 | 5 | E | 8:25 - 10:25 | walk/run at an easy pace. |
| Wednesday | 5 | 8 | HM | 8:25 | walk/run at your half marathon pace. |
| Thursday | 3 | 5 | M | 8:25 - 9:25 | walk/run at a medium pace. |
| Friday | Rest | Rest | Rest | Rest | Rest. |
| Saturday | 9 | 14 | S | 8:25 - 10:55 | walk/run at a slow pace. The most important piece of your long duration runs is finishing the run. |
| Sunday | Rest/CT | Rest/CT | Rest | Rest | Rest. If your body feels good, then go ahead and do some form of cross-training for 30 to 60 minutes. |

# Training - Week 9

**5K Pace: 7:30**     **5k Finish Time: 23 minutes**

| Day | Dist. Mile | Dist. KM | Difficulty | Pace (Range) | Instructions |
|---|---|---|---|---|---|
| Monday | Rest | Rest | Rest | Rest | Take it easy. Don't run. If you need to exercise, I recommend a walk for no longer than 30 minutes. |
| Tuesday | 3 | 5 | E | 8:25 - 10:25 | walk/run at an easy pace. |
| Wednesday | 5 | 8 | HM | 8:25 | walk/run at your half marathon pace. |
| Thursday | 3 | 5 | M | 8:25 - 9:25 | walk/run at a medium pace. |
| Friday | Rest | Rest | Rest | Rest | Rest. |
| Saturday | 8.5 | 13.5 | S | 8:25 - 10:55 | walk/run at a slow pace. The most important piece of your long duration runs is finishing the run. |
| Sunday | Rest/CT | Rest/CT | Rest | Rest | Rest. If your body feels good, then go ahead and do some form of cross-training for 30 to 60 minutes. |

## 13.1 Beta/Test Run Optional

| Day | Dist. Mile | Dist. KM | Difficulty | Pace (Range) | Instructions |
|---|---|---|---|---|---|
| Thursday | Rest | Rest | Rest | Rest | This is a rest day – it simulates race week |
| Friday | Rest | Rest | Rest | Rest | This is a rest day – it simulates race week |
| Saturday | 13.1 | 21 | S | 7:30 | I recommend that you attempt to go the full 13.1 miles (21 km) for a half marathon test run. <u>Only walk/run the first 10 miles (16 km) then walk the last 3.1 miles (5 km).</u> If you are successful, you will have a race ghost time to compete against. It will help energize and refocus your training on beating yourself in 3 weeks at the half marathon race. Also, it allows your mind to grasp the achievement of "completing the distance of a half marathon." |

# Training - Week 10

5K Pace: **7:30**     5k Finish Time: **23 minutes**

| Day | Dist. Mile | Dist. KM | Difficulty | Pace (Range) | Instructions |
|---|---|---|---|---|---|
| Monday | Rest | Rest | Rest | Rest | Take it easy. Don't run. If you need to exercise, I recommend a walk for no longer than 30 minutes. |
| Tuesday | 3 | 5 | E | 8:25 - 10:25 | walk/run at an easy pace. |
| Wednesday | 5 | 8 | HM | 8:25 | walk/run at your half marathon pace. |
| Thursday | 3 | 5 | M | 8:25 - 9:25 | walk/run at a medium pace. |
| Friday | Rest | Rest | Rest | Rest | Rest. |
| Saturday | 11 | 18 | S | 8:25 - 10:55 | walk/run at a slow pace. The most important piece of your long duration runs is finishing the run. |
| Sunday | Rest/CT | Rest/CT | Rest | Rest | Rest. If your body feels good, then go ahead and do some form of cross-training for 30 to 60 minutes. |

# Training - Week 11

| Day | Dist. Mile | Dist. KM | Difficulty | Pace (Range) | Instructions |
|---|---|---|---|---|---|
| Monday | Rest | Rest | Rest | Rest | Take it easy. Don't run. If you need to exercise, I recommend a walk for no longer than 30 minutes. |
| Tuesday | 3 | 5 | E | 8:25 - 10:25 | walk/run at an easy pace. |
| Wednesday | 5 | 8 | HM | 8:25 | walk/run at your half marathon pace. |
| Thursday | 3 | 5 | M | 8:25 - 9:25 | walk/run at a medium pace. |
| Friday | Rest | Rest | Rest | Rest | Rest. |
| Saturday | 12 | 20 | S | 8:25 - 10:55 | walk/run at a slow pace. The most important piece of your long duration runs is finishing the run. |
| Sunday | Rest/CT | Rest/CT | Rest | Rest | Rest. If your body feels good, then go ahead and do some form of cross-training for 30 to 60 minutes. |

# Training - Week 12

5K Pace: **7:30**   5k Finish Time: **23 minutes**

| Day | Dist. Mile | Dist. KM | Difficulty | Pace (Range) | Instructions |
|---|---|---|---|---|---|
| Monday | Rest | Rest | Rest | Rest | Take it easy. Don't run. If you need to exercise, I recommend a walk for no longer than 30 minutes. |
| Tuesday | 3 | 5 | E | 8:25 - 10:25 | walk/run at an easy pace. |
| Wednesday | 2 | 1.5 | HM | 8:25 | walk/run at your half marathon pace. |
| Thursday | Rest | Rest | Rest | Rest | Rest. |
| Friday | Rest | Rest | Rest | Rest | Rest. |
| Saturday | 13.1 | 21 | HM | 8:25 | RACE DAY! |
| Sunday | Rest | Rest | Rest | Rest | DRINK A VICTORY BEER! |

## NOTE:

- Get plenty of sleep the night before your long duration run.
- Try to run your long duration run early in the morning.
- After each run, it's important to stretch out your muscles.
- This week your body needs as much rest as possible.
- Don't run past Wednesday.

Half Marathon Training Schedule for

runners with a 5K finish time of 24 minutes

and a pace of *7:50* minutes/mile.

# Predicted Half Marathon Finish Time:

# *1* hour(s) *52* minutes

# PACING TABLES

| Pace | Pace (minutes/miles) |
|---:|---|
| 5k | 7:50 |
| Half marathon | 8:40 |
| Medium | Between 8:40 - 9:40 |
| Easy | Between 8:40 - 10:40 |
| Slow | Between 8:40 - 11:10 |

| Race | Finish Times (predicted) |
|---:|---|
| 5k | 24 minutes |
| Half marathon | 1 hour(s) 52 minutes |

| Determining your pace | |
|---|---|
| Slow Pace | Extremely easy to hold a conversation. |
| Easy Pace | You can hold a conversation with someone. Your breathing might break up some of the flow of the conversation. |
| Medium | You can hold a conversation with someone, but it's broken up into smaller sentences and smaller responses. |
| Half Marathon Pace | Conversation is difficult. One and two word responses back and forth at best. |

## Definitions in the table below:

CT = Cross Training

S = Slow Pace (long run pace)

E = Easy Pace

M = Medium Pace

HM = Half Marathon Pace

# Training - Week A (Optional)

5K Pace: **7:50**     5k Finish Time: **24 minutes**

| Day | Dist. Mile | Dist. KM | Difficulty | Pace (Range) | Instructions |
|---|---|---|---|---|---|
| Monday | Rest | Rest | Rest | Rest | Take it easy. Don't run. If you need to exercise, I recommend a walk for no longer than 30 minutes. |
| Tuesday | 1 | 1.5 | E | 8:40 - 10:40 | walk/run at an easy pace. |
| Wednesday | 1 | 1.5 | HM | 8:40 | walk/run at your half marathon pace. |
| Thursday | 1 | 1.5 | M | 8:40 - 9:40 | walk/run at a medium pace. |
| Friday | Rest | Rest | Rest | Rest | Rest. |
| Saturday | 1.5 | 2.5 | S | 8:40 - 11:10 | walk/run at a slow pace. The most important piece of your long duration runs is finishing the run. |
| Sunday | Rest/CT | Rest/CT | Rest | Rest | Rest. If your body feels good, then go ahead and do some form of cross-training for 30 to 60 minutes. |

## Training - Week B (Optional)

| Day | Dist. Mile | Dist. KM | Difficulty | Pace (Range) | Instructions |
|---|---|---|---|---|---|
| Monday | Rest | Rest | Rest | Rest | Take it easy. Don't run. If you need to exercise, I recommend a walk for no longer than 30 minutes. |
| Tuesday | 1.5 | 2.5 | E | 8:40 - 10:40 | walk/run at an easy pace. |
| Wednesday | 1.5 | 2.5 | HM | 8:40 | walk/run at your half marathon pace. |
| Thursday | 1.5 | 2.5 | M | 8:40 - 9:40 | walk/run at a medium pace. |
| Friday | Rest | Rest | Rest | Rest | Rest. |
| Saturday | 2 | 3 | S | 8:40 - 11:10 | walk/run at a slow pace. The most important piece of your long duration runs is finishing the run. |
| Sunday | Rest/CT | Rest/CT | Rest | Rest | Rest. If your body feels good, then go ahead and do some form of cross-training for 30 to 60 minutes. |

# Training - Week C (Optional)

5K Pace: **7:50**     5k Finish Time: **24 minutes**

| Day | Dist. Mile | Dist. KM | Difficulty | Pace (Range) | Instructions |
|---|---|---|---|---|---|
| Monday | Rest | Rest | Rest | Rest | Take it easy. Don't run. If you need to exercise, I recommend a walk for no longer than 30 minutes. |
| Tuesday | 2 | 3 | E | 8:40 - 10:40 | walk/run at an easy pace. |
| Wednesday | 2 | 3 | HM | 8:40 | walk/run at your half marathon pace. |
| Thursday | 2 | 3 | M | 8:40 - 9:40 | walk/run at a medium pace. |
| Friday | Rest | Rest | Rest | Rest | Rest. |
| Saturday | 3 | 5 | S | 8:40 - 11:10 | walk/run at a slow pace. The most important piece of your long duration runs is finishing the run. |
| Sunday | Rest/CT | Rest/CT | Rest | Rest | Rest. If your body feels good, then go ahead and do some form of cross-training for 30 to 60 minutes. |

# Training - Week 1

5K Pace: **7:50**    5k Finish Time: **24 minutes**

| Day | Dist. Mile | Dist. KM | Difficulty | Pace (Range) | Instructions |
|---|---|---|---|---|---|
| Monday | Rest | Rest | Rest | Rest | Take it easy. Don't run. If you need to exercise, I recommend a walk for no longer than 30 minutes. |
| Tuesday | 3 | 5 | E | 8:40 - 10:40 | walk/run at an easy pace. |
| Wednesday | 3 | 5 | HM | 8:40 | walk/run at your half marathon pace. |
| Thursday | 3 | 5 | M | 8:40 - 9:40 | walk/run at a medium pace. |
| Friday | Rest | Rest | Rest | Rest | Rest. |
| Saturday | 4 | 6 | S | 8:40 - 11:10 | walk/run at a slow pace. The most important piece of your long duration runs is finishing the run. |
| Sunday | Rest/CT | Rest/CT | Rest | Rest | Rest. If your body feels good, then go ahead and do some form of cross-training for 30 to 60 minutes. |

# Training - Week 2

| Day | Dist. Mile | Dist. KM | Difficulty | Pace (Range) | Instructions |
|---|---|---|---|---|---|
| Monday | Rest | Rest | Rest | Rest | Take it easy. Don't run. If you need to exercise, I recommend a walk for no longer than 30 minutes. |
| Tuesday | 3 | 5 | E | 8:40 - 10:40 | walk/run at an easy pace. |
| Wednesday | 3 | 5 | HM | 8:40 | walk/run at your half marathon pace. |
| Thursday | 3 | 5 | M | 8:40 - 9:40 | walk/run at a medium pace. |
| Friday | Rest | Rest | Rest | Rest | Rest. |
| Saturday | 5 | 8 | S | 8:40 - 11:10 | walk/run at a slow pace. The most important piece of your long duration runs is finishing the run. |
| Sunday | Rest/CT | Rest/CT | Rest | Rest | Rest. If your body feels good, then go ahead and do some form of cross-training for 30 to 60 minutes. |

# Training - Week 3

5K Pace: **7:50**     5k Finish Time: **24 minutes**

| Day | Dist. Mile | Dist. KM | Difficulty | Pace (Range) | Instructions |
|---|---|---|---|---|---|
| Monday | Rest | Rest | Rest | Rest | Take it easy. Don't run. If you need to exercise, I recommend a walk for no longer than 30 minutes. |
| Tuesday | 3 | 5 | E | 8:40 - 10:40 | walk/run at an easy pace. |
| Wednesday | 4 | 6 | HM | 8:40 | walk/run at your half marathon pace. |
| Thursday | 3 | 5 | M | 8:40 - 9:40 | walk/run at a medium pace. |
| Friday | Rest | Rest | Rest | Rest | Rest. |
| Saturday | 6 | 10 | S | 8:40 - 11:10 | walk/run at a slow pace. The most important piece of your long duration runs is finishing the run. |
| Sunday | Rest/CT | Rest/CT | Rest | Rest | Rest. If your body feels good, then go ahead and do some form of cross-training for 30 to 60 minutes. |

# Training - Week 4 (5K Optional)

5K Pace: **7:50**     5k Finish Time: **24 minutes**

| Day | Dist. Mile | Dist. KM | Difficulty | Pace (Range) | Instructions |
|---|---|---|---|---|---|
| Monday | Rest | Rest | Rest | Rest | Take it easy. Don't run. If you need to exercise, I recommend a walk for no longer than 30 minutes. |
| Tuesday | 3 | 5 | E | 8:40 - 10:40 | walk/run at an easy pace. |
| Wednesday | 4 | 6 | HM | 8:40 | walk/run at your half marathon pace. |
| Thursday | 3 | 5 | M | 8:40 - 9:40 | walk/run at a medium pace. |
| Friday | Rest | Rest | Rest | Rest | Rest. |
| Saturday | 6.5 | 10.5 | S | 8:40 - 11:10 | walk/run at a slow pace. The most important piece of your long duration runs is finishing the run. |
| Sunday | Rest/CT | Rest/CT | Rest | Rest | Rest. If your body feels good, then go ahead and do some form of cross-training for 30 to 60 minutes. |

# 5K Optional

| Day | Dist. Mile | Dist. KM | Difficulty | Pace (Range) | Instructions |
|---|---|---|---|---|---|
| Saturday | 3.1 | 5 | - | **7:50** | Run a 5k race instead of your long run. This is completely your choice. I recommend running a 5k race to help you get used to running races. You should see a difference in your race time if you have kept to your training schedule. Don't try for a personal best, run the 5K at your 5K pace. |

# Training - Week 5

5K Pace: **7:50**    5k Finish Time: **24 minutes**

| Day | Dist. Mile | Dist. KM | Difficulty | Pace (Range) | Instructions |
|---|---|---|---|---|---|
| Monday | Rest | Rest | Rest | Rest | Take it easy. Don't run. If you need to exercise, I recommend a walk for no longer than 30 minutes. |
| Tuesday | 3 | 5 | E | 8:40 - 10:40 | walk/run at an easy pace. |
| Wednesday | 4 | 6 | HM | 8:40 | walk/run at your half marathon pace. |
| Thursday | 3 | 5 | M | 8:40 - 9:40 | walk/run at a medium pace. |
| Friday | Rest | Rest | Rest | Rest | Rest. |
| Saturday | 7 | 11 | S | 8:40 - 11:10 | walk/run at a slow pace. The most important piece of your long duration runs is finishing the run. |
| Sunday | Rest/CT | Rest/CT | Rest | Rest | Rest. If your body feels good, then go ahead and do some form of cross-training for 30 to 60 minutes. |

## NOTE:

- Your long duration runs will begin to become more difficult for week 5 and beyond.
- If you get tired during a long duration run, walk for 1/10 mile or 3-5 minutes.

# Training - Week 6

5K Pace: **7:50**     5k Finish Time: **24 minutes**

| Day | Dist. Mile | Dist. KM | Difficulty | Pace (Range) | Instructions |
|---|---|---|---|---|---|
| Monday | Rest | Rest | Rest | Rest | Take it easy. Don't run. If you need to exercise, I recommend a walk for no longer than 30 minutes. |
| Tuesday | 3 | 5 | E | 8:40 - 10:40 | walk/run at an easy pace. |
| Wednesday | 4 | 6 | HM | 8:40 | walk/run at your half marathon pace. |
| Thursday | 3 | 5 | M | 8:40 - 9:40 | walk/run at a medium pace. |
| Friday | Rest | Rest | Rest | Rest | Rest. |
| Saturday | 8 | 13 | S | 8:40 - 11:10 | walk/run at a slow pace. The most important piece of your long duration runs is finishing the run. |
| Sunday | Rest/CT | Rest/CT | Rest | Rest | Rest. If your body feels good, then go ahead and do some form of cross-training for 30 to 60 minutes. |

# Training - Week 7

5K Pace: **7:50**     5k Finish Time: **24 minutes**

| Day | Dist. Mile | Dist. KM | Difficulty | Pace (Range) | Instructions |
|---|---|---|---|---|---|
| Monday | Rest | Rest | Rest | Rest | Take it easy. Don't run. If you need to exercise, I recommend a walk for no longer than 30 minutes. |
| Tuesday | 3 | 5 | E | 8:40 - 10:40 | walk/run at an easy pace. |
| Wednesday | 5 | 8 | HM | 8:40 | walk/run at your half marathon pace. |
| Thursday | 3 | 5 | M | 8:40 - 9:40 | walk/run at a medium pace. |
| Friday | Rest | Rest | Rest | Rest | Rest. |
| Saturday | 8.5 | 13.5 | S | 8:40 - 11:10 | walk/run at a slow pace. The most important piece of your long duration runs is finishing the run. |
| Sunday | Rest/CT | Rest/CT | Rest | Rest | Rest. If your body feels good, then go ahead and do some form of cross-training for 30 to 60 minutes. |

## 10K Optional

| Day | Dist. Mile | Dist. KM | Difficulty | Pace (Range) | Instructions |
|---|---|---|---|---|---|
| Thursday | 2 | 3 | E | 8:40 - 10:40 | If you run the optional 10K, either completely rest today or run 2 miles (3 km). |
| Saturday | 6.2 | 10K | - | 7:50 | Run a 10k race instead of your long run. This is completely your choice. I recommend running a 10k race to help you get used to running races. You should see a difference in your race time if you have kept to your training schedule. Don't try for a personal best, run the 10K at your 5K pace. |

# Training - Week 8

5K Pace: **7:50**     5k Finish Time: **24 minutes**

| Day | Dist. Mile | Dist. KM | Difficulty | Pace (Range) | Instructions |
|---|---|---|---|---|---|
| Monday | Rest | Rest | Rest | Rest | Take it easy. Don't run. If you need to exercise, I recommend a walk for no longer than 30 minutes. |
| Tuesday | 3 | 5 | E | 8:40 - 10:40 | walk/run at an easy pace. |
| Wednesday | 5 | 8 | HM | 8:40 | walk/run at your half marathon pace. |
| Thursday | 3 | 5 | M | 8:40 - 9:40 | walk/run at a medium pace. |
| Friday | Rest | Rest | Rest | Rest | Rest. |
| Saturday | 9 | 14 | S | 8:40 - 11:10 | walk/run at a slow pace. The most important piece of your long duration runs is finishing the run. |
| Sunday | Rest/CT | Rest/CT | Rest | Rest | Rest. If your body feels good, then go ahead and do some form of cross-training for 30 to 60 minutes. |

# Training - Week 9

5K Pace: **7:50**  5k Finish Time: **24 minutes**

| Day | Dist. Mile | Dist. KM | Difficulty | Pace (Range) | Instructions |
|---|---|---|---|---|---|
| Monday | Rest | Rest | Rest | Rest | Take it easy. Don't run. If you need to exercise, I recommend a walk for no longer than 30 minutes. |
| Tuesday | 3 | 5 | E | 8:40 - 10:40 | walk/run at an easy pace. |
| Wednesday | 5 | 8 | HM | 8:40 | walk/run at your half marathon pace. |
| Thursday | 3 | 5 | M | 8:40 - 9:40 | walk/run at a medium pace. |
| Friday | Rest | Rest | Rest | Rest | Rest. |
| Saturday | 8.5 | 13.5 | S | 8:40 - 11:10 | walk/run at a slow pace. The most important piece of your long duration runs is finishing the run. |
| Sunday | Rest/CT | Rest/CT | Rest | Rest | Rest. If your body feels good, then go ahead and do some form of cross-training for 30 to 60 minutes. |

## 13.1 Beta/Test Run Optional

| Day | Dist. Mile | Dist. KM | Difficulty | Pace (Range) | Instructions |
|---|---|---|---|---|---|
| Thursday | Rest | Rest | Rest | Rest | This is a rest day – it simulates race week |
| Friday | Rest | Rest | Rest | Rest | This is a rest day – it simulates race week |
| Saturday | 13.1 | 21 | S | 7:50 | I recommend that you attempt to go the full 13.1 miles (21 km) for a half marathon test run. <u>Only walk/run the first 10 miles (16 km) then walk the last 3.1 miles (5 km).</u> If you are successful, you will have a race ghost time to compete against. It will help energize and refocus your training on beating yourself in 3 weeks at the half marathon race. Also, it allows your mind to grasp the achievement of "completing the distance of a half marathon." |

# Training - Week 10

5K Pace: **7:50**     5k Finish Time: **24 minutes**

| Day | Dist. Mile | Dist. KM | Difficulty | Pace (Range) | Instructions |
|---|---|---|---|---|---|
| Monday | Rest | Rest | Rest | Rest | Take it easy. Don't run. If you need to exercise, I recommend a walk for no longer than 30 minutes. |
| Tuesday | 3 | 5 | E | 8:40 - 10:40 | walk/run at an easy pace. |
| Wednesday | 5 | 8 | HM | 8:40 | walk/run at your half marathon pace. |
| Thursday | 3 | 5 | M | 8:40 - 9:40 | walk/run at a medium pace. |
| Friday | Rest | Rest | Rest | Rest | Rest. |
| Saturday | 11 | 18 | S | 8:40 - 11:10 | walk/run at a slow pace. The most important piece of your long duration runs is finishing the run. |
| Sunday | Rest/CT | Rest/CT | Rest | Rest | Rest. If your body feels good, then go ahead and do some form of cross-training for 30 to 60 minutes. |

# Training - Week 11

| Day | Dist. Mile | Dist. KM | Difficulty | Pace (Range) | Instructions |
|---|---|---|---|---|---|
| Monday | Rest | Rest | Rest | Rest | Take it easy. Don't run. If you need to exercise, I recommend a walk for no longer than 30 minutes. |
| Tuesday | 3 | 5 | E | 8:40 - 10:40 | walk/run at an easy pace. |
| Wednesday | 5 | 8 | HM | 8:40 | walk/run at your half marathon pace. |
| Thursday | 3 | 5 | M | 8:40 - 9:40 | walk/run at a medium pace. |
| Friday | Rest | Rest | Rest | Rest | Rest. |
| Saturday | 12 | 20 | S | 8:40 - 11:10 | walk/run at a slow pace. The most important piece of your long duration runs is finishing the run. |
| Sunday | Rest/CT | Rest/CT | Rest | Rest | Rest. If your body feels good, then go ahead and do some form of cross-training for 30 to 60 minutes. |

# Training - Week 12

5K Pace: **7:50**     5k Finish Time: **24 minutes**

| Day | Dist. Mile | Dist. KM | Difficulty | Pace (Range) | Instructions |
|---|---|---|---|---|---|
| Monday | Rest | Rest | Rest | Rest | Take it easy. Don't run. If you need to exercise, I recommend a walk for no longer than 30 minutes. |
| Tuesday | 3 | 5 | E | 8:40 - 10:40 | walk/run at an easy pace. |
| Wednesday | 2 | 1.5 | HM | 8:40 | walk/run at your half marathon pace. |
| Thursday | Rest | Rest | Rest | Rest | Rest. |
| Friday | Rest | Rest | Rest | Rest | Rest. |
| Saturday | 13.1 | 21 | HM | 8:40 | RACE DAY! |
| Sunday | Rest | Rest | Rest | Rest | DRINK A VICTORY BEER! |

## NOTE:

- Get plenty of sleep the night before your long duration run.
- Try to run your long duration run early in the morning.
- After each run, it's important to stretch out your muscles.
- This week your body needs as much rest as possible.
- Don't run past Wednesday.

# BEGINNER TO FINISHER RUNNING

Half Marathon Training Schedule for runners with a 5K finish time of 25 minutes and a pace of *8:03* minutes/mile.

## Predicted Half Marathon Finish Time:
### *1* hour(s) *56* minutes

# PACING TABLES

| Pace | Pace (minutes/miles) |
|---:|---|
| 5k | 8:03 |
| Half marathon | 8:50 |
| Medium | Between 8:50 - 9:50 |
| Easy | Between 8:50 - 10:50 |
| Slow | Between 8:50 - 11:20 |

| Race | Finish Times (predicted) |
|---:|---|
| 5k | 25 minutes |
| Half marathon | 1 hour(s) 56 minutes |

| Determining your pace | |
|---|---|
| Slow Pace | Extremely easy to hold a conversation. |
| Easy Pace | You can hold a conversation with someone. Your breathing might break up some of the flow of the conversation. |
| Medium | You can hold a conversation with someone, but it's broken up into smaller sentences and smaller responses. |
| Half Marathon Pace | Conversation is difficult. One and two word responses back and forth at best. |

## Definitions in the table below:

CT = Cross Training

S = Slow Pace (long run pace)

E = Easy Pace

M = Medium Pace

HM = Half Marathon Pace

## Training - Week A (Optional)

5K Pace: **8:03**     5k Finish Time: **25 minutes**

| Day | Dist. Mile | Dist. KM | Difficulty | Pace (Range) | Instructions |
|---|---|---|---|---|---|
| Monday | Rest | Rest | Rest | Rest | Take it easy. Don't run. If you need to exercise, I recommend a walk for no longer than 30 minutes. |
| Tuesday | 1 | 1.5 | E | 8:50 - 10:50 | walk/run at an easy pace. |
| Wednesday | 1 | 1.5 | HM | 8:50 | walk/run at your half marathon pace. |
| Thursday | 1 | 1.5 | M | 8:50 - 9:50 | walk/run at a medium pace. |
| Friday | Rest | Rest | Rest | Rest | Rest. |
| Saturday | 1.5 | 2.5 | S | 8:50 - 11:20 | walk/run at a slow pace. The most important piece of your long duration runs is finishing the run. |
| Sunday | Rest/CT | Rest/CT | Rest | Rest | Rest. If your body feels good, then go ahead and do some form of cross-training for 30 to 60 minutes. |

## Training - Week B (Optional)

| Day | Dist. Mile | Dist. KM | Difficulty | Pace (Range) | Instructions |
|---|---|---|---|---|---|
| Monday | Rest | Rest | Rest | Rest | Take it easy. Don't run. If you need to exercise, I recommend a walk for no longer than 30 minutes. |
| Tuesday | 1.5 | 2.5 | E | 8:50 - 10:50 | walk/run at an easy pace. |
| Wednesday | 1.5 | 2.5 | HM | 8:50 | walk/run at your half marathon pace. |
| Thursday | 1.5 | 2.5 | M | 8:50 - 9:50 | walk/run at a medium pace. |
| Friday | Rest | Rest | Rest | Rest | Rest. |
| Saturday | 2 | 3 | S | 8:50 - 11:20 | walk/run at a slow pace. The most important piece of your long duration runs is finishing the run. |
| Sunday | Rest/CT | Rest/CT | Rest | Rest | Rest. If your body feels good, then go ahead and do some form of cross-training for 30 to 60 minutes. |

# Training - Week C (Optional)

5K Pace: **8:03**    5k Finish Time: **25 minutes**

| Day | Dist. Mile | Dist. KM | Difficulty | Pace (Range) | Instructions |
|---|---|---|---|---|---|
| Monday | Rest | Rest | Rest | Rest | Take it easy. Don't run. If you need to exercise, I recommend a walk for no longer than 30 minutes. |
| Tuesday | 2 | 3 | E | 8:50 - 10:50 | walk/run at an easy pace. |
| Wednesday | 2 | 3 | HM | 8:50 | walk/run at your half marathon pace. |
| Thursday | 2 | 3 | M | 8:50 - 9:50 | walk/run at a medium pace. |
| Friday | Rest | Rest | Rest | Rest | Rest. |
| Saturday | 3 | 5 | S | 8:50 - 11:20 | walk/run at a slow pace. The most important piece of your long duration runs is finishing the run. |
| Sunday | Rest/CT | Rest/CT | Rest | Rest | Rest. If your body feels good, then go ahead and do some form of cross-training for 30 to 60 minutes. |

# Training - Week 1

5K Pace: **8:03**     5k Finish Time: **25 minutes**

| Day | Dist. Mile | Dist. KM | Difficulty | Pace (Range) | Instructions |
|---|---|---|---|---|---|
| Monday | Rest | Rest | Rest | Rest | Take it easy. Don't run. If you need to exercise, I recommend a walk for no longer than 30 minutes. |
| Tuesday | 3 | 5 | E | 8:50 - 10:50 | walk/run at an easy pace. |
| Wednesday | 3 | 5 | HM | 8:50 | walk/run at your half marathon pace. |
| Thursday | 3 | 5 | M | 8:50 - 9:50 | walk/run at a medium pace. |
| Friday | Rest | Rest | Rest | Rest | Rest. |
| Saturday | 4 | 6 | S | 8:50 - 11:20 | walk/run at a slow pace. The most important piece of your long duration runs is finishing the run. |
| Sunday | Rest/CT | Rest/CT | Rest | Rest | Rest. If your body feels good, then go ahead and do some form of cross-training for 30 to 60 minutes. |

# Training - Week 2

| Day | Dist. Mile | Dist. KM | Difficulty | Pace (Range) | Instructions |
|---|---|---|---|---|---|
| Monday | Rest | Rest | Rest | Rest | Take it easy. Don't run. If you need to exercise, I recommend a walk for no longer than 30 minutes. |
| Tuesday | 3 | 5 | E | 8:50 - 10:50 | walk/run at an easy pace. |
| Wednesday | 3 | 5 | HM | 8:50 | walk/run at your half marathon pace. |
| Thursday | 3 | 5 | M | 8:50 - 9:50 | walk/run at a medium pace. |
| Friday | Rest | Rest | Rest | Rest | Rest. |
| Saturday | 5 | 8 | S | 8:50 - 11:20 | walk/run at a slow pace. The most important piece of your long duration runs is finishing the run. |
| Sunday | Rest/CT | Rest/CT | Rest | Rest | Rest. If your body feels good, then go ahead and do some form of cross-training for 30 to 60 minutes. |

# Training - Week 3

5K Pace: **8:03**     5k Finish Time: **25 minutes**

| Day | Dist. Mile | Dist. KM | Difficulty | Pace (Range) | Instructions |
|---|---|---|---|---|---|
| Monday | Rest | Rest | Rest | Rest | Take it easy. Don't run. If you need to exercise, I recommend a walk for no longer than 30 minutes. |
| Tuesday | 3 | 5 | E | 8:50 - 10:50 | walk/run at an easy pace. |
| Wednesday | 4 | 6 | HM | 8:50 | walk/run at your half marathon pace. |
| Thursday | 3 | 5 | M | 8:50 - 9:50 | walk/run at a medium pace. |
| Friday | Rest | Rest | Rest | Rest | Rest. |
| Saturday | 6 | 10 | S | 8:50 - 11:20 | walk/run at a slow pace. The most important piece of your long duration runs is finishing the run. |
| Sunday | Rest/CT | Rest/CT | Rest | Rest | Rest. If your body feels good, then go ahead and do some form of cross-training for 30 to 60 minutes. |

# Training - Week 4 (5K Optional)

**5K Pace:** **8:03**   **5k Finish Time:** **25 minutes**

| Day | Dist. Mile | Dist. KM | Difficulty | Pace (Range) | Instructions |
|---|---|---|---|---|---|
| Monday | Rest | Rest | Rest | Rest | Take it easy. Don't run. If you need to exercise, I recommend a walk for no longer than 30 minutes. |
| Tuesday | 3 | 5 | E | 8:50 - 10:50 | walk/run at an easy pace. |
| Wednesday | 4 | 6 | HM | 8:50 | walk/run at your half marathon pace. |
| Thursday | 3 | 5 | M | 8:50 - 9:50 | walk/run at a medium pace. |
| Friday | Rest | Rest | Rest | Rest | Rest. |
| Saturday | 6.5 | 10.5 | S | 8:50 - 11:20 | walk/run at a slow pace. The most important piece of your long duration runs is finishing the run. |
| Sunday | Rest/CT | Rest/CT | Rest | Rest | Rest. If your body feels good, then go ahead and do some form of cross-training for 30 to 60 minutes. |

## 5K Optional

| Day | Dist. Mile | Dist. KM | Difficulty | Pace (Range) | Instructions |
|---|---|---|---|---|---|
| Saturday | 3.1 | 5 | - | **8:03** | Run a 5k race instead of your long run. This is completely your choice. I recommend running a 5k race to help you get used to running races. You should see a difference in your race time if you have kept to your training schedule. Don't try for a personal best, run the 5K at your 5K pace. |

# Training - Week 5

**5K Pace: 8:03**     **5k Finish Time: 25 minutes**

| Day | Dist. Mile | Dist. KM | Difficulty | Pace (Range) | Instructions |
|---|---|---|---|---|---|
| Monday | Rest | Rest | Rest | Rest | Take it easy. Don't run. If you need to exercise, I recommend a walk for no longer than 30 minutes. |
| Tuesday | 3 | 5 | E | 8:50 - 10:50 | walk/run at an easy pace. |
| Wednesday | 4 | 6 | HM | 8:50 | walk/run at your half marathon pace. |
| Thursday | 3 | 5 | M | 8:50 - 9:50 | walk/run at a medium pace. |
| Friday | Rest | Rest | Rest | Rest | Rest. |
| Saturday | 7 | 11 | S | 8:50 - 11:20 | walk/run at a slow pace. The most important piece of your long duration runs is finishing the run. |
| Sunday | Rest/CT | Rest/CT | Rest | Rest | Rest. If your body feels good, then go ahead and do some form of cross-training for 30 to 60 minutes. |

## NOTE:

- Your long duration runs will begin to become more difficult for week 5 and beyond.
- If you get tired during a long duration run, walk for 1/10 mile or 3-5 minutes.

# Training - Week 6

5K Pace: **8:03**    5k Finish Time: **25 minutes**

| Day | Dist. Mile | Dist. KM | Difficulty | Pace (Range) | Instructions |
|---|---|---|---|---|---|
| Monday | Rest | Rest | Rest | Rest | Take it easy. Don't run. If you need to exercise, I recommend a walk for no longer than 30 minutes. |
| Tuesday | 3 | 5 | E | 8:50 - 10:50 | walk/run at an easy pace. |
| Wednesday | 4 | 6 | HM | 8:50 | walk/run at your half marathon pace. |
| Thursday | 3 | 5 | M | 8:50 - 9:50 | walk/run at a medium pace. |
| Friday | Rest | Rest | Rest | Rest | Rest. |
| Saturday | 8 | 13 | S | 8:50 - 11:20 | walk/run at a slow pace. The most important piece of your long duration runs is finishing the run. |
| Sunday | Rest/CT | Rest/CT | Rest | Rest | Rest. If your body feels good, then go ahead and do some form of cross-training for 30 to 60 minutes. |

# Training - Week 7

5K Pace: **8:03**     5k Finish Time: **25 minutes**

| Day | Dist. Mile | Dist. KM | Difficulty | Pace (Range) | Instructions |
|---|---|---|---|---|---|
| Monday | Rest | Rest | Rest | Rest | Take it easy. Don't run. If you need to exercise, I recommend a walk for no longer than 30 minutes. |
| Tuesday | 3 | 5 | E | 8:50 - 10:50 | walk/run at an easy pace. |
| Wednesday | 5 | 8 | HM | 8:50 | walk/run at your half marathon pace. |
| Thursday | 3 | 5 | M | 8:50 - 9:50 | walk/run at a medium pace. |
| Friday | Rest | Rest | Rest | Rest | Rest. |
| Saturday | 8.5 | 13.5 | S | 8:50 - 11:20 | walk/run at a slow pace. The most important piece of your long duration runs is finishing the run. |
| Sunday | Rest/CT | Rest/CT | Rest | Rest | Rest. If your body feels good, then go ahead and do some form of cross-training for 30 to 60 minutes. |

## 10K Optional

| Day | Dist. Mile | Dist. KM | Difficulty | Pace (Range) | Instructions |
|---|---|---|---|---|---|
| Thursday | 2 | 3 | E | 8:50 - 10:50 | If you run the optional 10K, either completely rest today or run 2 miles (3 km). |
| Saturday | 6.2 | 10K | - | 8:03 | Run a 10k race instead of your long run. This is completely your choice. I recommend running a 10k race to help you get used to running races. You should see a difference in your race time if you have kept to your training schedule. Don't try for a personal best, run the 10K at your 5K pace. |

# Training - Week 8

5K Pace: **8:03**     5k Finish Time: **25 minutes**

| Day | Dist. Mile | Dist. KM | Difficulty | Pace (Range) | Instructions |
|---|---|---|---|---|---|
| Monday | Rest | Rest | Rest | Rest | Take it easy. Don't run. If you need to exercise, I recommend a walk for no longer than 30 minutes. |
| Tuesday | 3 | 5 | E | 8:50 - 10:50 | walk/run at an easy pace. |
| Wednesday | 5 | 8 | HM | 8:50 | walk/run at your half marathon pace. |
| Thursday | 3 | 5 | M | 8:50 - 9:50 | walk/run at a medium pace. |
| Friday | Rest | Rest | Rest | Rest | Rest. |
| Saturday | 9 | 14 | S | 8:50 - 11:20 | walk/run at a slow pace. The most important piece of your long duration runs is finishing the run. |
| Sunday | Rest/CT | Rest/CT | Rest | Rest | Rest. If your body feels good, then go ahead and do some form of cross-training for 30 to 60 minutes. |

# Training - Week 9

5K Pace: **8:03**  5k Finish Time: **25 minutes**

| Day | Dist. Mile | Dist. KM | Difficulty | Pace (Range) | Instructions |
|---|---|---|---|---|---|
| Monday | Rest | Rest | Rest | Rest | Take it easy. Don't run. If you need to exercise, I recommend a walk for no longer than 30 minutes. |
| Tuesday | 3 | 5 | E | 8:50 - 10:50 | walk/run at an easy pace. |
| Wednesday | 5 | 8 | HM | 8:50 | walk/run at your half marathon pace. |
| Thursday | 3 | 5 | M | 8:50 - 9:50 | walk/run at a medium pace. |
| Friday | Rest | Rest | Rest | Rest | Rest. |
| Saturday | 8.5 | 13.5 | S | 8:50 - 11:20 | walk/run at a slow pace. The most important piece of your long duration runs is finishing the run. |
| Sunday | Rest/CT | Rest/CT | Rest | Rest | Rest. If your body feels good, then go ahead and do some form of cross-training for 30 to 60 minutes. |

## 13.1 Beta/Test Run Optional

| Day | Dist. Mile | Dist. KM | Difficulty | Pace (Range) | Instructions |
|---|---|---|---|---|---|
| Thursday | Rest | Rest | Rest | Rest | This is a rest day – it simulates race week |
| Friday | Rest | Rest | Rest | Rest | This is a rest day – it simulates race week |
| Saturday | 13.1 | 21 | S | 8:03 | I recommend that you attempt to go the full 13.1 miles (21 km) for a half marathon test run. <u>Only walk/run the first 10 miles (16 km) then walk the last 3.1 miles (5 km).</u> If you are successful, you will have a race ghost time to compete against. It will help energize and refocus your training on beating yourself in 3 weeks at the half marathon race. Also, it allows your mind to grasp the achievement of "completing the distance of a half marathon." |

# Training - Week 10

5K Pace: **8:03**     5k Finish Time: **25 minutes**

| Day | Dist. Mile | Dist. KM | Difficulty | Pace (Range) | Instructions |
|---|---|---|---|---|---|
| Monday | Rest | Rest | Rest | Rest | Take it easy. Don't run. If you need to exercise, I recommend a walk for no longer than 30 minutes. |
| Tuesday | 3 | 5 | E | 8:50 - 10:50 | walk/run at an easy pace. |
| Wednesday | 5 | 8 | HM | 8:50 | walk/run at your half marathon pace. |
| Thursday | 3 | 5 | M | 8:50 - 9:50 | walk/run at a medium pace. |
| Friday | Rest | Rest | Rest | Rest | Rest. |
| Saturday | 11 | 18 | S | 8:50 - 11:20 | walk/run at a slow pace. The most important piece of your long duration runs is finishing the run. |
| Sunday | Rest/CT | Rest/CT | Rest | Rest | Rest. If your body feels good, then go ahead and do some form of cross-training for 30 to 60 minutes. |

# Training - Week 11

| Day | Dist. Mile | Dist. KM | Difficulty | Pace (Range) | Instructions |
|---|---|---|---|---|---|
| Monday | Rest | Rest | Rest | Rest | Take it easy. Don't run. If you need to exercise, I recommend a walk for no longer than 30 minutes. |
| Tuesday | 3 | 5 | E | 8:50 - 10:50 | walk/run at an easy pace. |
| Wednesday | 5 | 8 | HM | 8:50 | walk/run at your half marathon pace. |
| Thursday | 3 | 5 | M | 8:50 - 9:50 | walk/run at a medium pace. |
| Friday | Rest | Rest | Rest | Rest | Rest. |
| Saturday | 12 | 20 | S | 8:50 - 11:20 | walk/run at a slow pace. The most important piece of your long duration runs is finishing the run. |
| Sunday | Rest/CT | Rest/CT | Rest | Rest | Rest. If your body feels good, then go ahead and do some form of cross-training for 30 to 60 minutes. |

# Training - Week 12

5K Pace: **8:03**  5k Finish Time: **25 minutes**

| Day | Dist. Mile | Dist. KM | Difficulty | Pace (Range) | Instructions |
|---|---|---|---|---|---|
| Monday | Rest | Rest | Rest | Rest | Take it easy. Don't run. If you need to exercise, I recommend a walk for no longer than 30 minutes. |
| Tuesday | 3 | 5 | E | 8:50 - 10:50 | walk/run at an easy pace. |
| Wednesday | 2 | 1.5 | HM | 8:50 | walk/run at your half marathon pace. |
| Thursday | Rest | Rest | Rest | Rest | Rest. |
| Friday | Rest | Rest | Rest | Rest | Rest. |
| Saturday | 13.1 | 21 | HM | 8:50 | RACE DAY! |
| Sunday | Rest | Rest | Rest | Rest | DRINK A VICTORY BEER! |

## NOTE:

- Get plenty of sleep the night before your long duration run.
- Try to run your long duration run early in the morning.
- After each run, it's important to stretch out your muscles.
- This week your body needs as much rest as possible.
- Don't run past Wednesday.

# BEGINNER TO FINISHER RUNNING

Half Marathon Training Schedule for

<u>runners with a 5K finish time of 26 minutes</u>

and a pace of *8:23* minutes/mile.

# Predicted Half Marathon Finish Time:

## <u>*2*</u> hour(s) <u>*00*</u> minutes

# PACING TABLES

| Pace | Pace (minutes/miles) |
|---:|---|
| 5k | 8:23 |
| Half marathon | 9:10 |
| Medium | Between 9:10 - 10:10 |
| Easy | Between 9:10 - 11:10 |
| Slow | Between 9:10 - 11:40 |

| Race | Finish Times (predicted) |
|---:|---|
| 5k | 26 minutes |
| Half marathon | 2 hour(s) 00 minutes |

| \ | Determining your pace |
|---|---|
| Slow Pace | Extremely easy to hold a conversation. |
| Easy Pace | You can hold a conversation with someone. Your breathing might break up some of the flow of the conversation. |
| Medium | You can hold a conversation with someone, but it's broken up into smaller sentences and smaller responses. |
| Half Marathon Pace | Conversation is difficult. One and two word responses back and forth at best. |

## Definitions in the table below:

CT = Cross Training

S = Slow Pace (long run pace)

E = Easy Pace

M = Medium Pace

HM = Half Marathon Pace

# Training - Week A (Optional)

5K Pace: **8:23**      5k Finish Time: **26 minutes**

| Day | Dist. Mile | Dist. KM | Difficulty | Pace (Range) | Instructions |
|---|---|---|---|---|---|
| Monday | Rest | Rest | Rest | Rest | Take it easy. Don't run. If you need to exercise, I recommend a walk for no longer than 30 minutes. |
| Tuesday | 1 | 1.5 | E | 9:10 - 11:10 | walk/run at an easy pace. |
| Wednesday | 1 | 1.5 | HM | 9:10 | walk/run at your half marathon pace. |
| Thursday | 1 | 1.5 | M | 9:10 - 10:10 | walk/run at a medium pace. |
| Friday | Rest | Rest | Rest | Rest | Rest. |
| Saturday | 1.5 | 2.5 | S | 9:10 - 11:40 | walk/run at a slow pace. The most important piece of your long duration runs is finishing the run. |
| Sunday | Rest/CT | Rest/CT | Rest | Rest | Rest. If your body feels good, then go ahead and do some form of cross-training for 30 to 60 minutes. |

# Training - Week B (Optional)

| Day | Dist. Mile | Dist. KM | Difficulty | Pace (Range) | Instructions |
|---|---|---|---|---|---|
| Monday | Rest | Rest | Rest | Rest | Take it easy. Don't run. If you need to exercise, I recommend a walk for no longer than 30 minutes. |
| Tuesday | 1.5 | 2.5 | E | 9:10 - 11:10 | walk/run at an easy pace. |
| Wednesday | 1.5 | 2.5 | HM | 9:10 | walk/run at your half marathon pace. |
| Thursday | 1.5 | 2.5 | M | 9:10 - 10:10 | walk/run at a medium pace. |
| Friday | Rest | Rest | Rest | Rest | Rest. |
| Saturday | 2 | 3 | S | 9:10 - 11:40 | walk/run at a slow pace. The most important piece of your long duration runs is finishing the run. |
| Sunday | Rest/CT | Rest/CT | Rest | Rest | Rest. If your body feels good, then go ahead and do some form of cross-training for 30 to 60 minutes. |

# Training - Week C (Optional)

5K Pace: **8:23**    5k Finish Time: **26 minutes**

| Day | Dist. Mile | Dist. KM | Difficulty | Pace (Range) | Instructions |
|---|---|---|---|---|---|
| Monday | Rest | Rest | Rest | Rest | Take it easy. Don't run. If you need to exercise, I recommend a walk for no longer than 30 minutes. |
| Tuesday | 2 | 3 | E | 9:10 - 11:10 | walk/run at an easy pace. |
| Wednesday | 2 | 3 | HM | 9:10 | walk/run at your half marathon pace. |
| Thursday | 2 | 3 | M | 9:10 - 10:10 | walk/run at a medium pace. |
| Friday | Rest | Rest | Rest | Rest | Rest. |
| Saturday | 3 | 5 | S | 9:10 - 11:40 | walk/run at a slow pace. The most important piece of your long duration runs is finishing the run. |
| Sunday | Rest/CT | Rest/CT | Rest | Rest | Rest. If your body feels good, then go ahead and do some form of cross-training for 30 to 60 minutes. |

# Training - Week 1

5K Pace: **8:23**     5k Finish Time: **26 minutes**

| Day | Dist. Mile | Dist. KM | Difficulty | Pace (Range) | Instructions |
|---|---|---|---|---|---|
| Monday | Rest | Rest | Rest | Rest | Take it easy. Don't run. If you need to exercise, I recommend a walk for no longer than 30 minutes. |
| Tuesday | 3 | 5 | E | 9:10 - 11:10 | walk/run at an easy pace. |
| Wednesday | 3 | 5 | HM | 9:10 | walk/run at your half marathon pace. |
| Thursday | 3 | 5 | M | 9:10 - 10:10 | walk/run at a medium pace. |
| Friday | Rest | Rest | Rest | Rest | Rest. |
| Saturday | 4 | 6 | S | 9:10 - 11:40 | walk/run at a slow pace. The most important piece of your long duration runs is finishing the run. |
| Sunday | Rest/CT | Rest/CT | Rest | Rest | Rest. If your body feels good, then go ahead and do some form of cross-training for 30 to 60 minutes. |

# Training - Week 2

| Day | Dist. Mile | Dist. KM | Difficulty | Pace (Range) | Instructions |
|---|---|---|---|---|---|
| Monday | Rest | Rest | Rest | Rest | Take it easy. Don't run. If you need to exercise, I recommend a walk for no longer than 30 minutes. |
| Tuesday | 3 | 5 | E | 9:10 - 11:10 | walk/run at an easy pace. |
| Wednesday | 3 | 5 | HM | 9:10 | walk/run at your half marathon pace. |
| Thursday | 3 | 5 | M | 9:10 - 10:10 | walk/run at a medium pace. |
| Friday | Rest | Rest | Rest | Rest | Rest. |
| Saturday | 5 | 8 | S | 9:10 - 11:40 | walk/run at a slow pace. The most important piece of your long duration runs is finishing the run. |
| Sunday | Rest/CT | Rest/CT | Rest | Rest | Rest. If your body feels good, then go ahead and do some form of cross-training for 30 to 60 minutes. |

# Training - Week 3

5K Pace: **8:23**     5k Finish Time: **26 minutes**

| Day | Dist. Mile | Dist. KM | Difficulty | Pace (Range) | Instructions |
|---|---|---|---|---|---|
| Monday | Rest | Rest | Rest | Rest | Take it easy. Don't run. If you need to exercise, I recommend a walk for no longer than 30 minutes. |
| Tuesday | 3 | 5 | E | 9:10 - 11:10 | walk/run at an easy pace. |
| Wednesday | 4 | 6 | HM | 9:10 | walk/run at your half marathon pace. |
| Thursday | 3 | 5 | M | 9:10 - 10:10 | walk/run at a medium pace. |
| Friday | Rest | Rest | Rest | Rest | Rest. |
| Saturday | 6 | 10 | S | 9:10 - 11:40 | walk/run at a slow pace. The most important piece of your long duration runs is finishing the run. |
| Sunday | Rest/CT | Rest/CT | Rest | Rest | Rest. If your body feels good, then go ahead and do some form of cross-training for 30 to 60 minutes. |

# Training - Week 4 (5K Optional)

5K Pace: **8:23**     5k Finish Time: **26 minutes**

| Day | Dist. Mile | Dist. KM | Difficulty | Pace (Range) | Instructions |
|---|---|---|---|---|---|
| Monday | Rest | Rest | Rest | Rest | Take it easy. Don't run. If you need to exercise, I recommend a walk for no longer than 30 minutes. |
| Tuesday | 3 | 5 | E | 9:10 - 11:10 | walk/run at an easy pace. |
| Wednesday | 4 | 6 | HM | 9:10 | walk/run at your half marathon pace. |
| Thursday | 3 | 5 | M | 9:10 - 10:10 | walk/run at a medium pace. |
| Friday | Rest | Rest | Rest | Rest | Rest. |
| Saturday | 6.5 | 10.5 | S | 9:10 - 11:40 | walk/run at a slow pace. The most important piece of your long duration runs is finishing the run. |
| Sunday | Rest/CT | Rest/CT | Rest | Rest | Rest. If your body feels good, then go ahead and do some form of cross-training for 30 to 60 minutes. |

## 5K Optional

| Day | Dist. Mile | Dist. KM | Difficulty | Pace (Range) | Instructions |
|---|---|---|---|---|---|
| Saturday | 3.1 | 5 | - | **8:23** | Run a 5k race instead of your long run. This is completely your choice. I recommend running a 5k race to help you get used to running races. You should see a difference in your race time if you have kept to your training schedule. Don't try for a personal best, run the 5K at your 5K pace. |

# Training - Week 5

5K Pace: **8:23**    5k Finish Time: **26 minutes**

| Day | Dist. Mile | Dist. KM | Difficulty | Pace (Range) | Instructions |
|---|---|---|---|---|---|
| Monday | Rest | Rest | Rest | Rest | Take it easy. Don't run. If you need to exercise, I recommend a walk for no longer than 30 minutes. |
| Tuesday | 3 | 5 | E | 9:10 - 11:10 | walk/run at an easy pace. |
| Wednesday | 4 | 6 | HM | 9:10 | walk/run at your half marathon pace. |
| Thursday | 3 | 5 | M | 9:10 - 10:10 | walk/run at a medium pace. |
| Friday | Rest | Rest | Rest | Rest | Rest. |
| Saturday | 7 | 11 | S | 9:10 - 11:40 | walk/run at a slow pace. The most important piece of your long duration runs is finishing the run. |
| Sunday | Rest/CT | Rest/CT | Rest | Rest | Rest. If your body feels good, then go ahead and do some form of cross-training for 30 to 60 minutes. |

## NOTE:

- Your long duration runs will begin to become more difficult for week 5 and beyond.
- If you get tired during a long duration run, walk for 1/10 mile or 3-5 minutes.

# Training - Week 6

5K Pace: **8:23**     5k Finish Time: **26 minutes**

| Day | Dist. Mile | Dist. KM | Difficulty | Pace (Range) | Instructions |
|---|---|---|---|---|---|
| Monday | Rest | Rest | Rest | Rest | Take it easy. Don't run. If you need to exercise, I recommend a walk for no longer than 30 minutes. |
| Tuesday | 3 | 5 | E | 9:10 - 11:10 | walk/run at an easy pace. |
| Wednesday | 4 | 6 | HM | 9:10 | walk/run at your half marathon pace. |
| Thursday | 3 | 5 | M | 9:10 - 10:10 | walk/run at a medium pace. |
| Friday | Rest | Rest | Rest | Rest | Rest. |
| Saturday | 8 | 13 | S | 9:10 - 11:40 | walk/run at a slow pace. The most important piece of your long duration runs is finishing the run. |
| Sunday | Rest/CT | Rest/CT | Rest | Rest | Rest. If your body feels good, then go ahead and do some form of cross-training for 30 to 60 minutes. |

# Training - Week 7

**5K Pace: 8:23**     **5k Finish Time: 26 minutes**

| Day | Dist. Mile | Dist. KM | Difficulty | Pace (Range) | Instructions |
|---|---|---|---|---|---|
| Monday | Rest | Rest | Rest | Rest | Take it easy. Don't run. If you need to exercise, I recommend a walk for no longer than 30 minutes. |
| Tuesday | 3 | 5 | E | 9:10 - 11:10 | walk/run at an easy pace. |
| Wednesday | 5 | 8 | HM | 9:10 | walk/run at your half marathon pace. |
| Thursday | 3 | 5 | M | 9:10 - 10:10 | walk/run at a medium pace. |
| Friday | Rest | Rest | Rest | Rest | Rest. |
| Saturday | 8.5 | 13.5 | S | 9:10 - 11:40 | walk/run at a slow pace. The most important piece of your long duration runs is finishing the run. |
| Sunday | Rest/CT | Rest/CT | Rest | Rest | Rest. If your body feels good, then go ahead and do some form of cross-training for 30 to 60 minutes. |

## 10K Optional

| Day | Dist. Mile | Dist. KM | Difficulty | Pace (Range) | Instructions |
|---|---|---|---|---|---|
| Thursday | 2 | 3 | E | 9:10 - 11:10 | If you run the optional 10K, either completely rest today or run 2 miles (3 km). |
| Saturday | 6.2 | 10K | - | 8:23 | Run a 10k race instead of your long run. This is completely your choice. I recommend running a 10k race to help you get used to running races. You should see a difference in your race time if you have kept to your training schedule. Don't try for a personal best, run the 10K at your 5K pace. |

# Training - Week 8

5K Pace: **8:23**     5k Finish Time: **26 minutes**

| Day | Dist. Mile | Dist. KM | Difficulty | Pace (Range) | Instructions |
|---|---|---|---|---|---|
| Monday | Rest | Rest | Rest | Rest | Take it easy. Don't run. If you need to exercise, I recommend a walk for no longer than 30 minutes. |
| Tuesday | 3 | 5 | E | 9:10 - 11:10 | walk/run at an easy pace. |
| Wednesday | 5 | 8 | HM | 9:10 | walk/run at your half marathon pace. |
| Thursday | 3 | 5 | M | 9:10 - 10:10 | walk/run at a medium pace. |
| Friday | Rest | Rest | Rest | Rest | Rest. |
| Saturday | 9 | 14 | S | 9:10 - 11:40 | walk/run at a slow pace. The most important piece of your long duration runs is finishing the run. |
| Sunday | Rest/CT | Rest/CT | Rest | Rest | Rest. If your body feels good, then go ahead and do some form of cross-training for 30 to 60 minutes. |

# Training - Week 9

5K Pace: **8:23**     5k Finish Time: **26 minutes**

| Day | Dist. Mile | Dist. KM | Difficulty | Pace (Range) | Instructions |
|---|---|---|---|---|---|
| Monday | Rest | Rest | Rest | Rest | Take it easy. Don't run. If you need to exercise, I recommend a walk for no longer than 30 minutes. |
| Tuesday | 3 | 5 | E | 9:10 - 11:10 | walk/run at an easy pace. |
| Wednesday | 5 | 8 | HM | 9:10 | walk/run at your half marathon pace. |
| Thursday | 3 | 5 | M | 9:10 - 10:10 | walk/run at a medium pace. |
| Friday | Rest | Rest | Rest | Rest | Rest. |
| Saturday | 8.5 | 13.5 | S | 9:10 - 11:40 | walk/run at a slow pace. The most important piece of your long duration runs is finishing the run. |
| Sunday | Rest/CT | Rest/CT | Rest | Rest | Rest. If your body feels good, then go ahead and do some form of cross-training for 30 to 60 minutes. |

## 13.1 Beta/Test Run Optional

| Day | Dist. Mile | Dist. KM | Difficulty | Pace (Range) | Instructions |
|---|---|---|---|---|---|
| Thursday | Rest | Rest | Rest | Rest | This is a rest day – it simulates race week |
| Friday | Rest | Rest | Rest | Rest | This is a rest day – it simulates race week |
| Saturday | 13.1 | 21 | S | 8:23 | I recommend that you attempt to go the full 13.1 miles (21 km) for a half marathon test run. Only walk/run the first 10 miles (16 km) then walk the last 3.1 miles (5 km). If you are successful, you will have a race ghost time to compete against. It will help energize and refocus your training on beating yourself in 3 weeks at the half marathon race. Also, it allows your mind to grasp the achievement of "completing the distance of a half marathon." |

# Training - Week 10

5K Pace: **8:23**     5k Finish Time: **26 minutes**

| Day | Dist. Mile | Dist. KM | Difficulty | Pace (Range) | Instructions |
|---|---|---|---|---|---|
| Monday | Rest | Rest | Rest | Rest | Take it easy. Don't run. If you need to exercise, I recommend a walk for no longer than 30 minutes. |
| Tuesday | 3 | 5 | E | 9:10 - 11:10 | walk/run at an easy pace. |
| Wednesday | 5 | 8 | HM | 9:10 | walk/run at your half marathon pace. |
| Thursday | 3 | 5 | M | 9:10 - 10:10 | walk/run at a medium pace. |
| Friday | Rest | Rest | Rest | Rest | Rest. |
| Saturday | 11 | 18 | S | 9:10 - 11:40 | walk/run at a slow pace. The most important piece of your long duration runs is finishing the run. |
| Sunday | Rest/CT | Rest/CT | Rest | Rest | Rest. If your body feels good, then go ahead and do some form of cross-training for 30 to 60 minutes. |

# Training - Week 11

| Day | Dist. Mile | Dist. KM | Difficulty | Pace (Range) | Instructions |
|---|---|---|---|---|---|
| Monday | Rest | Rest | Rest | Rest | Take it easy. Don't run. If you need to exercise, I recommend a walk for no longer than 30 minutes. |
| Tuesday | 3 | 5 | E | 9:10 - 11:10 | walk/run at an easy pace. |
| Wednesday | 5 | 8 | HM | 9:10 | walk/run at your half marathon pace. |
| Thursday | 3 | 5 | M | 9:10 - 10:10 | walk/run at a medium pace. |
| Friday | Rest | Rest | Rest | Rest | Rest. |
| Saturday | 12 | 20 | S | 9:10 - 11:40 | walk/run at a slow pace. The most important piece of your long duration runs is finishing the run. |
| Sunday | Rest/CT | Rest/CT | Rest | Rest | Rest. If your body feels good, then go ahead and do some form of cross-training for 30 to 60 minutes. |

# Training - Week 12

5K Pace: **8:23**     5k Finish Time: **26 minutes**

| Day | Dist. Mile | Dist. KM | Difficulty | Pace (Range) | Instructions |
|---|---|---|---|---|---|
| Monday | Rest | Rest | Rest | Rest | Take it easy. Don't run. If you need to exercise, I recommend a walk for no longer than 30 minutes. |
| Tuesday | 3 | 5 | E | 9:10 - 11:10 | walk/run at an easy pace. |
| Wednesday | 2 | 1.5 | HM | 9:10 | walk/run at your half marathon pace. |
| Thursday | Rest | Rest | Rest | Rest | Rest. |
| Friday | Rest | Rest | Rest | Rest | Rest. |
| Saturday | 13.1 | 21 | HM | 9:10 | RACE DAY! |
| Sunday | Rest | Rest | Rest | Rest | DRINK A VICTORY BEER! |

## NOTE:

- Get plenty of sleep the night before your long duration run.
- Try to run your long duration run early in the morning.
- After each run, it's important to stretch out your muscles.
- This week your body needs as much rest as possible.
- Don't run past Wednesday.

Half Marathon Training Schedule for

runners with a 5K finish time of 27 minutes

and a pace of *8:42* minutes/mile.

# Predicted Half Marathon Finish Time:

## *2* hour(s) *4* minutes

# PACING TABLES

| Pace | Pace (minutes/miles) |
|---:|---|
| 5k | 8:42 |
| Half marathon | 9:29 |
| Medium | Between 9:29 - 10:29 |
| Easy | Between 9:29 - 11:29 |
| Slow | Between 9:29 - 11:59 |

| Race | Finish Times (predicted) |
|---:|---|
| 5k | 27 minutes |
| Half marathon | 2 hour(s) 4 minutes |

| Determining your pace | |
|---|---|
| Slow Pace | Extremely easy to hold a conversation. |
| Easy Pace | You can hold a conversation with someone. Your breathing might break up some of the flow of the conversation. |
| Medium | You can hold a conversation with someone, but it's broken up into smaller sentences and smaller responses. |
| Half Marathon Pace | Conversation is difficult. One and two word responses back and forth at best. |

## Definitions in the table below:

CT = Cross Training

S = Slow Pace (long run pace)

E = Easy Pace

M = Medium Pace

HM = Half Marathon Pace

# Training - Week A (Optional)

5K Pace: **8:42**     5k Finish Time: **27 minutes**

| Day | Dist. Mile | Dist. KM | Difficulty | Pace (Range) | Instructions |
|---|---|---|---|---|---|
| Monday | Rest | Rest | Rest | Rest | Take it easy. Don't run. If you need to exercise, I recommend a walk for no longer than 30 minutes. |
| Tuesday | 1 | 1.5 | E | 9:29 - 11:29 | walk/run at an easy pace. |
| Wednesday | 1 | 1.5 | HM | 9:29 | walk/run at your half marathon pace. |
| Thursday | 1 | 1.5 | M | 9:29 - 10:29 | walk/run at a medium pace. |
| Friday | Rest | Rest | Rest | Rest | Rest. |
| Saturday | 1.5 | 2.5 | S | 9:29 - 11:59 | walk/run at a slow pace. The most important piece of your long duration runs is finishing the run. |
| Sunday | Rest/CT | Rest/CT | Rest | Rest | Rest. If your body feels good, then go ahead and do some form of cross-training for 30 to 60 minutes. |

# Training - Week B (Optional)

| Day | Dist. Mile | Dist. KM | Difficulty | Pace (Range) | Instructions |
|---|---|---|---|---|---|
| Monday | Rest | Rest | Rest | Rest | Take it easy. Don't run. If you need to exercise, I recommend a walk for no longer than 30 minutes. |
| Tuesday | 1.5 | 2.5 | E | 9:29 - 11:29 | walk/run at an easy pace. |
| Wednesday | 1.5 | 2.5 | HM | 9:29 | walk/run at your half marathon pace. |
| Thursday | 1.5 | 2.5 | M | 9:29 - 10:29 | walk/run at a medium pace. |
| Friday | Rest | Rest | Rest | Rest | Rest. |
| Saturday | 2 | 3 | S | 9:29 - 11:59 | walk/run at a slow pace. The most important piece of your long duration runs is finishing the run. |
| Sunday | Rest/CT | Rest/CT | Rest | Rest | Rest. If your body feels good, then go ahead and do some form of cross-training for 30 to 60 minutes. |

# Training - Week C (Optional)

5K Pace: **8:42**   5k Finish Time: **27 minutes**

| Day | Dist. Mile | Dist. KM | Difficulty | Pace (Range) | Instructions |
|---|---|---|---|---|---|
| Monday | Rest | Rest | Rest | Rest | Take it easy. Don't run. If you need to exercise, I recommend a walk for no longer than 30 minutes. |
| Tuesday | 2 | 3 | E | 9:29 - 11:29 | walk/run at an easy pace. |
| Wednesday | 2 | 3 | HM | 9:29 | walk/run at your half marathon pace. |
| Thursday | 2 | 3 | M | 9:29 - 10:29 | walk/run at a medium pace. |
| Friday | Rest | Rest | Rest | Rest | Rest. |
| Saturday | 3 | 5 | S | 9:29 - 11:59 | walk/run at a slow pace. The most important piece of your long duration runs is finishing the run. |
| Sunday | Rest/CT | Rest/CT | Rest | Rest | Rest. If your body feels good, then go ahead and do some form of cross-training for 30 to 60 minutes. |

# Training - Week 1

5K Pace: **8:42**     5k Finish Time: **27 minutes**

| Day | Dist. Mile | Dist. KM | Difficulty | Pace (Range) | Instructions |
|---|---|---|---|---|---|
| Monday | Rest | Rest | Rest | Rest | Take it easy. Don't run. If you need to exercise, I recommend a walk for no longer than 30 minutes. |
| Tuesday | 3 | 5 | E | 9:29 - 11:29 | walk/run at an easy pace. |
| Wednesday | 3 | 5 | HM | 9:29 | walk/run at your half marathon pace. |
| Thursday | 3 | 5 | M | 9:29 - 10:29 | walk/run at a medium pace. |
| Friday | Rest | Rest | Rest | Rest | Rest. |
| Saturday | 4 | 6 | S | 9:29 - 11:59 | walk/run at a slow pace. The most important piece of your long duration runs is finishing the run. |
| Sunday | Rest/CT | Rest/CT | Rest | Rest | Rest. If your body feels good, then go ahead and do some form of cross-training for 30 to 60 minutes. |

# Training - Week 2

| Day | Dist. Mile | Dist. KM | Difficulty | Pace (Range) | Instructions |
|---|---|---|---|---|---|
| Monday | Rest | Rest | Rest | Rest | Take it easy. Don't run. If you need to exercise, I recommend a walk for no longer than 30 minutes. |
| Tuesday | 3 | 5 | E | 9:29 - 11:29 | walk/run at an easy pace. |
| Wednesday | 3 | 5 | HM | 9:29 | walk/run at your half marathon pace. |
| Thursday | 3 | 5 | M | 9:29 - 10:29 | walk/run at a medium pace. |
| Friday | Rest | Rest | Rest | Rest | Rest. |
| Saturday | 5 | 8 | S | 9:29 - 11:59 | walk/run at a slow pace. The most important piece of your long duration runs is finishing the run. |
| Sunday | Rest/CT | Rest/CT | Rest | Rest | Rest. If your body feels good, then go ahead and do some form of cross-training for 30 to 60 minutes. |

# Training - Week 3

5K Pace: **8:42**     5k Finish Time: **27 minutes**

| Day | Dist. Mile | Dist. KM | Difficulty | Pace (Range) | Instructions |
|---|---|---|---|---|---|
| Monday | Rest | Rest | Rest | Rest | Take it easy. Don't run. If you need to exercise, I recommend a walk for no longer than 30 minutes. |
| Tuesday | 3 | 5 | E | 9:29 - 11:29 | walk/run at an easy pace. |
| Wednesday | 4 | 6 | HM | 9:29 | walk/run at your half marathon pace. |
| Thursday | 3 | 5 | M | 9:29 - 10:29 | walk/run at a medium pace. |
| Friday | Rest | Rest | Rest | Rest | Rest. |
| Saturday | 6 | 10 | S | 9:29 - 11:59 | walk/run at a slow pace. The most important piece of your long duration runs is finishing the run. |
| Sunday | Rest/CT | Rest/CT | Rest | Rest | Rest. If your body feels good, then go ahead and do some form of cross-training for 30 to 60 minutes. |

# Training - Week 4 (5K Optional)

5K Pace: **8:42**     5k Finish Time: **27 minutes**

| Day | Dist. Mile | Dist. KM | Difficulty | Pace (Range) | Instructions |
|---|---|---|---|---|---|
| Monday | Rest | Rest | Rest | Rest | Take it easy. Don't run. If you need to exercise, I recommend a walk for no longer than 30 minutes. |
| Tuesday | 3 | 5 | E | 9:29 - 11:29 | walk/run at an easy pace. |
| Wednesday | 4 | 6 | HM | 9:29 | walk/run at your half marathon pace. |
| Thursday | 3 | 5 | M | 9:29 - 10:29 | walk/run at a medium pace. |
| Friday | Rest | Rest | Rest | Rest | Rest. |
| Saturday | 6.5 | 10.5 | S | 9:29 - 11:59 | walk/run at a slow pace. The most important piece of your long duration runs is finishing the run. |
| Sunday | Rest/CT | Rest/CT | Rest | Rest | Rest. If your body feels good, then go ahead and do some form of cross-training for 30 to 60 minutes. |

## 5K Optional

| Day | Dist. Mile | Dist. KM | Difficulty | Pace (Range) | Instructions |
|---|---|---|---|---|---|
| Saturday | 3.1 | 5 | - | **8:42** | Run a 5k race instead of your long run. This is completely your choice. I recommend running a 5k race to help you get used to running races. You should see a difference in your race time if you have kept to your training schedule. Don't try for a personal best, run the 5K at your 5K pace. |

# Training - Week 5

5K Pace: **8:42**     5k Finish Time: **27 minutes**

| Day | Dist. Mile | Dist. KM | Difficulty | Pace (Range) | Instructions |
|---|---|---|---|---|---|
| Monday | Rest | Rest | Rest | Rest | Take it easy. Don't run. If you need to exercise, I recommend a walk for no longer than 30 minutes. |
| Tuesday | 3 | 5 | E | 9:29 - 11:29 | walk/run at an easy pace. |
| Wednesday | 4 | 6 | HM | 9:29 | walk/run at your half marathon pace. |
| Thursday | 3 | 5 | M | 9:29 - 10:29 | walk/run at a medium pace. |
| Friday | Rest | Rest | Rest | Rest | Rest. |
| Saturday | 7 | 11 | S | 9:29 - 11:59 | walk/run at a slow pace. The most important piece of your long duration runs is finishing the run. |
| Sunday | Rest/CT | Rest/CT | Rest | Rest | Rest. If your body feels good, then go ahead and do some form of cross-training for 30 to 60 minutes. |

## NOTE:

- Your long duration runs will begin to become more difficult for week 5 and beyond.
- If you get tired during a long duration run, walk for 1/10 mile or 3-5 minutes.

# Training - Week 6

5K Pace: **8:42**     5k Finish Time: **27 minutes**

| Day | Dist. Mile | Dist. KM | Difficulty | Pace (Range) | Instructions |
|---|---|---|---|---|---|
| Monday | Rest | Rest | Rest | Rest | Take it easy. Don't run. If you need to exercise, I recommend a walk for no longer than 30 minutes. |
| Tuesday | 3 | 5 | E | 9:29 - 11:29 | walk/run at an easy pace. |
| Wednesday | 4 | 6 | HM | 9:29 | walk/run at your half marathon pace. |
| Thursday | 3 | 5 | M | 9:29 - 10:29 | walk/run at a medium pace. |
| Friday | Rest | Rest | Rest | Rest | Rest. |
| Saturday | 8 | 13 | S | 9:29 - 11:59 | walk/run at a slow pace. The most important piece of your long duration runs is finishing the run. |
| Sunday | Rest/CT | Rest/CT | Rest | Rest | Rest. If your body feels good, then go ahead and do some form of cross-training for 30 to 60 minutes. |

# Training - Week 7

5K Pace: **8:42**     5k Finish Time: **27 minutes**

| Day | Dist. Mile | Dist. KM | Difficulty | Pace (Range) | Instructions |
|---|---|---|---|---|---|
| Monday | Rest | Rest | Rest | Rest | Take it easy. Don't run. If you need to exercise, I recommend a walk for no longer than 30 minutes. |
| Tuesday | 3 | 5 | E | 9:29 - 11:29 | walk/run at an easy pace. |
| Wednesday | 5 | 8 | HM | 9:29 | walk/run at your half marathon pace. |
| Thursday | 3 | 5 | M | 9:29 - 10:29 | walk/run at a medium pace. |
| Friday | Rest | Rest | Rest | Rest | Rest. |
| Saturday | 8.5 | 13.5 | S | 9:29 - 11:59 | walk/run at a slow pace. The most important piece of your long duration runs is finishing the run. |
| Sunday | Rest/CT | Rest/CT | Rest | Rest | Rest. If your body feels good, then go ahead and do some form of cross-training for 30 to 60 minutes. |

## 10K Optional

| Day | Dist. Mile | Dist. KM | Difficulty | Pace (Range) | Instructions |
|---|---|---|---|---|---|
| Thursday | 2 | 3 | E | 9:29 - 11:29 | If you run the optional 10K, either completely rest today or run 2 miles (3 km). |
| Saturday | 6.2 | 10K | - | **8:42** | Run a 10k race instead of your long run. This is completely your choice. I recommend running a 10k race to help you get used to running races. You should see a difference in your race time if you have kept to your training schedule. Don't try for a personal best, run the 10K at your 5K pace. |

# Training - Week 8

5K Pace: **8:42**       5k Finish Time: **27 minutes**

| Day | Dist. Mile | Dist. KM | Difficulty | Pace (Range) | Instructions |
|---|---|---|---|---|---|
| Monday | Rest | Rest | Rest | Rest | Take it easy. Don't run. If you need to exercise, I recommend a walk for no longer than 30 minutes. |
| Tuesday | 3 | 5 | E | 9:29 - 11:29 | walk/run at an easy pace. |
| Wednesday | 5 | 8 | HM | 9:29 | walk/run at your half marathon pace. |
| Thursday | 3 | 5 | M | 9:29 - 10:29 | walk/run at a medium pace. |
| Friday | Rest | Rest | Rest | Rest | Rest. |
| Saturday | 9 | 14 | S | 9:29 - 11:59 | walk/run at a slow pace. The most important piece of your long duration runs is finishing the run. |
| Sunday | Rest/CT | Rest/CT | Rest | Rest | Rest. If your body feels good, then go ahead and do some form of cross-training for 30 to 60 minutes. |

# Training - Week 9

5K Pace: **8:42**     5k Finish Time: **27 minutes**

| Day | Dist. Mile | Dist. KM | Difficulty | Pace (Range) | Instructions |
|---|---|---|---|---|---|
| Monday | Rest | Rest | Rest | Rest | Take it easy. Don't run. If you need to exercise, I recommend a walk for no longer than 30 minutes. |
| Tuesday | 3 | 5 | E | 9:29 - 11:29 | walk/run at an easy pace. |
| Wednesday | 5 | 8 | HM | 9:29 | walk/run at your half marathon pace. |
| Thursday | 3 | 5 | M | 9:29 - 10:29 | walk/run at a medium pace. |
| Friday | Rest | Rest | Rest | Rest | Rest. |
| Saturday | 8.5 | 13.5 | S | 9:29 - 11:59 | walk/run at a slow pace. The most important piece of your long duration runs is finishing the run. |
| Sunday | Rest/CT | Rest/CT | Rest | Rest | Rest. If your body feels good, then go ahead and do some form of cross-training for 30 to 60 minutes. |

## 13.1 Beta/Test Run Optional

| Day | Dist. Mile | Dist. KM | Difficulty | Pace (Range) | Instructions |
|---|---|---|---|---|---|
| Thursday | Rest | Rest | Rest | Rest | This is a rest day – it simulates race week |
| Friday | Rest | Rest | Rest | Rest | This is a rest day – it simulates race week |
| Saturday | 13.1 | 21 | S | 8:42 | I recommend that you attempt to go the full 13.1 miles (21 km) for a half marathon test run. <u>Only walk/run the first 10 miles (16 km) then walk the last 3.1 miles (5 km).</u> If you are successful, you will have a race ghost time to compete against. It will help energize and refocus your training on beating yourself in 3 weeks at the half marathon race. Also, it allows your mind to grasp the achievement of "completing the distance of a half marathon." |

# Training - Week 10

5K Pace: **8:42**     5k Finish Time: **27 minutes**

| Day | Dist. Mile | Dist. KM | Difficulty | Pace (Range) | Instructions |
|---|---|---|---|---|---|
| Monday | Rest | Rest | Rest | Rest | Take it easy. Don't run. If you need to exercise, I recommend a walk for no longer than 30 minutes. |
| Tuesday | 3 | 5 | E | 9:29 - 11:29 | walk/run at an easy pace. |
| Wednesday | 5 | 8 | HM | 9:29 | walk/run at your half marathon pace. |
| Thursday | 3 | 5 | M | 9:29 - 10:29 | walk/run at a medium pace. |
| Friday | Rest | Rest | Rest | Rest | Rest. |
| Saturday | 11 | 18 | S | 9:29 - 11:59 | walk/run at a slow pace. The most important piece of your long duration runs is finishing the run. |
| Sunday | Rest/CT | Rest/CT | Rest | Rest | Rest. If your body feels good, then go ahead and do some form of cross-training for 30 to 60 minutes. |

# Training - Week 11

| Day | Dist. Mile | Dist. KM | Difficulty | Pace (Range) | Instructions |
|---|---|---|---|---|---|
| Monday | Rest | Rest | Rest | Rest | Take it easy. Don't run. If you need to exercise, I recommend a walk for no longer than 30 minutes. |
| Tuesday | 3 | 5 | E | 9:29 - 11:29 | walk/run at an easy pace. |
| Wednesday | 5 | 8 | HM | 9:29 | walk/run at your half marathon pace. |
| Thursday | 3 | 5 | M | 9:29 - 10:29 | walk/run at a medium pace. |
| Friday | Rest | Rest | Rest | Rest | Rest. |
| Saturday | 12 | 20 | S | 9:29 - 11:59 | walk/run at a slow pace. The most important piece of your long duration runs is finishing the run. |
| Sunday | Rest/CT | Rest/CT | Rest | Rest | Rest. If your body feels good, then go ahead and do some form of cross-training for 30 to 60 minutes. |

# Training - Week 12

5K Pace: **8:42**    5k Finish Time: **27 minutes**

| Day | Dist. Mile | Dist. KM | Difficulty | Pace (Range) | Instructions |
|---|---|---|---|---|---|
| Monday | Rest | Rest | Rest | Rest | Take it easy. Don't run. If you need to exercise, I recommend a walk for no longer than 30 minutes. |
| Tuesday | 3 | 5 | E | 9:29 - 11:29 | walk/run at an easy pace. |
| Wednesday | 2 | 1.5 | HM | 9:29 | walk/run at your half marathon pace. |
| Thursday | Rest | Rest | Rest | Rest | Rest. |
| Friday | Rest | Rest | Rest | Rest | Rest. |
| Saturday | 13.1 | 21 | HM | 9:29 | RACE DAY! |
| Sunday | Rest | Rest | Rest | Rest | DRINK A VICTORY BEER! |

## NOTE:

- Get plenty of sleep the night before your long duration run.
- Try to run your long duration run early in the morning.
- After each run, it's important to stretch out your muscles.
- This week your body needs as much rest as possible.
- Don't run past Wednesday.

Half Marathon Training Schedule for

runners with a 5K finish time of 28 minutes

and a pace of *9:01* minutes/mile.

## Predicted Half Marathon Finish Time:

## *2* hour(s) *9* minutes

# PACING TABLES

| Pace | Pace (minutes/miles) |
|---:|---|
| 5k | 9:01 |
| Half marathon | 9:50 |
| Medium | Between 9:50 - 10:50 |
| Easy | Between 9:50 - 11:50 |
| Slow | Between 9:50 - 12:20 |

| Race | Finish Times (predicted) |
|---:|---|
| 5k | 28 minutes |
| Half marathon | 2 hour(s) 9 minutes |

| Determining your pace | |
|---|---|
| Slow Pace | Extremely easy to hold a conversation. |
| Easy Pace | You can hold a conversation with someone. Your breathing might break up some of the flow of the conversation. |
| Medium | You can hold a conversation with someone, but it's broken up into smaller sentences and smaller responses. |
| Half Marathon Pace | Conversation is difficult. One and two word responses back and forth at best. |

## Definitions in the table below:

CT = Cross Training

S = Slow Pace (long run pace)

E = Easy Pace

M = Medium Pace

HM = Half Marathon Pace

## Training - Week A (Optional)

5K Pace: **9:01**  5k Finish Time: **28 minutes**

| Day | Dist. Mile | Dist. KM | Difficulty | Pace (Range) | Instructions |
|---|---|---|---|---|---|
| Monday | Rest | Rest | Rest | Rest | Take it easy. Don't run. If you need to exercise, I recommend a walk for no longer than 30 minutes. |
| Tuesday | 1 | 1.5 | E | 9:50 - 11:50 | walk/run at an easy pace. |
| Wednesday | 1 | 1.5 | HM | 9:50 | walk/run at your half marathon pace. |
| Thursday | 1 | 1.5 | M | 9:50 - 10:50 | walk/run at a medium pace. |
| Friday | Rest | Rest | Rest | Rest | Rest. |
| Saturday | 1.5 | 2.5 | S | 9:50 - 12:20 | walk/run at a slow pace. The most important piece of your long duration runs is finishing the run. |
| Sunday | Rest/CT | Rest/CT | Rest | Rest | Rest. If your body feels good, then go ahead and do some form of cross-training for 30 to 60 minutes. |

## Training - Week B (Optional)

| Day | Dist. Mile | Dist. KM | Difficulty | Pace (Range) | Instructions |
|---|---|---|---|---|---|
| Monday | Rest | Rest | Rest | Rest | Take it easy. Don't run. If you need to exercise, I recommend a walk for no longer than 30 minutes. |
| Tuesday | 1.5 | 2.5 | E | 9:50 - 11:50 | walk/run at an easy pace. |
| Wednesday | 1.5 | 2.5 | HM | 9:50 | walk/run at your half marathon pace. |
| Thursday | 1.5 | 2.5 | M | 9:50 - 10:50 | walk/run at a medium pace. |
| Friday | Rest | Rest | Rest | Rest | Rest. |
| Saturday | 2 | 3 | S | 9:50 - 12:20 | walk/run at a slow pace. The most important piece of your long duration runs is finishing the run. |
| Sunday | Rest/CT | Rest/CT | Rest | Rest | Rest. If your body feels good, then go ahead and do some form of cross-training for 30 to 60 minutes. |

# Training - Week C (Optional)

5K Pace: **9:01**     5k Finish Time: **28 minutes**

| Day | Dist. Mile | Dist. KM | Difficulty | Pace (Range) | Instructions |
|---|---|---|---|---|---|
| Monday | Rest | Rest | Rest | Rest | Take it easy. Don't run. If you need to exercise, I recommend a walk for no longer than 30 minutes. |
| Tuesday | 2 | 3 | E | 9:50 - 11:50 | walk/run at an easy pace. |
| Wednesday | 2 | 3 | HM | 9:50 | walk/run at your half marathon pace. |
| Thursday | 2 | 3 | M | 9:50 - 10:50 | walk/run at a medium pace. |
| Friday | Rest | Rest | Rest | Rest | Rest. |
| Saturday | 3 | 5 | S | 9:50 - 12:20 | walk/run at a slow pace. The most important piece of your long duration runs is finishing the run. |
| Sunday | Rest/CT | Rest/CT | Rest | Rest | Rest. If your body feels good, then go ahead and do some form of cross-training for 30 to 60 minutes. |

# Training - Week 1

5K Pace: **9:01**     5k Finish Time: **28 minutes**

| Day | Dist. Mile | Dist. KM | Difficulty | Pace (Range) | Instructions |
|---|---|---|---|---|---|
| Monday | Rest | Rest | Rest | Rest | Take it easy. Don't run. If you need to exercise, I recommend a walk for no longer than 30 minutes. |
| Tuesday | 3 | 5 | E | 9:50 - 11:50 | walk/run at an easy pace. |
| Wednesday | 3 | 5 | HM | 9:50 | walk/run at your half marathon pace. |
| Thursday | 3 | 5 | M | 9:50 - 10:50 | walk/run at a medium pace. |
| Friday | Rest | Rest | Rest | Rest | Rest. |
| Saturday | 4 | 6 | S | 9:50 - 12:20 | walk/run at a slow pace. The most important piece of your long duration runs is finishing the run. |
| Sunday | Rest/CT | Rest/CT | Rest | Rest | Rest. If your body feels good, then go ahead and do some form of cross-training for 30 to 60 minutes. |

# Training - Week 2

| Day | Dist. Mile | Dist. KM | Difficulty | Pace (Range) | Instructions |
|---|---|---|---|---|---|
| Monday | Rest | Rest | Rest | Rest | Take it easy. Don't run. If you need to exercise, I recommend a walk for no longer than 30 minutes. |
| Tuesday | 3 | 5 | E | 9:50 - 11:50 | walk/run at an easy pace. |
| Wednesday | 3 | 5 | HM | 9:50 | walk/run at your half marathon pace. |
| Thursday | 3 | 5 | M | 9:50 - 10:50 | walk/run at a medium pace. |
| Friday | Rest | Rest | Rest | Rest | Rest. |
| Saturday | 5 | 8 | S | 9:50 - 12:20 | walk/run at a slow pace. The most important piece of your long duration runs is finishing the run. |
| Sunday | Rest/CT | Rest/CT | Rest | Rest | Rest. If your body feels good, then go ahead and do some form of cross-training for 30 to 60 minutes. |

# Training - Week 3

5K Pace: **9:01**     5k Finish Time: **28 minutes**

| Day | Dist. Mile | Dist. KM | Difficulty | Pace (Range) | Instructions |
|---|---|---|---|---|---|
| Monday | Rest | Rest | Rest | Rest | Take it easy. Don't run. If you need to exercise, I recommend a walk for no longer than 30 minutes. |
| Tuesday | 3 | 5 | E | 9:50 - 11:50 | walk/run at an easy pace. |
| Wednesday | 4 | 6 | HM | 9:50 | walk/run at your half marathon pace. |
| Thursday | 3 | 5 | M | 9:50 - 10:50 | walk/run at a medium pace. |
| Friday | Rest | Rest | Rest | Rest | Rest. |
| Saturday | 6 | 10 | S | 9:50 - 12:20 | walk/run at a slow pace. The most important piece of your long duration runs is finishing the run. |
| Sunday | Rest/CT | Rest/CT | Rest | Rest | Rest. If your body feels good, then go ahead and do some form of cross-training for 30 to 60 minutes. |

# Training - Week 4 (5K Optional)

5K Pace: **9:01**     5k Finish Time: **28 minutes**

| Day | Dist. Mile | Dist. KM | Difficulty | Pace (Range) | Instructions |
|---|---|---|---|---|---|
| Monday | Rest | Rest | Rest | Rest | Take it easy. Don't run. If you need to exercise, I recommend a walk for no longer than 30 minutes. |
| Tuesday | 3 | 5 | E | 9:50 - 11:50 | walk/run at an easy pace. |
| Wednesday | 4 | 6 | HM | 9:50 | walk/run at your half marathon pace. |
| Thursday | 3 | 5 | M | 9:50 - 10:50 | walk/run at a medium pace. |
| Friday | Rest | Rest | Rest | Rest | Rest. |
| Saturday | 6.5 | 10.5 | S | 9:50 - 12:20 | walk/run at a slow pace. The most important piece of your long duration runs is finishing the run. |
| Sunday | Rest/CT | Rest/CT | Rest | Rest | Rest. If your body feels good, then go ahead and do some form of cross-training for 30 to 60 minutes. |

## 5K Optional

| Day | Dist. Mile | Dist. KM | Difficulty | Pace (Range) | Instructions |
|---|---|---|---|---|---|
| Saturday | 3.1 | 5 | - | 9:01 | Run a 5k race instead of your long run. This is completely your choice. I recommend running a 5k race to help you get used to running races. You should see a difference in your race time if you have kept to your training schedule. Don't try for a personal best, run the 5K at your 5K pace. |

# Training - Week 5

5K Pace: **9:01**     5k Finish Time: **28 minutes**

| Day | Dist. Mile | Dist. KM | Difficulty | Pace (Range) | Instructions |
|---|---|---|---|---|---|
| Monday | Rest | Rest | Rest | Rest | Take it easy. Don't run. If you need to exercise, I recommend a walk for no longer than 30 minutes. |
| Tuesday | 3 | 5 | E | 9:50 - 11:50 | walk/run at an easy pace. |
| Wednesday | 4 | 6 | HM | 9:50 | walk/run at your half marathon pace. |
| Thursday | 3 | 5 | M | 9:50 - 10:50 | walk/run at a medium pace. |
| Friday | Rest | Rest | Rest | Rest | Rest. |
| Saturday | 7 | 11 | S | 9:50 - 12:20 | walk/run at a slow pace. The most important piece of your long duration runs is finishing the run. |
| Sunday | Rest/CT | Rest/CT | Rest | Rest | Rest. If your body feels good, then go ahead and do some form of cross-training for 30 to 60 minutes. |

## NOTE:

- Your long duration runs will begin to become more difficult for week 5 and beyond.
- If you get tired during a long duration run, walk for 1/10 mile or 3-5 minutes.

# Training - Week 6

5K Pace: **9:01**  5k Finish Time: **28 minutes**

| Day | Dist. Mile | Dist. KM | Difficulty | Pace (Range) | Instructions |
|---|---|---|---|---|---|
| Monday | Rest | Rest | Rest | Rest | Take it easy. Don't run. If you need to exercise, I recommend a walk for no longer than 30 minutes. |
| Tuesday | 3 | 5 | E | 9:50 - 11:50 | walk/run at an easy pace. |
| Wednesday | 4 | 6 | HM | 9:50 | walk/run at your half marathon pace. |
| Thursday | 3 | 5 | M | 9:50 - 10:50 | walk/run at a medium pace. |
| Friday | Rest | Rest | Rest | Rest | Rest. |
| Saturday | 8 | 13 | S | 9:50 - 12:20 | walk/run at a slow pace. The most important piece of your long duration runs is finishing the run. |
| Sunday | Rest/CT | Rest/CT | Rest | Rest | Rest. If your body feels good, then go ahead and do some form of cross-training for 30 to 60 minutes. |

# Training - Week 7

5K Pace: **9:01**     5k Finish Time: **28 minutes**

| Day | Dist. Mile | Dist. KM | Difficulty | Pace (Range) | Instructions |
|---|---|---|---|---|---|
| Monday | Rest | Rest | Rest | Rest | Take it easy. Don't run. If you need to exercise, I recommend a walk for no longer than 30 minutes. |
| Tuesday | 3 | 5 | E | 9:50 - 11:50 | walk/run at an easy pace. |
| Wednesday | 5 | 8 | HM | 9:50 | walk/run at your half marathon pace. |
| Thursday | 3 | 5 | M | 9:50 - 10:50 | walk/run at a medium pace. |
| Friday | Rest | Rest | Rest | Rest | Rest. |
| Saturday | 8.5 | 13.5 | S | 9:50 - 12:20 | walk/run at a slow pace. The most important piece of your long duration runs is finishing the run. |
| Sunday | Rest/CT | Rest/CT | Rest | Rest | Rest. If your body feels good, then go ahead and do some form of cross-training for 30 to 60 minutes. |

## 10K Optional

| Day | Dist. Mile | Dist. KM | Difficulty | Pace (Range) | Instructions |
|---|---|---|---|---|---|
| Thursday | 2 | 3 | E | 9:50 - 11:50 | If you run the optional 10K, either completely rest today or run 2 miles (3 km). |
| Saturday | 6.2 | 10K | - | 9:01 | Run a 10k race instead of your long run. This is completely your choice. I recommend running a 10k race to help you get used to running races. You should see a difference in your race time if you have kept to your training schedule. Don't try for a personal best, run the 10K at your 5K pace. |

# Training - Week 8

5K Pace: **9:01**  5k Finish Time: **28 minutes**

| Day | Dist. Mile | Dist. KM | Difficulty | Pace (Range) | Instructions |
|---|---|---|---|---|---|
| Monday | Rest | Rest | Rest | Rest | Take it easy. Don't run. If you need to exercise, I recommend a walk for no longer than 30 minutes. |
| Tuesday | 3 | 5 | E | 9:50 - 11:50 | walk/run at an easy pace. |
| Wednesday | 5 | 8 | HM | 9:50 | walk/run at your half marathon pace. |
| Thursday | 3 | 5 | M | 9:50 - 10:50 | walk/run at a medium pace. |
| Friday | Rest | Rest | Rest | Rest | Rest. |
| Saturday | 9 | 14 | S | 9:50 - 12:20 | walk/run at a slow pace. The most important piece of your long duration runs is finishing the run. |
| Sunday | Rest/CT | Rest/CT | Rest | Rest | Rest. If your body feels good, then go ahead and do some form of cross-training for 30 to 60 minutes. |

# Training - Week 9

5K Pace: **9:01**     5k Finish Time: **28 minutes**

| Day | Dist. Mile | Dist. KM | Difficulty | Pace (Range) | Instructions |
|---|---|---|---|---|---|
| Monday | Rest | Rest | Rest | Rest | Take it easy. Don't run. If you need to exercise, I recommend a walk for no longer than 30 minutes. |
| Tuesday | 3 | 5 | E | 9:50 - 11:50 | walk/run at an easy pace. |
| Wednesday | 5 | 8 | HM | 9:50 | walk/run at your half marathon pace. |
| Thursday | 3 | 5 | M | 9:50 - 10:50 | walk/run at a medium pace. |
| Friday | Rest | Rest | Rest | Rest | Rest. |
| Saturday | 8.5 | 13.5 | S | 9:50 - 12:20 | walk/run at a slow pace. The most important piece of your long duration runs is finishing the run. |
| Sunday | Rest/CT | Rest/CT | Rest | Rest | Rest. If your body feels good, then go ahead and do some form of cross-training for 30 to 60 minutes. |

## 13.1 Beta/Test Run Optional

| Day | Dist. Mile | Dist. KM | Difficulty | Pace (Range) | Instructions |
|---|---|---|---|---|---|
| Thursday | Rest | Rest | Rest | Rest | This is a rest day – it simulates race week |
| Friday | Rest | Rest | Rest | Rest | This is a rest day – it simulates race week |
| Saturday | 13.1 | 21 | S | 9:01 | I recommend that you attempt to go the full 13.1 miles (21 km) for a half marathon test run. Only walk/run the first 10 miles (16 km) then walk the last 3.1 miles (5 km). If you are successful, you will have a race ghost time to compete against. It will help energize and refocus your training on beating yourself in 3 weeks at the half marathon race. Also, it allows your mind to grasp the achievement of "completing the distance of a half marathon." |

# Training - Week 10

5K Pace: **9:01**    5k Finish Time: **28 minutes**

| Day | Dist. Mile | Dist. KM | Difficulty | Pace (Range) | Instructions |
|---|---|---|---|---|---|
| Monday | Rest | Rest | Rest | Rest | Take it easy. Don't run. If you need to exercise, I recommend a walk for no longer than 30 minutes. |
| Tuesday | 3 | 5 | E | 9:50 - 11:50 | walk/run at an easy pace. |
| Wednesday | 5 | 8 | HM | 9:50 | walk/run at your half marathon pace. |
| Thursday | 3 | 5 | M | 9:50 - 10:50 | walk/run at a medium pace. |
| Friday | Rest | Rest | Rest | Rest | Rest. |
| Saturday | 11 | 18 | S | 9:50 - 12:20 | walk/run at a slow pace. The most important piece of your long duration runs is finishing the run. |
| Sunday | Rest/CT | Rest/CT | Rest | Rest | Rest. If your body feels good, then go ahead and do some form of cross-training for 30 to 60 minutes. |

# Training - Week 11

| Day | Dist. Mile | Dist. KM | Difficulty | Pace (Range) | Instructions |
|---|---|---|---|---|---|
| Monday | Rest | Rest | Rest | Rest | Take it easy. Don't run. If you need to exercise, I recommend a walk for no longer than 30 minutes. |
| Tuesday | 3 | 5 | E | 9:50 - 11:50 | walk/run at an easy pace. |
| Wednesday | 5 | 8 | HM | 9:50 | walk/run at your half marathon pace. |
| Thursday | 3 | 5 | M | 9:50 - 10:50 | walk/run at a medium pace. |
| Friday | Rest | Rest | Rest | Rest | Rest. |
| Saturday | 12 | 20 | S | 9:50 - 12:20 | walk/run at a slow pace. The most important piece of your long duration runs is finishing the run. |
| Sunday | Rest/CT | Rest/CT | Rest | Rest | Rest. If your body feels good, then go ahead and do some form of cross-training for 30 to 60 minutes. |

# Training - Week 12

5K Pace: **9:01**    5k Finish Time: **28 minutes**

| Day | Dist. Mile | Dist. KM | Difficulty | Pace (Range) | Instructions |
|---|---|---|---|---|---|
| Monday | Rest | Rest | Rest | Rest | Take it easy. Don't run. If you need to exercise, I recommend a walk for no longer than 30 minutes. |
| Tuesday | 3 | 5 | E | 9:50 - 11:50 | walk/run at an easy pace. |
| Wednesday | 2 | 1.5 | HM | 9:50 | walk/run at your half marathon pace. |
| Thursday | Rest | Rest | Rest | Rest | Rest. |
| Friday | Rest | Rest | Rest | Rest | Rest. |
| Saturday | 13.1 | 21 | HM | 9:50 | RACE DAY! |
| Sunday | Rest | Rest | Rest | Rest | DRINK A VICTORY BEER! |

## NOTE:

- Get plenty of sleep the night before your long duration run.
- Try to run your long duration run early in the morning.
- After each run, it's important to stretch out your muscles.
- This week your body needs as much rest as possible.
- Don't run past Wednesday.

Half Marathon Training Schedule for runners with a 5K finish time of 29 minutes and a pace of *9:21* minutes/mile.

**Predicted Half Marathon Finish Time:**

*2* hour(s) *13* minutes

# PACING TABLES

| Pace | Pace (minutes/miles) |
|---:|---|
| 5k | 9:21 |
| Half marathon | 10:10 |
| Medium | Between 10:10 - 11:10 |
| Easy | Between 10:10 - 12:10 |
| Slow | Between 10:10 - 12:40 |

| Race | Finish Times (predicted) |
|---:|---|
| 5k | 29 minutes |
| Half marathon | 2 hour(s) 13 minutes |

| Determining your pace | |
|---|---|
| Slow Pace | Extremely easy to hold a conversation. |
| Easy Pace | You can hold a conversation with someone. Your breathing might break up some of the flow of the conversation. |
| Medium | You can hold a conversation with someone, but it's broken up into smaller sentences and smaller responses. |
| Half Marathon Pace | Conversation is difficult. One and two word responses back and forth at best. |

## Definitions in the table below:

CT = Cross Training

S = Slow Pace (long run pace)

E = Easy Pace

M = Medium Pace

HM = Half Marathon Pace

# Training - Week A (Optional)

5K Pace: **9:21**        5k Finish Time: **29 minutes**

| Day | Dist. Mile | Dist. KM | Difficulty | Pace (Range) | Instructions |
|---|---|---|---|---|---|
| Monday | Rest | Rest | Rest | Rest | Take it easy. Don't run. If you need to exercise, I recommend a walk for no longer than 30 minutes. |
| Tuesday | 1 | 1.5 | E | 10:10 - 12:10 | walk/run at an easy pace. |
| Wednesday | 1 | 1.5 | HM | 10:10 | walk/run at your half marathon pace. |
| Thursday | 1 | 1.5 | M | 10:10 - 11:10 | walk/run at a medium pace. |
| Friday | Rest | Rest | Rest | Rest | Rest. |
| Saturday | 1.5 | 2.5 | S | 10:10 - 12:40 | walk/run at a slow pace. The most important piece of your long duration runs is finishing the run. |
| Sunday | Rest/CT | Rest/CT | Rest | Rest | Rest. If your body feels good, then go ahead and do some form of cross-training for 30 to 60 minutes. |

# Training - Week B (Optional)

| Day | Dist. Mile | Dist. KM | Difficulty | Pace (Range) | Instructions |
|---|---|---|---|---|---|
| Monday | Rest | Rest | Rest | Rest | Take it easy. Don't run. If you need to exercise, I recommend a walk for no longer than 30 minutes. |
| Tuesday | 1.5 | 2.5 | E | 10:10 - 12:10 | walk/run at an easy pace. |
| Wednesday | 1.5 | 2.5 | HM | 10:10 | walk/run at your half marathon pace. |
| Thursday | 1.5 | 2.5 | M | 10:10 - 11:10 | walk/run at a medium pace. |
| Friday | Rest | Rest | Rest | Rest | Rest. |
| Saturday | 2 | 3 | S | 10:10 - 12:40 | walk/run at a slow pace. The most important piece of your long duration runs is finishing the run. |
| Sunday | Rest/CT | Rest/CT | Rest | Rest | Rest. If your body feels good, then go ahead and do some form of cross-training for 30 to 60 minutes. |

# Training - Week C (Optional)

5K Pace: **9:21**     5k Finish Time: **29 minutes**

| Day | Dist. Mile | Dist. KM | Difficulty | Pace (Range) | Instructions |
|---|---|---|---|---|---|
| Monday | Rest | Rest | Rest | Rest | Take it easy. Don't run. If you need to exercise, I recommend a walk for no longer than 30 minutes. |
| Tuesday | 2 | 3 | E | 10:10 - 12:10 | walk/run at an easy pace. |
| Wednesday | 2 | 3 | HM | 10:10 | walk/run at your half marathon pace. |
| Thursday | 2 | 3 | M | 10:10 - 11:10 | walk/run at a medium pace. |
| Friday | Rest | Rest | Rest | Rest | Rest. |
| Saturday | 3 | 5 | S | 10:10 - 12:40 | walk/run at a slow pace. The most important piece of your long duration runs is finishing the run. |
| Sunday | Rest/CT | Rest/CT | Rest | Rest | Rest. If your body feels good, then go ahead and do some form of cross-training for 30 to 60 minutes. |

# Training - Week 1

5K Pace: **9:21**     5k Finish Time: **29 minutes**

| Day | Dist. Mile | Dist. KM | Difficulty | Pace (Range) | Instructions |
|---|---|---|---|---|---|
| Monday | Rest | Rest | Rest | Rest | Take it easy. Don't run. If you need to exercise, I recommend a walk for no longer than 30 minutes. |
| Tuesday | 3 | 5 | E | 10:10 - 12:10 | walk/run at an easy pace. |
| Wednesday | 3 | 5 | HM | 10:10 | walk/run at your half marathon pace. |
| Thursday | 3 | 5 | M | 10:10 - 11:10 | walk/run at a medium pace. |
| Friday | Rest | Rest | Rest | Rest | Rest. |
| Saturday | 4 | 6 | S | 10:10 - 12:40 | walk/run at a slow pace. The most important piece of your long duration runs is finishing the run. |
| Sunday | Rest/CT | Rest/CT | Rest | Rest | Rest. If your body feels good, then go ahead and do some form of cross-training for 30 to 60 minutes. |

# Training - Week 2

| Day | Dist. Mile | Dist. KM | Difficulty | Pace (Range) | Instructions |
|---|---|---|---|---|---|
| Monday | Rest | Rest | Rest | Rest | Take it easy. Don't run. If you need to exercise, I recommend a walk for no longer than 30 minutes. |
| Tuesday | 3 | 5 | E | 10:10 - 12:10 | walk/run at an easy pace. |
| Wednesday | 3 | 5 | HM | 10:10 | walk/run at your half marathon pace. |
| Thursday | 3 | 5 | M | 10:10 - 11:10 | walk/run at a medium pace. |
| Friday | Rest | Rest | Rest | Rest | Rest. |
| Saturday | 5 | 8 | S | 10:10 - 12:40 | walk/run at a slow pace. The most important piece of your long duration runs is finishing the run. |
| Sunday | Rest/CT | Rest/CT | Rest | Rest | Rest. If your body feels good, then go ahead and do some form of cross-training for 30 to 60 minutes. |

# Training - Week 3

5K Pace: **9:21**     5k Finish Time: **29 minutes**

| Day | Dist. Mile | Dist. KM | Difficulty | Pace (Range) | Instructions |
|---|---|---|---|---|---|
| Monday | Rest | Rest | Rest | Rest | Take it easy. Don't run. If you need to exercise, I recommend a walk for no longer than 30 minutes. |
| Tuesday | 3 | 5 | E | 10:10 - 12:10 | walk/run at an easy pace. |
| Wednesday | 4 | 6 | HM | 10:10 | walk/run at your half marathon pace. |
| Thursday | 3 | 5 | M | 10:10 - 11:10 | walk/run at a medium pace. |
| Friday | Rest | Rest | Rest | Rest | Rest. |
| Saturday | 6 | 10 | S | 10:10 - 12:40 | walk/run at a slow pace. The most important piece of your long duration runs is finishing the run. |
| Sunday | Rest/CT | Rest/CT | Rest | Rest | Rest. If your body feels good, then go ahead and do some form of cross-training for 30 to 60 minutes. |

# Training - Week 4 (5K Optional)

5K Pace: **9:21**   5k Finish Time: **29 minutes**

| Day | Dist. Mile | Dist. KM | Difficulty | Pace (Range) | Instructions |
|---|---|---|---|---|---|
| Monday | Rest | Rest | Rest | Rest | Take it easy. Don't run. If you need to exercise, I recommend a walk for no longer than 30 minutes. |
| Tuesday | 3 | 5 | E | 10:10 - 12:10 | walk/run at an easy pace. |
| Wednesday | 4 | 6 | HM | 10:10 | walk/run at your half marathon pace. |
| Thursday | 3 | 5 | M | 10:10 - 11:10 | walk/run at a medium pace. |
| Friday | Rest | Rest | Rest | Rest | Rest. |
| Saturday | 6.5 | 10.5 | S | 10:10 - 12:40 | walk/run at a slow pace. The most important piece of your long duration runs is finishing the run. |
| Sunday | Rest/CT | Rest/CT | Rest | Rest | Rest. If your body feels good, then go ahead and do some form of cross-training for 30 to 60 minutes. |

## 5K Optional

| Day | Dist. Mile | Dist. KM | Difficulty | Pace (Range) | Instructions |
|---|---|---|---|---|---|
| Saturday | 3.1 | 5 | - | 9:21 | Run a 5k race instead of your long run. This is completely your choice. I recommend running a 5k race to help you get used to running races. You should see a difference in your race time if you have kept to your training schedule. Don't try for a personal best, run the 5K at your 5K pace. |

# Training - Week 5

5K Pace: **9:21**     5k Finish Time: **29 minutes**

| Day | Dist. Mile | Dist. KM | Difficulty | Pace (Range) | Instructions |
|---|---|---|---|---|---|
| Monday | Rest | Rest | Rest | Rest | Take it easy. Don't run. If you need to exercise, I recommend a walk for no longer than 30 minutes. |
| Tuesday | 3 | 5 | E | 10:10 - 12:10 | walk/run at an easy pace. |
| Wednesday | 4 | 6 | HM | 10:10 | walk/run at your half marathon pace. |
| Thursday | 3 | 5 | M | 10:10 - 11:10 | walk/run at a medium pace. |
| Friday | Rest | Rest | Rest | Rest | Rest. |
| Saturday | 7 | 11 | S | 10:10 - 12:40 | walk/run at a slow pace. The most important piece of your long duration runs is finishing the run. |
| Sunday | Rest/CT | Rest/CT | Rest | Rest | Rest. If your body feels good, then go ahead and do some form of cross-training for 30 to 60 minutes. |

## NOTE:

- Your long duration runs will begin to become more difficult for week 5 and beyond.
- If you get tired during a long duration run, walk for 1/10 mile or 3-5 minutes.

# Training - Week 6

5K Pace: **9:21**     5k Finish Time: **29 minutes**

| Day | Dist. Mile | Dist. KM | Difficulty | Pace (Range) | Instructions |
|---|---|---|---|---|---|
| Monday | Rest | Rest | Rest | Rest | Take it easy. Don't run. If you need to exercise, I recommend a walk for no longer than 30 minutes. |
| Tuesday | 3 | 5 | E | 10:10 - 12:10 | walk/run at an easy pace. |
| Wednesday | 4 | 6 | HM | 10:10 | walk/run at your half marathon pace. |
| Thursday | 3 | 5 | M | 10:10 - 11:10 | walk/run at a medium pace. |
| Friday | Rest | Rest | Rest | Rest | Rest. |
| Saturday | 8 | 13 | S | 10:10 - 12:40 | walk/run at a slow pace. The most important piece of your long duration runs is finishing the run. |
| Sunday | Rest/CT | Rest/CT | Rest | Rest | Rest. If your body feels good, then go ahead and do some form of cross-training for 30 to 60 minutes. |

# Training - Week 7

5K Pace: **9:21**     5k Finish Time: **29 minutes**

| Day | Dist. Mile | Dist. KM | Difficulty | Pace (Range) | Instructions |
|---|---|---|---|---|---|
| Monday | Rest | Rest | Rest | Rest | Take it easy. Don't run. If you need to exercise, I recommend a walk for no longer than 30 minutes. |
| Tuesday | 3 | 5 | E | 10:10 - 12:10 | walk/run at an easy pace. |
| Wednesday | 5 | 8 | HM | 10:10 | walk/run at your half marathon pace. |
| Thursday | 3 | 5 | M | 10:10 - 11:10 | walk/run at a medium pace. |
| Friday | Rest | Rest | Rest | Rest | Rest. |
| Saturday | 8.5 | 13.5 | S | 10:10 - 12:40 | walk/run at a slow pace. The most important piece of your long duration runs is finishing the run. |
| Sunday | Rest/CT | Rest/CT | Rest | Rest | Rest. If your body feels good, then go ahead and do some form of cross-training for 30 to 60 minutes. |

## 10K Optional

| Day | Dist. Mile | Dist. KM | Difficulty | Pace (Range) | Instructions |
|---|---|---|---|---|---|
| Thursday | 2 | 3 | E | 10:10 - 12:10 | If you run the optional 10K, either completely rest today or run 2 miles (3 km). |
| Saturday | 6.2 | 10K | - | 9:21 | Run a 10k race instead of your long run. This is completely your choice. I recommend running a 10k race to help you get used to running races. You should see a difference in your race time if you have kept to your training schedule. Don't try for a personal best, run the 10K at your 5K pace. |

# Training - Week 8

5K Pace: **9:21**     5k Finish Time: **29 minutes**

| Day | Dist. Mile | Dist. KM | Difficulty | Pace (Range) | Instructions |
|---|---|---|---|---|---|
| Monday | Rest | Rest | Rest | Rest | Take it easy. Don't run. If you need to exercise, I recommend a walk for no longer than 30 minutes. |
| Tuesday | 3 | 5 | E | 10:10 - 12:10 | walk/run at an easy pace. |
| Wednesday | 5 | 8 | HM | 10:10 | walk/run at your half marathon pace. |
| Thursday | 3 | 5 | M | 10:10 - 11:10 | walk/run at a medium pace. |
| Friday | Rest | Rest | Rest | Rest | Rest. |
| Saturday | 9 | 14 | S | 10:10 - 12:40 | walk/run at a slow pace. The most important piece of your long duration runs is finishing the run. |
| Sunday | Rest/CT | Rest/CT | Rest | Rest | Rest. If your body feels good, then go ahead and do some form of cross-training for 30 to 60 minutes. |

# Training - Week 9

5K Pace: **9:21**     5k Finish Time: **29 minutes**

| Day | Dist. Mile | Dist. KM | Difficulty | Pace (Range) | Instructions |
|---|---|---|---|---|---|
| Monday | Rest | Rest | Rest | Rest | Take it easy. Don't run. If you need to exercise, I recommend a walk for no longer than 30 minutes. |
| Tuesday | 3 | 5 | E | 10:10 - 12:10 | walk/run at an easy pace. |
| Wednesday | 5 | 8 | HM | 10:10 | walk/run at your half marathon pace. |
| Thursday | 3 | 5 | M | 10:10 - 11:10 | walk/run at a medium pace. |
| Friday | Rest | Rest | Rest | Rest | Rest. |
| Saturday | 8.5 | 13.5 | S | 10:10 - 12:40 | walk/run at a slow pace. The most important piece of your long duration runs is finishing the run. |
| Sunday | Rest/CT | Rest/CT | Rest | Rest | Rest. If your body feels good, then go ahead and do some form of cross-training for 30 to 60 minutes. |

## 13.1 Beta/Test Run Optional

| Day | Dist. Mile | Dist. KM | Difficulty | Pace (Range) | Instructions |
|---|---|---|---|---|---|
| Thursday | Rest | Rest | Rest | Rest | This is a rest day – it simulates race week |
| Friday | Rest | Rest | Rest | Rest | This is a rest day – it simulates race week |
| Saturday | 13.1 | 21 | S | 9:21 | I recommend that you attempt to go the full 13.1 miles (21 km) for a half marathon test run. <u>Only walk/run the first 10 miles (16 km) then walk the last 3.1 miles (5 km).</u> If you are successful, you will have a race ghost time to compete against. It will help energize and refocus your training on beating yourself in 3 weeks at the half marathon race. Also, it allows your mind to grasp the achievement of "completing the distance of a half marathon." |

# Training - Week 10

5K Pace: **9:21**     5k Finish Time: **29 minutes**

| Day | Dist. Mile | Dist. KM | Difficulty | Pace (Range) | Instructions |
|---|---|---|---|---|---|
| Monday | Rest | Rest | Rest | Rest | Take it easy. Don't run. If you need to exercise, I recommend a walk for no longer than 30 minutes. |
| Tuesday | 3 | 5 | E | 10:10 - 12:10 | walk/run at an easy pace. |
| Wednesday | 5 | 8 | HM | 10:10 | walk/run at your half marathon pace. |
| Thursday | 3 | 5 | M | 10:10 - 11:10 | walk/run at a medium pace. |
| Friday | Rest | Rest | Rest | Rest | Rest. |
| Saturday | 11 | 18 | S | 10:10 - 12:40 | walk/run at a slow pace. The most important piece of your long duration runs is finishing the run. |
| Sunday | Rest/CT | Rest/CT | Rest | Rest | Rest. If your body feels good, then go ahead and do some form of cross-training for 30 to 60 minutes. |

# Training - Week 11

| Day | Dist. Mile | Dist. KM | Difficulty | Pace (Range) | Instructions |
|---|---|---|---|---|---|
| Monday | Rest | Rest | Rest | Rest | Take it easy. Don't run. If you need to exercise, I recommend a walk for no longer than 30 minutes. |
| Tuesday | 3 | 5 | E | 10:10 - 12:10 | walk/run at an easy pace. |
| Wednesday | 5 | 8 | HM | 10:10 | walk/run at your half marathon pace. |
| Thursday | 3 | 5 | M | 10:10 - 11:10 | walk/run at a medium pace. |
| Friday | Rest | Rest | Rest | Rest | Rest. |
| Saturday | 12 | 20 | S | 10:10 - 12:40 | walk/run at a slow pace. The most important piece of your long duration runs is finishing the run. |
| Sunday | Rest/CT | Rest/CT | Rest | Rest | Rest. If your body feels good, then go ahead and do some form of cross-training for 30 to 60 minutes. |

# Training - Week 12

5K Pace: **9:21**     5k Finish Time: **29 minutes**

| Day | Dist. Mile | Dist. KM | Difficulty | Pace (Range) | Instructions |
|---|---|---|---|---|---|
| Monday | Rest | Rest | Rest | Rest | Take it easy. Don't run. If you need to exercise, I recommend a walk for no longer than 30 minutes. |
| Tuesday | 3 | 5 | E | 10:10 - 12:10 | walk/run at an easy pace. |
| Wednesday | 2 | 1.5 | HM | 10:10 | walk/run at your half marathon pace. |
| Thursday | Rest | Rest | Rest | Rest | Rest. |
| Friday | Rest | Rest | Rest | Rest | Rest. |
| Saturday | 13.1 | 21 | HM | 10:10 | RACE DAY! |
| Sunday | Rest | Rest | Rest | Rest | DRINK A VICTORY BEER! |

# NOTE:

- Get plenty of sleep the night before your long duration run.
- Try to run your long duration run early in the morning.
- After each run, it's important to stretch out your muscles.
- This week your body needs as much rest as possible.
- Don't run past Wednesday.

Half Marathon Training Schedule for
runners with a 5K finish time of 30 minutes
and a pace of *9:40* minutes/mile.

## Predicted Half Marathon Finish Time:
## *2* hour(s) *18* minutes

# PACING TABLES

| Pace | Pace (minutes/miles) |
|---:|---|
| 5k | 9:40 |
| Half marathon | 10:30 |
| Medium | Between 10:30 - 11:30 |
| Easy | Between 10:30 - 12:30 |
| Slow | Between 10:30 - 13:00 |

| Race | Finish Times (predicted) |
|---:|---|
| 5k | 30 minutes |
| Half marathon | 2 hour(s) 18 minutes |

| Determining your pace ||
|---|---|
| Slow Pace | Extremely easy to hold a conversation. |
| Easy Pace | You can hold a conversation with someone. Your breathing might break up some of the flow of the conversation. |
| Medium | You can hold a conversation with someone, but it's broken up into smaller sentences and smaller responses. |
| Half Marathon Pace | Conversation is difficult. One and two word responses back and forth at best. |

## Definitions in the table below:

CT = Cross Training

S = Slow Pace (long run pace)

E = Easy Pace

M = Medium Pace

HM = Half Marathon Pace

# Training - Week A (Optional)

5K Pace: **9:40**  5k Finish Time: **30 minutes**

| Day | Dist. Mile | Dist. KM | Difficulty | Pace (Range) | Instructions |
|---|---|---|---|---|---|
| Monday | Rest | Rest | Rest | Rest | Take it easy. Don't run. If you need to exercise, I recommend a walk for no longer than 30 minutes. |
| Tuesday | 1 | 1.5 | E | 10:30 - 12:30 | walk/run at an easy pace. |
| Wednesday | 1 | 1.5 | HM | 10:30 | walk/run at your half marathon pace. |
| Thursday | 1 | 1.5 | M | 10:30 - 11:30 | walk/run at a medium pace. |
| Friday | Rest | Rest | Rest | Rest | Rest. |
| Saturday | 1.5 | 2.5 | S | 10:30 - 13:00 | walk/run at a slow pace. The most important piece of your long duration runs is finishing the run. |
| Sunday | Rest/CT | Rest/CT | Rest | Rest | Rest. If your body feels good, then go ahead and do some form of cross-training for 30 to 60 minutes. |

# Training - Week B (Optional)

| Day | Dist. Mile | Dist. KM | Difficulty | Pace (Range) | Instructions |
|---|---|---|---|---|---|
| Monday | Rest | Rest | Rest | Rest | Take it easy. Don't run. If you need to exercise, I recommend a walk for no longer than 30 minutes. |
| Tuesday | 1.5 | 2.5 | E | 10:30 - 12:30 | walk/run at an easy pace. |
| Wednesday | 1.5 | 2.5 | HM | 10:30 | walk/run at your half marathon pace. |
| Thursday | 1.5 | 2.5 | M | 10:30 - 11:30 | walk/run at a medium pace. |
| Friday | Rest | Rest | Rest | Rest | Rest. |
| Saturday | 2 | 3 | S | 10:30 - 13:00 | walk/run at a slow pace. The most important piece of your long duration runs is finishing the run. |
| Sunday | Rest/CT | Rest/CT | Rest | Rest | Rest. If your body feels good, then go ahead and do some form of cross-training for 30 to 60 minutes. |

# Training - Week C (Optional)

5K Pace: **9:40**     5k Finish Time: **30 minutes**

| Day | Dist. Mile | Dist. KM | Difficulty | Pace (Range) | Instructions |
|---|---|---|---|---|---|
| Monday | Rest | Rest | Rest | Rest | Take it easy. Don't run. If you need to exercise, I recommend a walk for no longer than 30 minutes. |
| Tuesday | 2 | 3 | E | 10:30 - 12:30 | walk/run at an easy pace. |
| Wednesday | 2 | 3 | HM | 10:30 | walk/run at your half marathon pace. |
| Thursday | 2 | 3 | M | 10:30 - 11:30 | walk/run at a medium pace. |
| Friday | Rest | Rest | Rest | Rest | Rest. |
| Saturday | 3 | 5 | S | 10:30 - 13:00 | walk/run at a slow pace. The most important piece of your long duration runs is finishing the run. |
| Sunday | Rest/CT | Rest/CT | Rest | Rest | Rest. If your body feels good, then go ahead and do some form of cross-training for 30 to 60 minutes. |

# Training - Week 1

5K Pace: **9:40**     5k Finish Time: **30 minutes**

| Day | Dist. Mile | Dist. KM | Difficulty | Pace (Range) | Instructions |
|---|---|---|---|---|---|
| Monday | Rest | Rest | Rest | Rest | Take it easy. Don't run. If you need to exercise, I recommend a walk for no longer than 30 minutes. |
| Tuesday | 3 | 5 | E | 10:30 - 12:30 | walk/run at an easy pace. |
| Wednesday | 3 | 5 | HM | 10:30 | walk/run at your half marathon pace. |
| Thursday | 3 | 5 | M | 10:30 - 11:30 | walk/run at a medium pace. |
| Friday | Rest | Rest | Rest | Rest | Rest. |
| Saturday | 4 | 6 | S | 10:30 - 13:00 | walk/run at a slow pace. The most important piece of your long duration runs is finishing the run. |
| Sunday | Rest/CT | Rest/CT | Rest | Rest | Rest. If your body feels good, then go ahead and do some form of cross-training for 30 to 60 minutes. |

# Training - Week 2

| Day | Dist. Mile | Dist. KM | Difficulty | Pace (Range) | Instructions |
|---|---|---|---|---|---|
| Monday | Rest | Rest | Rest | Rest | Take it easy. Don't run. If you need to exercise, I recommend a walk for no longer than 30 minutes. |
| Tuesday | 3 | 5 | E | 10:30 - 12:30 | walk/run at an easy pace. |
| Wednesday | 3 | 5 | HM | 10:30 | walk/run at your half marathon pace. |
| Thursday | 3 | 5 | M | 10:30 - 11:30 | walk/run at a medium pace. |
| Friday | Rest | Rest | Rest | Rest | Rest. |
| Saturday | 5 | 8 | S | 10:30 - 13:00 | walk/run at a slow pace. The most important piece of your long duration runs is finishing the run. |
| Sunday | Rest/CT | Rest/CT | Rest | Rest | Rest. If your body feels good, then go ahead and do some form of cross-training for 30 to 60 minutes. |

# Training - Week 3

5K Pace: **9:40**     5k Finish Time: **30 minutes**

| Day | Dist. Mile | Dist. KM | Difficulty | Pace (Range) | Instructions |
|---|---|---|---|---|---|
| Monday | Rest | Rest | Rest | Rest | Take it easy. Don't run. If you need to exercise, I recommend a walk for no longer than 30 minutes. |
| Tuesday | 3 | 5 | E | 10:30 - 12:30 | walk/run at an easy pace. |
| Wednesday | 4 | 6 | HM | 10:30 | walk/run at your half marathon pace. |
| Thursday | 3 | 5 | M | 10:30 - 11:30 | walk/run at a medium pace. |
| Friday | Rest | Rest | Rest | Rest | Rest. |
| Saturday | 6 | 10 | S | 10:30 - 13:00 | walk/run at a slow pace. The most important piece of your long duration runs is finishing the run. |
| Sunday | Rest/CT | Rest/CT | Rest | Rest | Rest. If your body feels good, then go ahead and do some form of cross-training for 30 to 60 minutes. |

# Training - Week 4 (5K Optional)

5K Pace: **9:40**     5k Finish Time: **30 minutes**

| Day | Dist. Mile | Dist. KM | Difficulty | Pace (Range) | Instructions |
|---|---|---|---|---|---|
| Monday | Rest | Rest | Rest | Rest | Take it easy. Don't run. If you need to exercise, I recommend a walk for no longer than 30 minutes. |
| Tuesday | 3 | 5 | E | 10:30 - 12:30 | walk/run at an easy pace. |
| Wednesday | 4 | 6 | HM | 10:30 | walk/run at your half marathon pace. |
| Thursday | 3 | 5 | M | 10:30 - 11:30 | walk/run at a medium pace. |
| Friday | Rest | Rest | Rest | Rest | Rest. |
| Saturday | 6.5 | 10.5 | S | 10:30 - 13:00 | walk/run at a slow pace. The most important piece of your long duration runs is finishing the run. |
| Sunday | Rest/CT | Rest/CT | Rest | Rest | Rest. If your body feels good, then go ahead and do some form of cross-training for 30 to 60 minutes. |

## 5K Optional

| Day | Dist. Mile | Dist. KM | Difficulty | Pace (Range) | Instructions |
|---|---|---|---|---|---|
| Saturday | 3.1 | 5 | - | **9:40** | Run a 5k race instead of your long run. This is completely your choice. I recommend running a 5k race to help you get used to running races. You should see a difference in your race time if you have kept to your training schedule. Don't try for a personal best, run the 5K at your 5K pace. |

# Training - Week 5

5K Pace: **9:40**   5k Finish Time: **30 minutes**

| Day | Dist. Mile | Dist. KM | Difficulty | Pace (Range) | Instructions |
|---|---|---|---|---|---|
| Monday | Rest | Rest | Rest | Rest | Take it easy. Don't run. If you need to exercise, I recommend a walk for no longer than 30 minutes. |
| Tuesday | 3 | 5 | E | 10:30 - 12:30 | walk/run at an easy pace. |
| Wednesday | 4 | 6 | HM | 10:30 | walk/run at your half marathon pace. |
| Thursday | 3 | 5 | M | 10:30 - 11:30 | walk/run at a medium pace. |
| Friday | Rest | Rest | Rest | Rest | Rest. |
| Saturday | 7 | 11 | S | 10:30 - 13:00 | walk/run at a slow pace. The most important piece of your long duration runs is finishing the run. |
| Sunday | Rest/CT | Rest/CT | Rest | Rest | Rest. If your body feels good, then go ahead and do some form of cross-training for 30 to 60 minutes. |

## NOTE:

- Your long duration runs will begin to become more difficult for week 5 and beyond.
- If you get tired during a long duration run, walk for 1/10 mile or 3-5 minutes.

# Training - Week 6

5K Pace: **9:40**    5k Finish Time: **30 minutes**

| Day | Dist. Mile | Dist. KM | Difficulty | Pace (Range) | Instructions |
|---|---|---|---|---|---|
| Monday | Rest | Rest | Rest | Rest | Take it easy. Don't run. If you need to exercise, I recommend a walk for no longer than 30 minutes. |
| Tuesday | 3 | 5 | E | 10:30 - 12:30 | walk/run at an easy pace. |
| Wednesday | 4 | 6 | HM | 10:30 | walk/run at your half marathon pace. |
| Thursday | 3 | 5 | M | 10:30 - 11:30 | walk/run at a medium pace. |
| Friday | Rest | Rest | Rest | Rest | Rest. |
| Saturday | 8 | 13 | S | 10:30 - 13:00 | walk/run at a slow pace. The most important piece of your long duration runs is finishing the run. |
| Sunday | Rest/CT | Rest/CT | Rest | Rest | Rest. If your body feels good, then go ahead and do some form of cross-training for 30 to 60 minutes. |

# Training - Week 7

5K Pace: **9:40**     5k Finish Time: **30 minutes**

| Day | Dist. Mile | Dist. KM | Difficulty | Pace (Range) | Instructions |
|---|---|---|---|---|---|
| Monday | Rest | Rest | Rest | Rest | Take it easy. Don't run. If you need to exercise, I recommend a walk for no longer than 30 minutes. |
| Tuesday | 3 | 5 | E | 10:30 - 12:30 | walk/run at an easy pace. |
| Wednesday | 5 | 8 | HM | 10:30 | walk/run at your half marathon pace. |
| Thursday | 3 | 5 | M | 10:30 - 11:30 | walk/run at a medium pace. |
| Friday | Rest | Rest | Rest | Rest | Rest. |
| Saturday | 8.5 | 13.5 | S | 10:30 - 13:00 | walk/run at a slow pace. The most important piece of your long duration runs is finishing the run. |
| Sunday | Rest/CT | Rest/CT | Rest | Rest | Rest. If your body feels good, then go ahead and do some form of cross-training for 30 to 60 minutes. |

## 10K Optional

| Day | Dist. Mile | Dist. KM | Difficulty | Pace (Range) | Instructions |
|---|---|---|---|---|---|
| Thursday | 2 | 3 | E | 10:30 - 12:30 | If you run the optional 10K, either completely rest today or run 2 miles ( 3 km). |
| Saturday | 6.2 | 10K | - | **9:40** | Run a 10k race instead of your long run. This is completely your choice. I recommend running a 10k race to help you get used to running races. You should see a difference in your race time if you have kept to your training schedule. Don't try for a personal best, run the 10K at your 5K pace. |

# Training - Week 8

5K Pace: **9:40**    5k Finish Time: **30 minutes**

| Day | Dist. Mile | Dist. KM | Difficulty | Pace (Range) | Instructions |
|---|---|---|---|---|---|
| Monday | Rest | Rest | Rest | Rest | Take it easy. Don't run. If you need to exercise, I recommend a walk for no longer than 30 minutes. |
| Tuesday | 3 | 5 | E | 10:30 - 12:30 | walk/run at an easy pace. |
| Wednesday | 5 | 8 | HM | 10:30 | walk/run at your half marathon pace. |
| Thursday | 3 | 5 | M | 10:30 - 11:30 | walk/run at a medium pace. |
| Friday | Rest | Rest | Rest | Rest | Rest. |
| Saturday | 9 | 14 | S | 10:30 - 13:00 | walk/run at a slow pace. The most important piece of your long duration runs is finishing the run. |
| Sunday | Rest/CT | Rest/CT | Rest | Rest | Rest. If your body feels good, then go ahead and do some form of cross-training for 30 to 60 minutes. |

# Training - Week 9

5K Pace: **9:40**     5k Finish Time: **30 minutes**

| Day | Dist. Mile | Dist. KM | Difficulty | Pace (Range) | Instructions |
|---|---|---|---|---|---|
| Monday | Rest | Rest | Rest | Rest | Take it easy. Don't run. If you need to exercise, I recommend a walk for no longer than 30 minutes. |
| Tuesday | 3 | 5 | E | 10:30 - 12:30 | walk/run at an easy pace. |
| Wednesday | 5 | 8 | HM | 10:30 | walk/run at your half marathon pace. |
| Thursday | 3 | 5 | M | 10:30 - 11:30 | walk/run at a medium pace. |
| Friday | Rest | Rest | Rest | Rest | Rest. |
| Saturday | 8.5 | 13.5 | S | 10:30 - 13:00 | walk/run at a slow pace. The most important piece of your long duration runs is finishing the run. |
| Sunday | Rest/CT | Rest/CT | Rest | Rest | Rest. If your body feels good, then go ahead and do some form of cross-training for 30 to 60 minutes. |

## 13.1 Beta/Test Run Optional

| Day | Dist. Mile | Dist. KM | Difficulty | Pace (Range) | Instructions |
|---|---|---|---|---|---|
| Thursday | Rest | Rest | Rest | Rest | This is a rest day – it simulates race week |
| Friday | Rest | Rest | Rest | Rest | This is a rest day – it simulates race week |
| Saturday | 13.1 | 21 | S | 9:40 | I recommend that you attempt to go the full 13.1 miles (21 km) for a half marathon test run. <u>Only walk/run the first 10 miles (16 km) then walk the last 3.1 miles (5 km).</u> If you are successful, you will have a race ghost time to compete against. It will help energize and refocus your training on beating yourself in 3 weeks at the half marathon race. Also, it allows your mind to grasp the achievement of "completing the distance of a half marathon." |

# Training - Week 10

5K Pace: **9:40**     5k Finish Time: **30 minutes**

| Day | Dist. Mile | Dist. KM | Difficulty | Pace (Range) | Instructions |
|---|---|---|---|---|---|
| Monday | Rest | Rest | Rest | Rest | Take it easy. Don't run. If you need to exercise, I recommend a walk for no longer than 30 minutes. |
| Tuesday | 3 | 5 | E | 10:30 - 12:30 | walk/run at an easy pace. |
| Wednesday | 5 | 8 | HM | 10:30 | walk/run at your half marathon pace. |
| Thursday | 3 | 5 | M | 10:30 - 11:30 | walk/run at a medium pace. |
| Friday | Rest | Rest | Rest | Rest | Rest. |
| Saturday | 11 | 18 | S | 10:30 - 13:00 | walk/run at a slow pace. The most important piece of your long duration runs is finishing the run. |
| Sunday | Rest/CT | Rest/CT | Rest | Rest | Rest. If your body feels good, then go ahead and do some form of cross-training for 30 to 60 minutes. |

# Training - Week 11

| Day | Dist. Mile | Dist. KM | Difficulty | Pace (Range) | Instructions |
|---|---|---|---|---|---|
| Monday | Rest | Rest | Rest | Rest | Take it easy. Don't run. If you need to exercise, I recommend a walk for no longer than 30 minutes. |
| Tuesday | 3 | 5 | E | 10:30 - 12:30 | walk/run at an easy pace. |
| Wednesday | 5 | 8 | HM | 10:30 | walk/run at your half marathon pace. |
| Thursday | 3 | 5 | M | 10:30 - 11:30 | walk/run at a medium pace. |
| Friday | Rest | Rest | Rest | Rest | Rest. |
| Saturday | 12 | 20 | S | 10:30 - 13:00 | walk/run at a slow pace. The most important piece of your long duration runs is finishing the run. |
| Sunday | Rest/CT | Rest/CT | Rest | Rest | Rest. If your body feels good, then go ahead and do some form of cross-training for 30 to 60 minutes. |

# Training - Week 12

5K Pace: **9:40**     5k Finish Time: **30 minutes**

| Day | Dist. Mile | Dist. KM | Difficulty | Pace (Range) | Instructions |
|---|---|---|---|---|---|
| Monday | Rest | Rest | Rest | Rest | Take it easy. Don't run. If you need to exercise, I recommend a walk for no longer than 30 minutes. |
| Tuesday | 3 | 5 | E | 10:30 - 12:30 | walk/run at an easy pace. |
| Wednesday | 2 | 1.5 | HM | 10:30 | walk/run at your half marathon pace. |
| Thursday | Rest | Rest | Rest | Rest | Rest. |
| Friday | Rest | Rest | Rest | Rest | Rest. |
| Saturday | 13.1 | 21 | HM | 10:30 | RACE DAY! |
| Sunday | Rest | Rest | Rest | Rest | DRINK A VICTORY BEER! |

## NOTE:

- Get plenty of sleep the night before your long duration run.
- Try to run your long duration run early in the morning.
- After each run, it's important to stretch out your muscles.
- This week your body needs as much rest as possible.
- Don't run past Wednesday.

Half Marathon Training Schedule for

runners with a 5K finish time of 31 minutes

and a pace of *10:00* minutes/mile.

# Predicted Half Marathon Finish Time:

## *2* hour(s) *22* minutes

# PACING TABLES

| Pace | Pace (minutes/miles) |
|---:|:---|
| 5k | 10:00 |
| Half marathon | 10:50 |
| Medium | Between 10:50 - 11:50 |
| Easy | Between 10:50 - 12:50 |
| Slow | Between 10:50 - 13:20 |

| Race | Finish Times (predicted) |
|---:|:---|
| 5k | 31 minutes |
| Half marathon | 2 hour(s) 22 minutes |

| Determining your pace | |
|:---:|:---|
| Slow Pace | Extremely easy to hold a conversation. |
| Easy Pace | You can hold a conversation with someone. Your breathing might break up some of the flow of the conversation. |
| Medium | You can hold a conversation with someone, but it's broken up into smaller sentences and smaller responses. |
| Half Marathon Pace | Conversation is difficult. One and two word responses back and forth at best. |

## Definitions in the table below:

CT = Cross Training

S = Slow Pace (long run pace)

E = Easy Pace

M = Medium Pace

HM = Half Marathon Pace

# Training - Week A (Optional)

5K Pace: **10:00**         5k Finish Time: **31 minutes**

| Day | Dist. Mile | Dist. KM | Difficulty | Pace (Range) | Instructions |
|---|---|---|---|---|---|
| Monday | Rest | Rest | Rest | Rest | Take it easy. Don't run. If you need to exercise, I recommend a walk for no longer than 30 minutes. |
| Tuesday | 1 | 1.5 | E | 10:50 - 12:50 | walk/run at an easy pace. |
| Wednesday | 1 | 1.5 | HM | 10:50 | walk/run at your half marathon pace. |
| Thursday | 1 | 1.5 | M | 10:50 - 11:50 | walk/run at a medium pace. |
| Friday | Rest | Rest | Rest | Rest | Rest. |
| Saturday | 1.5 | 2.5 | S | 10:50 - 13:20 | walk/run at a slow pace. The most important piece of your long duration runs is finishing the run. |
| Sunday | Rest/CT | Rest/CT | Rest | Rest | Rest. If your body feels good, then go ahead and do some form of cross-training for 30 to 60 minutes. |

# Training - Week B (Optional)

| Day | Dist. Mile | Dist. KM | Difficulty | Pace (Range) | Instructions |
|---|---|---|---|---|---|
| Monday | Rest | Rest | Rest | Rest | Take it easy. Don't run. If you need to exercise, I recommend a walk for no longer than 30 minutes. |
| Tuesday | 1.5 | 2.5 | E | 10:50 - 12:50 | walk/run at an easy pace. |
| Wednesday | 1.5 | 2.5 | HM | 10:50 | walk/run at your half marathon pace. |
| Thursday | 1.5 | 2.5 | M | 10:50 - 11:50 | walk/run at a medium pace. |
| Friday | Rest | Rest | Rest | Rest | Rest. |
| Saturday | 2 | 3 | S | 10:50 - 13:20 | walk/run at a slow pace. The most important piece of your long duration runs is finishing the run. |
| Sunday | Rest/CT | Rest/CT | Rest | Rest | Rest. If your body feels good, then go ahead and do some form of cross-training for 30 to 60 minutes. |

# Training - Week C (Optional)

5K Pace: **10:00**     5k Finish Time: **31 minutes**

| Day | Dist. Mile | Dist. KM | Difficulty | Pace (Range) | Instructions |
|---|---|---|---|---|---|
| Monday | Rest | Rest | Rest | Rest | Take it easy. Don't run. If you need to exercise, I recommend a walk for no longer than 30 minutes. |
| Tuesday | 2 | 3 | E | 10:50 - 12:50 | walk/run at an easy pace. |
| Wednesday | 2 | 3 | HM | 10:50 | walk/run at your half marathon pace. |
| Thursday | 2 | 3 | M | 10:50 - 11:50 | walk/run at a medium pace. |
| Friday | Rest | Rest | Rest | Rest | Rest. |
| Saturday | 3 | 5 | S | 10:50 - 13:20 | walk/run at a slow pace. The most important piece of your long duration runs is finishing the run. |
| Sunday | Rest/CT | Rest/CT | Rest | Rest | Rest. If your body feels good, then go ahead and do some form of cross-training for 30 to 60 minutes. |

# Training - Week 1

5K Pace: **10:00**     5k Finish Time: **31 minutes**

| Day | Dist. Mile | Dist. KM | Difficulty | Pace (Range) | Instructions |
|---|---|---|---|---|---|
| Monday | Rest | Rest | Rest | Rest | Take it easy. Don't run. If you need to exercise, I recommend a walk for no longer than 30 minutes. |
| Tuesday | 3 | 5 | E | 10:50 - 12:50 | walk/run at an easy pace. |
| Wednesday | 3 | 5 | HM | 10:50 | walk/run at your half marathon pace. |
| Thursday | 3 | 5 | M | 10:50 - 11:50 | walk/run at a medium pace. |
| Friday | Rest | Rest | Rest | Rest | Rest. |
| Saturday | 4 | 6 | S | 10:50 - 13:20 | walk/run at a slow pace. The most important piece of your long duration runs is finishing the run. |
| Sunday | Rest/CT | Rest/CT | Rest | Rest | Rest. If your body feels good, then go ahead and do some form of cross-training for 30 to 60 minutes. |

# Training - Week 2

| Day | Dist. Mile | Dist. KM | Difficulty | Pace (Range) | Instructions |
|---|---|---|---|---|---|
| Monday | Rest | Rest | Rest | Rest | Take it easy. Don't run. If you need to exercise, I recommend a walk for no longer than 30 minutes. |
| Tuesday | 3 | 5 | E | 10:50 - 12:50 | walk/run at an easy pace. |
| Wednesday | 3 | 5 | HM | 10:50 | walk/run at your half marathon pace. |
| Thursday | 3 | 5 | M | 10:50 - 11:50 | walk/run at a medium pace. |
| Friday | Rest | Rest | Rest | Rest | Rest. |
| Saturday | 5 | 8 | S | 10:50 - 13:20 | walk/run at a slow pace. The most important piece of your long duration runs is finishing the run. |
| Sunday | Rest/CT | Rest/CT | Rest | Rest | Rest. If your body feels good, then go ahead and do some form of cross-training for 30 to 60 minutes. |

# Training - Week 3

5K Pace: **10:00**    5k Finish Time: **31 minutes**

| Day | Dist. Mile | Dist. KM | Difficulty | Pace (Range) | Instructions |
|---|---|---|---|---|---|
| Monday | Rest | Rest | Rest | Rest | Take it easy. Don't run. If you need to exercise, I recommend a walk for no longer than 30 minutes. |
| Tuesday | 3 | 5 | E | 10:50 - 12:50 | walk/run at an easy pace. |
| Wednesday | 4 | 6 | HM | 10:50 | walk/run at your half marathon pace. |
| Thursday | 3 | 5 | M | 10:50 - 11:50 | walk/run at a medium pace. |
| Friday | Rest | Rest | Rest | Rest | Rest. |
| Saturday | 6 | 10 | S | 10:50 - 13:20 | walk/run at a slow pace. The most important piece of your long duration runs is finishing the run. |
| Sunday | Rest/CT | Rest/CT | Rest | Rest | Rest. If your body feels good, then go ahead and do some form of cross-training for 30 to 60 minutes. |

# Training - Week 4 (5K Optional)

5K Pace: **10:00**     5k Finish Time: **31 minutes**

| Day | Dist. Mile | Dist. KM | Difficulty | Pace (Range) | Instructions |
|---|---|---|---|---|---|
| Monday | Rest | Rest | Rest | Rest | Take it easy. Don't run. If you need to exercise, I recommend a walk for no longer than 30 minutes. |
| Tuesday | 3 | 5 | E | 10:50 - 12:50 | walk/run at an easy pace. |
| Wednesday | 4 | 6 | HM | 10:50 | walk/run at your half marathon pace. |
| Thursday | 3 | 5 | M | 10:50 - 11:50 | walk/run at a medium pace. |
| Friday | Rest | Rest | Rest | Rest | Rest. |
| Saturday | 6.5 | 10.5 | S | 10:50 - 13:20 | walk/run at a slow pace. The most important piece of your long duration runs is finishing the run. |
| Sunday | Rest/CT | Rest/CT | Rest | Rest | Rest. If your body feels good, then go ahead and do some form of cross-training for 30 to 60 minutes. |

## 5K Optional

| Day | Dist. Mile | Dist. KM | Difficulty | Pace (Range) | Instructions |
|---|---|---|---|---|---|
| Saturday | 3.1 | 5 | - | **10:00** | Run a 5k race instead of your long run. This is completely your choice. I recommend running a 5k race to help you get used to running races. You should see a difference in your race time if you have kept to your training schedule. Don't try for a personal best, run the 5K at your 5K pace. |

# Training - Week 5

5K Pace: **10:00**    5k Finish Time: **31 minutes**

| Day | Dist. Mile | Dist. KM | Difficulty | Pace (Range) | Instructions |
|---|---|---|---|---|---|
| Monday | Rest | Rest | Rest | Rest | Take it easy. Don't run. If you need to exercise, I recommend a walk for no longer than 30 minutes. |
| Tuesday | 3 | 5 | E | 10:50 - 12:50 | walk/run at an easy pace. |
| Wednesday | 4 | 6 | HM | 10:50 | walk/run at your half marathon pace. |
| Thursday | 3 | 5 | M | 10:50 - 11:50 | walk/run at a medium pace. |
| Friday | Rest | Rest | Rest | Rest | Rest. |
| Saturday | 7 | 11 | S | 10:50 - 13:20 | walk/run at a slow pace. The most important piece of your long duration runs is finishing the run. |
| Sunday | Rest/CT | Rest/CT | Rest | Rest | Rest. If your body feels good, then go ahead and do some form of cross-training for 30 to 60 minutes. |

## NOTE:

- Your long duration runs will begin to become more difficult for week 5 and beyond.
- If you get tired during a long duration run, walk for 1/10 mile or 3-5 minutes.

# Training - Week 6

5K Pace: **10:00**     5k Finish Time: **31 minutes**

| Day | Dist. Mile | Dist. KM | Difficulty | Pace (Range) | Instructions |
|---|---|---|---|---|---|
| Monday | Rest | Rest | Rest | Rest | Take it easy. Don't run. If you need to exercise, I recommend a walk for no longer than 30 minutes. |
| Tuesday | 3 | 5 | E | 10:50 - 12:50 | walk/run at an easy pace. |
| Wednesday | 4 | 6 | HM | 10:50 | walk/run at your half marathon pace. |
| Thursday | 3 | 5 | M | 10:50 - 11:50 | walk/run at a medium pace. |
| Friday | Rest | Rest | Rest | Rest | Rest. |
| Saturday | 8 | 13 | S | 10:50 - 13:20 | walk/run at a slow pace. The most important piece of your long duration runs is finishing the run. |
| Sunday | Rest/CT | Rest/CT | Rest | Rest | Rest. If your body feels good, then go ahead and do some form of cross-training for 30 to 60 minutes. |

# Training - Week 7

5K Pace: **10:00**     5k Finish Time: **31 minutes**

| Day | Dist. Mile | Dist. KM | Difficulty | Pace (Range) | Instructions |
|---|---|---|---|---|---|
| Monday | Rest | Rest | Rest | Rest | Take it easy. Don't run. If you need to exercise, I recommend a walk for no longer than 30 minutes. |
| Tuesday | 3 | 5 | E | 10:50 - 12:50 | walk/run at an easy pace. |
| Wednesday | 5 | 8 | HM | 10:50 | walk/run at your half marathon pace. |
| Thursday | 3 | 5 | M | 10:50 - 11:50 | walk/run at a medium pace. |
| Friday | Rest | Rest | Rest | Rest | Rest. |
| Saturday | 8.5 | 13.5 | S | 10:50 - 13:20 | walk/run at a slow pace. The most important piece of your long duration runs is finishing the run. |
| Sunday | Rest/CT | Rest/CT | Rest | Rest | Rest. If your body feels good, then go ahead and do some form of cross-training for 30 to 60 minutes. |

## 10K Optional

| Day | Dist. Mile | Dist. KM | Difficulty | Pace (Range) | Instructions |
|---|---|---|---|---|---|
| Thursday | 2 | 3 | E | 10:50 - 12:50 | If you run the optional 10K, either completely rest today or run 2 miles (3 km). |
| Saturday | 6.2 | 10K | - | **10:00** | Run a 10k race instead of your long run. This is completely your choice. I recommend running a 10k race to help you get used to running races. You should see a difference in your race time if you have kept to your training schedule. Don't try for a personal best, run the 10K at your 5K pace. |

# Training - Week 8

5K Pace: **10:00**     5k Finish Time: **31 minutes**

| Day | Dist. Mile | Dist. KM | Difficulty | Pace (Range) | Instructions |
|---|---|---|---|---|---|
| Monday | Rest | Rest | Rest | Rest | Take it easy. Don't run. If you need to exercise, I recommend a walk for no longer than 30 minutes. |
| Tuesday | 3 | 5 | E | 10:50 - 12:50 | walk/run at an easy pace. |
| Wednesday | 5 | 8 | HM | 10:50 | walk/run at your half marathon pace. |
| Thursday | 3 | 5 | M | 10:50 - 11:50 | walk/run at a medium pace. |
| Friday | Rest | Rest | Rest | Rest | Rest. |
| Saturday | 9 | 14 | S | 10:50 - 13:20 | walk/run at a slow pace. The most important piece of your long duration runs is finishing the run. |
| Sunday | Rest/CT | Rest/CT | Rest | Rest | Rest. If your body feels good, then go ahead and do some form of cross-training for 30 to 60 minutes. |

# Training - Week 9

5K Pace: **10:00**     5k Finish Time: **31 minutes**

| Day | Dist. Mile | Dist. KM | Difficulty | Pace (Range) | Instructions |
|---|---|---|---|---|---|
| Monday | Rest | Rest | Rest | Rest | Take it easy. Don't run. If you need to exercise, I recommend a walk for no longer than 30 minutes. |
| Tuesday | 3 | 5 | E | 10:50 - 12:50 | walk/run at an easy pace. |
| Wednesday | 5 | 8 | HM | 10:50 | walk/run at your half marathon pace. |
| Thursday | 3 | 5 | M | 10:50 - 11:50 | walk/run at a medium pace. |
| Friday | Rest | Rest | Rest | Rest | Rest. |
| Saturday | 8.5 | 13.5 | S | 10:50 - 13:20 | walk/run at a slow pace. The most important piece of your long duration runs is finishing the run. |
| Sunday | Rest/CT | Rest/CT | Rest | Rest | Rest. If your body feels good, then go ahead and do some form of cross-training for 30 to 60 minutes. |

## 13.1 Beta/Test Run Optional

| Day | Dist. Mile | Dist. KM | Difficulty | Pace (Range) | Instructions |
|---|---|---|---|---|---|
| Thursday | Rest | Rest | Rest | Rest | This is a rest day – it simulates race week |
| Friday | Rest | Rest | Rest | Rest | This is a rest day – it simulates race week |
| Saturday | 13.1 | 21 | S | 10:00 | I recommend that you attempt to go the full 13.1 miles (21 km) for a half marathon test run. <u>Only walk/run the first 10 miles (16 km) then walk the last 3.1 miles (5 km)</u>. If you are successful, you will have a race ghost time to compete against. It will help energize and refocus your training on beating yourself in 3 weeks at the half marathon race. Also, it allows your mind to grasp the achievement of "completing the distance of a half marathon." |

# Training - Week 10

5K Pace: **10:00**     5k Finish Time: **31 minutes**

| Day | Dist. Mile | Dist. KM | Difficulty | Pace (Range) | Instructions |
|---|---|---|---|---|---|
| Monday | Rest | Rest | Rest | Rest | Take it easy. Don't run. If you need to exercise, I recommend a walk for no longer than 30 minutes. |
| Tuesday | 3 | 5 | E | 10:50 - 12:50 | walk/run at an easy pace. |
| Wednesday | 5 | 8 | HM | 10:50 | walk/run at your half marathon pace. |
| Thursday | 3 | 5 | M | 10:50 - 11:50 | walk/run at a medium pace. |
| Friday | Rest | Rest | Rest | Rest | Rest. |
| Saturday | 11 | 18 | S | 10:50 - 13:20 | walk/run at a slow pace. The most important piece of your long duration runs is finishing the run. |
| Sunday | Rest/CT | Rest/CT | Rest | Rest | Rest. If your body feels good, then go ahead and do some form of cross-training for 30 to 60 minutes. |

# Training - Week 11

| Day | Dist. Mile | Dist. KM | Difficulty | Pace (Range) | Instructions |
|---|---|---|---|---|---|
| Monday | Rest | Rest | Rest | Rest | Take it easy. Don't run. If you need to exercise, I recommend a walk for no longer than 30 minutes. |
| Tuesday | 3 | 5 | E | 10:50 - 12:50 | walk/run at an easy pace. |
| Wednesday | 5 | 8 | HM | 10:50 | walk/run at your half marathon pace. |
| Thursday | 3 | 5 | M | 10:50 - 11:50 | walk/run at a medium pace. |
| Friday | Rest | Rest | Rest | Rest | Rest. |
| Saturday | 12 | 20 | S | 10:50 - 13:20 | walk/run at a slow pace. The most important piece of your long duration runs is finishing the run. |
| Sunday | Rest/CT | Rest/CT | Rest | Rest | Rest. If your body feels good, then go ahead and do some form of cross-training for 30 to 60 minutes. |

# Training - Week 12

5K Pace: **10:00**    5k Finish Time: **31 minutes**

| Day | Dist. Mile | Dist. KM | Difficulty | Pace (Range) | Instructions |
|---|---|---|---|---|---|
| Monday | Rest | Rest | Rest | Rest | Take it easy. Don't run. If you need to exercise, I recommend a walk for no longer than 30 minutes. |
| Tuesday | 3 | 5 | E | 10:50 - 12:50 | walk/run at an easy pace. |
| Wednesday | 2 | 1.5 | HM | 10:50 | walk/run at your half marathon pace. |
| Thursday | Rest | Rest | Rest | Rest | Rest. |
| Friday | Rest | Rest | Rest | Rest | Rest. |
| Saturday | 13.1 | 21 | HM | 10:50 | RACE DAY! |
| Sunday | Rest | Rest | Rest | Rest | DRINK A VICTORY BEER! |

## NOTE:

- Get plenty of sleep the night before your long duration run.
- Try to run your long duration run early in the morning.
- After each run, it's important to stretch out your muscles.
- This week your body needs as much rest as possible.
- Don't run past Wednesday.

# BEGINNER TO FINISHER RUNNING

Half Marathon Training Schedule for runners with a 5K finish time of 32 minutes and a pace of *10:19* minutes/mile.

# Predicted Half Marathon Finish Time:
# *2* hour(s) *27* minutes

# PACING TABLES

| Pace | Pace (minutes/miles) |
|---:|---|
| 5k | 10:19 |
| Half marathon | 11:15 |
| Medium | Between 11:15 - 12:15 |
| Easy | Between 11:15 - 13:15 |
| Slow | Between 11:15 - 13:45 |

| Race | Finish Times (predicted) |
|---:|---|
| 5k | 32 minutes |
| Half marathon | 2 hour(s) 27 minutes |

| Determining your pace ||
|---|---|
| Slow Pace | Extremely easy to hold a conversation. |
| Easy Pace | You can hold a conversation with someone. Your breathing might break up some of the flow of the conversation. |
| Medium | You can hold a conversation with someone, but it's broken up into smaller sentences and smaller responses. |
| Half Marathon Pace | Conversation is difficult. One and two word responses back and forth at best. |

## Definitions in the table below:

CT = Cross Training

S = Slow Pace (long run pace)

E = Easy Pace

M = Medium Pace

HM = Half Marathon Pace

# Training - Week A (Optional)

5K Pace: **10:19**     5k Finish Time: **32 minutes**

| Day | Dist. Mile | Dist. KM | Difficulty | Pace (Range) | Instructions |
|---|---|---|---|---|---|
| Monday | Rest | Rest | Rest | Rest | Take it easy. Don't run. If you need to exercise, I recommend a walk for no longer than 30 minutes. |
| Tuesday | 1 | 1.5 | E | 11:15 - 13:15 | walk/run at an easy pace. |
| Wednesday | 1 | 1.5 | HM | 11:15 | walk/run at your half marathon pace. |
| Thursday | 1 | 1.5 | M | 11:15 - 12:15 | walk/run at a medium pace. |
| Friday | Rest | Rest | Rest | Rest | Rest. |
| Saturday | 1.5 | 2.5 | S | 11:15 - 13:45 | walk/run at a slow pace. The most important piece of your long duration runs is finishing the run. |
| Sunday | Rest/CT | Rest/CT | Rest | Rest | Rest. If your body feels good, then go ahead and do some form of cross-training for 30 to 60 minutes. |

# Training - Week B (Optional)

| Day | Dist. Mile | Dist. KM | Difficulty | Pace (Range) | Instructions |
|---|---|---|---|---|---|
| Monday | Rest | Rest | Rest | Rest | Take it easy. Don't run. If you need to exercise, I recommend a walk for no longer than 30 minutes. |
| Tuesday | 1.5 | 2.5 | E | 11:15 - 13:15 | walk/run at an easy pace. |
| Wednesday | 1.5 | 2.5 | HM | 11:15 | walk/run at your half marathon pace. |
| Thursday | 1.5 | 2.5 | M | 11:15 - 12:15 | walk/run at a medium pace. |
| Friday | Rest | Rest | Rest | Rest | Rest. |
| Saturday | 2 | 3 | S | 11:15 - 13:45 | walk/run at a slow pace. The most important piece of your long duration runs is finishing the run. |
| Sunday | Rest/CT | Rest/CT | Rest | Rest | Rest. If your body feels good, then go ahead and do some form of cross-training for 30 to 60 minutes. |

# Training - Week C (Optional)

5K Pace: **10:19**     5k Finish Time: **32 minutes**

| Day | Dist. Mile | Dist. KM | Difficulty | Pace (Range) | Instructions |
|---|---|---|---|---|---|
| Monday | Rest | Rest | Rest | Rest | Take it easy. Don't run. If you need to exercise, I recommend a walk for no longer than 30 minutes. |
| Tuesday | 2 | 3 | E | 11:15 - 13:15 | walk/run at an easy pace. |
| Wednesday | 2 | 3 | HM | 11:15 | walk/run at your half marathon pace. |
| Thursday | 2 | 3 | M | 11:15 - 12:15 | walk/run at a medium pace. |
| Friday | Rest | Rest | Rest | Rest | Rest. |
| Saturday | 3 | 5 | S | 11:15 - 13:45 | walk/run at a slow pace. The most important piece of your long duration runs is finishing the run. |
| Sunday | Rest/CT | Rest/CT | Rest | Rest | Rest. If your body feels good, then go ahead and do some form of cross-training for 30 to 60 minutes. |

# Training - Week 1

5K Pace: **10:19**    5k Finish Time: **32 minutes**

| Day | Dist. Mile | Dist. KM | Difficulty | Pace (Range) | Instructions |
|---|---|---|---|---|---|
| Monday | Rest | Rest | Rest | Rest | Take it easy. Don't run. If you need to exercise, I recommend a walk for no longer than 30 minutes. |
| Tuesday | 3 | 5 | E | 11:15 - 13:15 | walk/run at an easy pace. |
| Wednesday | 3 | 5 | HM | 11:15 | walk/run at your half marathon pace. |
| Thursday | 3 | 5 | M | 11:15 - 12:15 | walk/run at a medium pace. |
| Friday | Rest | Rest | Rest | Rest | Rest. |
| Saturday | 4 | 6 | S | 11:15 - 13:45 | walk/run at a slow pace. The most important piece of your long duration runs is finishing the run. |
| Sunday | Rest/CT | Rest/CT | Rest | Rest | Rest. If your body feels good, then go ahead and do some form of cross-training for 30 to 60 minutes. |

# Training - Week 2

| Day | Dist. Mile | Dist. KM | Difficulty | Pace (Range) | Instructions |
|---|---|---|---|---|---|
| Monday | Rest | Rest | Rest | Rest | Take it easy. Don't run. If you need to exercise, I recommend a walk for no longer than 30 minutes. |
| Tuesday | 3 | 5 | E | 11:15 - 13:15 | walk/run at an easy pace. |
| Wednesday | 3 | 5 | HM | 11:15 | walk/run at your half marathon pace. |
| Thursday | 3 | 5 | M | 11:15 - 12:15 | walk/run at a medium pace. |
| Friday | Rest | Rest | Rest | Rest | Rest. |
| Saturday | 5 | 8 | S | 11:15 - 13:45 | walk/run at a slow pace. The most important piece of your long duration runs is finishing the run. |
| Sunday | Rest/CT | Rest/CT | Rest | Rest | Rest. If your body feels good, then go ahead and do some form of cross-training for 30 to 60 minutes. |

# Training - Week 3

**5K Pace: 10:19**     5k Finish Time: **32 minutes**

| Day | Dist. Mile | Dist. KM | Difficulty | Pace (Range) | Instructions |
|---|---|---|---|---|---|
| Monday | Rest | Rest | Rest | Rest | Take it easy. Don't run. If you need to exercise, I recommend a walk for no longer than 30 minutes. |
| Tuesday | 3 | 5 | E | 11:15 - 13:15 | walk/run at an easy pace. |
| Wednesday | 4 | 6 | HM | 11:15 | walk/run at your half marathon pace. |
| Thursday | 3 | 5 | M | 11:15 - 12:15 | walk/run at a medium pace. |
| Friday | Rest | Rest | Rest | Rest | Rest. |
| Saturday | 6 | 10 | S | 11:15 - 13:45 | walk/run at a slow pace. The most important piece of your long duration runs is finishing the run. |
| Sunday | Rest/CT | Rest/CT | Rest | Rest | Rest. If your body feels good, then go ahead and do some form of cross-training for 30 to 60 minutes. |

# Training - Week 4 (5K Optional)

5K Pace: **10:19**     5k Finish Time: **32 minutes**

| Day | Dist. Mile | Dist. KM | Difficulty | Pace (Range) | Instructions |
|---|---|---|---|---|---|
| Monday | Rest | Rest | Rest | Rest | Take it easy. Don't run. If you need to exercise, I recommend a walk for no longer than 30 minutes. |
| Tuesday | 3 | 5 | E | 11:15 - 13:15 | walk/run at an easy pace. |
| Wednesday | 4 | 6 | HM | 11:15 | walk/run at your half marathon pace. |
| Thursday | 3 | 5 | M | 11:15 - 12:15 | walk/run at a medium pace. |
| Friday | Rest | Rest | Rest | Rest | Rest. |
| Saturday | 6.5 | 10.5 | S | 11:15 - 13:45 | walk/run at a slow pace. The most important piece of your long duration runs is finishing the run. |
| Sunday | Rest/CT | Rest/CT | Rest | Rest | Rest. If your body feels good, then go ahead and do some form of cross-training for 30 to 60 minutes. |

## 5K Optional

| Day | Dist. Mile | Dist. KM | Difficulty | Pace (Range) | Instructions |
|---|---|---|---|---|---|
| Saturday | 3.1 | 5 | - | 10:19 | Run a 5k race instead of your long run. This is completely your choice. I recommend running a 5k race to help you get used to running races. You should see a difference in your race time if you have kept to your training schedule. Don't try for a personal best, run the 5K at your 5K pace. |

# Training - Week 5

5K Pace: **10:19**     5k Finish Time: **32 minutes**

| Day | Dist. Mile | Dist. KM | Difficulty | Pace (Range) | Instructions |
|---|---|---|---|---|---|
| Monday | Rest | Rest | Rest | Rest | Take it easy. Don't run. If you need to exercise, I recommend a walk for no longer than 30 minutes. |
| Tuesday | 3 | 5 | E | 11:15 - 13:15 | walk/run at an easy pace. |
| Wednesday | 4 | 6 | HM | 11:15 | walk/run at your half marathon pace. |
| Thursday | 3 | 5 | M | 11:15 - 12:15 | walk/run at a medium pace. |
| Friday | Rest | Rest | Rest | Rest | Rest. |
| Saturday | 7 | 11 | S | 11:15 - 13:45 | walk/run at a slow pace. The most important piece of your long duration runs is finishing the run. |
| Sunday | Rest/CT | Rest/CT | Rest | Rest | Rest. If your body feels good, then go ahead and do some form of cross-training for 30 to 60 minutes. |

## NOTE:

- Your long duration runs will begin to become more difficult for week 5 and beyond.
- If you get tired during a long duration run, walk for 1/10 mile or 3-5 minutes.

# Training - Week 6

5K Pace: **10:19**    5k Finish Time: **32 minutes**

| Day | Dist. Mile | Dist. KM | Difficulty | Pace (Range) | Instructions |
|---|---|---|---|---|---|
| Monday | Rest | Rest | Rest | Rest | Take it easy. Don't run. If you need to exercise, I recommend a walk for no longer than 30 minutes. |
| Tuesday | 3 | 5 | E | 11:15 - 13:15 | walk/run at an easy pace. |
| Wednesday | 4 | 6 | HM | 11:15 | walk/run at your half marathon pace. |
| Thursday | 3 | 5 | M | 11:15 - 12:15 | walk/run at a medium pace. |
| Friday | Rest | Rest | Rest | Rest | Rest. |
| Saturday | 8 | 13 | S | 11:15 - 13:45 | walk/run at a slow pace. The most important piece of your long duration runs is finishing the run. |
| Sunday | Rest/CT | Rest/CT | Rest | Rest | Rest. If your body feels good, then go ahead and do some form of cross-training for 30 to 60 minutes. |

# Training - Week 7

5K Pace: **10:19**     5k Finish Time: **32 minutes**

| Day | Dist. Mile | Dist. KM | Difficulty | Pace (Range) | Instructions |
|---|---|---|---|---|---|
| Monday | Rest | Rest | Rest | Rest | Take it easy. Don't run. If you need to exercise, I recommend a walk for no longer than 30 minutes. |
| Tuesday | 3 | 5 | E | 11:15 - 13:15 | walk/run at an easy pace. |
| Wednesday | 5 | 8 | HM | 11:15 | walk/run at your half marathon pace. |
| Thursday | 3 | 5 | M | 11:15 - 12:15 | walk/run at a medium pace. |
| Friday | Rest | Rest | Rest | Rest | Rest. |
| Saturday | 8.5 | 13.5 | S | 11:15 - 13:45 | walk/run at a slow pace. The most important piece of your long duration runs is finishing the run. |
| Sunday | Rest/CT | Rest/CT | Rest | Rest | Rest. If your body feels good, then go ahead and do some form of cross-training for 30 to 60 minutes. |

## 10K Optional

| Day | Dist. Mile | Dist. KM | Difficulty | Pace (Range) | Instructions |
|---|---|---|---|---|---|
| Thursday | 2 | 3 | E | 11:15 - 13:15 | If you run the optional 10K, either completely rest today or run 2 miles (3 km). |
| Saturday | 6.2 | 10K | - | **10:19** | Run a 10k race instead of your long run. This is completely your choice. I recommend running a 10k race to help you get used to running races. You should see a difference in your race time if you have kept to your training schedule. Don't try for a personal best, run the 10K at your 5K pace. |

# Training - Week 8

5K Pace: **10:19**     5k Finish Time: **32 minutes**

| Day | Dist. Mile | Dist. KM | Difficulty | Pace (Range) | Instructions |
|---|---|---|---|---|---|
| Monday | Rest | Rest | Rest | Rest | Take it easy. Don't run. If you need to exercise, I recommend a walk for no longer than 30 minutes. |
| Tuesday | 3 | 5 | E | 11:15 - 13:15 | walk/run at an easy pace. |
| Wednesday | 5 | 8 | HM | 11:15 | walk/run at your half marathon pace. |
| Thursday | 3 | 5 | M | 11:15 - 12:15 | walk/run at a medium pace. |
| Friday | Rest | Rest | Rest | Rest | Rest. |
| Saturday | 9 | 14 | S | 11:15 - 13:45 | walk/run at a slow pace. The most important piece of your long duration runs is finishing the run. |
| Sunday | Rest/CT | Rest/CT | Rest | Rest | Rest. If your body feels good, then go ahead and do some form of cross-training for 30 to 60 minutes. |

# Training - Week 9

5K Pace: **10:19**     5k Finish Time: **32 minutes**

| Day | Dist. Mile | Dist. KM | Difficulty | Pace (Range) | Instructions |
|---|---|---|---|---|---|
| Monday | Rest | Rest | Rest | Rest | Take it easy. Don't run. If you need to exercise, I recommend a walk for no longer than 30 minutes. |
| Tuesday | 3 | 5 | E | 11:15 - 13:15 | walk/run at an easy pace. |
| Wednesday | 5 | 8 | HM | 11:15 | walk/run at your half marathon pace. |
| Thursday | 3 | 5 | M | 11:15 - 12:15 | walk/run at a medium pace. |
| Friday | Rest | Rest | Rest | Rest | Rest. |
| Saturday | 8.5 | 13.5 | S | 11:15 - 13:45 | walk/run at a slow pace. The most important piece of your long duration runs is finishing the run. |
| Sunday | Rest/CT | Rest/CT | Rest | Rest | Rest. If your body feels good, then go ahead and do some form of cross-training for 30 to 60 minutes. |

## 13.1 Beta/Test Run Optional

| Day | Dist. Mile | Dist. KM | Difficulty | Pace (Range) | Instructions |
|---|---|---|---|---|---|
| Thursday | Rest | Rest | Rest | Rest | This is a rest day – it simulates race week |
| Friday | Rest | Rest | Rest | Rest | This is a rest day – it simulates race week |
| Saturday | 13.1 | 21 | S | 10:19 | I recommend that you attempt to go the full 13.1 miles (21 km) for a half marathon test run. <u>Only walk/run the first 10 miles (16 km) then walk the last 3.1 miles (5 km).</u> If you are successful, you will have a race ghost time to compete against. It will help energize and refocus your training on beating yourself in 3 weeks at the half marathon race. Also, it allows your mind to grasp the achievement of "completing the distance of a half marathon." |

# Training - Week 10

5K Pace: **10:19**    5k Finish Time: **32 minutes**

| Day | Dist. Mile | Dist. KM | Difficulty | Pace (Range) | Instructions |
|---|---|---|---|---|---|
| Monday | Rest | Rest | Rest | Rest | Take it easy. Don't run. If you need to exercise, I recommend a walk for no longer than 30 minutes. |
| Tuesday | 3 | 5 | E | 11:15 - 13:15 | walk/run at an easy pace. |
| Wednesday | 5 | 8 | HM | 11:15 | walk/run at your half marathon pace. |
| Thursday | 3 | 5 | M | 11:15 - 12:15 | walk/run at a medium pace. |
| Friday | Rest | Rest | Rest | Rest | Rest. |
| Saturday | 11 | 18 | S | 11:15 - 13:45 | walk/run at a slow pace. The most important piece of your long duration runs is finishing the run. |
| Sunday | Rest/CT | Rest/CT | Rest | Rest | Rest. If your body feels good, then go ahead and do some form of cross-training for 30 to 60 minutes. |

# Training - Week 11

| Day | Dist. Mile | Dist. KM | Difficulty | Pace (Range) | Instructions |
|---|---|---|---|---|---|
| Monday | Rest | Rest | Rest | Rest | Take it easy. Don't run. If you need to exercise, I recommend a walk for no longer than 30 minutes. |
| Tuesday | 3 | 5 | E | 11:15 - 13:15 | walk/run at an easy pace. |
| Wednesday | 5 | 8 | HM | 11:15 | walk/run at your half marathon pace. |
| Thursday | 3 | 5 | M | 11:15 - 12:15 | walk/run at a medium pace. |
| Friday | Rest | Rest | Rest | Rest | Rest. |
| Saturday | 12 | 20 | S | 11:15 - 13:45 | walk/run at a slow pace. The most important piece of your long duration runs is finishing the run. |
| Sunday | Rest/CT | Rest/CT | Rest | Rest | Rest. If your body feels good, then go ahead and do some form of cross-training for 30 to 60 minutes. |

# Training - Week 12

5K Pace: **10:19**   5k Finish Time: **32 minutes**

| Day | Dist. Mile | Dist. KM | Difficulty | Pace (Range) | Instructions |
|---|---|---|---|---|---|
| Monday | Rest | Rest | Rest | Rest | Take it easy. Don't run. If you need to exercise, I recommend a walk for no longer than 30 minutes. |
| Tuesday | 3 | 5 | E | 11:15 - 13:15 | walk/run at an easy pace. |
| Wednesday | 2 | 1.5 | HM | 11:15 | walk/run at your half marathon pace. |
| Thursday | Rest | Rest | Rest | Rest | Rest. |
| Friday | Rest | Rest | Rest | Rest | Rest. |
| Saturday | 13.1 | 21 | HM | 11:15 | RACE DAY! |
| Sunday | Rest | Rest | Rest | Rest | DRINK A VICTORY BEER! |

## NOTE:

- Get plenty of sleep the night before your long duration run.
- Try to run your long duration run early in the morning.
- After each run, it's important to stretch out your muscles.
- This week your body needs as much rest as possible.
- Don't run past Wednesday.

Half Marathon Training Schedule for runners with a 5K finish time of 33 minutes and a pace of *10:38* minutes/mile.

## Predicted Half Marathon Finish Time:

## *2* hour(s) *31* minutes

# PACING TABLES

| Pace | Pace (minutes/miles) |
|---:|---|
| 5k | 10:38 |
| Half marathon | 11:33 |
| Medium | Between 11:33 - 12:33 |
| Easy | Between 11:33 - 13:33 |
| Slow | Between 11:33 - 14:03 |

| Race | Finish Times (predicted) |
|---:|---|
| 5k | 33 minutes |
| Half marathon | 2 hour(s) 31 minutes |

| Determining your pace ||
|---|---|
| Slow Pace | Extremely easy to hold a conversation. |
| Easy Pace | You can hold a conversation with someone. Your breathing might break up some of the flow of the conversation. |
| Medium | You can hold a conversation with someone, but it's broken up into smaller sentences and smaller responses. |
| Half Marathon Pace | Conversation is difficult. One and two word responses back and forth at best. |

## Definitions in the table below:

CT = Cross Training

S = Slow Pace (long run pace)

E = Easy Pace

M = Medium Pace

HM = Half Marathon Pace

## Training - Week A (Optional)

5K Pace: **10:38**        5k Finish Time: **33 minutes**

| Day | Dist. Mile | Dist. KM | Difficulty | Pace (Range) | Instructions |
|---|---|---|---|---|---|
| Monday | Rest | Rest | Rest | Rest | Take it easy. Don't run. If you need to exercise, I recommend a walk for no longer than 30 minutes. |
| Tuesday | 1 | 1.5 | E | 11:33 - 13:33 | walk/run at an easy pace. |
| Wednesday | 1 | 1.5 | HM | 11:33 | walk/run at your half marathon pace. |
| Thursday | 1 | 1.5 | M | 11:33 - 12:33 | walk/run at a medium pace. |
| Friday | Rest | Rest | Rest | Rest | Rest. |
| Saturday | 1.5 | 2.5 | S | 11:33 - 14:03 | walk/run at a slow pace. The most important piece of your long duration runs is finishing the run. |
| Sunday | Rest/CT | Rest/CT | Rest | Rest | Rest. If your body feels good, then go ahead and do some form of cross-training for 30 to 60 minutes. |

## Training - Week B (Optional)

| Day | Dist. Mile | Dist. KM | Difficulty | Pace (Range) | Instructions |
|---|---|---|---|---|---|
| Monday | Rest | Rest | Rest | Rest | Take it easy. Don't run. If you need to exercise, I recommend a walk for no longer than 30 minutes. |
| Tuesday | 1.5 | 2.5 | E | 11:33 - 13:33 | walk/run at an easy pace. |
| Wednesday | 1.5 | 2.5 | HM | 11:33 | walk/run at your half marathon pace. |
| Thursday | 1.5 | 2.5 | M | 11:33 - 12:33 | walk/run at a medium pace. |
| Friday | Rest | Rest | Rest | Rest | Rest. |
| Saturday | 2 | 3 | S | 11:33 - 14:03 | walk/run at a slow pace. The most important piece of your long duration runs is finishing the run. |
| Sunday | Rest/CT | Rest/CT | Rest | Rest | Rest. If your body feels good, then go ahead and do some form of cross-training for 30 to 60 minutes. |

# Training - Week C (Optional)

5K Pace: **10:38**     5k Finish Time: **33 minutes**

| Day | Dist. Mile | Dist. KM | Difficulty | Pace (Range) | Instructions |
|---|---|---|---|---|---|
| Monday | Rest | Rest | Rest | Rest | Take it easy. Don't run. If you need to exercise, I recommend a walk for no longer than 30 minutes. |
| Tuesday | 2 | 3 | E | 11:33 - 13:33 | walk/run at an easy pace. |
| Wednesday | 2 | 3 | HM | 11:33 | walk/run at your half marathon pace. |
| Thursday | 2 | 3 | M | 11:33 - 12:33 | walk/run at a medium pace. |
| Friday | Rest | Rest | Rest | Rest | Rest. |
| Saturday | 3 | 5 | S | 11:33 - 14:03 | walk/run at a slow pace. The most important piece of your long duration runs is finishing the run. |
| Sunday | Rest/CT | Rest/CT | Rest | Rest | Rest. If your body feels good, then go ahead and do some form of cross-training for 30 to 60 minutes. |

# Training - Week 1

5K Pace: **10:38**   5k Finish Time: **33 minutes**

| Day | Dist. Mile | Dist. KM | Difficulty | Pace (Range) | Instructions |
|---|---|---|---|---|---|
| Monday | Rest | Rest | Rest | Rest | Take it easy. Don't run. If you need to exercise, I recommend a walk for no longer than 30 minutes. |
| Tuesday | 3 | 5 | E | 11:33 - 13:33 | walk/run at an easy pace. |
| Wednesday | 3 | 5 | HM | 11:33 | walk/run at your half marathon pace. |
| Thursday | 3 | 5 | M | 11:33 - 12:33 | walk/run at a medium pace. |
| Friday | Rest | Rest | Rest | Rest | Rest. |
| Saturday | 4 | 6 | S | 11:33 - 14:03 | walk/run at a slow pace. The most important piece of your long duration runs is finishing the run. |
| Sunday | Rest/CT | Rest/CT | Rest | Rest | Rest. If your body feels good, then go ahead and do some form of cross-training for 30 to 60 minutes. |

# Training - Week 2

| Day | Dist. Mile | Dist. KM | Difficulty | Pace (Range) | Instructions |
|---|---|---|---|---|---|
| Monday | Rest | Rest | Rest | Rest | Take it easy. Don't run. If you need to exercise, I recommend a walk for no longer than 30 minutes. |
| Tuesday | 3 | 5 | E | 11:33 - 13:33 | walk/run at an easy pace. |
| Wednesday | 3 | 5 | HM | 11:33 | walk/run at your half marathon pace. |
| Thursday | 3 | 5 | M | 11:33 - 12:33 | walk/run at a medium pace. |
| Friday | Rest | Rest | Rest | Rest | Rest. |
| Saturday | 5 | 8 | S | 11:33 - 14:03 | walk/run at a slow pace. The most important piece of your long duration runs is finishing the run. |
| Sunday | Rest/CT | Rest/CT | Rest | Rest | Rest. If your body feels good, then go ahead and do some form of cross-training for 30 to 60 minutes. |

# Training - Week 3

5K Pace: **10:38**     5k Finish Time: **33 minutes**

| Day | Dist. Mile | Dist. KM | Difficulty | Pace (Range) | Instructions |
|---|---|---|---|---|---|
| Monday | Rest | Rest | Rest | Rest | Take it easy. Don't run. If you need to exercise, I recommend a walk for no longer than 30 minutes. |
| Tuesday | 3 | 5 | E | 11:33 - 13:33 | walk/run at an easy pace. |
| Wednesday | 4 | 6 | HM | 11:33 | walk/run at your half marathon pace. |
| Thursday | 3 | 5 | M | 11:33 - 12:33 | walk/run at a medium pace. |
| Friday | Rest | Rest | Rest | Rest | Rest. |
| Saturday | 6 | 10 | S | 11:33 - 14:03 | walk/run at a slow pace. The most important piece of your long duration runs is finishing the run. |
| Sunday | Rest/CT | Rest/CT | Rest | Rest | Rest. If your body feels good, then go ahead and do some form of cross-training for 30 to 60 minutes. |

# Training - Week 4 (5K Optional)

5K Pace: **10:38**     5k Finish Time: **33 minutes**

| Day | Dist. Mile | Dist. KM | Difficulty | Pace (Range) | Instructions |
|---|---|---|---|---|---|
| Monday | Rest | Rest | Rest | Rest | Take it easy. Don't run. If you need to exercise, I recommend a walk for no longer than 30 minutes. |
| Tuesday | 3 | 5 | E | 11:33 - 13:33 | walk/run at an easy pace. |
| Wednesday | 4 | 6 | HM | 11:33 | walk/run at your half marathon pace. |
| Thursday | 3 | 5 | M | 11:33 - 12:33 | walk/run at a medium pace. |
| Friday | Rest | Rest | Rest | Rest | Rest. |
| Saturday | 6.5 | 10.5 | S | 11:33 - 14:03 | walk/run at a slow pace. The most important piece of your long duration runs is finishing the run. |
| Sunday | Rest/CT | Rest/CT | Rest | Rest | Rest. If your body feels good, then go ahead and do some form of cross-training for 30 to 60 minutes. |

## 5K Optional

| Day | Dist. Mile | Dist. KM | Difficulty | Pace (Range) | Instructions |
|---|---|---|---|---|---|
| Saturday | 3.1 | 5 | - | 10:38 | Run a 5k race instead of your long run. This is completely your choice. I recommend running a 5k race to help you get used to running races. You should see a difference in your race time if you have kept to your training schedule. Don't try for a personal best, run the 5K at your 5K pace. |

# Training - Week 5

5K Pace: **10:38**     5k Finish Time: **33 minutes**

| Day | Dist. Mile | Dist. KM | Difficulty | Pace (Range) | Instructions |
|---|---|---|---|---|---|
| Monday | Rest | Rest | Rest | Rest | Take it easy. Don't run. If you need to exercise, I recommend a walk for no longer than 30 minutes. |
| Tuesday | 3 | 5 | E | 11:33 - 13:33 | walk/run at an easy pace. |
| Wednesday | 4 | 6 | HM | 11:33 | walk/run at your half marathon pace. |
| Thursday | 3 | 5 | M | 11:33 - 12:33 | walk/run at a medium pace. |
| Friday | Rest | Rest | Rest | Rest | Rest. |
| Saturday | 7 | 11 | S | 11:33 - 14:03 | walk/run at a slow pace. The most important piece of your long duration runs is finishing the run. |
| Sunday | Rest/CT | Rest/CT | Rest | Rest | Rest. If your body feels good, then go ahead and do some form of cross-training for 30 to 60 minutes. |

## NOTE:

- Your long duration runs will begin to become more difficult for week 5 and beyond.
- If you get tired during a long duration run, walk for 1/10 mile or 3-5 minutes.

# Training - Week 6

5K Pace: **10:38**     5k Finish Time: **33 minutes**

| Day | Dist. Mile | Dist. KM | Difficulty | Pace (Range) | Instructions |
|---|---|---|---|---|---|
| Monday | Rest | Rest | Rest | Rest | Take it easy. Don't run. If you need to exercise, I recommend a walk for no longer than 30 minutes. |
| Tuesday | 3 | 5 | E | 11:33 - 13:33 | walk/run at an easy pace. |
| Wednesday | 4 | 6 | HM | 11:33 | walk/run at your half marathon pace. |
| Thursday | 3 | 5 | M | 11:33 - 12:33 | walk/run at a medium pace. |
| Friday | Rest | Rest | Rest | Rest | Rest. |
| Saturday | 8 | 13 | S | 11:33 - 14:03 | walk/run at a slow pace. The most important piece of your long duration runs is finishing the run. |
| Sunday | Rest/CT | Rest/CT | Rest | Rest | Rest. If your body feels good, then go ahead and do some form of cross-training for 30 to 60 minutes. |

# Training - Week 7

5K Pace: **10:38**    5k Finish Time: **33 minutes**

| Day | Dist. Mile | Dist. KM | Difficulty | Pace (Range) | Instructions |
|---|---|---|---|---|---|
| Monday | Rest | Rest | Rest | Rest | Take it easy. Don't run. If you need to exercise, I recommend a walk for no longer than 30 minutes. |
| Tuesday | 3 | 5 | E | 11:33 - 13:33 | walk/run at an easy pace. |
| Wednesday | 5 | 8 | HM | 11:33 | walk/run at your half marathon pace. |
| Thursday | 3 | 5 | M | 11:33 - 12:33 | walk/run at a medium pace. |
| Friday | Rest | Rest | Rest | Rest | Rest. |
| Saturday | 8.5 | 13.5 | S | 11:33 - 14:03 | walk/run at a slow pace. The most important piece of your long duration runs is finishing the run. |
| Sunday | Rest/CT | Rest/CT | Rest | Rest | Rest. If your body feels good, then go ahead and do some form of cross-training for 30 to 60 minutes. |

## 10K Optional

| Day | Dist. Mile | Dist. KM | Difficulty | Pace (Range) | Instructions |
|---|---|---|---|---|---|
| Thursday | 2 | 3 | E | 11:33 - 13:33 | If you run the optional 10K, either completely rest today or run 2 miles ( 3 km). |
| Saturday | 6.2 | 10K | - | 10:38 | Run a 10k race instead of your long run. This is completely your choice. I recommend running a 10k race to help you get used to running races. You should see a difference in your race time if you have kept to your training schedule. Don't try for a personal best, run the 10K at your 5K pace. |

# Training - Week 8

5K Pace: **10:38**     5k Finish Time: **33 minutes**

| Day | Dist. Mile | Dist. KM | Difficulty | Pace (Range) | Instructions |
|---|---|---|---|---|---|
| Monday | Rest | Rest | Rest | Rest | Take it easy. Don't run. If you need to exercise, I recommend a walk for no longer than 30 minutes. |
| Tuesday | 3 | 5 | E | 11:33 - 13:33 | walk/run at an easy pace. |
| Wednesday | 5 | 8 | HM | 11:33 | walk/run at your half marathon pace. |
| Thursday | 3 | 5 | M | 11:33 - 12:33 | walk/run at a medium pace. |
| Friday | Rest | Rest | Rest | Rest | Rest. |
| Saturday | 9 | 14 | S | 11:33 - 14:03 | walk/run at a slow pace. The most important piece of your long duration runs is finishing the run. |
| Sunday | Rest/CT | Rest/CT | Rest | Rest | Rest. If your body feels good, then go ahead and do some form of cross-training for 30 to 60 minutes. |

# Training - Week 9

5K Pace: **10:38**     5k Finish Time: **33 minutes**

| Day | Dist. Mile | Dist. KM | Difficulty | Pace (Range) | Instructions |
|---|---|---|---|---|---|
| Monday | Rest | Rest | Rest | Rest | Take it easy. Don't run. If you need to exercise, I recommend a walk for no longer than 30 minutes. |
| Tuesday | 3 | 5 | E | 11:33 - 13:33 | walk/run at an easy pace. |
| Wednesday | 5 | 8 | HM | 11:33 | walk/run at your half marathon pace. |
| Thursday | 3 | 5 | M | 11:33 - 12:33 | walk/run at a medium pace. |
| Friday | Rest | Rest | Rest | Rest | Rest. |
| Saturday | 8.5 | 13.5 | S | 11:33 - 14:03 | walk/run at a slow pace. The most important piece of your long duration runs is finishing the run. |
| Sunday | Rest/CT | Rest/CT | Rest | Rest | Rest. If your body feels good, then go ahead and do some form of cross-training for 30 to 60 minutes. |

## 13.1 Beta/Test Run Optional

| Day | Dist. Mile | Dist. KM | Difficulty | Pace (Range) | Instructions |
|---|---|---|---|---|---|
| Thursday | Rest | Rest | Rest | Rest | This is a rest day – it simulates race week |
| Friday | Rest | Rest | Rest | Rest | This is a rest day – it simulates race week |
| Saturday | 13.1 | 21 | S | 10:38 | I recommend that you attempt to go the full 13.1 miles (21 km) for a half marathon test run. <u>Only walk/run the first 10 miles (16 km) then walk the last 3.1 miles (5 km).</u> If you are successful, you will have a race ghost time to compete against. It will help energize and refocus your training on beating yourself in 3 weeks at the half marathon race. Also, it allows your mind to grasp the achievement of "completing the distance of a half marathon." |

# Training - Week 10

5K Pace: **10:38**     5k Finish Time: **33 minutes**

| Day | Dist. Mile | Dist. KM | Difficulty | Pace (Range) | Instructions |
|---|---|---|---|---|---|
| Monday | Rest | Rest | Rest | Rest | Take it easy. Don't run. If you need to exercise, I recommend a walk for no longer than 30 minutes. |
| Tuesday | 3 | 5 | E | 11:33 - 13:33 | walk/run at an easy pace. |
| Wednesday | 5 | 8 | HM | 11:33 | walk/run at your half marathon pace. |
| Thursday | 3 | 5 | M | 11:33 - 12:33 | walk/run at a medium pace. |
| Friday | Rest | Rest | Rest | Rest | Rest. |
| Saturday | 11 | 18 | S | 11:33 - 14:03 | walk/run at a slow pace. The most important piece of your long duration runs is finishing the run. |
| Sunday | Rest/CT | Rest/CT | Rest | Rest | Rest. If your body feels good, then go ahead and do some form of cross-training for 30 to 60 minutes. |

# Training - Week 11

| Day | Dist. Mile | Dist. KM | Difficulty | Pace (Range) | Instructions |
|---|---|---|---|---|---|
| Monday | Rest | Rest | Rest | Rest | Take it easy. Don't run. If you need to exercise, I recommend a walk for no longer than 30 minutes. |
| Tuesday | 3 | 5 | E | 11:33 - 13:33 | walk/run at an easy pace. |
| Wednesday | 5 | 8 | HM | 11:33 | walk/run at your half marathon pace. |
| Thursday | 3 | 5 | M | 11:33 - 12:33 | walk/run at a medium pace. |
| Friday | Rest | Rest | Rest | Rest | Rest. |
| Saturday | 12 | 20 | S | 11:33 - 14:03 | walk/run at a slow pace. The most important piece of your long duration runs is finishing the run. |
| Sunday | Rest/CT | Rest/CT | Rest | Rest | Rest. If your body feels good, then go ahead and do some form of cross-training for 30 to 60 minutes. |

# Training - Week 12

5K Pace: **10:38**     5k Finish Time: **33 minutes**

| Day | Dist. Mile | Dist. KM | Difficulty | Pace (Range) | Instructions |
|---|---|---|---|---|---|
| Monday | Rest | Rest | Rest | Rest | Take it easy. Don't run. If you need to exercise, I recommend a walk for no longer than 30 minutes. |
| Tuesday | 3 | 5 | E | 11:33 - 13:33 | walk/run at an easy pace. |
| Wednesday | 2 | 1.5 | HM | 11:33 | walk/run at your half marathon pace. |
| Thursday | Rest | Rest | Rest | Rest | Rest. |
| Friday | Rest | Rest | Rest | Rest | Rest. |
| Saturday | 13.1 | 21 | HM | 11:33 | RACE DAY! |
| Sunday | Rest | Rest | Rest | Rest | DRINK A VICTORY BEER! |

## NOTE:

- Get plenty of sleep the night before your long duration run.
- Try to run your long duration run early in the morning.
- After each run, it's important to stretch out your muscles.
- This week your body needs as much rest as possible.
- Don't run past Wednesday.

# BEGINNER TO FINISHER RUNNING

Half Marathon Training Schedule for

runners with a 5K finish time of 34 minutes

and a pace of *10:58* minutes/mile.

## Predicted Half Marathon Finish Time:

## *2* hour(s) *36* minutes

# PACING TABLES

| Pace | Pace (minutes/miles) |
|---:|---|
| 5k | 10:58 |
| Half marathon | 11:55 |
| Medium | Between 11:55 - 12:55 |
| Easy | Between 11:55 - 13:55 |
| Slow | Between 11:55 - 14:25 |

| Race | Finish Times (predicted) |
|---:|---|
| 5k | 34 minutes |
| Half marathon | 2 hour(s) 36 minutes |

| Determining your pace | |
|---|---|
| Slow Pace | Extremely easy to hold a conversation. |
| Easy Pace | You can hold a conversation with someone. Your breathing might break up some of the flow of the conversation. |
| Medium | You can hold a conversation with someone, but it's broken up into smaller sentences and smaller responses. |
| Half Marathon Pace | Conversation is difficult. One and two word responses back and forth at best. |

## Definitions in the table below:

CT = Cross Training

S = Slow Pace (long run pace)

E = Easy Pace

M = Medium Pace

HM = Half Marathon Pace

## Training - Week A (Optional)

5K Pace: **10:58**     5k Finish Time: **34 minutes**

| Day | Dist. Mile | Dist. KM | Difficulty | Pace (Range) | Instructions |
|---|---|---|---|---|---|
| Monday | Rest | Rest | Rest | Rest | Take it easy. Don't run. If you need to exercise, I recommend a walk for no longer than 30 minutes. |
| Tuesday | 1 | 1.5 | E | 11:55 - 13:55 | walk/run at an easy pace. |
| Wednesday | 1 | 1.5 | HM | 11:55 | walk/run at your half marathon pace. |
| Thursday | 1 | 1.5 | M | 11:55 - 12:55 | walk/run at a medium pace. |
| Friday | Rest | Rest | Rest | Rest | Rest. |
| Saturday | 1.5 | 2.5 | S | 11:55 - 14:25 | walk/run at a slow pace. The most important piece of your long duration runs is finishing the run. |
| Sunday | Rest/CT | Rest/CT | Rest | Rest | Rest. If your body feels good, then go ahead and do some form of cross-training for 30 to 60 minutes. |

## Training - Week B (Optional)

| Day | Dist. Mile | Dist. KM | Difficulty | Pace (Range) | Instructions |
|---|---|---|---|---|---|
| Monday | Rest | Rest | Rest | Rest | Take it easy. Don't run. If you need to exercise, I recommend a walk for no longer than 30 minutes. |
| Tuesday | 1.5 | 2.5 | E | 11:55 - 13:55 | walk/run at an easy pace. |
| Wednesday | 1.5 | 2.5 | HM | 11:55 | walk/run at your half marathon pace. |
| Thursday | 1.5 | 2.5 | M | 11:55 - 12:55 | walk/run at a medium pace. |
| Friday | Rest | Rest | Rest | Rest | Rest. |
| Saturday | 2 | 3 | S | 11:55 - 14:25 | walk/run at a slow pace. The most important piece of your long duration runs is finishing the run. |
| Sunday | Rest/CT | Rest/CT | Rest | Rest | Rest. If your body feels good, then go ahead and do some form of cross-training for 30 to 60 minutes. |

# Training - Week C (Optional)

5K Pace: **10:58**     5k Finish Time: **34 minutes**

| Day | Dist. Mile | Dist. KM | Difficulty | Pace (Range) | Instructions |
|---|---|---|---|---|---|
| Monday | Rest | Rest | Rest | Rest | Take it easy. Don't run. If you need to exercise, I recommend a walk for no longer than 30 minutes. |
| Tuesday | 2 | 3 | E | 11:55 - 13:55 | walk/run at an easy pace. |
| Wednesday | 2 | 3 | HM | 11:55 | walk/run at your half marathon pace. |
| Thursday | 2 | 3 | M | 11:55 - 12:55 | walk/run at a medium pace. |
| Friday | Rest | Rest | Rest | Rest | Rest. |
| Saturday | 3 | 5 | S | 11:55 - 14:25 | walk/run at a slow pace. The most important piece of your long duration runs is finishing the run. |
| Sunday | Rest/CT | Rest/CT | Rest | Rest | Rest. If your body feels good, then go ahead and do some form of cross-training for 30 to 60 minutes. |

# Training - Week 1

5K Pace: **10:58**     5k Finish Time: **34 minutes**

| Day | Dist. Mile | Dist. KM | Difficulty | Pace (Range) | Instructions |
|---|---|---|---|---|---|
| Monday | Rest | Rest | Rest | Rest | Take it easy. Don't run. If you need to exercise, I recommend a walk for no longer than 30 minutes. |
| Tuesday | 3 | 5 | E | 11:55 - 13:55 | walk/run at an easy pace. |
| Wednesday | 3 | 5 | HM | 11:55 | walk/run at your half marathon pace. |
| Thursday | 3 | 5 | M | 11:55 - 12:55 | walk/run at a medium pace. |
| Friday | Rest | Rest | Rest | Rest | Rest. |
| Saturday | 4 | 6 | S | 11:55 - 14:25 | walk/run at a slow pace. The most important piece of your long duration runs is finishing the run. |
| Sunday | Rest/CT | Rest/CT | Rest | Rest | Rest. If your body feels good, then go ahead and do some form of cross-training for 30 to 60 minutes. |

# Training - Week 2

| Day | Dist. Mile | Dist. KM | Difficulty | Pace (Range) | Instructions |
|---|---|---|---|---|---|
| Monday | Rest | Rest | Rest | Rest | Take it easy. Don't run. If you need to exercise, I recommend a walk for no longer than 30 minutes. |
| Tuesday | 3 | 5 | E | 11:55 - 13:55 | walk/run at an easy pace. |
| Wednesday | 3 | 5 | HM | 11:55 | walk/run at your half marathon pace. |
| Thursday | 3 | 5 | M | 11:55 - 12:55 | walk/run at a medium pace. |
| Friday | Rest | Rest | Rest | Rest | Rest. |
| Saturday | 5 | 8 | S | 11:55 - 14:25 | walk/run at a slow pace. The most important piece of your long duration runs is finishing the run. |
| Sunday | Rest/CT | Rest/CT | Rest | Rest | Rest. If your body feels good, then go ahead and do some form of cross-training for 30 to 60 minutes. |

# Training - Week 3

5K Pace: **10:58**     5k Finish Time: **34 minutes**

| Day | Dist. Mile | Dist. KM | Difficulty | Pace (Range) | Instructions |
|---|---|---|---|---|---|
| Monday | Rest | Rest | Rest | Rest | Take it easy. Don't run. If you need to exercise, I recommend a walk for no longer than 30 minutes. |
| Tuesday | 3 | 5 | E | 11:55 - 13:55 | walk/run at an easy pace. |
| Wednesday | 4 | 6 | HM | 11:55 | walk/run at your half marathon pace. |
| Thursday | 3 | 5 | M | 11:55 - 12:55 | walk/run at a medium pace. |
| Friday | Rest | Rest | Rest | Rest | Rest. |
| Saturday | 6 | 10 | S | 11:55 - 14:25 | walk/run at a slow pace. The most important piece of your long duration runs is finishing the run. |
| Sunday | Rest/CT | Rest/CT | Rest | Rest | Rest. If your body feels good, then go ahead and do some form of cross-training for 30 to 60 minutes. |

# Training - Week 4 (5K Optional)

5K Pace: **10:58**     5k Finish Time: **34 minutes**

| Day | Dist. Mile | Dist. KM | Difficulty | Pace (Range) | Instructions |
|---|---|---|---|---|---|
| Monday | Rest | Rest | Rest | Rest | Take it easy. Don't run. If you need to exercise, I recommend a walk for no longer than 30 minutes. |
| Tuesday | 3 | 5 | E | 11:55 - 13:55 | walk/run at an easy pace. |
| Wednesday | 4 | 6 | HM | 11:55 | walk/run at your half marathon pace. |
| Thursday | 3 | 5 | M | 11:55 - 12:55 | walk/run at a medium pace. |
| Friday | Rest | Rest | Rest | Rest | Rest. |
| Saturday | 6.5 | 10.5 | S | 11:55 - 14:25 | walk/run at a slow pace. The most important piece of your long duration runs is finishing the run. |
| Sunday | Rest/CT | Rest/CT | Rest | Rest | Rest. If your body feels good, then go ahead and do some form of cross-training for 30 to 60 minutes. |

## 5K Optional

| Day | Dist. Mile | Dist. KM | Difficulty | Pace (Range) | Instructions |
|---|---|---|---|---|---|
| Saturday | 3.1 | 5 | - | 10:58 | Run a 5k race instead of your long run. This is completely your choice. I recommend running a 5k race to help you get used to running races. You should see a difference in your race time if you have kept to your training schedule. Don't try for a personal best, run the 5K at your 5K pace. |

# Training - Week 5

5K Pace: **10:58**  5k Finish Time: **34 minutes**

| Day | Dist. Mile | Dist. KM | Difficulty | Pace (Range) | Instructions |
|---|---|---|---|---|---|
| Monday | Rest | Rest | Rest | Rest | Take it easy. Don't run. If you need to exercise, I recommend a walk for no longer than 30 minutes. |
| Tuesday | 3 | 5 | E | 11:55 - 13:55 | walk/run at an easy pace. |
| Wednesday | 4 | 6 | HM | 11:55 | walk/run at your half marathon pace. |
| Thursday | 3 | 5 | M | 11:55 - 12:55 | walk/run at a medium pace. |
| Friday | Rest | Rest | Rest | Rest | Rest. |
| Saturday | 7 | 11 | S | 11:55 - 14:25 | walk/run at a slow pace. The most important piece of your long duration runs is finishing the run. |
| Sunday | Rest/CT | Rest/CT | Rest | Rest | Rest. If your body feels good, then go ahead and do some form of cross-training for 30 to 60 minutes. |

## NOTE:

- Your long duration runs will begin to become more difficult for week 5 and beyond.
- If you get tired during a long duration run, walk for 1/10 mile or 3-5 minutes.

# Training - Week 6

5K Pace: **10:58**     5k Finish Time: **34 minutes**

| Day | Dist. Mile | Dist. KM | Difficulty | Pace (Range) | Instructions |
|---|---|---|---|---|---|
| Monday | Rest | Rest | Rest | Rest | Take it easy. Don't run. If you need to exercise, I recommend a walk for no longer than 30 minutes. |
| Tuesday | 3 | 5 | E | 11:55 - 13:55 | walk/run at an easy pace. |
| Wednesday | 4 | 6 | HM | 11:55 | walk/run at your half marathon pace. |
| Thursday | 3 | 5 | M | 11:55 - 12:55 | walk/run at a medium pace. |
| Friday | Rest | Rest | Rest | Rest | Rest. |
| Saturday | 8 | 13 | S | 11:55 - 14:25 | walk/run at a slow pace. The most important piece of your long duration runs is finishing the run. |
| Sunday | Rest/CT | Rest/CT | Rest | Rest | Rest. If your body feels good, then go ahead and do some form of cross-training for 30 to 60 minutes. |

# Training - Week 7

5K Pace: **10:58**    5k Finish Time: **34 minutes**

| Day | Dist. Mile | Dist. KM | Difficulty | Pace (Range) | Instructions |
|---|---|---|---|---|---|
| Monday | Rest | Rest | Rest | Rest | Take it easy. Don't run. If you need to exercise, I recommend a walk for no longer than 30 minutes. |
| Tuesday | 3 | 5 | E | 11:55 - 13:55 | walk/run at an easy pace. |
| Wednesday | 5 | 8 | HM | 11:55 | walk/run at your half marathon pace. |
| Thursday | 3 | 5 | M | 11:55 - 12:55 | walk/run at a medium pace. |
| Friday | Rest | Rest | Rest | Rest | Rest. |
| Saturday | 8.5 | 13.5 | S | 11:55 - 14:25 | walk/run at a slow pace. The most important piece of your long duration runs is finishing the run. |
| Sunday | Rest/CT | Rest/CT | Rest | Rest | Rest. If your body feels good, then go ahead and do some form of cross-training for 30 to 60 minutes. |

## 10K Optional

| Day | Dist. Mile | Dist. KM | Difficulty | Pace (Range) | Instructions |
|---|---|---|---|---|---|
| Thursday | 2 | 3 | E | 11:55 - 13:55 | If you run the optional 10K, either completely rest today or run 2 miles ( 3 km). |
| Saturday | 6.2 | 10K | - | **10:58** | Run a 10k race instead of your long run. This is completely your choice. I recommend running a 10k race to help you get used to running races. You should see a difference in your race time if you have kept to your training schedule. Don't try for a personal best, run the 10K at your 5K pace. |

# Training - Week 8

5K Pace: **10:58**     5k Finish Time: **34 minutes**

| Day | Dist. Mile | Dist. KM | Difficulty | Pace (Range) | Instructions |
|---|---|---|---|---|---|
| Monday | Rest | Rest | Rest | Rest | Take it easy. Don't run. If you need to exercise, I recommend a walk for no longer than 30 minutes. |
| Tuesday | 3 | 5 | E | 11:55 - 13:55 | walk/run at an easy pace. |
| Wednesday | 5 | 8 | HM | 11:55 | walk/run at your half marathon pace. |
| Thursday | 3 | 5 | M | 11:55 - 12:55 | walk/run at a medium pace. |
| Friday | Rest | Rest | Rest | Rest | Rest. |
| Saturday | 9 | 14 | S | 11:55 - 14:25 | walk/run at a slow pace. The most important piece of your long duration runs is finishing the run. |
| Sunday | Rest/CT | Rest/CT | Rest | Rest | Rest. If your body feels good, then go ahead and do some form of cross-training for 30 to 60 minutes. |

# Training - Week 9

5K Pace: **10:58**     5k Finish Time: **34 minutes**

| Day | Dist. Mile | Dist. KM | Difficulty | Pace (Range) | Instructions |
|---|---|---|---|---|---|
| Monday | Rest | Rest | Rest | Rest | Take it easy. Don't run. If you need to exercise, I recommend a walk for no longer than 30 minutes. |
| Tuesday | 3 | 5 | E | 11:55 - 13:55 | walk/run at an easy pace. |
| Wednesday | 5 | 8 | HM | 11:55 | walk/run at your half marathon pace. |
| Thursday | 3 | 5 | M | 11:55 - 12:55 | walk/run at a medium pace. |
| Friday | Rest | Rest | Rest | Rest | Rest. |
| Saturday | 8.5 | 13.5 | S | 11:55 - 14:25 | walk/run at a slow pace. The most important piece of your long duration runs is finishing the run. |
| Sunday | Rest/CT | Rest/CT | Rest | Rest | Rest. If your body feels good, then go ahead and do some form of cross-training for 30 to 60 minutes. |

## 13.1 Beta/Test Run Optional

| Day | Dist. Mile | Dist. KM | Difficulty | Pace (Range) | Instructions |
|---|---|---|---|---|---|
| Thursday | Rest | Rest | Rest | Rest | This is a rest day – it simulates race week |
| Friday | Rest | Rest | Rest | Rest | This is a rest day – it simulates race week |
| Saturday | 13.1 | 21 | S | 10:58 | I recommend that you attempt to go the full 13.1 miles (21 km) for a half marathon test run. Only walk/run the first 10 miles (16 km) then walk the last 3.1 miles (5 km). If you are successful, you will have a race ghost time to compete against. It will help energize and refocus your training on beating yourself in 3 weeks at the half marathon race. Also, it allows your mind to grasp the achievement of "completing the distance of a half marathon." |

# Training - Week 10

5K Pace: **10:58**     5k Finish Time: **34 minutes**

| Day | Dist. Mile | Dist. KM | Difficulty | Pace (Range) | Instructions |
|---|---|---|---|---|---|
| Monday | Rest | Rest | Rest | Rest | Take it easy. Don't run. If you need to exercise, I recommend a walk for no longer than 30 minutes. |
| Tuesday | 3 | 5 | E | 11:55 - 13:55 | walk/run at an easy pace. |
| Wednesday | 5 | 8 | HM | 11:55 | walk/run at your half marathon pace. |
| Thursday | 3 | 5 | M | 11:55 - 12:55 | walk/run at a medium pace. |
| Friday | Rest | Rest | Rest | Rest | Rest. |
| Saturday | 11 | 18 | S | 11:55 - 14:25 | walk/run at a slow pace. The most important piece of your long duration runs is finishing the run. |
| Sunday | Rest/CT | Rest/CT | Rest | Rest | Rest. If your body feels good, then go ahead and do some form of cross-training for 30 to 60 minutes. |

# Training - Week 11

| Day | Dist. Mile | Dist. KM | Difficulty | Pace (Range) | Instructions |
|---|---|---|---|---|---|
| Monday | Rest | Rest | Rest | Rest | Take it easy. Don't run. If you need to exercise, I recommend a walk for no longer than 30 minutes. |
| Tuesday | 3 | 5 | E | 11:55 - 13:55 | walk/run at an easy pace. |
| Wednesday | 5 | 8 | HM | 11:55 | walk/run at your half marathon pace. |
| Thursday | 3 | 5 | M | 11:55 - 12:55 | walk/run at a medium pace. |
| Friday | Rest | Rest | Rest | Rest | Rest. |
| Saturday | 12 | 20 | S | 11:55 - 14:25 | walk/run at a slow pace. The most important piece of your long duration runs is finishing the run. |
| Sunday | Rest/CT | Rest/CT | Rest | Rest | Rest. If your body feels good, then go ahead and do some form of cross-training for 30 to 60 minutes. |

# Training - Week 12

5K Pace: **10:58**     5k Finish Time: **34 minutes**

| Day | Dist. Mile | Dist. KM | Difficulty | Pace (Range) | Instructions |
|---|---|---|---|---|---|
| Monday | Rest | Rest | Rest | Rest | Take it easy. Don't run. If you need to exercise, I recommend a walk for no longer than 30 minutes. |
| Tuesday | 3 | 5 | E | 11:55 - 13:55 | walk/run at an easy pace. |
| Wednesday | 2 | 1.5 | HM | 11:55 | walk/run at your half marathon pace. |
| Thursday | Rest | Rest | Rest | Rest | Rest. |
| Friday | Rest | Rest | Rest | Rest | Rest. |
| Saturday | 13.1 | 21 | HM | 11:55 | RACE DAY! |
| Sunday | Rest | Rest | Rest | Rest | DRINK A VICTORY BEER! |

# NOTE:

- Get plenty of sleep the night before your long duration run.
- Try to run your long duration run early in the morning.
- After each run, it's important to stretch out your muscles.
- This week your body needs as much rest as possible.
- Don't run past Wednesday.

Half Marathon Training Schedule for

runners with a 5K finish time of 35 minutes

and a pace of *11:17* minutes/mile.

# Predicted Half Marathon Finish Time:

## *2* hour(s) *40* minutes

# PACING TABLES

| Pace | Pace (minutes/miles) |
|---:|---|
| 5k | 11:17 |
| Half marathon | 12:15 |
| Medium | Between 12:15 - 13:15 |
| Easy | Between 12:15 - 14:15 |
| Slow | Between 12:15 - 14:45 |

| Race | Finish Times (predicted) |
|---:|---|
| 5k | 35 minutes |
| Half marathon | 2 hour(s) 40 minutes |

| Determining your pace | |
|---|---|
| Slow Pace | Extremely easy to hold a conversation. |
| Easy Pace | You can hold a conversation with someone. Your breathing might break up some of the flow of the conversation. |
| Medium | You can hold a conversation with someone, but it's broken up into smaller sentences and smaller responses. |
| Half Marathon Pace | Conversation is difficult. One and two word responses back and forth at best. |

## Definitions in the table below:

CT = Cross Training

S = Slow Pace (long run pace)

E = Easy Pace

M = Medium Pace

HM = Half Marathon Pace

# Training - Week A (Optional)

5K Pace: **11:17**     5k Finish Time: **35 minutes**

| Day | Dist. Mile | Dist. KM | Difficulty | Pace (Range) | Instructions |
|---|---|---|---|---|---|
| Monday | Rest | Rest | Rest | Rest | Take it easy. Don't run. If you need to exercise, I recommend a walk for no longer than 30 minutes. |
| Tuesday | 1 | 1.5 | E | 12:15 - 14:15 | walk/run at an easy pace. |
| Wednesday | 1 | 1.5 | HM | 12:15 | walk/run at your half marathon pace. |
| Thursday | 1 | 1.5 | M | 12:15 - 13:15 | walk/run at a medium pace. |
| Friday | Rest | Rest | Rest | Rest | Rest. |
| Saturday | 1.5 | 2.5 | S | 12:15 - 14:45 | walk/run at a slow pace. The most important piece of your long duration runs is finishing the run. |
| Sunday | Rest/CT | Rest/CT | Rest | Rest | Rest. If your body feels good, then go ahead and do some form of cross-training for 30 to 60 minutes. |

# Training - Week B (Optional)

| Day | Dist. Mile | Dist. KM | Difficulty | Pace (Range) | Instructions |
|---|---|---|---|---|---|
| Monday | Rest | Rest | Rest | Rest | Take it easy. Don't run. If you need to exercise, I recommend a walk for no longer than 30 minutes. |
| Tuesday | 1.5 | 2.5 | E | 12:15 - 14:15 | walk/run at an easy pace. |
| Wednesday | 1.5 | 2.5 | HM | 12:15 | walk/run at your half marathon pace. |
| Thursday | 1.5 | 2.5 | M | 12:15 - 13:15 | walk/run at a medium pace. |
| Friday | Rest | Rest | Rest | Rest | Rest. |
| Saturday | 2 | 3 | S | 12:15 - 14:45 | walk/run at a slow pace. The most important piece of your long duration runs is finishing the run. |
| Sunday | Rest/CT | Rest/CT | Rest | Rest | Rest. If your body feels good, then go ahead and do some form of cross-training for 30 to 60 minutes. |

# Training - Week C (Optional)

5K Pace: **11:17**     5k Finish Time: **35 minutes**

| Day | Dist. Mile | Dist. KM | Difficulty | Pace (Range) | Instructions |
|---|---|---|---|---|---|
| Monday | Rest | Rest | Rest | Rest | Take it easy. Don't run. If you need to exercise, I recommend a walk for no longer than 30 minutes. |
| Tuesday | 2 | 3 | E | 12:15 - 14:15 | walk/run at an easy pace. |
| Wednesday | 2 | 3 | HM | 12:15 | walk/run at your half marathon pace. |
| Thursday | 2 | 3 | M | 12:15 - 13:15 | walk/run at a medium pace. |
| Friday | Rest | Rest | Rest | Rest | Rest. |
| Saturday | 3 | 5 | S | 12:15 - 14:45 | walk/run at a slow pace. The most important piece of your long duration runs is finishing the run. |
| Sunday | Rest/CT | Rest/CT | Rest | Rest | Rest. If your body feels good, then go ahead and do some form of cross-training for 30 to 60 minutes. |

# Training - Week 1

5K Pace: **11:17**     5k Finish Time: **35 minutes**

| Day | Dist. Mile | Dist. KM | Difficulty | Pace (Range) | Instructions |
|---|---|---|---|---|---|
| Monday | Rest | Rest | Rest | Rest | Take it easy. Don't run. If you need to exercise, I recommend a walk for no longer than 30 minutes. |
| Tuesday | 3 | 5 | E | 12:15 - 14:15 | walk/run at an easy pace. |
| Wednesday | 3 | 5 | HM | 12:15 | walk/run at your half marathon pace. |
| Thursday | 3 | 5 | M | 12:15 - 13:15 | walk/run at a medium pace. |
| Friday | Rest | Rest | Rest | Rest | Rest. |
| Saturday | 4 | 6 | S | 12:15 - 14:45 | walk/run at a slow pace. The most important piece of your long duration runs is finishing the run. |
| Sunday | Rest/CT | Rest/CT | Rest | Rest | Rest. If your body feels good, then go ahead and do some form of cross-training for 30 to 60 minutes. |

# Training - Week 2

| Day | Dist. Mile | Dist. KM | Difficulty | Pace (Range) | Instructions |
|---|---|---|---|---|---|
| Monday | Rest | Rest | Rest | Rest | Take it easy. Don't run. If you need to exercise, I recommend a walk for no longer than 30 minutes. |
| Tuesday | 3 | 5 | E | 12:15 - 14:15 | walk/run at an easy pace. |
| Wednesday | 3 | 5 | HM | 12:15 | walk/run at your half marathon pace. |
| Thursday | 3 | 5 | M | 12:15 - 13:15 | walk/run at a medium pace. |
| Friday | Rest | Rest | Rest | Rest | Rest. |
| Saturday | 5 | 8 | S | 12:15 - 14:45 | walk/run at a slow pace. The most important piece of your long duration runs is finishing the run. |
| Sunday | Rest/CT | Rest/CT | Rest | Rest | Rest. If your body feels good, then go ahead and do some form of cross-training for 30 to 60 minutes. |

# Training - Week 3

5K Pace: **11:17**     5k Finish Time: **35 minutes**

| Day | Dist. Mile | Dist. KM | Difficulty | Pace (Range) | Instructions |
|---|---|---|---|---|---|
| Monday | Rest | Rest | Rest | Rest | Take it easy. Don't run. If you need to exercise, I recommend a walk for no longer than 30 minutes. |
| Tuesday | 3 | 5 | E | 12:15 - 14:15 | walk/run at an easy pace. |
| Wednesday | 4 | 6 | HM | 12:15 | walk/run at your half marathon pace. |
| Thursday | 3 | 5 | M | 12:15 - 13:15 | walk/run at a medium pace. |
| Friday | Rest | Rest | Rest | Rest | Rest. |
| Saturday | 6 | 10 | S | 12:15 - 14:45 | walk/run at a slow pace. The most important piece of your long duration runs is finishing the run. |
| Sunday | Rest/CT | Rest/CT | Rest | Rest | Rest. If your body feels good, then go ahead and do some form of cross-training for 30 to 60 minutes. |

# Training - Week 4 (5K Optional)

5K Pace: **11:17**    5k Finish Time: **35 minutes**

| Day | Dist. Mile | Dist. KM | Difficulty | Pace (Range) | Instructions |
|---|---|---|---|---|---|
| Monday | Rest | Rest | Rest | Rest | Take it easy. Don't run. If you need to exercise, I recommend a walk for no longer than 30 minutes. |
| Tuesday | 3 | 5 | E | 12:15 - 14:15 | walk/run at an easy pace. |
| Wednesday | 4 | 6 | HM | 12:15 | walk/run at your half marathon pace. |
| Thursday | 3 | 5 | M | 12:15 - 13:15 | walk/run at a medium pace. |
| Friday | Rest | Rest | Rest | Rest | Rest. |
| Saturday | 6.5 | 10.5 | S | 12:15 - 14:45 | walk/run at a slow pace. The most important piece of your long duration runs is finishing the run. |
| Sunday | Rest/CT | Rest/CT | Rest | Rest | Rest. If your body feels good, then go ahead and do some form of cross-training for 30 to 60 minutes. |

## 5K Optional

| Day | Dist. Mile | Dist. KM | Difficulty | Pace (Range) | Instructions |
|---|---|---|---|---|---|
| Saturday | 3.1 | 5 | - | 11:17 | Run a 5k race instead of your long run. This is completely your choice. I recommend running a 5k race to help you get used to running races. You should see a difference in your race time if you have kept to your training schedule. Don't try for a personal best, run the 5K at your 5K pace. |

# Training - Week 5

5K Pace: **11:17**  5k Finish Time: **35 minutes**

| Day | Dist. Mile | Dist. KM | Difficulty | Pace (Range) | Instructions |
|---|---|---|---|---|---|
| Monday | Rest | Rest | Rest | Rest | Take it easy. Don't run. If you need to exercise, I recommend a walk for no longer than 30 minutes. |
| Tuesday | 3 | 5 | E | 12:15 - 14:15 | walk/run at an easy pace. |
| Wednesday | 4 | 6 | HM | 12:15 | walk/run at your half marathon pace. |
| Thursday | 3 | 5 | M | 12:15 - 13:15 | walk/run at a medium pace. |
| Friday | Rest | Rest | Rest | Rest | Rest. |
| Saturday | 7 | 11 | S | 12:15 - 14:45 | walk/run at a slow pace. The most important piece of your long duration runs is finishing the run. |
| Sunday | Rest/CT | Rest/CT | Rest | Rest | Rest. If your body feels good, then go ahead and do some form of cross-training for 30 to 60 minutes. |

## NOTE:

- Your long duration runs will begin to become more difficult for week 5 and beyond.
- If you get tired during a long duration run, walk for 1/10 mile or 3-5 minutes.

# Training - Week 6

5K Pace: **11:17**    5k Finish Time: **35 minutes**

| Day | Dist. Mile | Dist. KM | Difficulty | Pace (Range) | Instructions |
|---|---|---|---|---|---|
| Monday | Rest | Rest | Rest | Rest | Take it easy. Don't run. If you need to exercise, I recommend a walk for no longer than 30 minutes. |
| Tuesday | 3 | 5 | E | 12:15 - 14:15 | walk/run at an easy pace. |
| Wednesday | 4 | 6 | HM | 12:15 | walk/run at your half marathon pace. |
| Thursday | 3 | 5 | M | 12:15 - 13:15 | walk/run at a medium pace. |
| Friday | Rest | Rest | Rest | Rest | Rest. |
| Saturday | 8 | 13 | S | 12:15 - 14:45 | walk/run at a slow pace. The most important piece of your long duration runs is finishing the run. |
| Sunday | Rest/CT | Rest/CT | Rest | Rest | Rest. If your body feels good, then go ahead and do some form of cross-training for 30 to 60 minutes. |

# Training - Week 7

5K Pace: **11:17**     5k Finish Time: **35 minutes**

| Day | Dist. Mile | Dist. KM | Difficulty | Pace (Range) | Instructions |
|---|---|---|---|---|---|
| Monday | Rest | Rest | Rest | Rest | Take it easy. Don't run. If you need to exercise, I recommend a walk for no longer than 30 minutes. |
| Tuesday | 3 | 5 | E | 12:15 - 14:15 | walk/run at an easy pace. |
| Wednesday | 5 | 8 | HM | 12:15 | walk/run at your half marathon pace. |
| Thursday | 3 | 5 | M | 12:15 - 13:15 | walk/run at a medium pace. |
| Friday | Rest | Rest | Rest | Rest | Rest. |
| Saturday | 8.5 | 13.5 | S | 12:15 - 14:45 | walk/run at a slow pace. The most important piece of your long duration runs is finishing the run. |
| Sunday | Rest/CT | Rest/CT | Rest | Rest | Rest. If your body feels good, then go ahead and do some form of cross-training for 30 to 60 minutes. |

## 10K Optional

| Day | Dist. Mile | Dist. KM | Difficulty | Pace (Range) | Instructions |
|---|---|---|---|---|---|
| Thursday | 2 | 3 | E | 12:15 - 14:15 | If you run the optional 10K, either completely rest today or run 2 miles (3 km). |
| Saturday | 6.2 | 10K | - | 11:17 | Run a 10k race instead of your long run. This is completely your choice. I recommend running a 10k race to help you get used to running races. You should see a difference in your race time if you have kept to your training schedule. Don't try for a personal best, run the 10K at your 5K pace. |

# Training - Week 8

5K Pace: **11:17**     5k Finish Time: **35 minutes**

| Day | Dist. Mile | Dist. KM | Difficulty | Pace (Range) | Instructions |
|---|---|---|---|---|---|
| Monday | Rest | Rest | Rest | Rest | Take it easy. Don't run. If you need to exercise, I recommend a walk for no longer than 30 minutes. |
| Tuesday | 3 | 5 | E | 12:15 - 14:15 | walk/run at an easy pace. |
| Wednesday | 5 | 8 | HM | 12:15 | walk/run at your half marathon pace. |
| Thursday | 3 | 5 | M | 12:15 - 13:15 | walk/run at a medium pace. |
| Friday | Rest | Rest | Rest | Rest | Rest. |
| Saturday | 9 | 14 | S | 12:15 - 14:45 | walk/run at a slow pace. The most important piece of your long duration runs is finishing the run. |
| Sunday | Rest/CT | Rest/CT | Rest | Rest | Rest. If your body feels good, then go ahead and do some form of cross-training for 30 to 60 minutes. |

# Training - Week 9

5K Pace: **11:17**    5k Finish Time: **35 minutes**

| Day | Dist. Mile | Dist. KM | Difficulty | Pace (Range) | Instructions |
|---|---|---|---|---|---|
| Monday | Rest | Rest | Rest | Rest | Take it easy. Don't run. If you need to exercise, I recommend a walk for no longer than 30 minutes. |
| Tuesday | 3 | 5 | E | 12:15 - 14:15 | walk/run at an easy pace. |
| Wednesday | 5 | 8 | HM | 12:15 | walk/run at your half marathon pace. |
| Thursday | 3 | 5 | M | 12:15 - 13:15 | walk/run at a medium pace. |
| Friday | Rest | Rest | Rest | Rest | Rest. |
| Saturday | 8.5 | 13.5 | S | 12:15 - 14:45 | walk/run at a slow pace. The most important piece of your long duration runs is finishing the run. |
| Sunday | Rest/CT | Rest/CT | Rest | Rest | Rest. If your body feels good, then go ahead and do some form of cross-training for 30 to 60 minutes. |

## 13.1 Beta/Test Run Optional

| Day | Dist. Mile | Dist. KM | Difficulty | Pace (Range) | Instructions |
|---|---|---|---|---|---|
| Thursday | Rest | Rest | Rest | Rest | This is a rest day – it simulates race week |
| Friday | Rest | Rest | Rest | Rest | This is a rest day – it simulates race week |
| Saturday | 13.1 | 21 | S | 11:17 | I recommend that you attempt to go the full 13.1 miles (21 km) for a half marathon test run. <u>Only walk/run the first 10 miles (16 km) then walk the last 3.1 miles (5 km)</u>. If you are successful, you will have a race ghost time to compete against. It will help energize and refocus your training on beating yourself in 3 weeks at the half marathon race. Also, it allows your mind to grasp the achievement of "completing the distance of a half marathon." |

# Training - Week 10

5K Pace: **11:17**     5k Finish Time: **35 minutes**

| Day | Dist. Mile | Dist. KM | Difficulty | Pace (Range) | Instructions |
|---|---|---|---|---|---|
| Monday | Rest | Rest | Rest | Rest | Take it easy. Don't run. If you need to exercise, I recommend a walk for no longer than 30 minutes. |
| Tuesday | 3 | 5 | E | 12:15 - 14:15 | walk/run at an easy pace. |
| Wednesday | 5 | 8 | HM | 12:15 | walk/run at your half marathon pace. |
| Thursday | 3 | 5 | M | 12:15 - 13:15 | walk/run at a medium pace. |
| Friday | Rest | Rest | Rest | Rest | Rest. |
| Saturday | 11 | 18 | S | 12:15 - 14:45 | walk/run at a slow pace. The most important piece of your long duration runs is finishing the run. |
| Sunday | Rest/CT | Rest/CT | Rest | Rest | Rest. If your body feels good, then go ahead and do some form of cross-training for 30 to 60 minutes. |

# Training - Week 11

| Day | Dist. Mile | Dist. KM | Difficulty | Pace (Range) | Instructions |
|---|---|---|---|---|---|
| Monday | Rest | Rest | Rest | Rest | Take it easy. Don't run. If you need to exercise, I recommend a walk for no longer than 30 minutes. |
| Tuesday | 3 | 5 | E | 12:15 - 14:15 | walk/run at an easy pace. |
| Wednesday | 5 | 8 | HM | 12:15 | walk/run at your half marathon pace. |
| Thursday | 3 | 5 | M | 12:15 - 13:15 | walk/run at a medium pace. |
| Friday | Rest | Rest | Rest | Rest | Rest. |
| Saturday | 12 | 20 | S | 12:15 - 14:45 | walk/run at a slow pace. The most important piece of your long duration runs is finishing the run. |
| Sunday | Rest/CT | Rest/CT | Rest | Rest | Rest. If your body feels good, then go ahead and do some form of cross-training for 30 to 60 minutes. |

# Training - Week 12

5K Pace: **11:17**     5k Finish Time: **35 minutes**

| Day | Dist. Mile | Dist. KM | Difficulty | Pace (Range) | Instructions |
|---|---|---|---|---|---|
| Monday | Rest | Rest | Rest | Rest | Take it easy. Don't run. If you need to exercise, I recommend a walk for no longer than 30 minutes. |
| Tuesday | 3 | 5 | E | 12:15 - 14:15 | walk/run at an easy pace. |
| Wednesday | 2 | 1.5 | HM | 12:15 | walk/run at your half marathon pace. |
| Thursday | Rest | Rest | Rest | Rest | Rest. |
| Friday | Rest | Rest | Rest | Rest | Rest. |
| Saturday | 13.1 | 21 | HM | 12:15 | RACE DAY! |
| Sunday | Rest | Rest | Rest | Rest | DRINK A VICTORY BEER! |

## NOTE:

- Get plenty of sleep the night before your long duration run.
- Try to run your long duration run early in the morning.
- After each run, it's important to stretch out your muscles.
- This week your body needs as much rest as possible.
- Don't run past Wednesday.

Half Marathon Training Schedule for runners with a 5K finish time of 36 minutes and a pace of *11:36* minutes/mile.

# Predicted Half Marathon Finish Time: *2* hour(s) *45* minutes

# PACING TABLES

| Pace | Pace (minutes/miles) |
|---:|---|
| 5k | 11:36 |
| Half marathon | 12:35 |
| Medium | Between 12:35 - 13:35 |
| Easy | Between 12:35 - 14:35 |
| Slow | Between 12:35 - 15:05 |

| Race | Finish Times (predicted) |
|---:|---|
| 5k | 36 minutes |
| Half marathon | 2 hour(s) 45 minutes |

| Determining your pace ||
|---|---|
| Slow Pace | Extremely easy to hold a conversation. |
| Easy Pace | You can hold a conversation with someone. Your breathing might break up some of the flow of the conversation. |
| Medium | You can hold a conversation with someone, but it's broken up into smaller sentences and smaller responses. |
| Half Marathon Pace | Conversation is difficult. One and two word responses back and forth at best. |

## Definitions in the table below:

CT = Cross Training

S = Slow Pace (long run pace)

E = Easy Pace

M = Medium Pace

HM = Half Marathon Pace

# Training - Week A (Optional)

5K Pace: **11:36**  5k Finish Time: **36 minutes**

| Day | Dist. Mile | Dist. KM | Difficulty | Pace (Range) | Instructions |
|---|---|---|---|---|---|
| Monday | Rest | Rest | Rest | Rest | Take it easy. Don't run. If you need to exercise, I recommend a walk for no longer than 30 minutes. |
| Tuesday | 1 | 1.5 | E | 12:35 - 14:35 | walk/run at an easy pace. |
| Wednesday | 1 | 1.5 | HM | 12:35 | walk/run at your half marathon pace. |
| Thursday | 1 | 1.5 | M | 12:35 - 13:35 | walk/run at a medium pace. |
| Friday | Rest | Rest | Rest | Rest | Rest. |
| Saturday | 1.5 | 2.5 | S | 12:35 - 15:05 | walk/run at a slow pace. The most important piece of your long duration runs is finishing the run. |
| Sunday | Rest/CT | Rest/CT | Rest | Rest | Rest. If your body feels good, then go ahead and do some form of cross-training for 30 to 60 minutes. |

# Training - Week B (Optional)

| Day | Dist. Mile | Dist. KM | Difficulty | Pace (Range) | Instructions |
|---|---|---|---|---|---|
| Monday | Rest | Rest | Rest | Rest | Take it easy. Don't run. If you need to exercise, I recommend a walk for no longer than 30 minutes. |
| Tuesday | 1.5 | 2.5 | E | 12:35 - 14:35 | walk/run at an easy pace. |
| Wednesday | 1.5 | 2.5 | HM | 12:35 | walk/run at your half marathon pace. |
| Thursday | 1.5 | 2.5 | M | 12:35 - 13:35 | walk/run at a medium pace. |
| Friday | Rest | Rest | Rest | Rest | Rest. |
| Saturday | 2 | 3 | S | 12:35 - 15:05 | walk/run at a slow pace. The most important piece of your long duration runs is finishing the run. |
| Sunday | Rest/CT | Rest/CT | Rest | Rest | Rest. If your body feels good, then go ahead and do some form of cross-training for 30 to 60 minutes. |

# Training - Week C (Optional)

5K Pace: **11:36**     5k Finish Time: **36 minutes**

| Day | Dist. Mile | Dist. KM | Difficulty | Pace (Range) | Instructions |
|---|---|---|---|---|---|
| Monday | Rest | Rest | Rest | Rest | Take it easy. Don't run. If you need to exercise, I recommend a walk for no longer than 30 minutes. |
| Tuesday | 2 | 3 | E | 12:35 - 14:35 | walk/run at an easy pace. |
| Wednesday | 2 | 3 | HM | 12:35 | walk/run at your half marathon pace. |
| Thursday | 2 | 3 | M | 12:35 - 13:35 | walk/run at a medium pace. |
| Friday | Rest | Rest | Rest | Rest | Rest. |
| Saturday | 3 | 5 | S | 12:35 - 15:05 | walk/run at a slow pace. The most important piece of your long duration runs is finishing the run. |
| Sunday | Rest/CT | Rest/CT | Rest | Rest | Rest. If your body feels good, then go ahead and do some form of cross-training for 30 to 60 minutes. |

# Training - Week 1

5K Pace: **11:36**     5k Finish Time: **36 minutes**

| Day | Dist. Mile | Dist. KM | Difficulty | Pace (Range) | Instructions |
|---|---|---|---|---|---|
| Monday | Rest | Rest | Rest | Rest | Take it easy. Don't run. If you need to exercise, I recommend a walk for no longer than 30 minutes. |
| Tuesday | 3 | 5 | E | 12:35 - 14:35 | walk/run at an easy pace. |
| Wednesday | 3 | 5 | HM | 12:35 | walk/run at your half marathon pace. |
| Thursday | 3 | 5 | M | 12:35 - 13:35 | walk/run at a medium pace. |
| Friday | Rest | Rest | Rest | Rest | Rest. |
| Saturday | 4 | 6 | S | 12:35 - 15:05 | walk/run at a slow pace. The most important piece of your long duration runs is finishing the run. |
| Sunday | Rest/CT | Rest/CT | Rest | Rest | Rest. If your body feels good, then go ahead and do some form of cross-training for 30 to 60 minutes. |

# Training - Week 2

| Day | Dist. Mile | Dist. KM | Difficulty | Pace (Range) | Instructions |
|---|---|---|---|---|---|
| Monday | Rest | Rest | Rest | Rest | Take it easy. Don't run. If you need to exercise, I recommend a walk for no longer than 30 minutes. |
| Tuesday | 3 | 5 | E | 12:35 - 14:35 | walk/run at an easy pace. |
| Wednesday | 3 | 5 | HM | 12:35 | walk/run at your half marathon pace. |
| Thursday | 3 | 5 | M | 12:35 - 13:35 | walk/run at a medium pace. |
| Friday | Rest | Rest | Rest | Rest | Rest. |
| Saturday | 5 | 8 | S | 12:35 - 15:05 | walk/run at a slow pace. The most important piece of your long duration runs is finishing the run. |
| Sunday | Rest/CT | Rest/CT | Rest | Rest | Rest. If your body feels good, then go ahead and do some form of cross-training for 30 to 60 minutes. |

# Training - Week 3

5K Pace: **11:36**     5k Finish Time: **36 minutes**

| Day | Dist. Mile | Dist. KM | Difficulty | Pace (Range) | Instructions |
|---|---|---|---|---|---|
| Monday | Rest | Rest | Rest | Rest | Take it easy. Don't run. If you need to exercise, I recommend a walk for no longer than 30 minutes. |
| Tuesday | 3 | 5 | E | 12:35 - 14:35 | walk/run at an easy pace. |
| Wednesday | 4 | 6 | HM | 12:35 | walk/run at your half marathon pace. |
| Thursday | 3 | 5 | M | 12:35 - 13:35 | walk/run at a medium pace. |
| Friday | Rest | Rest | Rest | Rest | Rest. |
| Saturday | 6 | 10 | S | 12:35 - 15:05 | walk/run at a slow pace. The most important piece of your long duration runs is finishing the run. |
| Sunday | Rest/CT | Rest/CT | Rest | Rest | Rest. If your body feels good, then go ahead and do some form of cross-training for 30 to 60 minutes. |

# Training - Week 4 (5K Optional)

5K Pace: **11:36**     5k Finish Time: **36 minutes**

| Day | Dist. Mile | Dist. KM | Difficulty | Pace (Range) | Instructions |
|---|---|---|---|---|---|
| Monday | Rest | Rest | Rest | Rest | Take it easy. Don't run. If you need to exercise, I recommend a walk for no longer than 30 minutes. |
| Tuesday | 3 | 5 | E | 12:35 - 14:35 | walk/run at an easy pace. |
| Wednesday | 4 | 6 | HM | 12:35 | walk/run at your half marathon pace. |
| Thursday | 3 | 5 | M | 12:35 - 13:35 | walk/run at a medium pace. |
| Friday | Rest | Rest | Rest | Rest | Rest. |
| Saturday | 6.5 | 10.5 | S | 12:35 - 15:05 | walk/run at a slow pace. The most important piece of your long duration runs is finishing the run. |
| Sunday | Rest/CT | Rest/CT | Rest | Rest | Rest. If your body feels good, then go ahead and do some form of cross-training for 30 to 60 minutes. |

## 5K Optional

| Day | Dist. Mile | Dist. KM | Difficulty | Pace (Range) | Instructions |
|---|---|---|---|---|---|
| Saturday | 3.1 | 5 | - | 11:36 | Run a 5k race instead of your long run. This is completely your choice. I recommend running a 5k race to help you get used to running races. You should see a difference in your race time if you have kept to your training schedule. Don't try for a personal best, run the 5K at your 5K pace. |

# Training - Week 5

5K Pace: **11:36**     5k Finish Time: **36 minutes**

| Day | Dist. Mile | Dist. KM | Difficulty | Pace (Range) | Instructions |
|---|---|---|---|---|---|
| Monday | Rest | Rest | Rest | Rest | Take it easy. Don't run. If you need to exercise, I recommend a walk for no longer than 30 minutes. |
| Tuesday | 3 | 5 | E | 12:35 - 14:35 | walk/run at an easy pace. |
| Wednesday | 4 | 6 | HM | 12:35 | walk/run at your half marathon pace. |
| Thursday | 3 | 5 | M | 12:35 - 13:35 | walk/run at a medium pace. |
| Friday | Rest | Rest | Rest | Rest | Rest. |
| Saturday | 7 | 11 | S | 12:35 - 15:05 | walk/run at a slow pace. The most important piece of your long duration runs is finishing the run. |
| Sunday | Rest/CT | Rest/CT | Rest | Rest | Rest. If your body feels good, then go ahead and do some form of cross-training for 30 to 60 minutes. |

## NOTE:

- Your long duration runs will begin to become more difficult for week 5 and beyond.
- If you get tired during a long duration run, walk for 1/10 mile or 3-5 minutes.

# Training - Week 6

5K Pace: **11:36**     5k Finish Time: **36 minutes**

| Day | Dist. Mile | Dist. KM | Difficulty | Pace (Range) | Instructions |
|---|---|---|---|---|---|
| Monday | Rest | Rest | Rest | Rest | Take it easy. Don't run. If you need to exercise, I recommend a walk for no longer than 30 minutes. |
| Tuesday | 3 | 5 | E | 12:35 - 14:35 | walk/run at an easy pace. |
| Wednesday | 4 | 6 | HM | 12:35 | walk/run at your half marathon pace. |
| Thursday | 3 | 5 | M | 12:35 - 13:35 | walk/run at a medium pace. |
| Friday | Rest | Rest | Rest | Rest | Rest. |
| Saturday | 8 | 13 | S | 12:35 - 15:05 | walk/run at a slow pace. The most important piece of your long duration runs is finishing the run. |
| Sunday | Rest/CT | Rest/CT | Rest | Rest | Rest. If your body feels good, then go ahead and do some form of cross-training for 30 to 60 minutes. |

# Training - Week 7

5K Pace: **11:36**  5k Finish Time: **36 minutes**

| Day | Dist. Mile | Dist. KM | Difficulty | Pace (Range) | Instructions |
|---|---|---|---|---|---|
| Monday | Rest | Rest | Rest | Rest | Take it easy. Don't run. If you need to exercise, I recommend a walk for no longer than 30 minutes. |
| Tuesday | 3 | 5 | E | 12:35 - 14:35 | walk/run at an easy pace. |
| Wednesday | 5 | 8 | HM | 12:35 | walk/run at your half marathon pace. |
| Thursday | 3 | 5 | M | 12:35 - 13:35 | walk/run at a medium pace. |
| Friday | Rest | Rest | Rest | Rest | Rest. |
| Saturday | 8.5 | 13.5 | S | 12:35 - 15:05 | walk/run at a slow pace. The most important piece of your long duration runs is finishing the run. |
| Sunday | Rest/CT | Rest/CT | Rest | Rest | Rest. If your body feels good, then go ahead and do some form of cross-training for 30 to 60 minutes. |

## 10K Optional

| Day | Dist. Mile | Dist. KM | Difficulty | Pace (Range) | Instructions |
|---|---|---|---|---|---|
| Thursday | 2 | 3 | E | 12:35 - 14:35 | If you run the optional 10K, either completely rest today or run 2 miles (3 km). |
| Saturday | 6.2 | 10K | - | **11:36** | Run a 10k race instead of your long run. This is completely your choice. I recommend running a 10k race to help you get used to running races. You should see a difference in your race time if you have kept to your training schedule. Don't try for a personal best, run the 10K at your 5K pace. |

# Training - Week 8

5K Pace: **11:36**     5k Finish Time: **36 minutes**

| Day | Dist. Mile | Dist. KM | Difficulty | Pace (Range) | Instructions |
|---|---|---|---|---|---|
| Monday | Rest | Rest | Rest | Rest | Take it easy. Don't run. If you need to exercise, I recommend a walk for no longer than 30 minutes. |
| Tuesday | 3 | 5 | E | 12:35 - 14:35 | walk/run at an easy pace. |
| Wednesday | 5 | 8 | HM | 12:35 | walk/run at your half marathon pace. |
| Thursday | 3 | 5 | M | 12:35 - 13:35 | walk/run at a medium pace. |
| Friday | Rest | Rest | Rest | Rest | Rest. |
| Saturday | 9 | 14 | S | 12:35 - 15:05 | walk/run at a slow pace. The most important piece of your long duration runs is finishing the run. |
| Sunday | Rest/CT | Rest/CT | Rest | Rest | Rest. If your body feels good, then go ahead and do some form of cross-training for 30 to 60 minutes. |

# Training - Week 9

5K Pace: **11:36**     5k Finish Time: **36 minutes**

| Day | Dist. Mile | Dist. KM | Difficulty | Pace (Range) | Instructions |
|---|---|---|---|---|---|
| Monday | Rest | Rest | Rest | Rest | Take it easy. Don't run. If you need to exercise, I recommend a walk for no longer than 30 minutes. |
| Tuesday | 3 | 5 | E | 12:35 - 14:35 | walk/run at an easy pace. |
| Wednesday | 5 | 8 | HM | 12:35 | walk/run at your half marathon pace. |
| Thursday | 3 | 5 | M | 12:35 - 13:35 | walk/run at a medium pace. |
| Friday | Rest | Rest | Rest | Rest | Rest. |
| Saturday | 8.5 | 13.5 | S | 12:35 - 15:05 | walk/run at a slow pace. The most important piece of your long duration runs is finishing the run. |
| Sunday | Rest/CT | Rest/CT | Rest | Rest | Rest. If your body feels good, then go ahead and do some form of cross-training for 30 to 60 minutes. |

## 13.1 Beta/Test Run Optional

| Day | Dist. Mile | Dist. KM | Difficulty | Pace (Range) | Instructions |
|---|---|---|---|---|---|
| Thursday | Rest | Rest | Rest | Rest | This is a rest day – it simulates race week |
| Friday | Rest | Rest | Rest | Rest | This is a rest day – it simulates race week |
| Saturday | 13.1 | 21 | S | 11:36 | I recommend that you attempt to go the full 13.1 miles (21 km) for a half marathon test run. <u>Only walk/run the first 10 miles (16 km) then walk the last 3.1 miles (5 km)</u>. If you are successful, you will have a race ghost time to compete against. It will help energize and refocus your training on beating yourself in 3 weeks at the half marathon race. Also, it allows your mind to grasp the achievement of "completing the distance of a half marathon." |

# Training - Week 10

5K Pace: **11:36**     5k Finish Time: **36 minutes**

| Day | Dist. Mile | Dist. KM | Difficulty | Pace (Range) | Instructions |
|---|---|---|---|---|---|
| Monday | Rest | Rest | Rest | Rest | Take it easy. Don't run. If you need to exercise, I recommend a walk for no longer than 30 minutes. |
| Tuesday | 3 | 5 | E | 12:35 - 14:35 | walk/run at an easy pace. |
| Wednesday | 5 | 8 | HM | 12:35 | walk/run at your half marathon pace. |
| Thursday | 3 | 5 | M | 12:35 - 13:35 | walk/run at a medium pace. |
| Friday | Rest | Rest | Rest | Rest | Rest. |
| Saturday | 11 | 18 | S | 12:35 - 15:05 | walk/run at a slow pace. The most important piece of your long duration runs is finishing the run. |
| Sunday | Rest/CT | Rest/CT | Rest | Rest | Rest. If your body feels good, then go ahead and do some form of cross-training for 30 to 60 minutes. |

# Training - Week 11

| Day | Dist. Mile | Dist. KM | Difficulty | Pace (Range) | Instructions |
|---|---|---|---|---|---|
| Monday | Rest | Rest | Rest | Rest | Take it easy. Don't run. If you need to exercise, I recommend a walk for no longer than 30 minutes. |
| Tuesday | 3 | 5 | E | 12:35 - 14:35 | walk/run at an easy pace. |
| Wednesday | 5 | 8 | HM | 12:35 | walk/run at your half marathon pace. |
| Thursday | 3 | 5 | M | 12:35 - 13:35 | walk/run at a medium pace. |
| Friday | Rest | Rest | Rest | Rest | Rest. |
| Saturday | 12 | 20 | S | 12:35 - 15:05 | walk/run at a slow pace. The most important piece of your long duration runs is finishing the run. |
| Sunday | Rest/CT | Rest/CT | Rest | Rest | Rest. If your body feels good, then go ahead and do some form of cross-training for 30 to 60 minutes. |

# Training - Week 12

5K Pace: **11:36**     5k Finish Time: **36 minutes**

| Day | Dist. Mile | Dist. KM | Difficulty | Pace (Range) | Instructions |
|---|---|---|---|---|---|
| Monday | Rest | Rest | Rest | Rest | Take it easy. Don't run. If you need to exercise, I recommend a walk for no longer than 30 minutes. |
| Tuesday | 3 | 5 | E | 12:35 - 14:35 | walk/run at an easy pace. |
| Wednesday | 2 | 1.5 | HM | 12:35 | walk/run at your half marathon pace. |
| Thursday | Rest | Rest | Rest | Rest | Rest. |
| Friday | Rest | Rest | Rest | Rest | Rest. |
| Saturday | 13.1 | 21 | HM | 12:35 | RACE DAY! |
| Sunday | Rest | Rest | Rest | Rest | DRINK A VICTORY BEER! |

## NOTE:

- Get plenty of sleep the night before your long duration run.
- Try to run your long duration run early in the morning.
- After each run, it's important to stretch out your muscles.
- This week your body needs as much rest as possible.
- Don't run past Wednesday.

Half Marathon Training Schedule for

runners with a 5K finish time of 37 minutes

and a pace of *11:56* minutes/mile.

# Predicted Half Marathon Finish Time:

# *2* hour(s) *51* minutes

# PACING TABLES

| Pace | Pace (minutes/miles) |
|---:|---|
| 5k | 11:56 |
| Half marathon | 13:05 |
| Medium | Between 13:05 - 14:05 |
| Easy | Between 13:05 - 15:05 |
| Slow | Between 13:05 - 15:35 |

| Race | Finish Times (predicted) |
|---:|---|
| 5k | 37 minutes |
| Half marathon | 2 hour(s) 51 minutes |

| \ | Determining your pace |
|---|---|
| Slow Pace | Extremely easy to hold a conversation. |
| Easy Pace | You can hold a conversation with someone. Your breathing might break up some of the flow of the conversation. |
| Medium | You can hold a conversation with someone, but it's broken up into smaller sentences and smaller responses. |
| Half Marathon Pace | Conversation is difficult. One and two word responses back and forth at best. |

## Definitions in the table below:

CT = Cross Training

S = Slow Pace (long run pace)

E = Easy Pace

M = Medium Pace

HM = Half Marathon Pace

# Training - Week A (Optional)

5K Pace: **11:56**     5k Finish Time: **37 minutes**

| Day | Dist. Mile | Dist. KM | Difficulty | Pace (Range) | Instructions |
|---|---|---|---|---|---|
| Monday | Rest | Rest | Rest | Rest | Take it easy. Don't run. If you need to exercise, I recommend a walk for no longer than 30 minutes. |
| Tuesday | 1 | 1.5 | E | 13:05 - 15:05 | walk/run at an easy pace. |
| Wednesday | 1 | 1.5 | HM | 13:05 | walk/run at your half marathon pace. |
| Thursday | 1 | 1.5 | M | 13:05 - 14:05 | walk/run at a medium pace. |
| Friday | Rest | Rest | Rest | Rest | Rest. |
| Saturday | 1.5 | 2.5 | S | 13:05 - 15:35 | walk/run at a slow pace. The most important piece of your long duration runs is finishing the run. |
| Sunday | Rest/CT | Rest/CT | Rest | Rest | Rest. If your body feels good, then go ahead and do some form of cross-training for 30 to 60 minutes. |

# Training - Week B (Optional)

| Day | Dist. Mile | Dist. KM | Difficulty | Pace (Range) | Instructions |
|---|---|---|---|---|---|
| Monday | Rest | Rest | Rest | Rest | Take it easy. Don't run. If you need to exercise, I recommend a walk for no longer than 30 minutes. |
| Tuesday | 1.5 | 2.5 | E | 13:05 - 15:05 | walk/run at an easy pace. |
| Wednesday | 1.5 | 2.5 | HM | 13:05 | walk/run at your half marathon pace. |
| Thursday | 1.5 | 2.5 | M | 13:05 - 14:05 | walk/run at a medium pace. |
| Friday | Rest | Rest | Rest | Rest | Rest. |
| Saturday | 2 | 3 | S | 13:05 - 15:35 | walk/run at a slow pace. The most important piece of your long duration runs is finishing the run. |
| Sunday | Rest/CT | Rest/CT | Rest | Rest | Rest. If your body feels good, then go ahead and do some form of cross-training for 30 to 60 minutes. |

# Training - Week C (Optional)

5K Pace: **11:56**    5k Finish Time: **37 minutes**

| Day | Dist. Mile | Dist. KM | Difficulty | Pace (Range) | Instructions |
|---|---|---|---|---|---|
| Monday | Rest | Rest | Rest | Rest | Take it easy. Don't run. If you need to exercise, I recommend a walk for no longer than 30 minutes. |
| Tuesday | 2 | 3 | E | 13:05 - 15:05 | walk/run at an easy pace. |
| Wednesday | 2 | 3 | HM | 13:05 | walk/run at your half marathon pace. |
| Thursday | 2 | 3 | M | 13:05 - 14:05 | walk/run at a medium pace. |
| Friday | Rest | Rest | Rest | Rest | Rest. |
| Saturday | 3 | 5 | S | 13:05 - 15:35 | walk/run at a slow pace. The most important piece of your long duration runs is finishing the run. |
| Sunday | Rest/CT | Rest/CT | Rest | Rest | Rest. If your body feels good, then go ahead and do some form of cross-training for 30 to 60 minutes. |

# Training - Week 1

5K Pace: **11:56**     5k Finish Time: **37 minutes**

| Day | Dist. Mile | Dist. KM | Difficulty | Pace (Range) | Instructions |
|---|---|---|---|---|---|
| Monday | Rest | Rest | Rest | Rest | Take it easy. Don't run. If you need to exercise, I recommend a walk for no longer than 30 minutes. |
| Tuesday | 3 | 5 | E | 13:05 - 15:05 | walk/run at an easy pace. |
| Wednesday | 3 | 5 | HM | 13:05 | walk/run at your half marathon pace. |
| Thursday | 3 | 5 | M | 13:05 - 14:05 | walk/run at a medium pace. |
| Friday | Rest | Rest | Rest | Rest | Rest. |
| Saturday | 4 | 6 | S | 13:05 - 15:35 | walk/run at a slow pace. The most important piece of your long duration runs is finishing the run. |
| Sunday | Rest/CT | Rest/CT | Rest | Rest | Rest. If your body feels good, then go ahead and do some form of cross-training for 30 to 60 minutes. |

# Training - Week 2

| Day | Dist. Mile | Dist. KM | Difficulty | Pace (Range) | Instructions |
|---|---|---|---|---|---|
| Monday | Rest | Rest | Rest | Rest | Take it easy. Don't run. If you need to exercise, I recommend a walk for no longer than 30 minutes. |
| Tuesday | 3 | 5 | E | 13:05 - 15:05 | walk/run at an easy pace. |
| Wednesday | 3 | 5 | HM | 13:05 | walk/run at your half marathon pace. |
| Thursday | 3 | 5 | M | 13:05 - 14:05 | walk/run at a medium pace. |
| Friday | Rest | Rest | Rest | Rest | Rest. |
| Saturday | 5 | 8 | S | 13:05 - 15:35 | walk/run at a slow pace. The most important piece of your long duration runs is finishing the run. |
| Sunday | Rest/CT | Rest/CT | Rest | Rest | Rest. If your body feels good, then go ahead and do some form of cross-training for 30 to 60 minutes. |

# Training - Week 3

5K Pace: **11:56**    5k Finish Time: **37 minutes**

| Day | Dist. Mile | Dist. KM | Difficulty | Pace (Range) | Instructions |
|---|---|---|---|---|---|
| Monday | Rest | Rest | Rest | Rest | Take it easy. Don't run. If you need to exercise, I recommend a walk for no longer than 30 minutes. |
| Tuesday | 3 | 5 | E | 13:05 - 15:05 | walk/run at an easy pace. |
| Wednesday | 4 | 6 | HM | 13:05 | walk/run at your half marathon pace. |
| Thursday | 3 | 5 | M | 13:05 - 14:05 | walk/run at a medium pace. |
| Friday | Rest | Rest | Rest | Rest | Rest. |
| Saturday | 6 | 10 | S | 13:05 - 15:35 | walk/run at a slow pace. The most important piece of your long duration runs is finishing the run. |
| Sunday | Rest/CT | Rest/CT | Rest | Rest | Rest. If your body feels good, then go ahead and do some form of cross-training for 30 to 60 minutes. |

# Training - Week 4 (5K Optional)

5K Pace: **11:56**     5k Finish Time: **37 minutes**

| Day | Dist. Mile | Dist. KM | Difficulty | Pace (Range) | Instructions |
|---|---|---|---|---|---|
| Monday | Rest | Rest | Rest | Rest | Take it easy. Don't run. If you need to exercise, I recommend a walk for no longer than 30 minutes. |
| Tuesday | 3 | 5 | E | 13:05 - 15:05 | walk/run at an easy pace. |
| Wednesday | 4 | 6 | HM | 13:05 | walk/run at your half marathon pace. |
| Thursday | 3 | 5 | M | 13:05 - 14:05 | walk/run at a medium pace. |
| Friday | Rest | Rest | Rest | Rest | Rest. |
| Saturday | 6.5 | 10.5 | S | 13:05 - 15:35 | walk/run at a slow pace. The most important piece of your long duration runs is finishing the run. |
| Sunday | Rest/CT | Rest/CT | Rest | Rest | Rest. If your body feels good, then go ahead and do some form of cross-training for 30 to 60 minutes. |

## 5K Optional

| Day | Dist. Mile | Dist. KM | Difficulty | Pace (Range) | Instructions |
|---|---|---|---|---|---|
| Saturday | 3.1 | 5 | - | 11:56 | Run a 5k race instead of your long run. This is completely your choice. I recommend running a 5k race to help you get used to running races. You should see a difference in your race time if you have kept to your training schedule. Don't try for a personal best, run the 5K at your 5K pace. |

# Training - Week 5

5K Pace: **11:56**     5k Finish Time: **37 minutes**

| Day | Dist. Mile | Dist. KM | Difficulty | Pace (Range) | Instructions |
|---|---|---|---|---|---|
| Monday | Rest | Rest | Rest | Rest | Take it easy. Don't run. If you need to exercise, I recommend a walk for no longer than 30 minutes. |
| Tuesday | 3 | 5 | E | 13:05 - 15:05 | walk/run at an easy pace. |
| Wednesday | 4 | 6 | HM | 13:05 | walk/run at your half marathon pace. |
| Thursday | 3 | 5 | M | 13:05 - 14:05 | walk/run at a medium pace. |
| Friday | Rest | Rest | Rest | Rest | Rest. |
| Saturday | 7 | 11 | S | 13:05 - 15:35 | walk/run at a slow pace. The most important piece of your long duration runs is finishing the run. |
| Sunday | Rest/CT | Rest/CT | Rest | Rest | Rest. If your body feels good, then go ahead and do some form of cross-training for 30 to 60 minutes. |

## NOTE:

- Your long duration runs will begin to become more difficult for week 5 and beyond.
- If you get tired during a long duration run, walk for 1/10 mile or 3-5 minutes.

# Training - Week 6

5K Pace: **11:56**     5k Finish Time: **37 minutes**

| Day | Dist. Mile | Dist. KM | Difficulty | Pace (Range) | Instructions |
|---|---|---|---|---|---|
| Monday | Rest | Rest | Rest | Rest | Take it easy. Don't run. If you need to exercise, I recommend a walk for no longer than 30 minutes. |
| Tuesday | 3 | 5 | E | 13:05 - 15:05 | walk/run at an easy pace. |
| Wednesday | 4 | 6 | HM | 13:05 | walk/run at your half marathon pace. |
| Thursday | 3 | 5 | M | 13:05 - 14:05 | walk/run at a medium pace. |
| Friday | Rest | Rest | Rest | Rest | Rest. |
| Saturday | 8 | 13 | S | 13:05 - 15:35 | walk/run at a slow pace. The most important piece of your long duration runs is finishing the run. |
| Sunday | Rest/CT | Rest/CT | Rest | Rest | Rest. If your body feels good, then go ahead and do some form of cross-training for 30 to 60 minutes. |

# Training - Week 7

5K Pace: **11:56**      5k Finish Time: **37 minutes**

| Day | Dist. Mile | Dist. KM | Difficulty | Pace (Range) | Instructions |
|---|---|---|---|---|---|
| Monday | Rest | Rest | Rest | Rest | Take it easy. Don't run. If you need to exercise, I recommend a walk for no longer than 30 minutes. |
| Tuesday | 3 | 5 | E | 13:05 - 15:05 | walk/run at an easy pace. |
| Wednesday | 5 | 8 | HM | 13:05 | walk/run at your half marathon pace. |
| Thursday | 3 | 5 | M | 13:05 - 14:05 | walk/run at a medium pace. |
| Friday | Rest | Rest | Rest | Rest | Rest. |
| Saturday | 8.5 | 13.5 | S | 13:05 - 15:35 | walk/run at a slow pace. The most important piece of your long duration runs is finishing the run. |
| Sunday | Rest/CT | Rest/CT | Rest | Rest | Rest. If your body feels good, then go ahead and do some form of cross-training for 30 to 60 minutes. |

## 10K Optional

| Day | Dist. Mile | Dist. KM | Difficulty | Pace (Range) | Instructions |
|---|---|---|---|---|---|
| Thursday | 2 | 3 | E | 13:05 - 15:05 | If you run the optional 10K, either completely rest today or run 2 miles (3 km). |
| Saturday | 6.2 | 10K | - | 11:56 | Run a 10k race instead of your long run. This is completely your choice. I recommend running a 10k race to help you get used to running races. You should see a difference in your race time if you have kept to your training schedule. Don't try for a personal best, run the 10K at your 5K pace. |

# Training - Week 8

5K Pace: **11:56**     5k Finish Time: **37 minutes**

| Day | Dist. Mile | Dist. KM | Difficulty | Pace (Range) | Instructions |
|---|---|---|---|---|---|
| Monday | Rest | Rest | Rest | Rest | Take it easy. Don't run. If you need to exercise, I recommend a walk for no longer than 30 minutes. |
| Tuesday | 3 | 5 | E | 13:05 - 15:05 | walk/run at an easy pace. |
| Wednesday | 5 | 8 | HM | 13:05 | walk/run at your half marathon pace. |
| Thursday | 3 | 5 | M | 13:05 - 14:05 | walk/run at a medium pace. |
| Friday | Rest | Rest | Rest | Rest | Rest. |
| Saturday | 9 | 14 | S | 13:05 - 15:35 | walk/run at a slow pace. The most important piece of your long duration runs is finishing the run. |
| Sunday | Rest/CT | Rest/CT | Rest | Rest | Rest. If your body feels good, then go ahead and do some form of cross-training for 30 to 60 minutes. |

# Training - Week 9

5K Pace: **11:56**     5k Finish Time: **37 minutes**

| Day | Dist. Mile | Dist. KM | Difficulty | Pace (Range) | Instructions |
|---|---|---|---|---|---|
| Monday | Rest | Rest | Rest | Rest | Take it easy. Don't run. If you need to exercise, I recommend a walk for no longer than 30 minutes. |
| Tuesday | 3 | 5 | E | 13:05 - 15:05 | walk/run at an easy pace. |
| Wednesday | 5 | 8 | HM | 13:05 | walk/run at your half marathon pace. |
| Thursday | 3 | 5 | M | 13:05 - 14:05 | walk/run at a medium pace. |
| Friday | Rest | Rest | Rest | Rest | Rest. |
| Saturday | 8.5 | 13.5 | S | 13:05 - 15:35 | walk/run at a slow pace. The most important piece of your long duration runs is finishing the run. |
| Sunday | Rest/CT | Rest/CT | Rest | Rest | Rest. If your body feels good, then go ahead and do some form of cross-training for 30 to 60 minutes. |

# 13.1 Beta/Test Run Optional

| Day | Dist. Mile | Dist. KM | Difficulty | Pace (Range) | Instructions |
|---|---|---|---|---|---|
| Thursday | Rest | Rest | Rest | Rest | This is a rest day – it simulates race week |
| Friday | Rest | Rest | Rest | Rest | This is a rest day – it simulates race week |
| Saturday | 13.1 | 21 | S | 11:56 | I recommend that you attempt to go the full 13.1 miles (21 km) for a half marathon test run. <u>Only walk/run the first 10 miles (16 km) then walk the last 3.1 miles (5 km)</u>. If you are successful, you will have a race ghost time to compete against. It will help energize and refocus your training on beating yourself in 3 weeks at the half marathon race. Also, it allows your mind to grasp the achievement of "completing the distance of a half marathon." |

# Training - Week 10

5K Pace: **11:56**     5k Finish Time: **37 minutes**

| Day | Dist. Mile | Dist. KM | Difficulty | Pace (Range) | Instructions |
|---|---|---|---|---|---|
| Monday | Rest | Rest | Rest | Rest | Take it easy. Don't run. If you need to exercise, I recommend a walk for no longer than 30 minutes. |
| Tuesday | 3 | 5 | E | 13:05 - 15:05 | walk/run at an easy pace. |
| Wednesday | 5 | 8 | HM | 13:05 | walk/run at your half marathon pace. |
| Thursday | 3 | 5 | M | 13:05 - 14:05 | walk/run at a medium pace. |
| Friday | Rest | Rest | Rest | Rest | Rest. |
| Saturday | 11 | 18 | S | 13:05 - 15:35 | walk/run at a slow pace. The most important piece of your long duration runs is finishing the run. |
| Sunday | Rest/CT | Rest/CT | Rest | Rest | Rest. If your body feels good, then go ahead and do some form of cross-training for 30 to 60 minutes. |

# Training - Week 11

| Day | Dist. Mile | Dist. KM | Difficulty | Pace (Range) | Instructions |
|---|---|---|---|---|---|
| Monday | Rest | Rest | Rest | Rest | Take it easy. Don't run. If you need to exercise, I recommend a walk for no longer than 30 minutes. |
| Tuesday | 3 | 5 | E | 13:05 - 15:05 | walk/run at an easy pace. |
| Wednesday | 5 | 8 | HM | 13:05 | walk/run at your half marathon pace. |
| Thursday | 3 | 5 | M | 13:05 - 14:05 | walk/run at a medium pace. |
| Friday | Rest | Rest | Rest | Rest | Rest. |
| Saturday | 12 | 20 | S | 13:05 - 15:35 | walk/run at a slow pace. The most important piece of your long duration runs is finishing the run. |
| Sunday | Rest/CT | Rest/CT | Rest | Rest | Rest. If your body feels good, then go ahead and do some form of cross-training for 30 to 60 minutes. |

# Training - Week 12

5K Pace: **11:56**     5k Finish Time: **37 minutes**

| Day | Dist. Mile | Dist. KM | Difficulty | Pace (Range) | Instructions |
|---|---|---|---|---|---|
| Monday | Rest | Rest | Rest | Rest | Take it easy. Don't run. If you need to exercise, I recommend a walk for no longer than 30 minutes. |
| Tuesday | 3 | 5 | E | 13:05 - 15:05 | walk/run at an easy pace. |
| Wednesday | 2 | 1.5 | HM | 13:05 | walk/run at your half marathon pace. |
| Thursday | Rest | Rest | Rest | Rest | Rest. |
| Friday | Rest | Rest | Rest | Rest | Rest. |
| Saturday | 13.1 | 21 | HM | 13:05 | RACE DAY! |
| Sunday | Rest | Rest | Rest | Rest | DRINK A VICTORY BEER! |

## NOTE:

- Get plenty of sleep the night before your long duration run.
- Try to run your long duration run early in the morning.
- After each run, it's important to stretch out your muscles.
- This week your body needs as much rest as possible.
- Don't run past Wednesday.

Half Marathon Training Schedule for runners with a 5K finish time of 38 minutes and a pace of *12:15* minutes/mile.

**Predicted Half Marathon Finish Time:**

*2* hour(s) *54* minutes

# PACING TABLES

| Pace | Pace (minutes/miles) |
|---:|---|
| 5k | 12:15 |
| Half marathon | 13:15 |
| Medium | Between 13:15 - 14:15 |
| Easy | Between 13:15 - 15:15 |
| Slow | Between 13:15 - 15:45 |

| Race | Finish Times (predicted) |
|---:|---|
| 5k | 38 minutes |
| Half marathon | 2 hour(s) 54 minutes |

| Determining your pace | |
|---|---|
| Slow Pace | Extremely easy to hold a conversation. |
| Easy Pace | You can hold a conversation with someone. Your breathing might break up some of the flow of the conversation. |
| Medium | You can hold a conversation with someone, but it's broken up into smaller sentences and smaller responses. |
| Half Marathon Pace | Conversation is difficult. One and two word responses back and forth at best. |

## Definitions in the table below:

CT = Cross Training

S = Slow Pace (long run pace)

E = Easy Pace

M = Medium Pace

HM = Half Marathon Pace

## Training - Week A (Optional)

5K Pace: **12:15**          5k Finish Time: **38 minutes**

| Day | Dist. Mile | Dist. KM | Difficulty | Pace (Range) | Instructions |
|---|---|---|---|---|---|
| Monday | Rest | Rest | Rest | Rest | Take it easy. Don't run. If you need to exercise, I recommend a walk for no longer than 30 minutes. |
| Tuesday | 1 | 1.5 | E | 13:15 - 15:15 | walk/run at an easy pace. |
| Wednesday | 1 | 1.5 | HM | 13:15 | walk/run at your half marathon pace. |
| Thursday | 1 | 1.5 | M | 13:15 - 14:15 | walk/run at a medium pace. |
| Friday | Rest | Rest | Rest | Rest | Rest. |
| Saturday | 1.5 | 2.5 | S | 13:15 - 15:45 | walk/run at a slow pace. The most important piece of your long duration runs is finishing the run. |
| Sunday | Rest/CT | Rest/CT | Rest | Rest | Rest. If your body feels good, then go ahead and do some form of cross-training for 30 to 60 minutes. |

## Training - Week B (Optional)

| Day | Dist. Mile | Dist. KM | Difficulty | Pace (Range) | Instructions |
|---|---|---|---|---|---|
| Monday | Rest | Rest | Rest | Rest | Take it easy. Don't run. If you need to exercise, I recommend a walk for no longer than 30 minutes. |
| Tuesday | 1.5 | 2.5 | E | 13:15 - 15:15 | walk/run at an easy pace. |
| Wednesday | 1.5 | 2.5 | HM | 13:15 | walk/run at your half marathon pace. |
| Thursday | 1.5 | 2.5 | M | 13:15 - 14:15 | walk/run at a medium pace. |
| Friday | Rest | Rest | Rest | Rest | Rest. |
| Saturday | 2 | 3 | S | 13:15 - 15:45 | walk/run at a slow pace. The most important piece of your long duration runs is finishing the run. |
| Sunday | Rest/CT | Rest/CT | Rest | Rest | Rest. If your body feels good, then go ahead and do some form of cross-training for 30 to 60 minutes. |

# Training - Week C (Optional)

5K Pace: **12:15**     5k Finish Time: **38 minutes**

| Day | Dist. Mile | Dist. KM | Difficulty | Pace (Range) | Instructions |
|---|---|---|---|---|---|
| Monday | Rest | Rest | Rest | Rest | Take it easy. Don't run. If you need to exercise, I recommend a walk for no longer than 30 minutes. |
| Tuesday | 2 | 3 | E | 13:15 - 15:15 | walk/run at an easy pace. |
| Wednesday | 2 | 3 | HM | 13:15 | walk/run at your half marathon pace. |
| Thursday | 2 | 3 | M | 13:15 - 14:15 | walk/run at a medium pace. |
| Friday | Rest | Rest | Rest | Rest | Rest. |
| Saturday | 3 | 5 | S | 13:15 - 15:45 | walk/run at a slow pace. The most important piece of your long duration runs is finishing the run. |
| Sunday | Rest/CT | Rest/CT | Rest | Rest | Rest. If your body feels good, then go ahead and do some form of cross-training for 30 to 60 minutes. |

# Training - Week 1

5K Pace: **12:15**    5k Finish Time: **38 minutes**

| Day | Dist. Mile | Dist. KM | Difficulty | Pace (Range) | Instructions |
|---|---|---|---|---|---|
| Monday | Rest | Rest | Rest | Rest | Take it easy. Don't run. If you need to exercise, I recommend a walk for no longer than 30 minutes. |
| Tuesday | 3 | 5 | E | 13:15 - 15:15 | walk/run at an easy pace. |
| Wednesday | 3 | 5 | HM | 13:15 | walk/run at your half marathon pace. |
| Thursday | 3 | 5 | M | 13:15 - 14:15 | walk/run at a medium pace. |
| Friday | Rest | Rest | Rest | Rest | Rest. |
| Saturday | 4 | 6 | S | 13:15 - 15:45 | walk/run at a slow pace. The most important piece of your long duration runs is finishing the run. |
| Sunday | Rest/CT | Rest/CT | Rest | Rest | Rest. If your body feels good, then go ahead and do some form of cross-training for 30 to 60 minutes. |

# Training - Week 2

| Day | Dist. Mile | Dist. KM | Difficulty | Pace (Range) | Instructions |
|---|---|---|---|---|---|
| Monday | Rest | Rest | Rest | Rest | Take it easy. Don't run. If you need to exercise, I recommend a walk for no longer than 30 minutes. |
| Tuesday | 3 | 5 | E | 13:15 - 15:15 | walk/run at an easy pace. |
| Wednesday | 3 | 5 | HM | 13:15 | walk/run at your half marathon pace. |
| Thursday | 3 | 5 | M | 13:15 - 14:15 | walk/run at a medium pace. |
| Friday | Rest | Rest | Rest | Rest | Rest. |
| Saturday | 5 | 8 | S | 13:15 - 15:45 | walk/run at a slow pace. The most important piece of your long duration runs is finishing the run. |
| Sunday | Rest/CT | Rest/CT | Rest | Rest | Rest. If your body feels good, then go ahead and do some form of cross-training for 30 to 60 minutes. |

# Training - Week 3

5K Pace: **12:15**     5k Finish Time: **38 minutes**

| Day | Dist. Mile | Dist. KM | Difficulty | Pace (Range) | Instructions |
|---|---|---|---|---|---|
| Monday | Rest | Rest | Rest | Rest | Take it easy. Don't run. If you need to exercise, I recommend a walk for no longer than 30 minutes. |
| Tuesday | 3 | 5 | E | 13:15 - 15:15 | walk/run at an easy pace. |
| Wednesday | 4 | 6 | HM | 13:15 | walk/run at your half marathon pace. |
| Thursday | 3 | 5 | M | 13:15 - 14:15 | walk/run at a medium pace. |
| Friday | Rest | Rest | Rest | Rest | Rest. |
| Saturday | 6 | 10 | S | 13:15 - 15:45 | walk/run at a slow pace. The most important piece of your long duration runs is finishing the run. |
| Sunday | Rest/CT | Rest/CT | Rest | Rest | Rest. If your body feels good, then go ahead and do some form of cross-training for 30 to 60 minutes. |

# Training - Week 4 (5K Optional)

5K Pace: **12:15**     5k Finish Time: **38 minutes**

| Day | Dist. Mile | Dist. KM | Difficulty | Pace (Range) | Instructions |
|---|---|---|---|---|---|
| Monday | Rest | Rest | Rest | Rest | Take it easy. Don't run. If you need to exercise, I recommend a walk for no longer than 30 minutes. |
| Tuesday | 3 | 5 | E | 13:15 - 15:15 | walk/run at an easy pace. |
| Wednesday | 4 | 6 | HM | 13:15 | walk/run at your half marathon pace. |
| Thursday | 3 | 5 | M | 13:15 - 14:15 | walk/run at a medium pace. |
| Friday | Rest | Rest | Rest | Rest | Rest. |
| Saturday | 6.5 | 10.5 | S | 13:15 - 15:45 | walk/run at a slow pace. The most important piece of your long duration runs is finishing the run. |
| Sunday | Rest/CT | Rest/CT | Rest | Rest | Rest. If your body feels good, then go ahead and do some form of cross-training for 30 to 60 minutes. |

## 5K Optional

| Day | Dist. Mile | Dist. KM | Difficulty | Pace (Range) | Instructions |
|---|---|---|---|---|---|
| Saturday | 3.1 | 5 | - | 12:15 | Run a 5k race instead of your long run. This is completely your choice. I recommend running a 5k race to help you get used to running races. You should see a difference in your race time if you have kept to your training schedule. Don't try for a personal best, run the 5K at your 5K pace. |

# Training - Week 5

5K Pace: **12:15**    5k Finish Time: **38 minutes**

| Day | Dist. Mile | Dist. KM | Difficulty | Pace (Range) | Instructions |
|---|---|---|---|---|---|
| Monday | Rest | Rest | Rest | Rest | Take it easy. Don't run. If you need to exercise, I recommend a walk for no longer than 30 minutes. |
| Tuesday | 3 | 5 | E | 13:15 - 15:15 | walk/run at an easy pace. |
| Wednesday | 4 | 6 | HM | 13:15 | walk/run at your half marathon pace. |
| Thursday | 3 | 5 | M | 13:15 - 14:15 | walk/run at a medium pace. |
| Friday | Rest | Rest | Rest | Rest | Rest. |
| Saturday | 7 | 11 | S | 13:15 - 15:45 | walk/run at a slow pace. The most important piece of your long duration runs is finishing the run. |
| Sunday | Rest/CT | Rest/CT | Rest | Rest | Rest. If your body feels good, then go ahead and do some form of cross-training for 30 to 60 minutes. |

## NOTE:

- Your long duration runs will begin to become more difficult for week 5 and beyond.
- If you get tired during a long duration run, walk for 1/10 mile or 3-5 minutes.

# Training - Week 6

5K Pace: **12:15**   5k Finish Time: **38 minutes**

| Day | Dist. Mile | Dist. KM | Difficulty | Pace (Range) | Instructions |
|---|---|---|---|---|---|
| Monday | Rest | Rest | Rest | Rest | Take it easy. Don't run. If you need to exercise, I recommend a walk for no longer than 30 minutes. |
| Tuesday | 3 | 5 | E | 13:15 - 15:15 | walk/run at an easy pace. |
| Wednesday | 4 | 6 | HM | 13:15 | walk/run at your half marathon pace. |
| Thursday | 3 | 5 | M | 13:15 - 14:15 | walk/run at a medium pace. |
| Friday | Rest | Rest | Rest | Rest | Rest. |
| Saturday | 8 | 13 | S | 13:15 - 15:45 | walk/run at a slow pace. The most important piece of your long duration runs is finishing the run. |
| Sunday | Rest/CT | Rest/CT | Rest | Rest | Rest. If your body feels good, then go ahead and do some form of cross-training for 30 to 60 minutes. |

# Training - Week 7

5K Pace: **12:15**     5k Finish Time: **38 minutes**

| Day | Dist. Mile | Dist. KM | Difficulty | Pace (Range) | Instructions |
|---|---|---|---|---|---|
| Monday | Rest | Rest | Rest | Rest | Take it easy. Don't run. If you need to exercise, I recommend a walk for no longer than 30 minutes. |
| Tuesday | 3 | 5 | E | 13:15 - 15:15 | walk/run at an easy pace. |
| Wednesday | 5 | 8 | HM | 13:15 | walk/run at your half marathon pace. |
| Thursday | 3 | 5 | M | 13:15 - 14:15 | walk/run at a medium pace. |
| Friday | Rest | Rest | Rest | Rest | Rest. |
| Saturday | 8.5 | 13.5 | S | 13:15 - 15:45 | walk/run at a slow pace. The most important piece of your long duration runs is finishing the run. |
| Sunday | Rest/CT | Rest/CT | Rest | Rest | Rest. If your body feels good, then go ahead and do some form of cross-training for 30 to 60 minutes. |

## 10K Optional

| Day | Dist. Mile | Dist. KM | Difficulty | Pace (Range) | Instructions |
|---|---|---|---|---|---|
| Thursday | 2 | 3 | E | 13:15 - 15:15 | If you run the optional 10K, either completely rest today or run 2 miles ( 3 km). |
| Saturday | 6.2 | 10K | - | 12:15 | Run a 10k race instead of your long run. This is completely your choice. I recommend running a 10k race to help you get used to running races. You should see a difference in your race time if you have kept to your training schedule. Don't try for a personal best, run the 10K at your 5K pace. |

# Training - Week 8

5K Pace: **12:15**     5k Finish Time: **38 minutes**

| Day | Dist. Mile | Dist. KM | Difficulty | Pace (Range) | Instructions |
|---|---|---|---|---|---|
| Monday | Rest | Rest | Rest | Rest | Take it easy. Don't run. If you need to exercise, I recommend a walk for no longer than 30 minutes. |
| Tuesday | 3 | 5 | E | 13:15 - 15:15 | walk/run at an easy pace. |
| Wednesday | 5 | 8 | HM | 13:15 | walk/run at your half marathon pace. |
| Thursday | 3 | 5 | M | 13:15 - 14:15 | walk/run at a medium pace. |
| Friday | Rest | Rest | Rest | Rest | Rest. |
| Saturday | 9 | 14 | S | 13:15 - 15:45 | walk/run at a slow pace. The most important piece of your long duration runs is finishing the run. |
| Sunday | Rest/CT | Rest/CT | Rest | Rest | Rest. If your body feels good, then go ahead and do some form of cross-training for 30 to 60 minutes. |

# Training - Week 9

5K Pace: **12:15**     5k Finish Time: **38 minutes**

| Day | Dist. Mile | Dist. KM | Difficulty | Pace (Range) | Instructions |
|---|---|---|---|---|---|
| Monday | Rest | Rest | Rest | Rest | Take it easy. Don't run. If you need to exercise, I recommend a walk for no longer than 30 minutes. |
| Tuesday | 3 | 5 | E | 13:15 - 15:15 | walk/run at an easy pace. |
| Wednesday | 5 | 8 | HM | 13:15 | walk/run at your half marathon pace. |
| Thursday | 3 | 5 | M | 13:15 - 14:15 | walk/run at a medium pace. |
| Friday | Rest | Rest | Rest | Rest | Rest. |
| Saturday | 8.5 | 13.5 | S | 13:15 - 15:45 | walk/run at a slow pace. The most important piece of your long duration runs is finishing the run. |
| Sunday | Rest/CT | Rest/CT | Rest | Rest | Rest. If your body feels good, then go ahead and do some form of cross-training for 30 to 60 minutes. |

## 13.1 Beta/Test Run Optional

| Day | Dist. Mile | Dist. KM | Difficulty | Pace (Range) | Instructions |
|---|---|---|---|---|---|
| Thursday | Rest | Rest | Rest | Rest | This is a rest day – it simulates race week |
| Friday | Rest | Rest | Rest | Rest | This is a rest day – it simulates race week |
| Saturday | 13.1 | 21 | S | 12:15 | I recommend that you attempt to go the full 13.1 miles (21 km) for a half marathon test run. <u>Only walk/run the first 10 miles (16 km) then walk the last 3.1 miles (5 km)</u>. If you are successful, you will have a race ghost time to compete against. It will help energize and refocus your training on beating yourself in 3 weeks at the half marathon race. Also, it allows your mind to grasp the achievement of "completing the distance of a half marathon." |

# Training - Week 10

5K Pace: **12:15**    5k Finish Time: **38 minutes**

| Day | Dist. Mile | Dist. KM | Difficulty | Pace (Range) | Instructions |
|---|---|---|---|---|---|
| Monday | Rest | Rest | Rest | Rest | Take it easy. Don't run. If you need to exercise, I recommend a walk for no longer than 30 minutes. |
| Tuesday | 3 | 5 | E | 13:15 - 15:15 | walk/run at an easy pace. |
| Wednesday | 5 | 8 | HM | 13:15 | walk/run at your half marathon pace. |
| Thursday | 3 | 5 | M | 13:15 - 14:15 | walk/run at a medium pace. |
| Friday | Rest | Rest | Rest | Rest | Rest. |
| Saturday | 11 | 18 | S | 13:15 - 15:45 | walk/run at a slow pace. The most important piece of your long duration runs is finishing the run. |
| Sunday | Rest/CT | Rest/CT | Rest | Rest | Rest. If your body feels good, then go ahead and do some form of cross-training for 30 to 60 minutes. |

# Training - Week 11

| Day | Dist. Mile | Dist. KM | Difficulty | Pace (Range) | Instructions |
|---|---|---|---|---|---|
| Monday | Rest | Rest | Rest | Rest | Take it easy. Don't run. If you need to exercise, I recommend a walk for no longer than 30 minutes. |
| Tuesday | 3 | 5 | E | 13:15 - 15:15 | walk/run at an easy pace. |
| Wednesday | 5 | 8 | HM | 13:15 | walk/run at your half marathon pace. |
| Thursday | 3 | 5 | M | 13:15 - 14:15 | walk/run at a medium pace. |
| Friday | Rest | Rest | Rest | Rest | Rest. |
| Saturday | 12 | 20 | S | 13:15 - 15:45 | walk/run at a slow pace. The most important piece of your long duration runs is finishing the run. |
| Sunday | Rest/CT | Rest/CT | Rest | Rest | Rest. If your body feels good, then go ahead and do some form of cross-training for 30 to 60 minutes. |

# Training - Week 12

5K Pace: **12:15**     5k Finish Time: **38 minutes**

| Day | Dist. Mile | Dist. KM | Difficulty | Pace (Range) | Instructions |
|---|---|---|---|---|---|
| Monday | Rest | Rest | Rest | Rest | Take it easy. Don't run. If you need to exercise, I recommend a walk for no longer than 30 minutes. |
| Tuesday | 3 | 5 | E | 13:15 - 15:15 | walk/run at an easy pace. |
| Wednesday | 2 | 1.5 | HM | 13:15 | walk/run at your half marathon pace. |
| Thursday | Rest | Rest | Rest | Rest | Rest. |
| Friday | Rest | Rest | Rest | Rest | Rest. |
| Saturday | 13.1 | 21 | HM | 13:15 | RACE DAY! |
| Sunday | Rest | Rest | Rest | Rest | DRINK A VICTORY BEER! |

## NOTE:

- Get plenty of sleep the night before your long duration run.
- Try to run your long duration run early in the morning.
- After each run, it's important to stretch out your muscles.
- This week your body needs as much rest as possible.
- Don't run past Wednesday.

Half Marathon Training Schedule for

runners with a 5K finish time of 39 minutes

and a pace of *12:34* minutes/mile.

# Predicted Half Marathon Finish Time:

## *2* hour(s) *59* minutes

# PACING TABLES

| Pace | Pace (minutes/miles) |
|---:|:---|
| **5k** | 12:34 |
| **Half marathon** | 13:40 |
| **Medium** | Between 13:40 - 14:30 |
| **Easy** | Between 13:40 - 15:30 |
| **Slow** | Between 13:40 - 16:00 |

| Race | Finish Times (predicted) |
|---:|:---|
| **5k** | 39 minutes |
| **Half marathon** | 2 hour(s) 59 minutes |

| \multicolumn{2}{c}{Determining your pace} ||
|:---:|:---|
| Slow Pace | Extremely easy to hold a conversation. |
| Easy Pace | You can hold a conversation with someone. Your breathing might break up some of the flow of the conversation. |
| Medium | You can hold a conversation with someone, but it's broken up into smaller sentences and smaller responses. |
| Half Marathon Pace | Conversation is difficult. One and two word responses back and forth at best. |

## Definitions in the table below:

CT = Cross Training

S = Slow Pace (long run pace)

E = Easy Pace

M = Medium Pace

HM = Half Marathon Pace

## Training - Week A (Optional)

5K Pace: **12:34**    5k Finish Time: **39 minutes**

| Day | Dist. Mile | Dist. KM | Difficulty | Pace (Range) | Instructions |
|---|---|---|---|---|---|
| Monday | Rest | Rest | Rest | Rest | Take it easy. Don't run. If you need to exercise, I recommend a walk for no longer than 30 minutes. |
| Tuesday | 1 | 1.5 | E | 13:40 - 15:30 | walk/run at an easy pace. |
| Wednesday | 1 | 1.5 | HM | 13:40 | walk/run at your half marathon pace. |
| Thursday | 1 | 1.5 | M | 13:40 - 14:30 | walk/run at a medium pace. |
| Friday | Rest | Rest | Rest | Rest | Rest. |
| Saturday | 1.5 | 2.5 | S | 13:40 - 16:00 | walk/run at a slow pace. The most important piece of your long duration runs is finishing the run. |
| Sunday | Rest/CT | Rest/CT | Rest | Rest | Rest. If your body feels good, then go ahead and do some form of cross-training for 30 to 60 minutes. |

## Training - Week B (Optional)

| Day | Dist. Mile | Dist. KM | Difficulty | Pace (Range) | Instructions |
|---|---|---|---|---|---|
| Monday | Rest | Rest | Rest | Rest | Take it easy. Don't run. If you need to exercise, I recommend a walk for no longer than 30 minutes. |
| Tuesday | 1.5 | 2.5 | E | 13:40 - 15:30 | walk/run at an easy pace. |
| Wednesday | 1.5 | 2.5 | HM | 13:40 | walk/run at your half marathon pace. |
| Thursday | 1.5 | 2.5 | M | 13:40 - 14:30 | walk/run at a medium pace. |
| Friday | Rest | Rest | Rest | Rest | Rest. |
| Saturday | 2 | 3 | S | 13:40 - 16:00 | walk/run at a slow pace. The most important piece of your long duration runs is finishing the run. |
| Sunday | Rest/CT | Rest/CT | Rest | Rest | Rest. If your body feels good, then go ahead and do some form of cross-training for 30 to 60 minutes. |

# Training - Week C (Optional)

5K Pace: **12:34**     5k Finish Time: **39 minutes**

| Day | Dist. Mile | Dist. KM | Difficulty | Pace (Range) | Instructions |
|---|---|---|---|---|---|
| Monday | Rest | Rest | Rest | Rest | Take it easy. Don't run. If you need to exercise, I recommend a walk for no longer than 30 minutes. |
| Tuesday | 2 | 3 | E | 13:40 - 15:30 | walk/run at an easy pace. |
| Wednesday | 2 | 3 | HM | 13:40 | walk/run at your half marathon pace. |
| Thursday | 2 | 3 | M | 13:40 - 14:30 | walk/run at a medium pace. |
| Friday | Rest | Rest | Rest | Rest | Rest. |
| Saturday | 3 | 5 | S | 13:40 - 16:00 | walk/run at a slow pace. The most important piece of your long duration runs is finishing the run. |
| Sunday | Rest/CT | Rest/CT | Rest | Rest | Rest. If your body feels good, then go ahead and do some form of cross-training for 30 to 60 minutes. |

# Training - Week 1

5K Pace: **12:34**     5k Finish Time: **39 minutes**

| Day | Dist. Mile | Dist. KM | Difficulty | Pace (Range) | Instructions |
|---|---|---|---|---|---|
| Monday | Rest | Rest | Rest | Rest | Take it easy. Don't run. If you need to exercise, I recommend a walk for no longer than 30 minutes. |
| Tuesday | 3 | 5 | E | 13:40 - 15:30 | walk/run at an easy pace. |
| Wednesday | 3 | 5 | HM | 13:40 | walk/run at your half marathon pace. |
| Thursday | 3 | 5 | M | 13:40 - 14:30 | walk/run at a medium pace. |
| Friday | Rest | Rest | Rest | Rest | Rest. |
| Saturday | 4 | 6 | S | 13:40 - 16:00 | walk/run at a slow pace. The most important piece of your long duration runs is finishing the run. |
| Sunday | Rest/CT | Rest/CT | Rest | Rest | Rest. If your body feels good, then go ahead and do some form of cross-training for 30 to 60 minutes. |

# Training - Week 2

| Day | Dist. Mile | Dist. KM | Difficulty | Pace (Range) | Instructions |
|---|---|---|---|---|---|
| Monday | Rest | Rest | Rest | Rest | Take it easy. Don't run. If you need to exercise, I recommend a walk for no longer than 30 minutes. |
| Tuesday | 3 | 5 | E | 13:40 - 15:30 | walk/run at an easy pace. |
| Wednesday | 3 | 5 | HM | 13:40 | walk/run at your half marathon pace. |
| Thursday | 3 | 5 | M | 13:40 - 14:30 | walk/run at a medium pace. |
| Friday | Rest | Rest | Rest | Rest | Rest. |
| Saturday | 5 | 8 | S | 13:40 - 16:00 | walk/run at a slow pace. The most important piece of your long duration runs is finishing the run. |
| Sunday | Rest/CT | Rest/CT | Rest | Rest | Rest. If your body feels good, then go ahead and do some form of cross-training for 30 to 60 minutes. |

# Training - Week 3

5K Pace: **12:34**     5k Finish Time: **39 minutes**

| Day | Dist. Mile | Dist. KM | Difficulty | Pace (Range) | Instructions |
|---|---|---|---|---|---|
| Monday | Rest | Rest | Rest | Rest | Take it easy. Don't run. If you need to exercise, I recommend a walk for no longer than 30 minutes. |
| Tuesday | 3 | 5 | E | 13:40 - 15:30 | walk/run at an easy pace. |
| Wednesday | 4 | 6 | HM | 13:40 | walk/run at your half marathon pace. |
| Thursday | 3 | 5 | M | 13:40 - 14:30 | walk/run at a medium pace. |
| Friday | Rest | Rest | Rest | Rest | Rest. |
| Saturday | 6 | 10 | S | 13:40 - 16:00 | walk/run at a slow pace. The most important piece of your long duration runs is finishing the run. |
| Sunday | Rest/CT | Rest/CT | Rest | Rest | Rest. If your body feels good, then go ahead and do some form of cross-training for 30 to 60 minutes. |

# Training - Week 4 (5K Optional)

5K Pace: **12:34**     5k Finish Time: **39 minutes**

| Day | Dist. Mile | Dist. KM | Difficulty | Pace (Range) | Instructions |
|---|---|---|---|---|---|
| Monday | Rest | Rest | Rest | Rest | Take it easy. Don't run. If you need to exercise, I recommend a walk for no longer than 30 minutes. |
| Tuesday | 3 | 5 | E | 13:40 - 15:30 | walk/run at an easy pace. |
| Wednesday | 4 | 6 | HM | 13:40 | walk/run at your half marathon pace. |
| Thursday | 3 | 5 | M | 13:40 - 14:30 | walk/run at a medium pace. |
| Friday | Rest | Rest | Rest | Rest | Rest. |
| Saturday | 6.5 | 10.5 | S | 13:40 - 16:00 | walk/run at a slow pace. The most important piece of your long duration runs is finishing the run. |
| Sunday | Rest/CT | Rest/CT | Rest | Rest | Rest. If your body feels good, then go ahead and do some form of cross-training for 30 to 60 minutes. |

## 5K Optional

| Day | Dist. Mile | Dist. KM | Difficulty | Pace (Range) | Instructions |
|---|---|---|---|---|---|
| Saturday | 3.1 | 5 | - | 12:34 | Run a 5k race instead of your long run. This is completely your choice. I recommend running a 5k race to help you get used to running races. You should see a difference in your race time if you have kept to your training schedule. Don't try for a personal best, run the 5K at your 5K pace. |

# Training - Week 5

5K Pace: **12:34**     5k Finish Time: **39 minutes**

| Day | Dist. Mile | Dist. KM | Difficulty | Pace (Range) | Instructions |
|---|---|---|---|---|---|
| Monday | Rest | Rest | Rest | Rest | Take it easy. Don't run. If you need to exercise, I recommend a walk for no longer than 30 minutes. |
| Tuesday | 3 | 5 | E | 13:40 - 15:30 | walk/run at an easy pace. |
| Wednesday | 4 | 6 | HM | 13:40 | walk/run at your half marathon pace. |
| Thursday | 3 | 5 | M | 13:40 - 14:30 | walk/run at a medium pace. |
| Friday | Rest | Rest | Rest | Rest | Rest. |
| Saturday | 7 | 11 | S | 13:40 - 16:00 | walk/run at a slow pace. The most important piece of your long duration runs is finishing the run. |
| Sunday | Rest/CT | Rest/CT | Rest | Rest | Rest. If your body feels good, then go ahead and do some form of cross-training for 30 to 60 minutes. |

## NOTE:

- Your long duration runs will begin to become more difficult for week 5 and beyond.
- If you get tired during a long duration run, walk for 1/10 mile or 3-5 minutes.

# Training - Week 6

5K Pace: **12:34**     5k Finish Time: **39 minutes**

| Day | Dist. Mile | Dist. KM | Difficulty | Pace (Range) | Instructions |
|---|---|---|---|---|---|
| Monday | Rest | Rest | Rest | Rest | Take it easy. Don't run. If you need to exercise, I recommend a walk for no longer than 30 minutes. |
| Tuesday | 3 | 5 | E | 13:40 - 15:30 | walk/run at an easy pace. |
| Wednesday | 4 | 6 | HM | 13:40 | walk/run at your half marathon pace. |
| Thursday | 3 | 5 | M | 13:40 - 14:30 | walk/run at a medium pace. |
| Friday | Rest | Rest | Rest | Rest | Rest. |
| Saturday | 8 | 13 | S | 13:40 - 16:00 | walk/run at a slow pace. The most important piece of your long duration runs is finishing the run. |
| Sunday | Rest/CT | Rest/CT | Rest | Rest | Rest. If your body feels good, then go ahead and do some form of cross-training for 30 to 60 minutes. |

# Training - Week 7

5K Pace: **12:34**     5k Finish Time: **39 minutes**

| Day | Dist. Mile | Dist. KM | Difficulty | Pace (Range) | Instructions |
|---|---|---|---|---|---|
| Monday | Rest | Rest | Rest | Rest | Take it easy. Don't run. If you need to exercise, I recommend a walk for no longer than 30 minutes. |
| Tuesday | 3 | 5 | E | 13:40 - 15:30 | walk/run at an easy pace. |
| Wednesday | 5 | 8 | HM | 13:40 | walk/run at your half marathon pace. |
| Thursday | 3 | 5 | M | 13:40 - 14:30 | walk/run at a medium pace. |
| Friday | Rest | Rest | Rest | Rest | Rest. |
| Saturday | 8.5 | 13.5 | S | 13:40 - 16:00 | walk/run at a slow pace. The most important piece of your long duration runs is finishing the run. |
| Sunday | Rest/CT | Rest/CT | Rest | Rest | Rest. If your body feels good, then go ahead and do some form of cross-training for 30 to 60 minutes. |

## 10K Optional

| Day | Dist. Mile | Dist. KM | Difficulty | Pace (Range) | Instructions |
|---|---|---|---|---|---|
| Thursday | 2 | 3 | E | 13:40 - 15:30 | If you run the optional 10K, either completely rest today or run 2 miles (3 km). |
| Saturday | 6.2 | 10K | - | 12:34 | Run a 10k race instead of your long run. This is completely your choice. I recommend running a 10k race to help you get used to running races. You should see a difference in your race time if you have kept to your training schedule. Don't try for a personal best, run the 10K at your 5K pace. |

# Training - Week 8

5K Pace: **12:34**     5k Finish Time: **39 minutes**

| Day | Dist. Mile | Dist. KM | Difficulty | Pace (Range) | Instructions |
|---|---|---|---|---|---|
| Monday | Rest | Rest | Rest | Rest | Take it easy. Don't run. If you need to exercise, I recommend a walk for no longer than 30 minutes. |
| Tuesday | 3 | 5 | E | 13:40 - 15:30 | walk/run at an easy pace. |
| Wednesday | 5 | 8 | HM | 13:40 | walk/run at your half marathon pace. |
| Thursday | 3 | 5 | M | 13:40 - 14:30 | walk/run at a medium pace. |
| Friday | Rest | Rest | Rest | Rest | Rest. |
| Saturday | 9 | 14 | S | 13:40 - 16:00 | walk/run at a slow pace. The most important piece of your long duration runs is finishing the run. |
| Sunday | Rest/CT | Rest/CT | Rest | Rest | Rest. If your body feels good, then go ahead and do some form of cross-training for 30 to 60 minutes. |

# Training - Week 9

**5K Pace: 12:34**     **5k Finish Time: 39 minutes**

| Day | Dist. Mile | Dist. KM | Difficulty | Pace (Range) | Instructions |
|---|---|---|---|---|---|
| Monday | Rest | Rest | Rest | Rest | Take it easy. Don't run. If you need to exercise, I recommend a walk for no longer than 30 minutes. |
| Tuesday | 3 | 5 | E | 13:40 - 15:30 | walk/run at an easy pace. |
| Wednesday | 5 | 8 | HM | 13:40 | walk/run at your half marathon pace. |
| Thursday | 3 | 5 | M | 13:40 - 14:30 | walk/run at a medium pace. |
| Friday | Rest | Rest | Rest | Rest | Rest. |
| Saturday | 8.5 | 13.5 | S | 13:40 - 16:00 | walk/run at a slow pace. The most important piece of your long duration runs is finishing the run. |
| Sunday | Rest/CT | Rest/CT | Rest | Rest | Rest. If your body feels good, then go ahead and do some form of cross-training for 30 to 60 minutes. |

## 13.1 Beta/Test Run Optional

| Day | Dist. Mile | Dist. KM | Difficulty | Pace (Range) | Instructions |
|---|---|---|---|---|---|
| Thursday | Rest | Rest | Rest | Rest | This is a rest day – it simulates race week |
| Friday | Rest | Rest | Rest | Rest | This is a rest day – it simulates race week |
| Saturday | 13.1 | 21 | S | 12:34 | I recommend that you attempt to go the full 13.1 miles (21 km) for a half marathon test run. <u>Only walk/run the first 10 miles (16 km) then walk the last 3.1 miles (5 km)</u>. If you are successful, you will have a race ghost time to compete against. It will help energize and refocus your training on beating yourself in 3 weeks at the half marathon race. Also, it allows your mind to grasp the achievement of "completing the distance of a half marathon." |

# Training - Week 10

5K Pace: **12:34**     5k Finish Time: **39 minutes**

| Day | Dist. Mile | Dist. KM | Difficulty | Pace (Range) | Instructions |
|---|---|---|---|---|---|
| Monday | Rest | Rest | Rest | Rest | Take it easy. Don't run. If you need to exercise, I recommend a walk for no longer than 30 minutes. |
| Tuesday | 3 | 5 | E | 13:40 - 15:30 | walk/run at an easy pace. |
| Wednesday | 5 | 8 | HM | 13:40 | walk/run at your half marathon pace. |
| Thursday | 3 | 5 | M | 13:40 - 14:30 | walk/run at a medium pace. |
| Friday | Rest | Rest | Rest | Rest | Rest. |
| Saturday | 11 | 18 | S | 13:40 - 16:00 | walk/run at a slow pace. The most important piece of your long duration runs is finishing the run. |
| Sunday | Rest/CT | Rest/CT | Rest | Rest | Rest. If your body feels good, then go ahead and do some form of cross-training for 30 to 60 minutes. |

# Training - Week 11

| Day | Dist. Mile | Dist. KM | Difficulty | Pace (Range) | Instructions |
|---|---|---|---|---|---|
| Monday | Rest | Rest | Rest | Rest | Take it easy. Don't run. If you need to exercise, I recommend a walk for no longer than 30 minutes. |
| Tuesday | 3 | 5 | E | 13:40 - 15:30 | walk/run at an easy pace. |
| Wednesday | 5 | 8 | HM | 13:40 | walk/run at your half marathon pace. |
| Thursday | 3 | 5 | M | 13:40 - 14:30 | walk/run at a medium pace. |
| Friday | Rest | Rest | Rest | Rest | Rest. |
| Saturday | 12 | 20 | S | 13:40 - 16:00 | walk/run at a slow pace. The most important piece of your long duration runs is finishing the run. |
| Sunday | Rest/CT | Rest/CT | Rest | Rest | Rest. If your body feels good, then go ahead and do some form of cross-training for 30 to 60 minutes. |

# Training - Week 12

5K Pace: **12:34**     5k Finish Time: **39 minutes**

| Day | Dist. Mile | Dist. KM | Difficulty | Pace (Range) | Instructions |
|---|---|---|---|---|---|
| Monday | Rest | Rest | Rest | Rest | Take it easy. Don't run. If you need to exercise, I recommend a walk for no longer than 30 minutes. |
| Tuesday | 3 | 5 | E | 13:40 - 15:30 | walk/run at an easy pace. |
| Wednesday | 2 | 1.5 | HM | 13:40 | walk/run at your half marathon pace. |
| Thursday | Rest | Rest | Rest | Rest | Rest. |
| Friday | Rest | Rest | Rest | Rest | Rest. |
| Saturday | 13.1 | 21 | HM | 13:40 | RACE DAY! |
| Sunday | Rest | Rest | Rest | Rest | DRINK A VICTORY BEER! |

## NOTE:

- Get plenty of sleep the night before your long duration run.
- Try to run your long duration run early in the morning.
- After each run, it's important to stretch out your muscles.
- This week your body needs as much rest as possible.
- Don't run past Wednesday.

# BEGINNER TO FINISHER RUNNING

Half Marathon Training Schedule for runners with a 5K finish time of 40 minutes and a pace of *12:54* minutes/mile.

**Predicted Half Marathon Finish Time:**

*3* hour(s) *3* minutes

# PACING TABLES

| Pace | Pace (minutes/miles) |
|---:|:---|
| 5k | 12:54 |
| Half marathon | 14:00 |
| Medium | Between 14:00 - 15:00 |
| Easy | Between 14:00 - 16:00 |
| Slow | Between 14:00 - 16:30 |

| Race | Finish Times (predicted) |
|---:|:---|
| 5k | 40 minutes |
| Half marathon | 3 hour(s) 3 minutes |

| Determining your pace | |
|:---:|:---|
| Slow Pace | Extremely easy to hold a conversation. |
| Easy Pace | You can hold a conversation with someone. Your breathing might break up some of the flow of the conversation. |
| Medium | You can hold a conversation with someone, but it's broken up into smaller sentences and smaller responses. |
| Half Marathon Pace | Conversation is difficult. One and two word responses back and forth at best. |

## Definitions in the table below:

CT = Cross Training

S = Slow Pace (long run pace)

E = Easy Pace

M = Medium Pace

HM = Half Marathon Pace

# Training - Week A (Optional)

5K Pace: **12:54**  5k Finish Time: **40 minutes**

| Day | Dist. Mile | Dist. KM | Difficulty | Pace (Range) | Instructions |
|---|---|---|---|---|---|
| Monday | Rest | Rest | Rest | Rest | Take it easy. Don't run. If you need to exercise, I recommend a walk for no longer than 30 minutes. |
| Tuesday | 1 | 1.5 | E | 14:00 - 16:00 | walk/run at an easy pace. |
| Wednesday | 1 | 1.5 | HM | 14:00 | walk/run at your half marathon pace. |
| Thursday | 1 | 1.5 | M | 14:00 - 15:00 | walk/run at a medium pace. |
| Friday | Rest | Rest | Rest | Rest | Rest. |
| Saturday | 1.5 | 2.5 | S | 14:00 - 16:30 | walk/run at a slow pace. The most important piece of your long duration runs is finishing the run. |
| Sunday | Rest/CT | Rest/CT | Rest | Rest | Rest. If your body feels good, then go ahead and do some form of cross-training for 30 to 60 minutes. |

# Training - Week B (Optional)

| Day | Dist. Mile | Dist. KM | Difficulty | Pace (Range) | Instructions |
|---|---|---|---|---|---|
| Monday | Rest | Rest | Rest | Rest | Take it easy. Don't run. If you need to exercise, I recommend a walk for no longer than 30 minutes. |
| Tuesday | 1.5 | 2.5 | E | 14:00 - 16:00 | walk/run at an easy pace. |
| Wednesday | 1.5 | 2.5 | HM | 14:00 | walk/run at your half marathon pace. |
| Thursday | 1.5 | 2.5 | M | 14:00 - 15:00 | walk/run at a medium pace. |
| Friday | Rest | Rest | Rest | Rest | Rest. |
| Saturday | 2 | 3 | S | 14:00 - 16:30 | walk/run at a slow pace. The most important piece of your long duration runs is finishing the run. |
| Sunday | Rest/CT | Rest/CT | Rest | Rest | Rest. If your body feels good, then go ahead and do some form of cross-training for 30 to 60 minutes. |

# Training - Week C (Optional)

5K Pace: **12:54**     5k Finish Time: **40 minutes**

| Day | Dist. Mile | Dist. KM | Difficulty | Pace (Range) | Instructions |
|---|---|---|---|---|---|
| Monday | Rest | Rest | Rest | Rest | Take it easy. Don't run. If you need to exercise, I recommend a walk for no longer than 30 minutes. |
| Tuesday | 2 | 3 | E | 14:00 - 16:00 | walk/run at an easy pace. |
| Wednesday | 2 | 3 | HM | 14:00 | walk/run at your half marathon pace. |
| Thursday | 2 | 3 | M | 14:00 - 15:00 | walk/run at a medium pace. |
| Friday | Rest | Rest | Rest | Rest | Rest. |
| Saturday | 3 | 5 | S | 14:00 - 16:30 | walk/run at a slow pace. The most important piece of your long duration runs is finishing the run. |
| Sunday | Rest/CT | Rest/CT | Rest | Rest | Rest. If your body feels good, then go ahead and do some form of cross-training for 30 to 60 minutes. |

# Training - Week 1

5K Pace: **12:54**      5k Finish Time: **40 minutes**

| Day | Dist. Mile | Dist. KM | Difficulty | Pace (Range) | Instructions |
|---|---|---|---|---|---|
| Monday | Rest | Rest | Rest | Rest | Take it easy. Don't run. If you need to exercise, I recommend a walk for no longer than 30 minutes. |
| Tuesday | 3 | 5 | E | 14:00 - 16:00 | walk/run at an easy pace. |
| Wednesday | 3 | 5 | HM | 14:00 | walk/run at your half marathon pace. |
| Thursday | 3 | 5 | M | 14:00 - 15:00 | walk/run at a medium pace. |
| Friday | Rest | Rest | Rest | Rest | Rest. |
| Saturday | 4 | 6 | S | 14:00 - 16:30 | walk/run at a slow pace. The most important piece of your long duration runs is finishing the run. |
| Sunday | Rest/CT | Rest/CT | Rest | Rest | Rest. If your body feels good, then go ahead and do some form of cross-training for 30 to 60 minutes. |

# Training - Week 2

| Day | Dist. Mile | Dist. KM | Difficulty | Pace (Range) | Instructions |
|---|---|---|---|---|---|
| Monday | Rest | Rest | Rest | Rest | Take it easy. Don't run. If you need to exercise, I recommend a walk for no longer than 30 minutes. |
| Tuesday | 3 | 5 | E | 14:00 - 16:00 | walk/run at an easy pace. |
| Wednesday | 3 | 5 | HM | 14:00 | walk/run at your half marathon pace. |
| Thursday | 3 | 5 | M | 14:00 - 15:00 | walk/run at a medium pace. |
| Friday | Rest | Rest | Rest | Rest | Rest. |
| Saturday | 5 | 8 | S | 14:00 - 16:30 | walk/run at a slow pace. The most important piece of your long duration runs is finishing the run. |
| Sunday | Rest/CT | Rest/CT | Rest | Rest | Rest. If your body feels good, then go ahead and do some form of cross-training for 30 to 60 minutes. |

# Training - Week 3

5K Pace: **12:54**     5k Finish Time: **40 minutes**

| Day | Dist. Mile | Dist. KM | Difficulty | Pace (Range) | Instructions |
|---|---|---|---|---|---|
| Monday | Rest | Rest | Rest | Rest | Take it easy. Don't run. If you need to exercise, I recommend a walk for no longer than 30 minutes. |
| Tuesday | 3 | 5 | E | 14:00 - 16:00 | walk/run at an easy pace. |
| Wednesday | 4 | 6 | HM | 14:00 | walk/run at your half marathon pace. |
| Thursday | 3 | 5 | M | 14:00 - 15:00 | walk/run at a medium pace. |
| Friday | Rest | Rest | Rest | Rest | Rest. |
| Saturday | 6 | 10 | S | 14:00 - 16:30 | walk/run at a slow pace. The most important piece of your long duration runs is finishing the run. |
| Sunday | Rest/CT | Rest/CT | Rest | Rest | Rest. If your body feels good, then go ahead and do some form of cross-training for 30 to 60 minutes. |

# Training - Week 4 (5K Optional)

5K Pace: **12:54**     5k Finish Time: **40 minutes**

| Day | Dist. Mile | Dist. KM | Difficulty | Pace (Range) | Instructions |
|---|---|---|---|---|---|
| Monday | Rest | Rest | Rest | Rest | Take it easy. Don't run. If you need to exercise, I recommend a walk for no longer than 30 minutes. |
| Tuesday | 3 | 5 | E | 14:00 - 16:00 | walk/run at an easy pace. |
| Wednesday | 4 | 6 | HM | 14:00 | walk/run at your half marathon pace. |
| Thursday | 3 | 5 | M | 14:00 - 15:00 | walk/run at a medium pace. |
| Friday | Rest | Rest | Rest | Rest | Rest. |
| Saturday | 6.5 | 10.5 | S | 14:00 - 16:30 | walk/run at a slow pace. The most important piece of your long duration runs is finishing the run. |
| Sunday | Rest/CT | Rest/CT | Rest | Rest | Rest. If your body feels good, then go ahead and do some form of cross-training for 30 to 60 minutes. |

## 5K Optional

| Day | Dist. Mile | Dist. KM | Difficulty | Pace (Range) | Instructions |
|---|---|---|---|---|---|
| Saturday | 3.1 | 5 | - | 12:54 | Run a 5k race instead of your long run. This is completely your choice. I recommend running a 5k race to help you get used to running races. You should see a difference in your race time if you have kept to your training schedule. Don't try for a personal best, run the 5K at your 5K pace. |

# Training - Week 5

5K Pace: **12:54**     5k Finish Time: **40 minutes**

| Day | Dist. Mile | Dist. KM | Difficulty | Pace (Range) | Instructions |
|---|---|---|---|---|---|
| Monday | Rest | Rest | Rest | Rest | Take it easy. Don't run. If you need to exercise, I recommend a walk for no longer than 30 minutes. |
| Tuesday | 3 | 5 | E | 14:00 - 16:00 | walk/run at an easy pace. |
| Wednesday | 4 | 6 | HM | 14:00 | walk/run at your half marathon pace. |
| Thursday | 3 | 5 | M | 14:00 - 15:00 | walk/run at a medium pace. |
| Friday | Rest | Rest | Rest | Rest | Rest. |
| Saturday | 7 | 11 | S | 14:00 - 16:30 | walk/run at a slow pace. The most important piece of your long duration runs is finishing the run. |
| Sunday | Rest/CT | Rest/CT | Rest | Rest | Rest. If your body feels good, then go ahead and do some form of cross-training for 30 to 60 minutes. |

## NOTE:

- Your long duration runs will begin to become more difficult for week 5 and beyond.
- If you get tired during a long duration run, walk for 1/10 mile or 3-5 minutes.

# Training - Week 6

5K Pace: **12:54**     5k Finish Time: **40 minutes**

| Day | Dist. Mile | Dist. KM | Difficulty | Pace (Range) | Instructions |
|---|---|---|---|---|---|
| Monday | Rest | Rest | Rest | Rest | Take it easy. Don't run. If you need to exercise, I recommend a walk for no longer than 30 minutes. |
| Tuesday | 3 | 5 | E | 14:00 - 16:00 | walk/run at an easy pace. |
| Wednesday | 4 | 6 | HM | 14:00 | walk/run at your half marathon pace. |
| Thursday | 3 | 5 | M | 14:00 - 15:00 | walk/run at a medium pace. |
| Friday | Rest | Rest | Rest | Rest | Rest. |
| Saturday | 8 | 13 | S | 14:00 - 16:30 | walk/run at a slow pace. The most important piece of your long duration runs is finishing the run. |
| Sunday | Rest/CT | Rest/CT | Rest | Rest | Rest. If your body feels good, then go ahead and do some form of cross-training for 30 to 60 minutes. |

# Training - Week 7

5K Pace: **12:54**    5k Finish Time: **40 minutes**

| Day | Dist. Mile | Dist. KM | Difficulty | Pace (Range) | Instructions |
|---|---|---|---|---|---|
| Monday | Rest | Rest | Rest | Rest | Take it easy. Don't run. If you need to exercise, I recommend a walk for no longer than 30 minutes. |
| Tuesday | 3 | 5 | E | 14:00 - 16:00 | walk/run at an easy pace. |
| Wednesday | 5 | 8 | HM | 14:00 | walk/run at your half marathon pace. |
| Thursday | 3 | 5 | M | 14:00 - 15:00 | walk/run at a medium pace. |
| Friday | Rest | Rest | Rest | Rest | Rest. |
| Saturday | 8.5 | 13.5 | S | 14:00 - 16:30 | walk/run at a slow pace. The most important piece of your long duration runs is finishing the run. |
| Sunday | Rest/CT | Rest/CT | Rest | Rest | Rest. If your body feels good, then go ahead and do some form of cross-training for 30 to 60 minutes. |

## 10K Optional

| Day | Dist. Mile | Dist. KM | Difficulty | Pace (Range) | Instructions |
|---|---|---|---|---|---|
| Thursday | 2 | 3 | E | 14:00 - 16:00 | If you run the optional 10K, either completely rest today or run 2 miles (3 km). |
| Saturday | 6.2 | 10K | - | 12:54 | Run a 10k race instead of your long run. This is completely your choice. I recommend running a 10k race to help you get used to running races. You should see a difference in your race time if you have kept to your training schedule. Don't try for a personal best, run the 10K at your 5K pace. |

# Training - Week 8

5K Pace: **12:54**  5k Finish Time: **40 minutes**

| Day | Dist. Mile | Dist. KM | Difficulty | Pace (Range) | Instructions |
|---|---|---|---|---|---|
| Monday | Rest | Rest | Rest | Rest | Take it easy. Don't run. If you need to exercise, I recommend a walk for no longer than 30 minutes. |
| Tuesday | 3 | 5 | E | 14:00 - 16:00 | walk/run at an easy pace. |
| Wednesday | 5 | 8 | HM | 14:00 | walk/run at your half marathon pace. |
| Thursday | 3 | 5 | M | 14:00 - 15:00 | walk/run at a medium pace. |
| Friday | Rest | Rest | Rest | Rest | Rest. |
| Saturday | 9 | 14 | S | 14:00 - 16:30 | walk/run at a slow pace. The most important piece of your long duration runs is finishing the run. |
| Sunday | Rest/CT | Rest/CT | Rest | Rest | Rest. If your body feels good, then go ahead and do some form of cross-training for 30 to 60 minutes. |

# Training - Week 9

5K Pace: **12:54**     5k Finish Time: **40 minutes**

| Day | Dist. Mile | Dist. KM | Difficulty | Pace (Range) | Instructions |
|---|---|---|---|---|---|
| Monday | Rest | Rest | Rest | Rest | Take it easy. Don't run. If you need to exercise, I recommend a walk for no longer than 30 minutes. |
| Tuesday | 3 | 5 | E | 14:00 - 16:00 | walk/run at an easy pace. |
| Wednesday | 5 | 8 | HM | 14:00 | walk/run at your half marathon pace. |
| Thursday | 3 | 5 | M | 14:00 - 15:00 | walk/run at a medium pace. |
| Friday | Rest | Rest | Rest | Rest | Rest. |
| Saturday | 8.5 | 13.5 | S | 14:00 - 16:30 | walk/run at a slow pace. The most important piece of your long duration runs is finishing the run. |
| Sunday | Rest/CT | Rest/CT | Rest | Rest | Rest. If your body feels good, then go ahead and do some form of cross-training for 30 to 60 minutes. |

## 13.1 Beta/Test Run Optional

| Day | Dist. Mile | Dist. KM | Difficulty | Pace (Range) | Instructions |
|---|---|---|---|---|---|
| Thursday | Rest | Rest | Rest | Rest | This is a rest day – it simulates race week |
| Friday | Rest | Rest | Rest | Rest | This is a rest day – it simulates race week |
| Saturday | 13.1 | 21 | S | 12:54 | I recommend that you attempt to go the full 13.1 miles (21 km) for a half marathon test run. Only walk/run the first 10 miles (16 km) then walk the last 3.1 miles (5 km). If you are successful, you will have a race ghost time to compete against. It will help energize and refocus your training on beating yourself in 3 weeks at the half marathon race. Also, it allows your mind to grasp the achievement of "completing the distance of a half marathon." |

# Training - Week 10

5K Pace: **12:54**    5k Finish Time: **40 minutes**

| Day | Dist. Mile | Dist. KM | Difficulty | Pace (Range) | Instructions |
|---|---|---|---|---|---|
| Monday | Rest | Rest | Rest | Rest | Take it easy. Don't run. If you need to exercise, I recommend a walk for no longer than 30 minutes. |
| Tuesday | 3 | 5 | E | 14:00 - 16:00 | walk/run at an easy pace. |
| Wednesday | 5 | 8 | HM | 14:00 | walk/run at your half marathon pace. |
| Thursday | 3 | 5 | M | 14:00 - 15:00 | walk/run at a medium pace. |
| Friday | Rest | Rest | Rest | Rest | Rest. |
| Saturday | 11 | 18 | S | 14:00 - 16:30 | walk/run at a slow pace. The most important piece of your long duration runs is finishing the run. |
| Sunday | Rest/CT | Rest/CT | Rest | Rest | Rest. If your body feels good, then go ahead and do some form of cross-training for 30 to 60 minutes. |

# Training - Week 11

| Day | Dist. Mile | Dist. KM | Difficulty | Pace (Range) | Instructions |
|---|---|---|---|---|---|
| Monday | Rest | Rest | Rest | Rest | Take it easy. Don't run. If you need to exercise, I recommend a walk for no longer than 30 minutes. |
| Tuesday | 3 | 5 | E | 14:00 - 16:00 | walk/run at an easy pace. |
| Wednesday | 5 | 8 | HM | 14:00 | walk/run at your half marathon pace. |
| Thursday | 3 | 5 | M | 14:00 - 15:00 | walk/run at a medium pace. |
| Friday | Rest | Rest | Rest | Rest | Rest. |
| Saturday | 12 | 20 | S | 14:00 - 16:30 | walk/run at a slow pace. The most important piece of your long duration runs is finishing the run. |
| Sunday | Rest/CT | Rest/CT | Rest | Rest | Rest. If your body feels good, then go ahead and do some form of cross-training for 30 to 60 minutes. |

# Training - Week 12

5K Pace: **12:54**     5k Finish Time: **40 minutes**

| Day | Dist. Mile | Dist. KM | Difficulty | Pace (Range) | Instructions |
|---|---|---|---|---|---|
| Monday | Rest | Rest | Rest | Rest | Take it easy. Don't run. If you need to exercise, I recommend a walk for no longer than 30 minutes. |
| Tuesday | 3 | 5 | E | 14:00 - 16:00 | walk/run at an easy pace. |
| Wednesday | 2 | 1.5 | HM | 14:00 | walk/run at your half marathon pace. |
| Thursday | Rest | Rest | Rest | Rest | Rest. |
| Friday | Rest | Rest | Rest | Rest | Rest. |
| Saturday | 13.1 | 21 | HM | 14:00 | RACE DAY! |
| Sunday | Rest | Rest | Rest | Rest | DRINK A VICTORY BEER! |

## NOTE:

- Get plenty of sleep the night before your long duration run.
- Try to run your long duration run early in the morning.
- After each run, it's important to stretch out your muscles.
- This week your body needs as much rest as possible.
- Don't run past Wednesday.

# BEGINNER TO FINISHER RUNNING

Half Marathon Training Schedule for

runners with a 5K finish time of 41 minutes

and a pace of *13:13* minutes/mile.

# Predicted Half Marathon Finish Time:

## *3* hour(s) *8* minutes

# PACING TABLES

| Pace | Pace (minutes/miles) |
|---:|---|
| 5k | 13:13 |
| Half marathon | 14:22 |
| Medium | Between 14:22 - 15:22 |
| Easy | Between 14:22 - 16:22 |
| Slow | Between 14:22 - 16:52 |

| Race | Finish Times (predicted) |
|---:|---|
| 5k | 41 minutes |
| Half marathon | 3 hour(s) 8 minutes |

| Determining your pace | |
|---|---|
| Slow Pace | Extremely easy to hold a conversation. |
| Easy Pace | You can hold a conversation with someone. Your breathing might break up some of the flow of the conversation. |
| Medium | You can hold a conversation with someone, but it's broken up into smaller sentences and smaller responses. |
| Half Marathon Pace | Conversation is difficult. One and two word responses back and forth at best. |

## Definitions in the table below:

CT = Cross Training

S = Slow Pace (long run pace)

E = Easy Pace

M = Medium Pace

HM = Half Marathon Pace

# Training - Week A (Optional)

5K Pace: **13:13**     5k Finish Time: **41 minutes**

| Day | Dist. Mile | Dist. KM | Difficulty | Pace (Range) | Instructions |
|---|---|---|---|---|---|
| Monday | Rest | Rest | Rest | Rest | Take it easy. Don't run. If you need to exercise, I recommend a walk for no longer than 30 minutes. |
| Tuesday | 1 | 1.5 | E | 14:22 - 16:22 | walk/run at an easy pace. |
| Wednesday | 1 | 1.5 | HM | 14:22 | walk/run at your half marathon pace. |
| Thursday | 1 | 1.5 | M | 14:22 - 15:22 | walk/run at a medium pace. |
| Friday | Rest | Rest | Rest | Rest | Rest. |
| Saturday | 1.5 | 2.5 | S | 14:22 - 16:52 | walk/run at a slow pace. The most important piece of your long duration runs is finishing the run. |
| Sunday | Rest/CT | Rest/CT | Rest | Rest | Rest. If your body feels good, then go ahead and do some form of cross-training for 30 to 60 minutes. |

# Training - Week B (Optional)

| Day | Dist. Mile | Dist. KM | Difficulty | Pace (Range) | Instructions |
|---|---|---|---|---|---|
| Monday | Rest | Rest | Rest | Rest | Take it easy. Don't run. If you need to exercise, I recommend a walk for no longer than 30 minutes. |
| Tuesday | 1.5 | 2.5 | E | 14:22 - 16:22 | walk/run at an easy pace. |
| Wednesday | 1.5 | 2.5 | HM | 14:22 | walk/run at your half marathon pace. |
| Thursday | 1.5 | 2.5 | M | 14:22 - 15:22 | walk/run at a medium pace. |
| Friday | Rest | Rest | Rest | Rest | Rest. |
| Saturday | 2 | 3 | S | 14:22 - 16:52 | walk/run at a slow pace. The most important piece of your long duration runs is finishing the run. |
| Sunday | Rest/CT | Rest/CT | Rest | Rest | Rest. If your body feels good, then go ahead and do some form of cross-training for 30 to 60 minutes. |

# Training - Week C (Optional)

5K Pace: **13:13**     5k Finish Time: **41 minutes**

| Day | Dist. Mile | Dist. KM | Difficulty | Pace (Range) | Instructions |
|---|---|---|---|---|---|
| Monday | Rest | Rest | Rest | Rest | Take it easy. Don't run. If you need to exercise, I recommend a walk for no longer than 30 minutes. |
| Tuesday | 2 | 3 | E | 14:22 - 16:22 | walk/run at an easy pace. |
| Wednesday | 2 | 3 | HM | 14:22 | walk/run at your half marathon pace. |
| Thursday | 2 | 3 | M | 14:22 - 15:22 | walk/run at a medium pace. |
| Friday | Rest | Rest | Rest | Rest | Rest. |
| Saturday | 3 | 5 | S | 14:22 - 16:52 | walk/run at a slow pace. The most important piece of your long duration runs is finishing the run. |
| Sunday | Rest/CT | Rest/CT | Rest | Rest | Rest. If your body feels good, then go ahead and do some form of cross-training for 30 to 60 minutes. |

# Training - Week 1

5K Pace: **13:13**     5k Finish Time: **41 minutes**

| Day | Dist. Mile | Dist. KM | Difficulty | Pace (Range) | Instructions |
|---|---|---|---|---|---|
| Monday | Rest | Rest | Rest | Rest | Take it easy. Don't run. If you need to exercise, I recommend a walk for no longer than 30 minutes. |
| Tuesday | 3 | 5 | E | 14:22 - 16:22 | walk/run at an easy pace. |
| Wednesday | 3 | 5 | HM | 14:22 | walk/run at your half marathon pace. |
| Thursday | 3 | 5 | M | 14:22 - 15:22 | walk/run at a medium pace. |
| Friday | Rest | Rest | Rest | Rest | Rest. |
| Saturday | 4 | 6 | S | 14:22 - 16:52 | walk/run at a slow pace. The most important piece of your long duration runs is finishing the run. |
| Sunday | Rest/CT | Rest/CT | Rest | Rest | Rest. If your body feels good, then go ahead and do some form of cross-training for 30 to 60 minutes. |

# Training - Week 2

| Day | Dist. Mile | Dist. KM | Difficulty | Pace (Range) | Instructions |
|---|---|---|---|---|---|
| Monday | Rest | Rest | Rest | Rest | Take it easy. Don't run. If you need to exercise, I recommend a walk for no longer than 30 minutes. |
| Tuesday | 3 | 5 | E | 14:22 - 16:22 | walk/run at an easy pace. |
| Wednesday | 3 | 5 | HM | 14:22 | walk/run at your half marathon pace. |
| Thursday | 3 | 5 | M | 14:22 - 15:22 | walk/run at a medium pace. |
| Friday | Rest | Rest | Rest | Rest | Rest. |
| Saturday | 5 | 8 | S | 14:22 - 16:52 | walk/run at a slow pace. The most important piece of your long duration runs is finishing the run. |
| Sunday | Rest/CT | Rest/CT | Rest | Rest | Rest. If your body feels good, then go ahead and do some form of cross-training for 30 to 60 minutes. |

# Training - Week 3

5K Pace: **13:13**     5k Finish Time: **41 minutes**

| Day | Dist. Mile | Dist. KM | Difficulty | Pace (Range) | Instructions |
|---|---|---|---|---|---|
| Monday | Rest | Rest | Rest | Rest | Take it easy. Don't run. If you need to exercise, I recommend a walk for no longer than 30 minutes. |
| Tuesday | 3 | 5 | E | 14:22 - 16:22 | walk/run at an easy pace. |
| Wednesday | 4 | 6 | HM | 14:22 | walk/run at your half marathon pace. |
| Thursday | 3 | 5 | M | 14:22 - 15:22 | walk/run at a medium pace. |
| Friday | Rest | Rest | Rest | Rest | Rest. |
| Saturday | 6 | 10 | S | 14:22 - 16:52 | walk/run at a slow pace. The most important piece of your long duration runs is finishing the run. |
| Sunday | Rest/CT | Rest/CT | Rest | Rest | Rest. If your body feels good, then go ahead and do some form of cross-training for 30 to 60 minutes. |

# Training - Week 4 (5K Optional)

5K Pace: **13:13**     5k Finish Time: **41 minutes**

| Day | Dist. Mile | Dist. KM | Difficulty | Pace (Range) | Instructions |
|---|---|---|---|---|---|
| Monday | Rest | Rest | Rest | Rest | Take it easy. Don't run. If you need to exercise, I recommend a walk for no longer than 30 minutes. |
| Tuesday | 3 | 5 | E | 14:22 - 16:22 | walk/run at an easy pace. |
| Wednesday | 4 | 6 | HM | 14:22 | walk/run at your half marathon pace. |
| Thursday | 3 | 5 | M | 14:22 - 15:22 | walk/run at a medium pace. |
| Friday | Rest | Rest | Rest | Rest | Rest. |
| Saturday | 6.5 | 10.5 | S | 14:22 - 16:52 | walk/run at a slow pace. The most important piece of your long duration runs is finishing the run. |
| Sunday | Rest/CT | Rest/CT | Rest | Rest | Rest. If your body feels good, then go ahead and do some form of cross-training for 30 to 60 minutes. |

## 5K Optional

| Day | Dist. Mile | Dist. KM | Difficulty | Pace (Range) | Instructions |
|---|---|---|---|---|---|
| Saturday | 3.1 | 5 | - | 13:13 | Run a 5k race instead of your long run. This is completely your choice. I recommend running a 5k race to help you get used to running races. You should see a difference in your race time if you have kept to your training schedule. Don't try for a personal best, run the 5K at your 5K pace. |

# Training - Week 5

5K Pace: **13:13**     5k Finish Time: **41 minutes**

| Day | Dist. Mile | Dist. KM | Difficulty | Pace (Range) | Instructions |
|---|---|---|---|---|---|
| Monday | Rest | Rest | Rest | Rest | Take it easy. Don't run. If you need to exercise, I recommend a walk for no longer than 30 minutes. |
| Tuesday | 3 | 5 | E | 14:22 - 16:22 | walk/run at an easy pace. |
| Wednesday | 4 | 6 | HM | 14:22 | walk/run at your half marathon pace. |
| Thursday | 3 | 5 | M | 14:22 - 15:22 | walk/run at a medium pace. |
| Friday | Rest | Rest | Rest | Rest | Rest. |
| Saturday | 7 | 11 | S | 14:22 - 16:52 | walk/run at a slow pace. The most important piece of your long duration runs is finishing the run. |
| Sunday | Rest/CT | Rest/CT | Rest | Rest | Rest. If your body feels good, then go ahead and do some form of cross-training for 30 to 60 minutes. |

## NOTE:

- Your long duration runs will begin to become more difficult for week 5 and beyond.
- If you get tired during a long duration run, walk for 1/10 mile or 3-5 minutes.

# Training - Week 6

5K Pace: **13:13**     5k Finish Time: **41 minutes**

| Day | Dist. Mile | Dist. KM | Difficulty | Pace (Range) | Instructions |
|---|---|---|---|---|---|
| Monday | Rest | Rest | Rest | Rest | Take it easy. Don't run. If you need to exercise, I recommend a walk for no longer than 30 minutes. |
| Tuesday | 3 | 5 | E | 14:22 - 16:22 | walk/run at an easy pace. |
| Wednesday | 4 | 6 | HM | 14:22 | walk/run at your half marathon pace. |
| Thursday | 3 | 5 | M | 14:22 - 15:22 | walk/run at a medium pace. |
| Friday | Rest | Rest | Rest | Rest | Rest. |
| Saturday | 8 | 13 | S | 14:22 - 16:52 | walk/run at a slow pace. The most important piece of your long duration runs is finishing the run. |
| Sunday | Rest/CT | Rest/CT | Rest | Rest | Rest. If your body feels good, then go ahead and do some form of cross-training for 30 to 60 minutes. |

# Training - Week 7

5K Pace: **13:13**     5k Finish Time: **41 minutes**

| Day | Dist. Mile | Dist. KM | Difficulty | Pace (Range) | Instructions |
|---|---|---|---|---|---|
| Monday | Rest | Rest | Rest | Rest | Take it easy. Don't run. If you need to exercise, I recommend a walk for no longer than 30 minutes. |
| Tuesday | 3 | 5 | E | 14:22 - 16:22 | walk/run at an easy pace. |
| Wednesday | 5 | 8 | HM | 14:22 | walk/run at your half marathon pace. |
| Thursday | 3 | 5 | M | 14:22 - 15:22 | walk/run at a medium pace. |
| Friday | Rest | Rest | Rest | Rest | Rest. |
| Saturday | 8.5 | 13.5 | S | 14:22 - 16:52 | walk/run at a slow pace. The most important piece of your long duration runs is finishing the run. |
| Sunday | Rest/CT | Rest/CT | Rest | Rest | Rest. If your body feels good, then go ahead and do some form of cross-training for 30 to 60 minutes. |

## 10K Optional

| Day | Dist. Mile | Dist. KM | Difficulty | Pace (Range) | Instructions |
|---|---|---|---|---|---|
| Thursday | 2 | 3 | E | 14:22 - 16:22 | If you run the optional 10K, either completely rest today or run 2 miles (3 km). |
| Saturday | 6.2 | 10K | - | 13:13 | Run a 10k race instead of your long run. This is completely your choice. I recommend running a 10k race to help you get used to running races. You should see a difference in your race time if you have kept to your training schedule. Don't try for a personal best, run the 10K at your 5K pace. |

# Training - Week 8

5K Pace: **13:13**     5k Finish Time: **41 minutes**

| Day | Dist. Mile | Dist. KM | Difficulty | Pace (Range) | Instructions |
|---|---|---|---|---|---|
| Monday | Rest | Rest | Rest | Rest | Take it easy. Don't run. If you need to exercise, I recommend a walk for no longer than 30 minutes. |
| Tuesday | 3 | 5 | E | 14:22 - 16:22 | walk/run at an easy pace. |
| Wednesday | 5 | 8 | HM | 14:22 | walk/run at your half marathon pace. |
| Thursday | 3 | 5 | M | 14:22 - 15:22 | walk/run at a medium pace. |
| Friday | Rest | Rest | Rest | Rest | Rest. |
| Saturday | 9 | 14 | S | 14:22 - 16:52 | walk/run at a slow pace. The most important piece of your long duration runs is finishing the run. |
| Sunday | Rest/CT | Rest/CT | Rest | Rest | Rest. If your body feels good, then go ahead and do some form of cross-training for 30 to 60 minutes. |

# Training - Week 9

5K Pace: **13:13**     5k Finish Time: **41 minutes**

| Day | Dist. Mile | Dist. KM | Difficulty | Pace (Range) | Instructions |
|---|---|---|---|---|---|
| Monday | Rest | Rest | Rest | Rest | Take it easy. Don't run. If you need to exercise, I recommend a walk for no longer than 30 minutes. |
| Tuesday | 3 | 5 | E | 14:22 - 16:22 | walk/run at an easy pace. |
| Wednesday | 5 | 8 | HM | 14:22 | walk/run at your half marathon pace. |
| Thursday | 3 | 5 | M | 14:22 - 15:22 | walk/run at a medium pace. |
| Friday | Rest | Rest | Rest | Rest | Rest. |
| Saturday | 8.5 | 13.5 | S | 14:22 - 16:52 | walk/run at a slow pace. The most important piece of your long duration runs is finishing the run. |
| Sunday | Rest/CT | Rest/CT | Rest | Rest | Rest. If your body feels good, then go ahead and do some form of cross-training for 30 to 60 minutes. |

## 13.1 Beta/Test Run Optional

| Day | Dist. Mile | Dist. KM | Difficulty | Pace (Range) | Instructions |
|---|---|---|---|---|---|
| Thursday | Rest | Rest | Rest | Rest | This is a rest day – it simulates race week |
| Friday | Rest | Rest | Rest | Rest | This is a rest day – it simulates race week |
| Saturday | 13.1 | 21 | S | 13:13 | I recommend that you attempt to go the full 13.1 miles (21 km) for a half marathon test run. <u>Only walk/run the first 10 miles (16 km) then walk the last 3.1 miles (5 km)</u>. If you are successful, you will have a race ghost time to compete against. It will help energize and refocus your training on beating yourself in 3 weeks at the half marathon race. Also, it allows your mind to grasp the achievement of "completing the distance of a half marathon." |

# Training - Week 10

5K Pace: **13:13**    5k Finish Time: **41 minutes**

| Day | Dist. Mile | Dist. KM | Difficulty | Pace (Range) | Instructions |
|---|---|---|---|---|---|
| Monday | Rest | Rest | Rest | Rest | Take it easy. Don't run. If you need to exercise, I recommend a walk for no longer than 30 minutes. |
| Tuesday | 3 | 5 | E | 14:22 - 16:22 | walk/run at an easy pace. |
| Wednesday | 5 | 8 | HM | 14:22 | walk/run at your half marathon pace. |
| Thursday | 3 | 5 | M | 14:22 - 15:22 | walk/run at a medium pace. |
| Friday | Rest | Rest | Rest | Rest | Rest. |
| Saturday | 11 | 18 | S | 14:22 - 16:52 | walk/run at a slow pace. The most important piece of your long duration runs is finishing the run. |
| Sunday | Rest/CT | Rest/CT | Rest | Rest | Rest. If your body feels good, then go ahead and do some form of cross-training for 30 to 60 minutes. |

# Training - Week 11

| Day | Dist. Mile | Dist. KM | Difficulty | Pace (Range) | Instructions |
|---|---|---|---|---|---|
| Monday | Rest | Rest | Rest | Rest | Take it easy. Don't run. If you need to exercise, I recommend a walk for no longer than 30 minutes. |
| Tuesday | 3 | 5 | E | 14:22 - 16:22 | walk/run at an easy pace. |
| Wednesday | 5 | 8 | HM | 14:22 | walk/run at your half marathon pace. |
| Thursday | 3 | 5 | M | 14:22 - 15:22 | walk/run at a medium pace. |
| Friday | Rest | Rest | Rest | Rest | Rest. |
| Saturday | 12 | 20 | S | 14:22 - 16:52 | walk/run at a slow pace. The most important piece of your long duration runs is finishing the run. |
| Sunday | Rest/CT | Rest/CT | Rest | Rest | Rest. If your body feels good, then go ahead and do some form of cross-training for 30 to 60 minutes. |

# Training - Week 12

5K Pace: **13:13**     5k Finish Time: **41 minutes**

| Day | Dist. Mile | Dist. KM | Difficulty | Pace (Range) | Instructions |
|---|---|---|---|---|---|
| Monday | Rest | Rest | Rest | Rest | Take it easy. Don't run. If you need to exercise, I recommend a walk for no longer than 30 minutes. |
| Tuesday | 3 | 5 | E | 14:22 - 16:22 | walk/run at an easy pace. |
| Wednesday | 2 | 1.5 | HM | 14:22 | walk/run at your half marathon pace. |
| Thursday | Rest | Rest | Rest | Rest | Rest. |
| Friday | Rest | Rest | Rest | Rest | Rest. |
| Saturday | 13.1 | 21 | HM | 14:22 | RACE DAY! |
| Sunday | Rest | Rest | Rest | Rest | DRINK A VICTORY BEER! |

## NOTE:

- Get plenty of sleep the night before your long duration run.
- Try to run your long duration run early in the morning.
- After each run, it's important to stretch out your muscles.
- This week your body needs as much rest as possible.
- Don't run past Wednesday.

Half Marathon Training Schedule for

<u>runners with a 5K finish time of 42 minutes</u>

and a pace of *13:32* minutes/mile.

# Predicted Half Marathon Finish Time:

<u>*3* hour(s) *13* minutes</u>

# PACING TABLES

| Pace | Pace (minutes/miles) |
|---:|---|
| 5k | 13:32 |
| Half marathon | 14:45 |
| Medium | Between 14:45 - 15:45 |
| Easy | Between 14:45 - 16:45 |
| Slow | Between 14:45 - 17:15 |

| Race | Finish Times (predicted) |
|---:|---|
| 5k | 42 minutes |
| Half marathon | 3 hour(s) 13 minutes |

| Determining your pace ||
|---|---|
| Slow Pace | Extremely easy to hold a conversation. |
| Easy Pace | You can hold a conversation with someone. Your breathing might break up some of the flow of the conversation. |
| Medium | You can hold a conversation with someone, but it's broken up into smaller sentences and smaller responses. |
| Half Marathon Pace | Conversation is difficult. One and two word responses back and forth at best. |

## Definitions in the table below:

CT = Cross Training

S = Slow Pace (long run pace)

E = Easy Pace

M = Medium Pace

HM = Half Marathon Pace

# Training - Week A (Optional)

5K Pace: **13:32**          5k Finish Time: **42 minutes**

| Day | Dist. Mile | Dist. KM | Difficulty | Pace (Range) | Instructions |
|---|---|---|---|---|---|
| Monday | Rest | Rest | Rest | Rest | Take it easy. Don't run. If you need to exercise, I recommend a walk for no longer than 30 minutes. |
| Tuesday | 1 | 1.5 | E | 14:45 - 16:45 | walk/run at an easy pace. |
| Wednesday | 1 | 1.5 | HM | 14:45 | walk/run at your half marathon pace. |
| Thursday | 1 | 1.5 | M | 14:45 - 15:45 | walk/run at a medium pace. |
| Friday | Rest | Rest | Rest | Rest | Rest. |
| Saturday | 1.5 | 2.5 | S | 14:45 - 17:15 | walk/run at a slow pace. The most important piece of your long duration runs is finishing the run. |
| Sunday | Rest/CT | Rest/CT | Rest | Rest | Rest. If your body feels good, then go ahead and do some form of cross-training for 30 to 60 minutes. |

# Training - Week B (Optional)

| Day | Dist. Mile | Dist. KM | Difficulty | Pace (Range) | Instructions |
|---|---|---|---|---|---|
| Monday | Rest | Rest | Rest | Rest | Take it easy. Don't run. If you need to exercise, I recommend a walk for no longer than 30 minutes. |
| Tuesday | 1.5 | 2.5 | E | 14:45 - 16:45 | walk/run at an easy pace. |
| Wednesday | 1.5 | 2.5 | HM | 14:45 | walk/run at your half marathon pace. |
| Thursday | 1.5 | 2.5 | M | 14:45 - 15:45 | walk/run at a medium pace. |
| Friday | Rest | Rest | Rest | Rest | Rest. |
| Saturday | 2 | 3 | S | 14:45 - 17:15 | walk/run at a slow pace. The most important piece of your long duration runs is finishing the run. |
| Sunday | Rest/CT | Rest/CT | Rest | Rest | Rest. If your body feels good, then go ahead and do some form of cross-training for 30 to 60 minutes. |

# Training - Week C (Optional)

5K Pace: **13:32**     5k Finish Time: **42 minutes**

| Day | Dist. Mile | Dist. KM | Difficulty | Pace (Range) | Instructions |
|---|---|---|---|---|---|
| Monday | Rest | Rest | Rest | Rest | Take it easy. Don't run. If you need to exercise, I recommend a walk for no longer than 30 minutes. |
| Tuesday | 2 | 3 | E | 14:45 - 16:45 | walk/run at an easy pace. |
| Wednesday | 2 | 3 | HM | 14:45 | walk/run at your half marathon pace. |
| Thursday | 2 | 3 | M | 14:45 - 15:45 | walk/run at a medium pace. |
| Friday | Rest | Rest | Rest | Rest | Rest. |
| Saturday | 3 | 5 | S | 14:45 - 17:15 | walk/run at a slow pace. The most important piece of your long duration runs is finishing the run. |
| Sunday | Rest/CT | Rest/CT | Rest | Rest | Rest. If your body feels good, then go ahead and do some form of cross-training for 30 to 60 minutes. |

# Training - Week 1

5K Pace: **13:32**   5k Finish Time: **42 minutes**

| Day | Dist. Mile | Dist. KM | Difficulty | Pace (Range) | Instructions |
|---|---|---|---|---|---|
| Monday | Rest | Rest | Rest | Rest | Take it easy. Don't run. If you need to exercise, I recommend a walk for no longer than 30 minutes. |
| Tuesday | 3 | 5 | E | 14:45 - 16:45 | walk/run at an easy pace. |
| Wednesday | 3 | 5 | HM | 14:45 | walk/run at your half marathon pace. |
| Thursday | 3 | 5 | M | 14:45 - 15:45 | walk/run at a medium pace. |
| Friday | Rest | Rest | Rest | Rest | Rest. |
| Saturday | 4 | 6 | S | 14:45 - 17:15 | walk/run at a slow pace. The most important piece of your long duration runs is finishing the run. |
| Sunday | Rest/CT | Rest/CT | Rest | Rest | Rest. If your body feels good, then go ahead and do some form of cross-training for 30 to 60 minutes. |

# Training - Week 2

| Day | Dist. Mile | Dist. KM | Difficulty | Pace (Range) | Instructions |
|---|---|---|---|---|---|
| Monday | Rest | Rest | Rest | Rest | Take it easy. Don't run. If you need to exercise, I recommend a walk for no longer than 30 minutes. |
| Tuesday | 3 | 5 | E | 14:45 - 16:45 | walk/run at an easy pace. |
| Wednesday | 3 | 5 | HM | 14:45 | walk/run at your half marathon pace. |
| Thursday | 3 | 5 | M | 14:45 - 15:45 | walk/run at a medium pace. |
| Friday | Rest | Rest | Rest | Rest | Rest. |
| Saturday | 5 | 8 | S | 14:45 - 17:15 | walk/run at a slow pace. The most important piece of your long duration runs is finishing the run. |
| Sunday | Rest/CT | Rest/CT | Rest | Rest | Rest. If your body feels good, then go ahead and do some form of cross-training for 30 to 60 minutes. |

# Training - Week 3

5K Pace: **13:32**     5k Finish Time: **42 minutes**

| Day | Dist. Mile | Dist. KM | Difficulty | Pace (Range) | Instructions |
|---|---|---|---|---|---|
| Monday | Rest | Rest | Rest | Rest | Take it easy. Don't run. If you need to exercise, I recommend a walk for no longer than 30 minutes. |
| Tuesday | 3 | 5 | E | 14:45 - 16:45 | walk/run at an easy pace. |
| Wednesday | 4 | 6 | HM | 14:45 | walk/run at your half marathon pace. |
| Thursday | 3 | 5 | M | 14:45 - 15:45 | walk/run at a medium pace. |
| Friday | Rest | Rest | Rest | Rest | Rest. |
| Saturday | 6 | 10 | S | 14:45 - 17:15 | walk/run at a slow pace. The most important piece of your long duration runs is finishing the run. |
| Sunday | Rest/CT | Rest/CT | Rest | Rest | Rest. If your body feels good, then go ahead and do some form of cross-training for 30 to 60 minutes. |

# Training - Week 4 (5K Optional)

5K Pace: **13:32**     5k Finish Time: **42 minutes**

| Day | Dist. Mile | Dist. KM | Difficulty | Pace (Range) | Instructions |
|---|---|---|---|---|---|
| Monday | Rest | Rest | Rest | Rest | Take it easy. Don't run. If you need to exercise, I recommend a walk for no longer than 30 minutes. |
| Tuesday | 3 | 5 | E | 14:45 - 16:45 | walk/run at an easy pace. |
| Wednesday | 4 | 6 | HM | 14:45 | walk/run at your half marathon pace. |
| Thursday | 3 | 5 | M | 14:45 - 15:45 | walk/run at a medium pace. |
| Friday | Rest | Rest | Rest | Rest | Rest. |
| Saturday | 6.5 | 10.5 | S | 14:45 - 17:15 | walk/run at a slow pace. The most important piece of your long duration runs is finishing the run. |
| Sunday | Rest/CT | Rest/CT | Rest | Rest | Rest. If your body feels good, then go ahead and do some form of cross-training for 30 to 60 minutes. |

## 5K Optional

| Day | Dist. Mile | Dist. KM | Difficulty | Pace (Range) | Instructions |
|---|---|---|---|---|---|
| Saturday | 3.1 | 5 | - | 13:32 | Run a 5k race instead of your long run. This is completely your choice. I recommend running a 5k race to help you get used to running races. You should see a difference in your race time if you have kept to your training schedule. Don't try for a personal best, run the 5K at your 5K pace. |

# Training - Week 5

5K Pace: **13:32**   5k Finish Time: **42 minutes**

| Day | Dist. Mile | Dist. KM | Difficulty | Pace (Range) | Instructions |
|---|---|---|---|---|---|
| Monday | Rest | Rest | Rest | Rest | Take it easy. Don't run. If you need to exercise, I recommend a walk for no longer than 30 minutes. |
| Tuesday | 3 | 5 | E | 14:45 - 16:45 | walk/run at an easy pace. |
| Wednesday | 4 | 6 | HM | 14:45 | walk/run at your half marathon pace. |
| Thursday | 3 | 5 | M | 14:45 - 15:45 | walk/run at a medium pace. |
| Friday | Rest | Rest | Rest | Rest | Rest. |
| Saturday | 7 | 11 | S | 14:45 - 17:15 | walk/run at a slow pace. The most important piece of your long duration runs is finishing the run. |
| Sunday | Rest/CT | Rest/CT | Rest | Rest | Rest. If your body feels good, then go ahead and do some form of cross-training for 30 to 60 minutes. |

## NOTE:

- Your long duration runs will begin to become more difficult for week 5 and beyond.
- If you get tired during a long duration run, walk for 1/10 mile or 3-5 minutes.

# Training - Week 6

5K Pace: **13:32**     5k Finish Time: **42 minutes**

| Day | Dist. Mile | Dist. KM | Difficulty | Pace (Range) | Instructions |
|---|---|---|---|---|---|
| Monday | Rest | Rest | Rest | Rest | Take it easy. Don't run. If you need to exercise, I recommend a walk for no longer than 30 minutes. |
| Tuesday | 3 | 5 | E | 14:45 - 16:45 | walk/run at an easy pace. |
| Wednesday | 4 | 6 | HM | 14:45 | walk/run at your half marathon pace. |
| Thursday | 3 | 5 | M | 14:45 - 15:45 | walk/run at a medium pace. |
| Friday | Rest | Rest | Rest | Rest | Rest. |
| Saturday | 8 | 13 | S | 14:45 - 17:15 | walk/run at a slow pace. The most important piece of your long duration runs is finishing the run. |
| Sunday | Rest/CT | Rest/CT | Rest | Rest | Rest. If your body feels good, then go ahead and do some form of cross-training for 30 to 60 minutes. |

# Training - Week 7

5K Pace: **13:32**     5k Finish Time: **42 minutes**

| Day | Dist. Mile | Dist. KM | Difficulty | Pace (Range) | Instructions |
|---|---|---|---|---|---|
| Monday | Rest | Rest | Rest | Rest | Take it easy. Don't run. If you need to exercise, I recommend a walk for no longer than 30 minutes. |
| Tuesday | 3 | 5 | E | 14:45 - 16:45 | walk/run at an easy pace. |
| Wednesday | 5 | 8 | HM | 14:45 | walk/run at your half marathon pace. |
| Thursday | 3 | 5 | M | 14:45 - 15:45 | walk/run at a medium pace. |
| Friday | Rest | Rest | Rest | Rest | Rest. |
| Saturday | 8.5 | 13.5 | S | 14:45 - 17:15 | walk/run at a slow pace. The most important piece of your long duration runs is finishing the run. |
| Sunday | Rest/CT | Rest/CT | Rest | Rest | Rest. If your body feels good, then go ahead and do some form of cross-training for 30 to 60 minutes. |

## 10K Optional

| Day | Dist. Mile | Dist. KM | Difficulty | Pace (Range) | Instructions |
|---|---|---|---|---|---|
| Thursday | 2 | 3 | E | 14:45 - 16:45 | If you run the optional 10K, either completely rest today or run 2 miles (3 km). |
| Saturday | 6.2 | 10K | - | 13:32 | Run a 10k race instead of your long run. This is completely your choice. I recommend running a 10k race to help you get used to running races. You should see a difference in your race time if you have kept to your training schedule. Don't try for a personal best, run the 10K at your 5K pace. |

# Training - Week 8

5K Pace: **13:32**     5k Finish Time: **42 minutes**

| Day | Dist. Mile | Dist. KM | Difficulty | Pace (Range) | Instructions |
|---|---|---|---|---|---|
| Monday | Rest | Rest | Rest | Rest | Take it easy. Don't run. If you need to exercise, I recommend a walk for no longer than 30 minutes. |
| Tuesday | 3 | 5 | E | 14:45 - 16:45 | walk/run at an easy pace. |
| Wednesday | 5 | 8 | HM | 14:45 | walk/run at your half marathon pace. |
| Thursday | 3 | 5 | M | 14:45 - 15:45 | walk/run at a medium pace. |
| Friday | Rest | Rest | Rest | Rest | Rest. |
| Saturday | 9 | 14 | S | 14:45 - 17:15 | walk/run at a slow pace. The most important piece of your long duration runs is finishing the run. |
| Sunday | Rest/CT | Rest/CT | Rest | Rest | Rest. If your body feels good, then go ahead and do some form of cross-training for 30 to 60 minutes. |

# Training - Week 9

5K Pace: **13:32**     5k Finish Time: **42 minutes**

| Day | Dist. Mile | Dist. KM | Difficulty | Pace (Range) | Instructions |
|---|---|---|---|---|---|
| Monday | Rest | Rest | Rest | Rest | Take it easy. Don't run. If you need to exercise, I recommend a walk for no longer than 30 minutes. |
| Tuesday | 3 | 5 | E | 14:45 - 16:45 | walk/run at an easy pace. |
| Wednesday | 5 | 8 | HM | 14:45 | walk/run at your half marathon pace. |
| Thursday | 3 | 5 | M | 14:45 - 15:45 | walk/run at a medium pace. |
| Friday | Rest | Rest | Rest | Rest | Rest. |
| Saturday | 8.5 | 13.5 | S | 14:45 - 17:15 | walk/run at a slow pace. The most important piece of your long duration runs is finishing the run. |
| Sunday | Rest/CT | Rest/CT | Rest | Rest | Rest. If your body feels good, then go ahead and do some form of cross-training for 30 to 60 minutes. |

## 13.1 Beta/Test Run Optional

| Day | Dist. Mile | Dist. KM | Difficulty | Pace (Range) | Instructions |
|---|---|---|---|---|---|
| Thursday | Rest | Rest | Rest | Rest | This is a rest day – it simulates race week |
| Friday | Rest | Rest | Rest | Rest | This is a rest day – it simulates race week |
| Saturday | 13.1 | 21 | S | 13:32 | I recommend that you attempt to go the full 13.1 miles (21 km) for a half marathon test run. Only walk/run the first 10 miles (16 km) then walk the last 3.1 miles (5 km). If you are successful, you will have a race ghost time to compete against. It will help energize and refocus your training on beating yourself in 3 weeks at the half marathon race. Also, it allows your mind to grasp the achievement of "completing the distance of a half marathon." |

# Training - Week 10

5K Pace: **13:32**     5k Finish Time: **42 minutes**

| Day | Dist. Mile | Dist. KM | Difficulty | Pace (Range) | Instructions |
|---|---|---|---|---|---|
| Monday | Rest | Rest | Rest | Rest | Take it easy. Don't run. If you need to exercise, I recommend a walk for no longer than 30 minutes. |
| Tuesday | 3 | 5 | E | 14:45 - 16:45 | walk/run at an easy pace. |
| Wednesday | 5 | 8 | HM | 14:45 | walk/run at your half marathon pace. |
| Thursday | 3 | 5 | M | 14:45 - 15:45 | walk/run at a medium pace. |
| Friday | Rest | Rest | Rest | Rest | Rest. |
| Saturday | 11 | 18 | S | 14:45 - 17:15 | walk/run at a slow pace. The most important piece of your long duration runs is finishing the run. |
| Sunday | Rest/CT | Rest/CT | Rest | Rest | Rest. If your body feels good, then go ahead and do some form of cross-training for 30 to 60 minutes. |

# Training - Week 11

| Day | Dist. Mile | Dist. KM | Difficulty | Pace (Range) | Instructions |
|---|---|---|---|---|---|
| Monday | Rest | Rest | Rest | Rest | Take it easy. Don't run. If you need to exercise, I recommend a walk for no longer than 30 minutes. |
| Tuesday | 3 | 5 | E | 14:45 - 16:45 | walk/run at an easy pace. |
| Wednesday | 5 | 8 | HM | 14:45 | walk/run at your half marathon pace. |
| Thursday | 3 | 5 | M | 14:45 - 15:45 | walk/run at a medium pace. |
| Friday | Rest | Rest | Rest | Rest | Rest. |
| Saturday | 12 | 20 | S | 14:45 - 17:15 | walk/run at a slow pace. The most important piece of your long duration runs is finishing the run. |
| Sunday | Rest/CT | Rest/CT | Rest | Rest | Rest. If your body feels good, then go ahead and do some form of cross-training for 30 to 60 minutes. |

# Training - Week 12

5K Pace: **13:32**     5k Finish Time: **42 minutes**

| Day | Dist. Mile | Dist. KM | Difficulty | Pace (Range) | Instructions |
|---|---|---|---|---|---|
| Monday | Rest | Rest | Rest | Rest | Take it easy. Don't run. If you need to exercise, I recommend a walk for no longer than 30 minutes. |
| Tuesday | 3 | 5 | E | 14:45 - 16:45 | walk/run at an easy pace. |
| Wednesday | 2 | 1.5 | HM | 14:45 | walk/run at your half marathon pace. |
| Thursday | Rest | Rest | Rest | Rest | Rest. |
| Friday | Rest | Rest | Rest | Rest | Rest. |
| Saturday | 13.1 | 21 | HM | 14:45 | RACE DAY! |
| Sunday | Rest | Rest | Rest | Rest | DRINK A VICTORY BEER! |

## NOTE:

- Get plenty of sleep the night before your long duration run.
- Try to run your long duration run early in the morning.
- After each run, it's important to stretch out your muscles.
- This week your body needs as much rest as possible.
- Don't run past Wednesday.

Half Marathon Training Schedule for

runners with a 5K finish time of 43 minutes

and a pace of *13:52* minutes/mile.

# Predicted Half Marathon Finish Time:

## *3* hour(s)  *18* minutes

# PACING TABLES

| Pace | Pace (minutes/miles) |
|---:|---|
| 5k | 13:52 |
| Half marathon | 15:05 |
| Medium | Between 15:05 - 16:05 |
| Easy | Between 15:05 - 17:05 |
| Slow | Between 15:05 - 15:35 |

| Race | Finish Times (predicted) |
|---:|---|
| 5k | 43 minutes |
| Half marathon | 3 hour(s) 18 minutes |

| Determining your pace | |
|---|---|
| Slow Pace | Extremely easy to hold a conversation. |
| Easy Pace | You can hold a conversation with someone. Your breathing might break up some of the flow of the conversation. |
| Medium | You can hold a conversation with someone, but it's broken up into smaller sentences and smaller responses. |
| Half Marathon Pace | Conversation is difficult. One and two word responses back and forth at best. |

## Definitions in the table below:

CT = Cross Training

S = Slow Pace (long run pace)

E = Easy Pace

M = Medium Pace

HM = Half Marathon Pace

## Training - Week A (Optional)

5K Pace: **13:52**    5k Finish Time: **43 minutes**

| Day | Dist. Mile | Dist. KM | Difficulty | Pace (Range) | Instructions |
|---|---|---|---|---|---|
| Monday | Rest | Rest | Rest | Rest | Take it easy. Don't run. If you need to exercise, I recommend a walk for no longer than 30 minutes. |
| Tuesday | 1 | 1.5 | E | 15:05 - 17:05 | walk/run at an easy pace. |
| Wednesday | 1 | 1.5 | HM | 15:05 | walk/run at your half marathon pace. |
| Thursday | 1 | 1.5 | M | 15:05 - 16:05 | walk/run at a medium pace. |
| Friday | Rest | Rest | Rest | Rest | Rest. |
| Saturday | 1.5 | 2.5 | S | 15:05 - 15:35 | walk/run at a slow pace. The most important piece of your long duration runs is finishing the run. |
| Sunday | Rest/CT | Rest/CT | Rest | Rest | Rest. If your body feels good, then go ahead and do some form of cross-training for 30 to 60 minutes. |

## Training - Week B (Optional)

| Day | Dist. Mile | Dist. KM | Difficulty | Pace (Range) | Instructions |
|---|---|---|---|---|---|
| Monday | Rest | Rest | Rest | Rest | Take it easy. Don't run. If you need to exercise, I recommend a walk for no longer than 30 minutes. |
| Tuesday | 1.5 | 2.5 | E | 15:05 - 17:05 | walk/run at an easy pace. |
| Wednesday | 1.5 | 2.5 | HM | 15:05 | walk/run at your half marathon pace. |
| Thursday | 1.5 | 2.5 | M | 15:05 - 16:05 | walk/run at a medium pace. |
| Friday | Rest | Rest | Rest | Rest | Rest. |
| Saturday | 2 | 3 | S | 15:05 - 15:35 | walk/run at a slow pace. The most important piece of your long duration runs is finishing the run. |
| Sunday | Rest/CT | Rest/CT | Rest | Rest | Rest. If your body feels good, then go ahead and do some form of cross-training for 30 to 60 minutes. |

# Training - Week C (Optional)

5K Pace: **13:52**     5k Finish Time: **43 minutes**

| Day | Dist. Mile | Dist. KM | Difficulty | Pace (Range) | Instructions |
|---|---|---|---|---|---|
| Monday | Rest | Rest | Rest | Rest | Take it easy. Don't run. If you need to exercise, I recommend a walk for no longer than 30 minutes. |
| Tuesday | 2 | 3 | E | 15:05 - 17:05 | walk/run at an easy pace. |
| Wednesday | 2 | 3 | HM | 15:05 | walk/run at your half marathon pace. |
| Thursday | 2 | 3 | M | 15:05 - 16:05 | walk/run at a medium pace. |
| Friday | Rest | Rest | Rest | Rest | Rest. |
| Saturday | 3 | 5 | S | 15:05 - 15:35 | walk/run at a slow pace. The most important piece of your long duration runs is finishing the run. |
| Sunday | Rest/CT | Rest/CT | Rest | Rest | Rest. If your body feels good, then go ahead and do some form of cross-training for 30 to 60 minutes. |

# Training - Week 1

5K Pace: **13:52**   5k Finish Time: **43 minutes**

| Day | Dist. Mile | Dist. KM | Difficulty | Pace (Range) | Instructions |
|---|---|---|---|---|---|
| Monday | Rest | Rest | Rest | Rest | Take it easy. Don't run. If you need to exercise, I recommend a walk for no longer than 30 minutes. |
| Tuesday | 3 | 5 | E | 15:05 - 17:05 | walk/run at an easy pace. |
| Wednesday | 3 | 5 | HM | 15:05 | walk/run at your half marathon pace. |
| Thursday | 3 | 5 | M | 15:05 - 16:05 | walk/run at a medium pace. |
| Friday | Rest | Rest | Rest | Rest | Rest. |
| Saturday | 4 | 6 | S | 15:05 - 15:35 | walk/run at a slow pace. The most important piece of your long duration runs is finishing the run. |
| Sunday | Rest/CT | Rest/CT | Rest | Rest | Rest. If your body feels good, then go ahead and do some form of cross-training for 30 to 60 minutes. |

# Training - Week 2

| Day | Dist. Mile | Dist. KM | Difficulty | Pace (Range) | Instructions |
|---|---|---|---|---|---|
| Monday | Rest | Rest | Rest | Rest | Take it easy. Don't run. If you need to exercise, I recommend a walk for no longer than 30 minutes. |
| Tuesday | 3 | 5 | E | 15:05 - 17:05 | walk/run at an easy pace. |
| Wednesday | 3 | 5 | HM | 15:05 | walk/run at your half marathon pace. |
| Thursday | 3 | 5 | M | 15:05 - 16:05 | walk/run at a medium pace. |
| Friday | Rest | Rest | Rest | Rest | Rest. |
| Saturday | 5 | 8 | S | 15:05 - 15:35 | walk/run at a slow pace. The most important piece of your long duration runs is finishing the run. |
| Sunday | Rest/CT | Rest/CT | Rest | Rest | Rest. If your body feels good, then go ahead and do some form of cross-training for 30 to 60 minutes. |

# Training - Week 3

5K Pace: **13:52**     5k Finish Time: **43 minutes**

| Day | Dist. Mile | Dist. KM | Difficulty | Pace (Range) | Instructions |
|---|---|---|---|---|---|
| Monday | Rest | Rest | Rest | Rest | Take it easy. Don't run. If you need to exercise, I recommend a walk for no longer than 30 minutes. |
| Tuesday | 3 | 5 | E | 15:05 - 17:05 | walk/run at an easy pace. |
| Wednesday | 4 | 6 | HM | 15:05 | walk/run at your half marathon pace. |
| Thursday | 3 | 5 | M | 15:05 - 16:05 | walk/run at a medium pace. |
| Friday | Rest | Rest | Rest | Rest | Rest. |
| Saturday | 6 | 10 | S | 15:05 - 15:35 | walk/run at a slow pace. The most important piece of your long duration runs is finishing the run. |
| Sunday | Rest/CT | Rest/CT | Rest | Rest | Rest. If your body feels good, then go ahead and do some form of cross-training for 30 to 60 minutes. |

# Training - Week 4 (5K Optional)

5K Pace: **13:52**     5k Finish Time: **43 minutes**

| Day | Dist. Mile | Dist. KM | Difficulty | Pace (Range) | Instructions |
|---|---|---|---|---|---|
| Monday | Rest | Rest | Rest | Rest | Take it easy. Don't run. If you need to exercise, I recommend a walk for no longer than 30 minutes. |
| Tuesday | 3 | 5 | E | 15:05 - 17:05 | walk/run at an easy pace. |
| Wednesday | 4 | 6 | HM | 15:05 | walk/run at your half marathon pace. |
| Thursday | 3 | 5 | M | 15:05 - 16:05 | walk/run at a medium pace. |
| Friday | Rest | Rest | Rest | Rest | Rest. |
| Saturday | 6.5 | 10.5 | S | 15:05 - 15:35 | walk/run at a slow pace. The most important piece of your long duration runs is finishing the run. |
| Sunday | Rest/CT | Rest/CT | Rest | Rest | Rest. If your body feels good, then go ahead and do some form of cross-training for 30 to 60 minutes. |

## 5K Optional

| Day | Dist. Mile | Dist. KM | Difficulty | Pace (Range) | Instructions |
|---|---|---|---|---|---|
| Saturday | 3.1 | 5 | - | 13:52 | Run a 5k race instead of your long run. This is completely your choice. I recommend running a 5k race to help you get used to running races. You should see a difference in your race time if you have kept to your training schedule. Don't try for a personal best, run the 5K at your 5K pace. |

# Training - Week 5

5K Pace: **13:52**     5k Finish Time: **43 minutes**

| Day | Dist. Mile | Dist. KM | Difficulty | Pace (Range) | Instructions |
|---|---|---|---|---|---|
| Monday | Rest | Rest | Rest | Rest | Take it easy. Don't run. If you need to exercise, I recommend a walk for no longer than 30 minutes. |
| Tuesday | 3 | 5 | E | 15:05 - 17:05 | walk/run at an easy pace. |
| Wednesday | 4 | 6 | HM | 15:05 | walk/run at your half marathon pace. |
| Thursday | 3 | 5 | M | 15:05 - 16:05 | walk/run at a medium pace. |
| Friday | Rest | Rest | Rest | Rest | Rest. |
| Saturday | 7 | 11 | S | 15:05 - 15:35 | walk/run at a slow pace. The most important piece of your long duration runs is finishing the run. |
| Sunday | Rest/CT | Rest/CT | Rest | Rest | Rest. If your body feels good, then go ahead and do some form of cross-training for 30 to 60 minutes. |

## NOTE:

- Your long duration runs will begin to become more difficult for week 5 and beyond.
- If you get tired during a long duration run, walk for 1/10 mile or 3-5 minutes.

# Training - Week 6

5K Pace: **13:52**      5k Finish Time: **43 minutes**

| Day | Dist. Mile | Dist. KM | Difficulty | Pace (Range) | Instructions |
|---|---|---|---|---|---|
| Monday | Rest | Rest | Rest | Rest | Take it easy. Don't run. If you need to exercise, I recommend a walk for no longer than 30 minutes. |
| Tuesday | 3 | 5 | E | 15:05 - 17:05 | walk/run at an easy pace. |
| Wednesday | 4 | 6 | HM | 15:05 | walk/run at your half marathon pace. |
| Thursday | 3 | 5 | M | 15:05 - 16:05 | walk/run at a medium pace. |
| Friday | Rest | Rest | Rest | Rest | Rest. |
| Saturday | 8 | 13 | S | 15:05 - 15:35 | walk/run at a slow pace. The most important piece of your long duration runs is finishing the run. |
| Sunday | Rest/CT | Rest/CT | Rest | Rest | Rest. If your body feels good, then go ahead and do some form of cross-training for 30 to 60 minutes. |

# Training - Week 7

5K Pace: **13:52**     5k Finish Time: **43 minutes**

| Day | Dist. Mile | Dist. KM | Difficulty | Pace (Range) | Instructions |
|---|---|---|---|---|---|
| Monday | Rest | Rest | Rest | Rest | Take it easy. Don't run. If you need to exercise, I recommend a walk for no longer than 30 minutes. |
| Tuesday | 3 | 5 | E | 15:05 - 17:05 | walk/run at an easy pace. |
| Wednesday | 5 | 8 | HM | 15:05 | walk/run at your half marathon pace. |
| Thursday | 3 | 5 | M | 15:05 - 16:05 | walk/run at a medium pace. |
| Friday | Rest | Rest | Rest | Rest | Rest. |
| Saturday | 8.5 | 13.5 | S | 15:05 - 15:35 | walk/run at a slow pace. The most important piece of your long duration runs is finishing the run. |
| Sunday | Rest/CT | Rest/CT | Rest | Rest | Rest. If your body feels good, then go ahead and do some form of cross-training for 30 to 60 minutes. |

## 10K Optional

| Day | Dist. Mile | Dist. KM | Difficulty | Pace (Range) | Instructions |
|---|---|---|---|---|---|
| Thursday | 2 | 3 | E | 15:05 - 17:05 | If you run the optional 10K, either completely rest today or run 2 miles (3 km). |
| Saturday | 6.2 | 10K | - | 13:52 | Run a 10k race instead of your long run. This is completely your choice. I recommend running a 10k race to help you get used to running races. You should see a difference in your race time if you have kept to your training schedule. Don't try for a personal best, run the 10K at your 5K pace. |

# Training - Week 8

5K Pace: **13:52**     5k Finish Time: **43 minutes**

| Day | Dist. Mile | Dist. KM | Difficulty | Pace (Range) | Instructions |
|---|---|---|---|---|---|
| Monday | Rest | Rest | Rest | Rest | Take it easy. Don't run. If you need to exercise, I recommend a walk for no longer than 30 minutes. |
| Tuesday | 3 | 5 | E | 15:05 - 17:05 | walk/run at an easy pace. |
| Wednesday | 5 | 8 | HM | 15:05 | walk/run at your half marathon pace. |
| Thursday | 3 | 5 | M | 15:05 - 16:05 | walk/run at a medium pace. |
| Friday | Rest | Rest | Rest | Rest | Rest. |
| Saturday | 9 | 14 | S | 15:05 - 15:35 | walk/run at a slow pace. The most important piece of your long duration runs is finishing the run. |
| Sunday | Rest/CT | Rest/CT | Rest | Rest | Rest. If your body feels good, then go ahead and do some form of cross-training for 30 to 60 minutes. |

# Training - Week 9

**5K Pace: 13:52**     **5k Finish Time: 43 minutes**

| Day | Dist. Mile | Dist. KM | Difficulty | Pace (Range) | Instructions |
|---|---|---|---|---|---|
| Monday | Rest | Rest | Rest | Rest | Take it easy. Don't run. If you need to exercise, I recommend a walk for no longer than 30 minutes. |
| Tuesday | 3 | 5 | E | 15:05 - 17:05 | walk/run at an easy pace. |
| Wednesday | 5 | 8 | HM | 15:05 | walk/run at your half marathon pace. |
| Thursday | 3 | 5 | M | 15:05 - 16:05 | walk/run at a medium pace. |
| Friday | Rest | Rest | Rest | Rest | Rest. |
| Saturday | 8.5 | 13.5 | S | 15:05 - 15:35 | walk/run at a slow pace. The most important piece of your long duration runs is finishing the run. |
| Sunday | Rest/CT | Rest/CT | Rest | Rest | Rest. If your body feels good, then go ahead and do some form of cross-training for 30 to 60 minutes. |

## 13.1 Beta/Test Run Optional

| Day | Dist. Mile | Dist. KM | Difficulty | Pace (Range) | Instructions |
|---|---|---|---|---|---|
| Thursday | Rest | Rest | Rest | Rest | This is a rest day – it simulates race week |
| Friday | Rest | Rest | Rest | Rest | This is a rest day – it simulates race week |
| Saturday | 13.1 | 21 | S | 13:52 | I recommend that you attempt to go the full 13.1 miles (21 km) for a half marathon test run. <u>Only walk/run the first 10 miles (16 km) then walk the last 3.1 miles (5 km)</u>. If you are successful, you will have a race ghost time to compete against. It will help energize and refocus your training on beating yourself in 3 weeks at the half marathon race. Also, it allows your mind to grasp the achievement of "completing the distance of a half marathon." |

# Training - Week 10

5K Pace: **13:52**    5k Finish Time: **43 minutes**

| Day | Dist. Mile | Dist. KM | Difficulty | Pace (Range) | Instructions |
|---|---|---|---|---|---|
| Monday | Rest | Rest | Rest | Rest | Take it easy. Don't run. If you need to exercise, I recommend a walk for no longer than 30 minutes. |
| Tuesday | 3 | 5 | E | 15:05 - 17:05 | walk/run at an easy pace. |
| Wednesday | 5 | 8 | HM | 15:05 | walk/run at your half marathon pace. |
| Thursday | 3 | 5 | M | 15:05 - 16:05 | walk/run at a medium pace. |
| Friday | Rest | Rest | Rest | Rest | Rest. |
| Saturday | 11 | 18 | S | 15:05 - 15:35 | walk/run at a slow pace. The most important piece of your long duration runs is finishing the run. |
| Sunday | Rest/CT | Rest/CT | Rest | Rest | Rest. If your body feels good, then go ahead and do some form of cross-training for 30 to 60 minutes. |

# Training - Week 11

| Day | Dist. Mile | Dist. KM | Difficulty | Pace (Range) | Instructions |
|---|---|---|---|---|---|
| Monday | Rest | Rest | Rest | Rest | Take it easy. Don't run. If you need to exercise, I recommend a walk for no longer than 30 minutes. |
| Tuesday | 3 | 5 | E | 15:05 - 17:05 | walk/run at an easy pace. |
| Wednesday | 5 | 8 | HM | 15:05 | walk/run at your half marathon pace. |
| Thursday | 3 | 5 | M | 15:05 - 16:05 | walk/run at a medium pace. |
| Friday | Rest | Rest | Rest | Rest | Rest. |
| Saturday | 12 | 20 | S | 15:05 - 15:35 | walk/run at a slow pace. The most important piece of your long duration runs is finishing the run. |
| Sunday | Rest/CT | Rest/CT | Rest | Rest | Rest. If your body feels good, then go ahead and do some form of cross-training for 30 to 60 minutes. |

# Training - Week 12

5K Pace: **13:52**     5k Finish Time: **43 minutes**

| Day | Dist. Mile | Dist. KM | Difficulty | Pace (Range) | Instructions |
|---|---|---|---|---|---|
| Monday | Rest | Rest | Rest | Rest | Take it easy. Don't run. If you need to exercise, I recommend a walk for no longer than 30 minutes. |
| Tuesday | 3 | 5 | E | 15:05 - 17:05 | walk/run at an easy pace. |
| Wednesday | 2 | 1.5 | HM | 15:05 | walk/run at your half marathon pace. |
| Thursday | Rest | Rest | Rest | Rest | Rest. |
| Friday | Rest | Rest | Rest | Rest | Rest. |
| Saturday | 13.1 | 21 | HM | 15:05 | RACE DAY! |
| Sunday | Rest | Rest | Rest | Rest | DRINK A VICTORY BEER! |

## NOTE:

- Get plenty of sleep the night before your long duration run.
- Try to run your long duration run early in the morning.
- After each run, it's important to stretch out your muscles.
- This week your body needs as much rest as possible.
- Don't run past Wednesday.

## BEGINNER TO FINISHER RUNNING

Half Marathon Training Schedule for

runners with a 5K finish time of 44 minutes

and a pace of *14:11* minutes/mile.

# Predicted Half Marathon Finish Time:

# *3* hour(s) *23* minutes

# PACING TABLES

| Pace | Pace (minutes/miles) |
|---:|---|
| 5k | 14:11 |
| Half marathon | 15:30 |
| Medium | Between 15:30 - 16:30 |
| Easy | Between 15:30 - 17:30 |
| Slow | Between 15:30 - 18:00 |

| Race | Finish Times (predicted) |
|---:|---|
| 5k | 44 minutes |
| Half marathon | 3 hour(s) 23 minutes |

| | Determining your pace |
|---|---|
| Slow Pace | Extremely easy to hold a conversation. |
| Easy Pace | You can hold a conversation with someone. Your breathing might break up some of the flow of the conversation. |
| Medium | You can hold a conversation with someone, but it's broken up into smaller sentences and smaller responses. |
| Half Marathon Pace | Conversation is difficult. One and two word responses back and forth at best. |

## Definitions in the table below:

CT = Cross Training

S = Slow Pace (long run pace)

E = Easy Pace

M = Medium Pace

HM = Half Marathon Pace

## Training - Week A (Optional)

5K Pace: **14:11**     5k Finish Time: **44 minutes**

| Day | Dist. Mile | Dist. KM | Difficulty | Pace (Range) | Instructions |
|---|---|---|---|---|---|
| Monday | Rest | Rest | Rest | Rest | Take it easy. Don't run. If you need to exercise, I recommend a walk for no longer than 30 minutes. |
| Tuesday | 1 | 1.5 | E | 15:30 - 17:30 | walk/run at an easy pace. |
| Wednesday | 1 | 1.5 | HM | 15:30 | walk/run at your half marathon pace. |
| Thursday | 1 | 1.5 | M | 15:30 - 16:30 | walk/run at a medium pace. |
| Friday | Rest | Rest | Rest | Rest | Rest. |
| Saturday | 1.5 | 2.5 | S | 15:30 - 18:00 | walk/run at a slow pace. The most important piece of your long duration runs is finishing the run. |
| Sunday | Rest/CT | Rest/CT | Rest | Rest | Rest. If your body feels good, then go ahead and do some form of cross-training for 30 to 60 minutes. |

## Training - Week B (Optional)

| Day | Dist. Mile | Dist. KM | Difficulty | Pace (Range) | Instructions |
|---|---|---|---|---|---|
| Monday | Rest | Rest | Rest | Rest | Take it easy. Don't run. If you need to exercise, I recommend a walk for no longer than 30 minutes. |
| Tuesday | 1.5 | 2.5 | E | 15:30 - 17:30 | walk/run at an easy pace. |
| Wednesday | 1.5 | 2.5 | HM | 15:30 | walk/run at your half marathon pace. |
| Thursday | 1.5 | 2.5 | M | 15:30 - 16:30 | walk/run at a medium pace. |
| Friday | Rest | Rest | Rest | Rest | Rest. |
| Saturday | 2 | 3 | S | 15:30 - 18:00 | walk/run at a slow pace. The most important piece of your long duration runs is finishing the run. |
| Sunday | Rest/CT | Rest/CT | Rest | Rest | Rest. If your body feels good, then go ahead and do some form of cross-training for 30 to 60 minutes. |

# Training - Week C (Optional)

5K Pace: **14:11**  5k Finish Time: **44 minutes**

| Day | Dist. Mile | Dist. KM | Difficulty | Pace (Range) | Instructions |
|---|---|---|---|---|---|
| Monday | Rest | Rest | Rest | Rest | Take it easy. Don't run. If you need to exercise, I recommend a walk for no longer than 30 minutes. |
| Tuesday | 2 | 3 | E | 15:30 - 17:30 | walk/run at an easy pace. |
| Wednesday | 2 | 3 | HM | 15:30 | walk/run at your half marathon pace. |
| Thursday | 2 | 3 | M | 15:30 - 16:30 | walk/run at a medium pace. |
| Friday | Rest | Rest | Rest | Rest | Rest. |
| Saturday | 3 | 5 | S | 15:30 - 18:00 | walk/run at a slow pace. The most important piece of your long duration runs is finishing the run. |
| Sunday | Rest/CT | Rest/CT | Rest | Rest | Rest. If your body feels good, then go ahead and do some form of cross-training for 30 to 60 minutes. |

# Training - Week 1

5K Pace: **14:11**     5k Finish Time: **44 minutes**

| Day | Dist. Mile | Dist. KM | Difficulty | Pace (Range) | Instructions |
|---|---|---|---|---|---|
| Monday | Rest | Rest | Rest | Rest | Take it easy. Don't run. If you need to exercise, I recommend a walk for no longer than 30 minutes. |
| Tuesday | 3 | 5 | E | 15:30 - 17:30 | walk/run at an easy pace. |
| Wednesday | 3 | 5 | HM | 15:30 | walk/run at your half marathon pace. |
| Thursday | 3 | 5 | M | 15:30 - 16:30 | walk/run at a medium pace. |
| Friday | Rest | Rest | Rest | Rest | Rest. |
| Saturday | 4 | 6 | S | 15:30 - 18:00 | walk/run at a slow pace. The most important piece of your long duration runs is finishing the run. |
| Sunday | Rest/CT | Rest/CT | Rest | Rest | Rest. If your body feels good, then go ahead and do some form of cross-training for 30 to 60 minutes. |

# Training - Week 2

| Day | Dist. Mile | Dist. KM | Difficulty | Pace (Range) | Instructions |
|---|---|---|---|---|---|
| Monday | Rest | Rest | Rest | Rest | Take it easy. Don't run. If you need to exercise, I recommend a walk for no longer than 30 minutes. |
| Tuesday | 3 | 5 | E | 15:30 - 17:30 | walk/run at an easy pace. |
| Wednesday | 3 | 5 | HM | 15:30 | walk/run at your half marathon pace. |
| Thursday | 3 | 5 | M | 15:30 - 16:30 | walk/run at a medium pace. |
| Friday | Rest | Rest | Rest | Rest | Rest. |
| Saturday | 5 | 8 | S | 15:30 - 18:00 | walk/run at a slow pace. The most important piece of your long duration runs is finishing the run. |
| Sunday | Rest/CT | Rest/CT | Rest | Rest | Rest. If your body feels good, then go ahead and do some form of cross-training for 30 to 60 minutes. |

# Training - Week 3

5K Pace: **14:11**     5k Finish Time: **44 minutes**

| Day | Dist. Mile | Dist. KM | Difficulty | Pace (Range) | Instructions |
|---|---|---|---|---|---|
| Monday | Rest | Rest | Rest | Rest | Take it easy. Don't run. If you need to exercise, I recommend a walk for no longer than 30 minutes. |
| Tuesday | 3 | 5 | E | 15:30 - 17:30 | walk/run at an easy pace. |
| Wednesday | 4 | 6 | HM | 15:30 | walk/run at your half marathon pace. |
| Thursday | 3 | 5 | M | 15:30 - 16:30 | walk/run at a medium pace. |
| Friday | Rest | Rest | Rest | Rest | Rest. |
| Saturday | 6 | 10 | S | 15:30 - 18:00 | walk/run at a slow pace. The most important piece of your long duration runs is finishing the run. |
| Sunday | Rest/CT | Rest/CT | Rest | Rest | Rest. If your body feels good, then go ahead and do some form of cross-training for 30 to 60 minutes. |

# Training - Week 4 (5K Optional)

5K Pace: **14:11**     5k Finish Time: **44 minutes**

| Day | Dist. Mile | Dist. KM | Difficulty | Pace (Range) | Instructions |
|---|---|---|---|---|---|
| Monday | Rest | Rest | Rest | Rest | Take it easy. Don't run. If you need to exercise, I recommend a walk for no longer than 30 minutes. |
| Tuesday | 3 | 5 | E | 15:30 - 17:30 | walk/run at an easy pace. |
| Wednesday | 4 | 6 | HM | 15:30 | walk/run at your half marathon pace. |
| Thursday | 3 | 5 | M | 15:30 - 16:30 | walk/run at a medium pace. |
| Friday | Rest | Rest | Rest | Rest | Rest. |
| Saturday | 6.5 | 10.5 | S | 15:30 - 18:00 | walk/run at a slow pace. The most important piece of your long duration runs is finishing the run. |
| Sunday | Rest/CT | Rest/CT | Rest | Rest | Rest. If your body feels good, then go ahead and do some form of cross-training for 30 to 60 minutes. |

## 5K Optional

| Day | Dist. Mile | Dist. KM | Difficulty | Pace (Range) | Instructions |
|---|---|---|---|---|---|
| Saturday | 3.1 | 5 | - | 14:11 | Run a 5k race instead of your long run. This is completely your choice. I recommend running a 5k race to help you get used to running races. You should see a difference in your race time if you have kept to your training schedule. Don't try for a personal best, run the 5K at your 5K pace. |

# Training - Week 5

5K Pace: **14:11**     5k Finish Time: **44 minutes**

| Day | Dist. Mile | Dist. KM | Difficulty | Pace (Range) | Instructions |
|---|---|---|---|---|---|
| Monday | Rest | Rest | Rest | Rest | Take it easy. Don't run. If you need to exercise, I recommend a walk for no longer than 30 minutes. |
| Tuesday | 3 | 5 | E | 15:30 - 17:30 | walk/run at an easy pace. |
| Wednesday | 4 | 6 | HM | 15:30 | walk/run at your half marathon pace. |
| Thursday | 3 | 5 | M | 15:30 - 16:30 | walk/run at a medium pace. |
| Friday | Rest | Rest | Rest | Rest | Rest. |
| Saturday | 7 | 11 | S | 15:30 - 18:00 | walk/run at a slow pace. The most important piece of your long duration runs is finishing the run. |
| Sunday | Rest/CT | Rest/CT | Rest | Rest | Rest. If your body feels good, then go ahead and do some form of cross-training for 30 to 60 minutes. |

## NOTE:

- Your long duration runs will begin to become more difficult for week 5 and beyond.
- If you get tired during a long duration run, walk for 1/10 mile or 3-5 minutes.

# Training - Week 6

5K Pace: **14:11**     5k Finish Time: **44 minutes**

| Day | Dist. Mile | Dist. KM | Difficulty | Pace (Range) | Instructions |
|---|---|---|---|---|---|
| Monday | Rest | Rest | Rest | Rest | Take it easy. Don't run. If you need to exercise, I recommend a walk for no longer than 30 minutes. |
| Tuesday | 3 | 5 | E | 15:30 - 17:30 | walk/run at an easy pace. |
| Wednesday | 4 | 6 | HM | 15:30 | walk/run at your half marathon pace. |
| Thursday | 3 | 5 | M | 15:30 - 16:30 | walk/run at a medium pace. |
| Friday | Rest | Rest | Rest | Rest | Rest. |
| Saturday | 8 | 13 | S | 15:30 - 18:00 | walk/run at a slow pace. The most important piece of your long duration runs is finishing the run. |
| Sunday | Rest/CT | Rest/CT | Rest | Rest | Rest. If your body feels good, then go ahead and do some form of cross-training for 30 to 60 minutes. |

# Training - Week 7

5K Pace: **14:11**     5k Finish Time: **44 minutes**

| Day | Dist. Mile | Dist. KM | Difficulty | Pace (Range) | Instructions |
|---|---|---|---|---|---|
| Monday | Rest | Rest | Rest | Rest | Take it easy. Don't run. If you need to exercise, I recommend a walk for no longer than 30 minutes. |
| Tuesday | 3 | 5 | E | 15:30 - 17:30 | walk/run at an easy pace. |
| Wednesday | 5 | 8 | HM | 15:30 | walk/run at your half marathon pace. |
| Thursday | 3 | 5 | M | 15:30 - 16:30 | walk/run at a medium pace. |
| Friday | Rest | Rest | Rest | Rest | Rest. |
| Saturday | 8.5 | 13.5 | S | 15:30 - 18:00 | walk/run at a slow pace. The most important piece of your long duration runs is finishing the run. |
| Sunday | Rest/CT | Rest/CT | Rest | Rest | Rest. If your body feels good, then go ahead and do some form of cross-training for 30 to 60 minutes. |

## 10K Optional

| Day | Dist. Mile | Dist. KM | Difficulty | Pace (Range) | Instructions |
|---|---|---|---|---|---|
| Thursday | 2 | 3 | E | 15:30 - 17:30 | If you run the optional 10K, either completely rest today or run 2 miles (3 km). |
| Saturday | 6.2 | 10K | - | 14:11 | Run a 10k race instead of your long run. This is completely your choice. I recommend running a 10k race to help you get used to running races. You should see a difference in your race time if you have kept to your training schedule. Don't try for a personal best, run the 10K at your 5K pace. |

# Training - Week 8

5K Pace: **14:11**     5k Finish Time: **44 minutes**

| Day | Dist. Mile | Dist. KM | Difficulty | Pace (Range) | Instructions |
|---|---|---|---|---|---|
| Monday | Rest | Rest | Rest | Rest | Take it easy. Don't run. If you need to exercise, I recommend a walk for no longer than 30 minutes. |
| Tuesday | 3 | 5 | E | 15:30 - 17:30 | walk/run at an easy pace. |
| Wednesday | 5 | 8 | HM | 15:30 | walk/run at your half marathon pace. |
| Thursday | 3 | 5 | M | 15:30 - 16:30 | walk/run at a medium pace. |
| Friday | Rest | Rest | Rest | Rest | Rest. |
| Saturday | 9 | 14 | S | 15:30 - 18:00 | walk/run at a slow pace. The most important piece of your long duration runs is finishing the run. |
| Sunday | Rest/CT | Rest/CT | Rest | Rest | Rest. If your body feels good, then go ahead and do some form of cross-training for 30 to 60 minutes. |

# Training - Week 9

5K Pace: **14:11**     5k Finish Time: **44 minutes**

| Day | Dist. Mile | Dist. KM | Difficulty | Pace (Range) | Instructions |
|---|---|---|---|---|---|
| Monday | Rest | Rest | Rest | Rest | Take it easy. Don't run. If you need to exercise, I recommend a walk for no longer than 30 minutes. |
| Tuesday | 3 | 5 | E | 15:30 - 17:30 | walk/run at an easy pace. |
| Wednesday | 5 | 8 | HM | 15:30 | walk/run at your half marathon pace. |
| Thursday | 3 | 5 | M | 15:30 - 16:30 | walk/run at a medium pace. |
| Friday | Rest | Rest | Rest | Rest | Rest. |
| Saturday | 8.5 | 13.5 | S | 15:30 - 18:00 | walk/run at a slow pace. The most important piece of your long duration runs is finishing the run. |
| Sunday | Rest/CT | Rest/CT | Rest | Rest | Rest. If your body feels good, then go ahead and do some form of cross-training for 30 to 60 minutes. |

## 13.1 Beta/Test Run Optional

| Day | Dist. Mile | Dist. KM | Difficulty | Pace (Range) | Instructions |
|---|---|---|---|---|---|
| Thursday | Rest | Rest | Rest | Rest | This is a rest day – it simulates race week |
| Friday | Rest | Rest | Rest | Rest | This is a rest day – it simulates race week |
| Saturday | 13.1 | 21 | S | 14:11 | I recommend that you attempt to go the full 13.1 miles (21 km) for a half marathon test run. <u>Only walk/run the first 10 miles (16 km) then walk the last 3.1 miles (5 km)</u>. If you are successful, you will have a race ghost time to compete against. It will help energize and refocus your training on beating yourself in 3 weeks at the half marathon race. Also, it allows your mind to grasp the achievement of "completing the distance of a half marathon." |

# Training - Week 10

5K Pace: **14:11**     5k Finish Time: **44 minutes**

| Day | Dist. Mile | Dist. KM | Difficulty | Pace (Range) | Instructions |
|---|---|---|---|---|---|
| Monday | Rest | Rest | Rest | Rest | Take it easy. Don't run. If you need to exercise, I recommend a walk for no longer than 30 minutes. |
| Tuesday | 3 | 5 | E | 15:30 - 17:30 | walk/run at an easy pace. |
| Wednesday | 5 | 8 | HM | 15:30 | walk/run at your half marathon pace. |
| Thursday | 3 | 5 | M | 15:30 - 16:30 | walk/run at a medium pace. |
| Friday | Rest | Rest | Rest | Rest | Rest. |
| Saturday | 11 | 18 | S | 15:30 - 18:00 | walk/run at a slow pace. The most important piece of your long duration runs is finishing the run. |
| Sunday | Rest/CT | Rest/CT | Rest | Rest | Rest. If your body feels good, then go ahead and do some form of cross-training for 30 to 60 minutes. |

# Training - Week 11

| Day | Dist. Mile | Dist. KM | Difficulty | Pace (Range) | Instructions |
|---|---|---|---|---|---|
| Monday | Rest | Rest | Rest | Rest | Take it easy. Don't run. If you need to exercise, I recommend a walk for no longer than 30 minutes. |
| Tuesday | 3 | 5 | E | 15:30 - 17:30 | walk/run at an easy pace. |
| Wednesday | 5 | 8 | HM | 15:30 | walk/run at your half marathon pace. |
| Thursday | 3 | 5 | M | 15:30 - 16:30 | walk/run at a medium pace. |
| Friday | Rest | Rest | Rest | Rest | Rest. |
| Saturday | 12 | 20 | S | 15:30 - 18:00 | walk/run at a slow pace. The most important piece of your long duration runs is finishing the run. |
| Sunday | Rest/CT | Rest/CT | Rest | Rest | Rest. If your body feels good, then go ahead and do some form of cross-training for 30 to 60 minutes. |

# Training - Week 12

5K Pace: **14:11**    5k Finish Time: **44 minutes**

| Day | Dist. Mile | Dist. KM | Difficulty | Pace (Range) | Instructions |
|---|---|---|---|---|---|
| Monday | Rest | Rest | Rest | Rest | Take it easy. Don't run. If you need to exercise, I recommend a walk for no longer than 30 minutes. |
| Tuesday | 3 | 5 | E | 15:30 - 17:30 | walk/run at an easy pace. |
| Wednesday | 2 | 1.5 | HM | 15:30 | walk/run at your half marathon pace. |
| Thursday | Rest | Rest | Rest | Rest | Rest. |
| Friday | Rest | Rest | Rest | Rest | Rest. |
| Saturday | 13.1 | 21 | HM | 15:30 | RACE DAY! |
| Sunday | Rest | Rest | Rest | Rest | DRINK A VICTORY BEER! |

## NOTE:

- Get plenty of sleep the night before your long duration run.
- Try to run your long duration run early in the morning.
- After each run, it's important to stretch out your muscles.
- This week your body needs as much rest as possible.
- Don't run past Wednesday.

Half Marathon Training Schedule for runners with a 5K finish time of 45 minutes and a pace of *14:30* minutes/mile.

## Predicted Half Marathon Finish Time:

*3* hour(s) *27* minutes

# PACING TABLES

| Pace | Pace (minutes/miles) |
|---:|---|
| 5k | 14:30 |
| Half marathon | 15:50 |
| Medium | Between 15:50 - 16:50 |
| Easy | Between 15:50 - 17:50 |
| Slow | Between 15:50 - 18:20 |

| Race | Finish Times (predicted) |
|---:|---|
| 5k | 45 minutes |
| Half marathon | 3 hour(s) 27 minutes |

| Determining your pace ||
|---|---|
| Slow Pace | Extremely easy to hold a conversation. |
| Easy Pace | You can hold a conversation with someone. Your breathing might break up some of the flow of the conversation. |
| Medium | You can hold a conversation with someone, but it's broken up into smaller sentences and smaller responses. |
| Half Marathon Pace | Conversation is difficult. One and two word responses back and forth at best. |

## Definitions in the table below:

CT = Cross Training

S = Slow Pace (long run pace)

E = Easy Pace

M = Medium Pace

HM = Half Marathon Pace

## Training - Week A (Optional)

5K Pace: **14:30**  5k Finish Time: **45 minutes**

| Day | Dist. Mile | Dist. KM | Difficulty | Pace (Range) | Instructions |
|---|---|---|---|---|---|
| Monday | Rest | Rest | Rest | Rest | Take it easy. Don't run. If you need to exercise, I recommend a walk for no longer than 30 minutes. |
| Tuesday | 1 | 1.5 | E | 15:50 - 17:50 | walk/run at an easy pace. |
| Wednesday | 1 | 1.5 | HM | 15:50 | walk/run at your half marathon pace. |
| Thursday | 1 | 1.5 | M | 15:50 - 16:50 | walk/run at a medium pace. |
| Friday | Rest | Rest | Rest | Rest | Rest. |
| Saturday | 1.5 | 2.5 | S | 15:50 - 18:20 | walk/run at a slow pace. The most important piece of your long duration runs is finishing the run. |
| Sunday | Rest/CT | Rest/CT | Rest | Rest | Rest. If your body feels good, then go ahead and do some form of cross-training for 30 to 60 minutes. |

## Training - Week B (Optional)

| Day | Dist. Mile | Dist. KM | Difficulty | Pace (Range) | Instructions |
|---|---|---|---|---|---|
| Monday | Rest | Rest | Rest | Rest | Take it easy. Don't run. If you need to exercise, I recommend a walk for no longer than 30 minutes. |
| Tuesday | 1.5 | 2.5 | E | 15:50 - 17:50 | walk/run at an easy pace. |
| Wednesday | 1.5 | 2.5 | HM | 15:50 | walk/run at your half marathon pace. |
| Thursday | 1.5 | 2.5 | M | 15:50 - 16:50 | walk/run at a medium pace. |
| Friday | Rest | Rest | Rest | Rest | Rest. |
| Saturday | 2 | 3 | S | 15:50 - 18:20 | walk/run at a slow pace. The most important piece of your long duration runs is finishing the run. |
| Sunday | Rest/CT | Rest/CT | Rest | Rest | Rest. If your body feels good, then go ahead and do some form of cross-training for 30 to 60 minutes. |

# Training - Week C (Optional)

5K Pace: **14:30**     5k Finish Time: **45 minutes**

| Day | Dist. Mile | Dist. KM | Difficulty | Pace (Range) | Instructions |
|---|---|---|---|---|---|
| Monday | Rest | Rest | Rest | Rest | Take it easy. Don't run. If you need to exercise, I recommend a walk for no longer than 30 minutes. |
| Tuesday | 2 | 3 | E | 15:50 - 17:50 | walk/run at an easy pace. |
| Wednesday | 2 | 3 | HM | 15:50 | walk/run at your half marathon pace. |
| Thursday | 2 | 3 | M | 15:50 - 16:50 | walk/run at a medium pace. |
| Friday | Rest | Rest | Rest | Rest | Rest. |
| Saturday | 3 | 5 | S | 15:50 - 18:20 | walk/run at a slow pace. The most important piece of your long duration runs is finishing the run. |
| Sunday | Rest/CT | Rest/CT | Rest | Rest | Rest. If your body feels good, then go ahead and do some form of cross-training for 30 to 60 minutes. |

# Training - Week 1

5K Pace: **14:30**     5k Finish Time: **45 minutes**

| Day | Dist. Mile | Dist. KM | Difficulty | Pace (Range) | Instructions |
|---|---|---|---|---|---|
| Monday | Rest | Rest | Rest | Rest | Take it easy. Don't run. If you need to exercise, I recommend a walk for no longer than 30 minutes. |
| Tuesday | 3 | 5 | E | 15:50 - 17:50 | walk/run at an easy pace. |
| Wednesday | 3 | 5 | HM | 15:50 | walk/run at your half marathon pace. |
| Thursday | 3 | 5 | M | 15:50 - 16:50 | walk/run at a medium pace. |
| Friday | Rest | Rest | Rest | Rest | Rest. |
| Saturday | 4 | 6 | S | 15:50 - 18:20 | walk/run at a slow pace. The most important piece of your long duration runs is finishing the run. |
| Sunday | Rest/CT | Rest/CT | Rest | Rest | Rest. If your body feels good, then go ahead and do some form of cross-training for 30 to 60 minutes. |

# Training - Week 2

| Day | Dist. Mile | Dist. KM | Difficulty | Pace (Range) | Instructions |
|---|---|---|---|---|---|
| Monday | Rest | Rest | Rest | Rest | Take it easy. Don't run. If you need to exercise, I recommend a walk for no longer than 30 minutes. |
| Tuesday | 3 | 5 | E | 15:50 - 17:50 | walk/run at an easy pace. |
| Wednesday | 3 | 5 | HM | 15:50 | walk/run at your half marathon pace. |
| Thursday | 3 | 5 | M | 15:50 - 16:50 | walk/run at a medium pace. |
| Friday | Rest | Rest | Rest | Rest | Rest. |
| Saturday | 5 | 8 | S | 15:50 - 18:20 | walk/run at a slow pace. The most important piece of your long duration runs is finishing the run. |
| Sunday | Rest/CT | Rest/CT | Rest | Rest | Rest. If your body feels good, then go ahead and do some form of cross-training for 30 to 60 minutes. |

# Training - Week 3

5K Pace: **14:30**     5k Finish Time: **45 minutes**

| Day | Dist. Mile | Dist. KM | Difficulty | Pace (Range) | Instructions |
|---|---|---|---|---|---|
| Monday | Rest | Rest | Rest | Rest | Take it easy. Don't run. If you need to exercise, I recommend a walk for no longer than 30 minutes. |
| Tuesday | 3 | 5 | E | 15:50 - 17:50 | walk/run at an easy pace. |
| Wednesday | 4 | 6 | HM | 15:50 | walk/run at your half marathon pace. |
| Thursday | 3 | 5 | M | 15:50 - 16:50 | walk/run at a medium pace. |
| Friday | Rest | Rest | Rest | Rest | Rest. |
| Saturday | 6 | 10 | S | 15:50 - 18:20 | walk/run at a slow pace. The most important piece of your long duration runs is finishing the run. |
| Sunday | Rest/CT | Rest/CT | Rest | Rest | Rest. If your body feels good, then go ahead and do some form of cross-training for 30 to 60 minutes. |

# Training - Week 4 (5K Optional)

5K Pace: **14:30**     5k Finish Time: **45 minutes**

| Day | Dist. Mile | Dist. KM | Difficulty | Pace (Range) | Instructions |
|---|---|---|---|---|---|
| Monday | Rest | Rest | Rest | Rest | Take it easy. Don't run. If you need to exercise, I recommend a walk for no longer than 30 minutes. |
| Tuesday | 3 | 5 | E | 15:50 - 17:50 | walk/run at an easy pace. |
| Wednesday | 4 | 6 | HM | 15:50 | walk/run at your half marathon pace. |
| Thursday | 3 | 5 | M | 15:50 - 16:50 | walk/run at a medium pace. |
| Friday | Rest | Rest | Rest | Rest | Rest. |
| Saturday | 6.5 | 10.5 | S | 15:50 - 18:20 | walk/run at a slow pace. The most important piece of your long duration runs is finishing the run. |
| Sunday | Rest/CT | Rest/CT | Rest | Rest | Rest. If your body feels good, then go ahead and do some form of cross-training for 30 to 60 minutes. |

## 5K Optional

| Day | Dist. Mile | Dist. KM | Difficulty | Pace (Range) | Instructions |
|---|---|---|---|---|---|
| Saturday | 3.1 | 5 | - | **14:30** | Run a 5k race instead of your long run. This is completely your choice. I recommend running a 5k race to help you get used to running races. You should see a difference in your race time if you have kept to your training schedule. Don't try for a personal best, run the 5K at your 5K pace. |

# Training - Week 5

5K Pace: **14:30**     5k Finish Time: **45 minutes**

| Day | Dist. Mile | Dist. KM | Difficulty | Pace (Range) | Instructions |
|---|---|---|---|---|---|
| Monday | Rest | Rest | Rest | Rest | Take it easy. Don't run. If you need to exercise, I recommend a walk for no longer than 30 minutes. |
| Tuesday | 3 | 5 | E | 15:50 - 17:50 | walk/run at an easy pace. |
| Wednesday | 4 | 6 | HM | 15:50 | walk/run at your half marathon pace. |
| Thursday | 3 | 5 | M | 15:50 - 16:50 | walk/run at a medium pace. |
| Friday | Rest | Rest | Rest | Rest | Rest. |
| Saturday | 7 | 11 | S | 15:50 - 18:20 | walk/run at a slow pace. The most important piece of your long duration runs is finishing the run. |
| Sunday | Rest/CT | Rest/CT | Rest | Rest | Rest. If your body feels good, then go ahead and do some form of cross-training for 30 to 60 minutes. |

## NOTE:

- Your long duration runs will begin to become more difficult for week 5 and beyond.
- If you get tired during a long duration run, walk for 1/10 mile or 3-5 minutes.

# Training - Week 6

5K Pace: **14:30**  5k Finish Time: **45 minutes**

| Day | Dist. Mile | Dist. KM | Difficulty | Pace (Range) | Instructions |
|---|---|---|---|---|---|
| Monday | Rest | Rest | Rest | Rest | Take it easy. Don't run. If you need to exercise, I recommend a walk for no longer than 30 minutes. |
| Tuesday | 3 | 5 | E | 15:50 - 17:50 | walk/run at an easy pace. |
| Wednesday | 4 | 6 | HM | 15:50 | walk/run at your half marathon pace. |
| Thursday | 3 | 5 | M | 15:50 - 16:50 | walk/run at a medium pace. |
| Friday | Rest | Rest | Rest | Rest | Rest. |
| Saturday | 8 | 13 | S | 15:50 - 18:20 | walk/run at a slow pace. The most important piece of your long duration runs is finishing the run. |
| Sunday | Rest/CT | Rest/CT | Rest | Rest | Rest. If your body feels good, then go ahead and do some form of cross-training for 30 to 60 minutes. |

# Training - Week 7

5K Pace: **14:30**     5k Finish Time: **45 minutes**

| Day | Dist. Mile | Dist. KM | Difficulty | Pace (Range) | Instructions |
|---|---|---|---|---|---|
| Monday | Rest | Rest | Rest | Rest | Take it easy. Don't run. If you need to exercise, I recommend a walk for no longer than 30 minutes. |
| Tuesday | 3 | 5 | E | 15:50 - 17:50 | walk/run at an easy pace. |
| Wednesday | 5 | 8 | HM | 15:50 | walk/run at your half marathon pace. |
| Thursday | 3 | 5 | M | 15:50 - 16:50 | walk/run at a medium pace. |
| Friday | Rest | Rest | Rest | Rest | Rest. |
| Saturday | 8.5 | 13.5 | S | 15:50 - 18:20 | walk/run at a slow pace. The most important piece of your long duration runs is finishing the run. |
| Sunday | Rest/CT | Rest/CT | Rest | Rest | Rest. If your body feels good, then go ahead and do some form of cross-training for 30 to 60 minutes. |

## 10K Optional

| Day | Dist. Mile | Dist. KM | Difficulty | Pace (Range) | Instructions |
|---|---|---|---|---|---|
| Thursday | 2 | 3 | E | 15:50 - 17:50 | If you run the optional 10K, either completely rest today or run 2 miles (3 km). |
| Saturday | 6.2 | 10K | - | 14:30 | Run a 10k race instead of your long run. This is completely your choice. I recommend running a 10k race to help you get used to running races. You should see a difference in your race time if you have kept to your training schedule. Don't try for a personal best, run the 10K at your 5K pace. |

# Training - Week 8

5K Pace: **14:30**   5k Finish Time: **45 minutes**

| Day | Dist. Mile | Dist. KM | Difficulty | Pace (Range) | Instructions |
|---|---|---|---|---|---|
| Monday | Rest | Rest | Rest | Rest | Take it easy. Don't run. If you need to exercise, I recommend a walk for no longer than 30 minutes. |
| Tuesday | 3 | 5 | E | 15:50 - 17:50 | walk/run at an easy pace. |
| Wednesday | 5 | 8 | HM | 15:50 | walk/run at your half marathon pace. |
| Thursday | 3 | 5 | M | 15:50 - 16:50 | walk/run at a medium pace. |
| Friday | Rest | Rest | Rest | Rest | Rest. |
| Saturday | 9 | 14 | S | 15:50 - 18:20 | walk/run at a slow pace. The most important piece of your long duration runs is finishing the run. |
| Sunday | Rest/CT | Rest/CT | Rest | Rest | Rest. If your body feels good, then go ahead and do some form of cross-training for 30 to 60 minutes. |

# Training - Week 9

5K Pace: **14:30**     5k Finish Time: **45 minutes**

| Day | Dist. Mile | Dist. KM | Difficulty | Pace (Range) | Instructions |
|---|---|---|---|---|---|
| Monday | Rest | Rest | Rest | Rest | Take it easy. Don't run. If you need to exercise, I recommend a walk for no longer than 30 minutes. |
| Tuesday | 3 | 5 | E | 15:50 - 17:50 | walk/run at an easy pace. |
| Wednesday | 5 | 8 | HM | 15:50 | walk/run at your half marathon pace. |
| Thursday | 3 | 5 | M | 15:50 - 16:50 | walk/run at a medium pace. |
| Friday | Rest | Rest | Rest | Rest | Rest. |
| Saturday | 8.5 | 13.5 | S | 15:50 - 18:20 | walk/run at a slow pace. The most important piece of your long duration runs is finishing the run. |
| Sunday | Rest/CT | Rest/CT | Rest | Rest | Rest. If your body feels good, then go ahead and do some form of cross-training for 30 to 60 minutes. |

## 13.1 Beta/Test Run Optional

| Day | Dist. Mile | Dist. KM | Difficulty | Pace (Range) | Instructions |
|---|---|---|---|---|---|
| Thursday | Rest | Rest | Rest | Rest | This is a rest day – it simulates race week |
| Friday | Rest | Rest | Rest | Rest | This is a rest day – it simulates race week |
| Saturday | 13.1 | 21 | S | 14:30 | I recommend that you attempt to go the full 13.1 miles (21 km) for a half marathon test run. <u>Only walk/run the first 10 miles (16 km) then walk the last 3.1 miles (5 km)</u>. If you are successful, you will have a race ghost time to compete against. It will help energize and refocus your training on beating yourself in 3 weeks at the half marathon race. Also, it allows your mind to grasp the achievement of "completing the distance of a half marathon." |

# Training - Week 10

5K Pace: **14:30**   5k Finish Time: **45 minutes**

| Day | Dist. Mile | Dist. KM | Difficulty | Pace (Range) | Instructions |
|---|---|---|---|---|---|
| Monday | Rest | Rest | Rest | Rest | Take it easy. Don't run. If you need to exercise, I recommend a walk for no longer than 30 minutes. |
| Tuesday | 3 | 5 | E | 15:50 - 17:50 | walk/run at an easy pace. |
| Wednesday | 5 | 8 | HM | 15:50 | walk/run at your half marathon pace. |
| Thursday | 3 | 5 | M | 15:50 - 16:50 | walk/run at a medium pace. |
| Friday | Rest | Rest | Rest | Rest | Rest. |
| Saturday | 11 | 18 | S | 15:50 - 18:20 | walk/run at a slow pace. The most important piece of your long duration runs is finishing the run. |
| Sunday | Rest/CT | Rest/CT | Rest | Rest | Rest. If your body feels good, then go ahead and do some form of cross-training for 30 to 60 minutes. |

# Training - Week 11

| Day | Dist. Mile | Dist. KM | Difficulty | Pace (Range) | Instructions |
|---|---|---|---|---|---|
| Monday | Rest | Rest | Rest | Rest | Take it easy. Don't run. If you need to exercise, I recommend a walk for no longer than 30 minutes. |
| Tuesday | 3 | 5 | E | 15:50 - 17:50 | walk/run at an easy pace. |
| Wednesday | 5 | 8 | HM | 15:50 | walk/run at your half marathon pace. |
| Thursday | 3 | 5 | M | 15:50 - 16:50 | walk/run at a medium pace. |
| Friday | Rest | Rest | Rest | Rest | Rest. |
| Saturday | 12 | 20 | S | 15:50 - 18:20 | walk/run at a slow pace. The most important piece of your long duration runs is finishing the run. |
| Sunday | Rest/CT | Rest/CT | Rest | Rest | Rest. If your body feels good, then go ahead and do some form of cross-training for 30 to 60 minutes. |

# Training - Week 12

5K Pace: **14:30**     5k Finish Time: **45 minutes**

| Day | Dist. Mile | Dist. KM | Difficulty | Pace (Range) | Instructions |
|---|---|---|---|---|---|
| Monday | Rest | Rest | Rest | Rest | Take it easy. Don't run. If you need to exercise, I recommend a walk for no longer than 30 minutes. |
| Tuesday | 3 | 5 | E | 15:50 - 17:50 | walk/run at an easy pace. |
| Wednesday | 2 | 1.5 | HM | 15:50 | walk/run at your half marathon pace. |
| Thursday | Rest | Rest | Rest | Rest | Rest. |
| Friday | Rest | Rest | Rest | Rest | Rest. |
| Saturday | 13.1 | 21 | HM | 15:50 | RACE DAY! |
| Sunday | Rest | Rest | Rest | Rest | DRINK A VICTORY BEER! |

# NOTE:

- Get plenty of sleep the night before your long duration run.
- Try to run your long duration run early in the morning.
- After each run, it's important to stretch out your muscles.
- This week your body needs as much rest as possible.
- Don't run past Wednesday.

Half Marathon Training Schedule for runners with a 5K finish time of 46 minutes and a pace of *14:50* minutes/mile.

**Predicted Half Marathon Finish Time:**

*3* hour(s) *31* minutes

# PACING TABLES

| Pace | Pace (minutes/miles) |
|---:|---|
| 5k | 14:50 |
| Half marathon | 16:08 |
| Medium | Between 16:08 - 17:08 |
| Easy | Between 16:08 - 18:08 |
| Slow | Between 16:08 - 18:38 |

| Race | Finish Times (predicted) |
|---:|---|
| 5k | 46 minutes |
| Half marathon | 3 hour(s) 31 minutes |

| Determining your pace | |
|---|---|
| Slow Pace | Extremely easy to hold a conversation. |
| Easy Pace | You can hold a conversation with someone. Your breathing might break up some of the flow of the conversation. |
| Medium | You can hold a conversation with someone, but it's broken up into smaller sentences and smaller responses. |
| Half Marathon Pace | Conversation is difficult. One and two word responses back and forth at best. |

## Definitions in the table below:

CT = Cross Training

S = Slow Pace (long run pace)

E = Easy Pace

M = Medium Pace

HM = Half Marathon Pace

# Training - Week A (Optional)

5K Pace: **14:50**     5k Finish Time: **46 minutes**

| Day | Dist. Mile | Dist. KM | Difficulty | Pace (Range) | Instructions |
|---|---|---|---|---|---|
| Monday | Rest | Rest | Rest | Rest | Take it easy. Don't run. If you need to exercise, I recommend a walk for no longer than 30 minutes. |
| Tuesday | 1 | 1.5 | E | 16:08 - 18:08 | walk/run at an easy pace. |
| Wednesday | 1 | 1.5 | HM | 16:08 | walk/run at your half marathon pace. |
| Thursday | 1 | 1.5 | M | 16:08 - 17:08 | walk/run at a medium pace. |
| Friday | Rest | Rest | Rest | Rest | Rest. |
| Saturday | 1.5 | 2.5 | S | 16:08 - 18:38 | walk/run at a slow pace. The most important piece of your long duration runs is finishing the run. |
| Sunday | Rest/CT | Rest/CT | Rest | Rest | Rest. If your body feels good, then go ahead and do some form of cross-training for 30 to 60 minutes. |

# Training - Week B (Optional)

| Day | Dist. Mile | Dist. KM | Difficulty | Pace (Range) | Instructions |
|---|---|---|---|---|---|
| Monday | Rest | Rest | Rest | Rest | Take it easy. Don't run. If you need to exercise, I recommend a walk for no longer than 30 minutes. |
| Tuesday | 1.5 | 2.5 | E | 16:08 - 18:08 | walk/run at an easy pace. |
| Wednesday | 1.5 | 2.5 | HM | 16:08 | walk/run at your half marathon pace. |
| Thursday | 1.5 | 2.5 | M | 16:08 - 17:08 | walk/run at a medium pace. |
| Friday | Rest | Rest | Rest | Rest | Rest. |
| Saturday | 2 | 3 | S | 16:08 - 18:38 | walk/run at a slow pace. The most important piece of your long duration runs is finishing the run. |
| Sunday | Rest/CT | Rest/CT | Rest | Rest | Rest. If your body feels good, then go ahead and do some form of cross-training for 30 to 60 minutes. |

# Training - Week C (Optional)

5K Pace: **14:50**      5k Finish Time: **46 minutes**

| Day | Dist. Mile | Dist. KM | Difficulty | Pace (Range) | Instructions |
|---|---|---|---|---|---|
| Monday | Rest | Rest | Rest | Rest | Take it easy. Don't run. If you need to exercise, I recommend a walk for no longer than 30 minutes. |
| Tuesday | 2 | 3 | E | 16:08 - 18:08 | walk/run at an easy pace. |
| Wednesday | 2 | 3 | HM | 16:08 | walk/run at your half marathon pace. |
| Thursday | 2 | 3 | M | 16:08 - 17:08 | walk/run at a medium pace. |
| Friday | Rest | Rest | Rest | Rest | Rest. |
| Saturday | 3 | 5 | S | 16:08 - 18:38 | walk/run at a slow pace. The most important piece of your long duration runs is finishing the run. |
| Sunday | Rest/CT | Rest/CT | Rest | Rest | Rest. If your body feels good, then go ahead and do some form of cross-training for 30 to 60 minutes. |

# Training - Week 1

5K Pace: **14:50**    5k Finish Time: **46 minutes**

| Day | Dist. Mile | Dist. KM | Difficulty | Pace (Range) | Instructions |
|---|---|---|---|---|---|
| Monday | Rest | Rest | Rest | Rest | Take it easy. Don't run. If you need to exercise, I recommend a walk for no longer than 30 minutes. |
| Tuesday | 3 | 5 | E | 16:08 - 18:08 | walk/run at an easy pace. |
| Wednesday | 3 | 5 | HM | 16:08 | walk/run at your half marathon pace. |
| Thursday | 3 | 5 | M | 16:08 - 17:08 | walk/run at a medium pace. |
| Friday | Rest | Rest | Rest | Rest | Rest. |
| Saturday | 4 | 6 | S | 16:08 - 18:38 | walk/run at a slow pace. The most important piece of your long duration runs is finishing the run. |
| Sunday | Rest/CT | Rest/CT | Rest | Rest | Rest. If your body feels good, then go ahead and do some form of cross-training for 30 to 60 minutes. |

# Training - Week 2

| Day | Dist. Mile | Dist. KM | Difficulty | Pace (Range) | Instructions |
|---|---|---|---|---|---|
| Monday | Rest | Rest | Rest | Rest | Take it easy. Don't run. If you need to exercise, I recommend a walk for no longer than 30 minutes. |
| Tuesday | 3 | 5 | E | 16:08 - 18:08 | walk/run at an easy pace. |
| Wednesday | 3 | 5 | HM | 16:08 | walk/run at your half marathon pace. |
| Thursday | 3 | 5 | M | 16:08 - 17:08 | walk/run at a medium pace. |
| Friday | Rest | Rest | Rest | Rest | Rest. |
| Saturday | 5 | 8 | S | 16:08 - 18:38 | walk/run at a slow pace. The most important piece of your long duration runs is finishing the run. |
| Sunday | Rest/CT | Rest/CT | Rest | Rest | Rest. If your body feels good, then go ahead and do some form of cross-training for 30 to 60 minutes. |

# Training - Week 3

5K Pace: **14:50**     5k Finish Time: **46 minutes**

| Day | Dist. Mile | Dist. KM | Difficulty | Pace (Range) | Instructions |
|---|---|---|---|---|---|
| Monday | Rest | Rest | Rest | Rest | Take it easy. Don't run. If you need to exercise, I recommend a walk for no longer than 30 minutes. |
| Tuesday | 3 | 5 | E | 16:08 - 18:08 | walk/run at an easy pace. |
| Wednesday | 4 | 6 | HM | 16:08 | walk/run at your half marathon pace. |
| Thursday | 3 | 5 | M | 16:08 - 17:08 | walk/run at a medium pace. |
| Friday | Rest | Rest | Rest | Rest | Rest. |
| Saturday | 6 | 10 | S | 16:08 - 18:38 | walk/run at a slow pace. The most important piece of your long duration runs is finishing the run. |
| Sunday | Rest/CT | Rest/CT | Rest | Rest | Rest. If your body feels good, then go ahead and do some form of cross-training for 30 to 60 minutes. |

# Training - Week 4 (5K Optional)

5K Pace: **14:50**    5k Finish Time: **46 minutes**

| Day | Dist. Mile | Dist. KM | Difficulty | Pace (Range) | Instructions |
|---|---|---|---|---|---|
| Monday | Rest | Rest | Rest | Rest | Take it easy. Don't run. If you need to exercise, I recommend a walk for no longer than 30 minutes. |
| Tuesday | 3 | 5 | E | 16:08 - 18:08 | walk/run at an easy pace. |
| Wednesday | 4 | 6 | HM | 16:08 | walk/run at your half marathon pace. |
| Thursday | 3 | 5 | M | 16:08 - 17:08 | walk/run at a medium pace. |
| Friday | Rest | Rest | Rest | Rest | Rest. |
| Saturday | 6.5 | 10.5 | S | 16:08 - 18:38 | walk/run at a slow pace. The most important piece of your long duration runs is finishing the run. |
| Sunday | Rest/CT | Rest/CT | Rest | Rest | Rest. If your body feels good, then go ahead and do some form of cross-training for 30 to 60 minutes. |

## 5K Optional

| Day | Dist. Mile | Dist. KM | Difficulty | Pace (Range) | Instructions |
|---|---|---|---|---|---|
| Saturday | 3.1 | 5 | - | **14:50** | Run a 5k race instead of your long run. This is completely your choice. I recommend running a 5k race to help you get used to running races. You should see a difference in your race time if you have kept to your training schedule. Don't try for a personal best, run the 5K at your 5K pace. |

# Training - Week 5

5K Pace: **14:50**     5k Finish Time: **46 minutes**

| Day | Dist. Mile | Dist. KM | Difficulty | Pace (Range) | Instructions |
|---|---|---|---|---|---|
| Monday | Rest | Rest | Rest | Rest | Take it easy. Don't run. If you need to exercise, I recommend a walk for no longer than 30 minutes. |
| Tuesday | 3 | 5 | E | 16:08 - 18:08 | walk/run at an easy pace. |
| Wednesday | 4 | 6 | HM | 16:08 | walk/run at your half marathon pace. |
| Thursday | 3 | 5 | M | 16:08 - 17:08 | walk/run at a medium pace. |
| Friday | Rest | Rest | Rest | Rest | Rest. |
| Saturday | 7 | 11 | S | 16:08 - 18:38 | walk/run at a slow pace. The most important piece of your long duration runs is finishing the run. |
| Sunday | Rest/CT | Rest/CT | Rest | Rest | Rest. If your body feels good, then go ahead and do some form of cross-training for 30 to 60 minutes. |

## NOTE:

- Your long duration runs will begin to become more difficult for week 5 and beyond.
- If you get tired during a long duration run, walk for 1/10 mile or 3-5 minutes.

# Training - Week 6

5K Pace: **14:50**   5k Finish Time: **46 minutes**

| Day | Dist. Mile | Dist. KM | Difficulty | Pace (Range) | Instructions |
|---|---|---|---|---|---|
| Monday | Rest | Rest | Rest | Rest | Take it easy. Don't run. If you need to exercise, I recommend a walk for no longer than 30 minutes. |
| Tuesday | 3 | 5 | E | 16:08 - 18:08 | walk/run at an easy pace. |
| Wednesday | 4 | 6 | HM | 16:08 | walk/run at your half marathon pace. |
| Thursday | 3 | 5 | M | 16:08 - 17:08 | walk/run at a medium pace. |
| Friday | Rest | Rest | Rest | Rest | Rest. |
| Saturday | 8 | 13 | S | 16:08 - 18:38 | walk/run at a slow pace. The most important piece of your long duration runs is finishing the run. |
| Sunday | Rest/CT | Rest/CT | Rest | Rest | Rest. If your body feels good, then go ahead and do some form of cross-training for 30 to 60 minutes. |

# Training - Week 7

5K Pace: **14:50**     5k Finish Time: **46 minutes**

| Day | Dist. Mile | Dist. KM | Difficulty | Pace (Range) | Instructions |
|---|---|---|---|---|---|
| Monday | Rest | Rest | Rest | Rest | Take it easy. Don't run. If you need to exercise, I recommend a walk for no longer than 30 minutes. |
| Tuesday | 3 | 5 | E | 16:08 - 18:08 | walk/run at an easy pace. |
| Wednesday | 5 | 8 | HM | 16:08 | walk/run at your half marathon pace. |
| Thursday | 3 | 5 | M | 16:08 - 17:08 | walk/run at a medium pace. |
| Friday | Rest | Rest | Rest | Rest | Rest. |
| Saturday | 8.5 | 13.5 | S | 16:08 - 18:38 | walk/run at a slow pace. The most important piece of your long duration runs is finishing the run. |
| Sunday | Rest/CT | Rest/CT | Rest | Rest | Rest. If your body feels good, then go ahead and do some form of cross-training for 30 to 60 minutes. |

## 10K Optional

| Day | Dist. Mile | Dist. KM | Difficulty | Pace (Range) | Instructions |
|---|---|---|---|---|---|
| Thursday | 2 | 3 | E | 16:08 - 18:08 | If you run the optional 10K, either completely rest today or run 2 miles (3 km). |
| Saturday | 6.2 | 10K | - | 14:50 | Run a 10k race instead of your long run. This is completely your choice. I recommend running a 10k race to help you get used to running races. You should see a difference in your race time if you have kept to your training schedule. Don't try for a personal best, run the 10K at your 5K pace. |

# Training - Week 8

5K Pace: **14:50**     5k Finish Time: **46 minutes**

| Day | Dist. Mile | Dist. KM | Difficulty | Pace (Range) | Instructions |
|---|---|---|---|---|---|
| Monday | Rest | Rest | Rest | Rest | Take it easy. Don't run. If you need to exercise, I recommend a walk for no longer than 30 minutes. |
| Tuesday | 3 | 5 | E | 16:08 - 18:08 | walk/run at an easy pace. |
| Wednesday | 5 | 8 | HM | 16:08 | walk/run at your half marathon pace. |
| Thursday | 3 | 5 | M | 16:08 - 17:08 | walk/run at a medium pace. |
| Friday | Rest | Rest | Rest | Rest | Rest. |
| Saturday | 9 | 14 | S | 16:08 - 18:38 | walk/run at a slow pace. The most important piece of your long duration runs is finishing the run. |
| Sunday | Rest/CT | Rest/CT | Rest | Rest | Rest. If your body feels good, then go ahead and do some form of cross-training for 30 to 60 minutes. |

# Training - Week 9

5K Pace: **14:50**     5k Finish Time: **46 minutes**

| Day | Dist. Mile | Dist. KM | Difficulty | Pace (Range) | Instructions |
|---|---|---|---|---|---|
| Monday | Rest | Rest | Rest | Rest | Take it easy. Don't run. If you need to exercise, I recommend a walk for no longer than 30 minutes. |
| Tuesday | 3 | 5 | E | 16:08 - 18:08 | walk/run at an easy pace. |
| Wednesday | 5 | 8 | HM | 16:08 | walk/run at your half marathon pace. |
| Thursday | 3 | 5 | M | 16:08 - 17:08 | walk/run at a medium pace. |
| Friday | Rest | Rest | Rest | Rest | Rest. |
| Saturday | 8.5 | 13.5 | S | 16:08 - 18:38 | walk/run at a slow pace. The most important piece of your long duration runs is finishing the run. |
| Sunday | Rest/CT | Rest/CT | Rest | Rest | Rest. If your body feels good, then go ahead and do some form of cross-training for 30 to 60 minutes. |

## 13.1 Beta/Test Run Optional

| Day | Dist. Mile | Dist. KM | Difficulty | Pace (Range) | Instructions |
|---|---|---|---|---|---|
| Thursday | Rest | Rest | Rest | Rest | This is a rest day – it simulates race week |
| Friday | Rest | Rest | Rest | Rest | This is a rest day – it simulates race week |
| Saturday | 13.1 | 21 | S | 14:50 | I recommend that you attempt to go the full 13.1 miles (21 km) for a half marathon test run. <u>Only walk/run the first 10 miles (16 km) then walk the last 3.1 miles (5 km).</u> If you are successful, you will have a race ghost time to compete against. It will help energize and refocus your training on beating yourself in 3 weeks at the half marathon race. Also, it allows your mind to grasp the achievement of "completing the distance of a half marathon." |

# Training - Week 10

5K Pace: **14:50**     5k Finish Time: **46 minutes**

| Day | Dist. Mile | Dist. KM | Difficulty | Pace (Range) | Instructions |
|---|---|---|---|---|---|
| Monday | Rest | Rest | Rest | Rest | Take it easy. Don't run. If you need to exercise, I recommend a walk for no longer than 30 minutes. |
| Tuesday | 3 | 5 | E | 16:08 - 18:08 | walk/run at an easy pace. |
| Wednesday | 5 | 8 | HM | 16:08 | walk/run at your half marathon pace. |
| Thursday | 3 | 5 | M | 16:08 - 17:08 | walk/run at a medium pace. |
| Friday | Rest | Rest | Rest | Rest | Rest. |
| Saturday | 11 | 18 | S | 16:08 - 18:38 | walk/run at a slow pace. The most important piece of your long duration runs is finishing the run. |
| Sunday | Rest/CT | Rest/CT | Rest | Rest | Rest. If your body feels good, then go ahead and do some form of cross-training for 30 to 60 minutes. |

# Training - Week 11

| Day | Dist. Mile | Dist. KM | Difficulty | Pace (Range) | Instructions |
|---|---|---|---|---|---|
| Monday | Rest | Rest | Rest | Rest | Take it easy. Don't run. If you need to exercise, I recommend a walk for no longer than 30 minutes. |
| Tuesday | 3 | 5 | E | 16:08 - 18:08 | walk/run at an easy pace. |
| Wednesday | 5 | 8 | HM | 16:08 | walk/run at your half marathon pace. |
| Thursday | 3 | 5 | M | 16:08 - 17:08 | walk/run at a medium pace. |
| Friday | Rest | Rest | Rest | Rest | Rest. |
| Saturday | 12 | 20 | S | 16:08 - 18:38 | walk/run at a slow pace. The most important piece of your long duration runs is finishing the run. |
| Sunday | Rest/CT | Rest/CT | Rest | Rest | Rest. If your body feels good, then go ahead and do some form of cross-training for 30 to 60 minutes. |

# Training - Week 12

5K Pace: **14:50**     5k Finish Time: **46 minutes**

| Day | Dist. Mile | Dist. KM | Difficulty | Pace (Range) | Instructions |
|---|---|---|---|---|---|
| Monday | Rest | Rest | Rest | Rest | Take it easy. Don't run. If you need to exercise, I recommend a walk for no longer than 30 minutes. |
| Tuesday | 3 | 5 | E | 16:08 - 18:08 | walk/run at an easy pace. |
| Wednesday | 2 | 1.5 | HM | 16:08 | walk/run at your half marathon pace. |
| Thursday | Rest | Rest | Rest | Rest | Rest. |
| Friday | Rest | Rest | Rest | Rest | Rest. |
| Saturday | 13.1 | 21 | HM | 16:08 | RACE DAY! |
| Sunday | Rest | Rest | Rest | Rest | DRINK A VICTORY BEER! |

## NOTE:

- Get plenty of sleep the night before your long duration run.
- Try to run your long duration run early in the morning.
- After each run, it's important to stretch out your muscles.
- This week your body needs as much rest as possible.
- Don't run past Wednesday.

Half Marathon Training Schedule for

runners with a 5K finish time of 47 minutes

and a pace of *15:09* minutes/mile.

# Predicted Half Marathon Finish Time:

## *3* hour(s) *36* minutes

# PACING TABLES

| Pace | Pace (minutes/miles) |
|---:|---|
| 5k | 15:09 |
| Half marathon | 16:30 |
| Medium | Between 16:30 - 17:30 |
| Easy | Between 16:30 - 18:30 |
| Slow | Between 16:30 - 19:00 |

| Race | Finish Times (predicted) |
|---:|---|
| 5k | 47 minutes |
| Half marathon | 3 hour(s) 36 minutes |

| \ | Determining your pace |
|---|---|
| Slow Pace | Extremely easy to hold a conversation. |
| Easy Pace | You can hold a conversation with someone. Your breathing might break up some of the flow of the conversation. |
| Medium | You can hold a conversation with someone, but it's broken up into smaller sentences and smaller responses. |
| Half Marathon Pace | Conversation is difficult. One and two word responses back and forth at best. |

## Definitions in the table below:

CT = Cross Training

S = Slow Pace (long run pace)

E = Easy Pace

M = Medium Pace

HM = Half Marathon Pace

## Training - Week A (Optional)

5K Pace: **15:09**         5k Finish Time: **47 minutes**

| Day | Dist. Mile | Dist. KM | Difficulty | Pace (Range) | Instructions |
|---|---|---|---|---|---|
| Monday | Rest | Rest | Rest | Rest | Take it easy. Don't run. If you need to exercise, I recommend a walk for no longer than 30 minutes. |
| Tuesday | 1 | 1.5 | E | 16:30 - 18:30 | walk/run at an easy pace. |
| Wednesday | 1 | 1.5 | HM | 16:30 | walk/run at your half marathon pace. |
| Thursday | 1 | 1.5 | M | 16:30 - 17:30 | walk/run at a medium pace. |
| Friday | Rest | Rest | Rest | Rest | Rest. |
| Saturday | 1.5 | 2.5 | S | 16:30 - 19:00 | walk/run at a slow pace. The most important piece of your long duration runs is finishing the run. |
| Sunday | Rest/CT | Rest/CT | Rest | Rest | Rest. If your body feels good, then go ahead and do some form of cross-training for 30 to 60 minutes. |

## Training - Week B (Optional)

| Day | Dist. Mile | Dist. KM | Difficulty | Pace (Range) | Instructions |
|---|---|---|---|---|---|
| Monday | Rest | Rest | Rest | Rest | Take it easy. Don't run. If you need to exercise, I recommend a walk for no longer than 30 minutes. |
| Tuesday | 1.5 | 2.5 | E | 16:30 - 18:30 | walk/run at an easy pace. |
| Wednesday | 1.5 | 2.5 | HM | 16:30 | walk/run at your half marathon pace. |
| Thursday | 1.5 | 2.5 | M | 16:30 - 17:30 | walk/run at a medium pace. |
| Friday | Rest | Rest | Rest | Rest | Rest. |
| Saturday | 2 | 3 | S | 16:30 - 19:00 | walk/run at a slow pace. The most important piece of your long duration runs is finishing the run. |
| Sunday | Rest/CT | Rest/CT | Rest | Rest | Rest. If your body feels good, then go ahead and do some form of cross-training for 30 to 60 minutes. |

# Training - Week C (Optional)

5K Pace: **15:09**     5k Finish Time: **47 minutes**

| Day | Dist. Mile | Dist. KM | Difficulty | Pace (Range) | Instructions |
|---|---|---|---|---|---|
| Monday | Rest | Rest | Rest | Rest | Take it easy. Don't run. If you need to exercise, I recommend a walk for no longer than 30 minutes. |
| Tuesday | 2 | 3 | E | 16:30 - 18:30 | walk/run at an easy pace. |
| Wednesday | 2 | 3 | HM | 16:30 | walk/run at your half marathon pace. |
| Thursday | 2 | 3 | M | 16:30 - 17:30 | walk/run at a medium pace. |
| Friday | Rest | Rest | Rest | Rest | Rest. |
| Saturday | 3 | 5 | S | 16:30 - 19:00 | walk/run at a slow pace. The most important piece of your long duration runs is finishing the run. |
| Sunday | Rest/CT | Rest/CT | Rest | Rest | Rest. If your body feels good, then go ahead and do some form of cross-training for 30 to 60 minutes. |

# Training - Week 1

5K Pace: **15:09**     5k Finish Time: **47 minutes**

| Day | Dist. Mile | Dist. KM | Difficulty | Pace (Range) | Instructions |
|---|---|---|---|---|---|
| Monday | Rest | Rest | Rest | Rest | Take it easy. Don't run. If you need to exercise, I recommend a walk for no longer than 30 minutes. |
| Tuesday | 3 | 5 | E | 16:30 - 18:30 | walk/run at an easy pace. |
| Wednesday | 3 | 5 | HM | 16:30 | walk/run at your half marathon pace. |
| Thursday | 3 | 5 | M | 16:30 - 17:30 | walk/run at a medium pace. |
| Friday | Rest | Rest | Rest | Rest | Rest. |
| Saturday | 4 | 6 | S | 16:30 - 19:00 | walk/run at a slow pace. The most important piece of your long duration runs is finishing the run. |
| Sunday | Rest/CT | Rest/CT | Rest | Rest | Rest. If your body feels good, then go ahead and do some form of cross-training for 30 to 60 minutes. |

# Training - Week 2

| Day | Dist. Mile | Dist. KM | Difficulty | Pace (Range) | Instructions |
|---|---|---|---|---|---|
| Monday | Rest | Rest | Rest | Rest | Take it easy. Don't run. If you need to exercise, I recommend a walk for no longer than 30 minutes. |
| Tuesday | 3 | 5 | E | 16:30 - 18:30 | walk/run at an easy pace. |
| Wednesday | 3 | 5 | HM | 16:30 | walk/run at your half marathon pace. |
| Thursday | 3 | 5 | M | 16:30 - 17:30 | walk/run at a medium pace. |
| Friday | Rest | Rest | Rest | Rest | Rest. |
| Saturday | 5 | 8 | S | 16:30 - 19:00 | walk/run at a slow pace. The most important piece of your long duration runs is finishing the run. |
| Sunday | Rest/CT | Rest/CT | Rest | Rest | Rest. If your body feels good, then go ahead and do some form of cross-training for 30 to 60 minutes. |

# Training - Week 3

5K Pace: **15:09**     5k Finish Time: **47 minutes**

| Day | Dist. Mile | Dist. KM | Difficulty | Pace (Range) | Instructions |
|---|---|---|---|---|---|
| Monday | Rest | Rest | Rest | Rest | Take it easy. Don't run. If you need to exercise, I recommend a walk for no longer than 30 minutes. |
| Tuesday | 3 | 5 | E | 16:30 - 18:30 | walk/run at an easy pace. |
| Wednesday | 4 | 6 | HM | 16:30 | walk/run at your half marathon pace. |
| Thursday | 3 | 5 | M | 16:30 - 17:30 | walk/run at a medium pace. |
| Friday | Rest | Rest | Rest | Rest | Rest. |
| Saturday | 6 | 10 | S | 16:30 - 19:00 | walk/run at a slow pace. The most important piece of your long duration runs is finishing the run. |
| Sunday | Rest/CT | Rest/CT | Rest | Rest | Rest. If your body feels good, then go ahead and do some form of cross-training for 30 to 60 minutes. |

# Training - Week 4 (5K Optional)

5K Pace: **15:09**     5k Finish Time: **47 minutes**

| Day | Dist. Mile | Dist. KM | Difficulty | Pace (Range) | Instructions |
|---|---|---|---|---|---|
| Monday | Rest | Rest | Rest | Rest | Take it easy. Don't run. If you need to exercise, I recommend a walk for no longer than 30 minutes. |
| Tuesday | 3 | 5 | E | 16:30 - 18:30 | walk/run at an easy pace. |
| Wednesday | 4 | 6 | HM | 16:30 | walk/run at your half marathon pace. |
| Thursday | 3 | 5 | M | 16:30 - 17:30 | walk/run at a medium pace. |
| Friday | Rest | Rest | Rest | Rest | Rest. |
| Saturday | 6.5 | 10.5 | S | 16:30 - 19:00 | walk/run at a slow pace. The most important piece of your long duration runs is finishing the run. |
| Sunday | Rest/CT | Rest/CT | Rest | Rest | Rest. If your body feels good, then go ahead and do some form of cross-training for 30 to 60 minutes. |

## 5K Optional

| Day | Dist. Mile | Dist. KM | Difficulty | Pace (Range) | Instructions |
|---|---|---|---|---|---|
| Saturday | 3.1 | 5 | - | 15:09 | Run a 5k race instead of your long run. This is completely your choice. I recommend running a 5k race to help you get used to running races. You should see a difference in your race time if you have kept to your training schedule. Don't try for a personal best, run the 5K at your 5K pace. |

# Training - Week 5

5K Pace: **15:09**     5k Finish Time: **47 minutes**

| Day | Dist. Mile | Dist. KM | Difficulty | Pace (Range) | Instructions |
|---|---|---|---|---|---|
| Monday | Rest | Rest | Rest | Rest | Take it easy. Don't run. If you need to exercise, I recommend a walk for no longer than 30 minutes. |
| Tuesday | 3 | 5 | E | 16:30 - 18:30 | walk/run at an easy pace. |
| Wednesday | 4 | 6 | HM | 16:30 | walk/run at your half marathon pace. |
| Thursday | 3 | 5 | M | 16:30 - 17:30 | walk/run at a medium pace. |
| Friday | Rest | Rest | Rest | Rest | Rest. |
| Saturday | 7 | 11 | S | 16:30 - 19:00 | walk/run at a slow pace. The most important piece of your long duration runs is finishing the run. |
| Sunday | Rest/CT | Rest/CT | Rest | Rest | Rest. If your body feels good, then go ahead and do some form of cross-training for 30 to 60 minutes. |

## NOTE:

- Your long duration runs will begin to become more difficult for week 5 and beyond.
- If you get tired during a long duration run, walk for 1/10 mile or 3-5 minutes.

# Training - Week 6

5K Pace: **15:09**     5k Finish Time: **47 minutes**

| Day | Dist. Mile | Dist. KM | Difficulty | Pace (Range) | Instructions |
|---|---|---|---|---|---|
| Monday | Rest | Rest | Rest | Rest | Take it easy. Don't run. If you need to exercise, I recommend a walk for no longer than 30 minutes. |
| Tuesday | 3 | 5 | E | 16:30 - 18:30 | walk/run at an easy pace. |
| Wednesday | 4 | 6 | HM | 16:30 | walk/run at your half marathon pace. |
| Thursday | 3 | 5 | M | 16:30 - 17:30 | walk/run at a medium pace. |
| Friday | Rest | Rest | Rest | Rest | Rest. |
| Saturday | 8 | 13 | S | 16:30 - 19:00 | walk/run at a slow pace. The most important piece of your long duration runs is finishing the run. |
| Sunday | Rest/CT | Rest/CT | Rest | Rest | Rest. If your body feels good, then go ahead and do some form of cross-training for 30 to 60 minutes. |

# Training - Week 7

5K Pace: **15:09**     5k Finish Time: **47 minutes**

| Day | Dist. Mile | Dist. KM | Difficulty | Pace (Range) | Instructions |
|---|---|---|---|---|---|
| Monday | Rest | Rest | Rest | Rest | Take it easy. Don't run. If you need to exercise, I recommend a walk for no longer than 30 minutes. |
| Tuesday | 3 | 5 | E | 16:30 - 18:30 | walk/run at an easy pace. |
| Wednesday | 5 | 8 | HM | 16:30 | walk/run at your half marathon pace. |
| Thursday | 3 | 5 | M | 16:30 - 17:30 | walk/run at a medium pace. |
| Friday | Rest | Rest | Rest | Rest | Rest. |
| Saturday | 8.5 | 13.5 | S | 16:30 - 19:00 | walk/run at a slow pace. The most important piece of your long duration runs is finishing the run. |
| Sunday | Rest/CT | Rest/CT | Rest | Rest | Rest. If your body feels good, then go ahead and do some form of cross-training for 30 to 60 minutes. |

## 10K Optional

| Day | Dist. Mile | Dist. KM | Difficulty | Pace (Range) | Instructions |
|---|---|---|---|---|---|
| Thursday | 2 | 3 | E | 16:30 - 18:30 | If you run the optional 10K, either completely rest today or run 2 miles (3 km). |
| Saturday | 6.2 | 10K | - | **15:09** | Run a 10k race instead of your long run. This is completely your choice. I recommend running a 10k race to help you get used to running races. You should see a difference in your race time if you have kept to your training schedule. Don't try for a personal best, run the 10K at your 5K pace. |

# Training - Week 8

5K Pace: **15:09**     5k Finish Time: **47 minutes**

| Day | Dist. Mile | Dist. KM | Difficulty | Pace (Range) | Instructions |
|---|---|---|---|---|---|
| Monday | Rest | Rest | Rest | Rest | Take it easy. Don't run. If you need to exercise, I recommend a walk for no longer than 30 minutes. |
| Tuesday | 3 | 5 | E | 16:30 - 18:30 | walk/run at an easy pace. |
| Wednesday | 5 | 8 | HM | 16:30 | walk/run at your half marathon pace. |
| Thursday | 3 | 5 | M | 16:30 - 17:30 | walk/run at a medium pace. |
| Friday | Rest | Rest | Rest | Rest | Rest. |
| Saturday | 9 | 14 | S | 16:30 - 19:00 | walk/run at a slow pace. The most important piece of your long duration runs is finishing the run. |
| Sunday | Rest/CT | Rest/CT | Rest | Rest | Rest. If your body feels good, then go ahead and do some form of cross-training for 30 to 60 minutes. |

# Training - Week 9

5K Pace: **15:09**   5k Finish Time: **47 minutes**

| Day | Dist. Mile | Dist. KM | Difficulty | Pace (Range) | Instructions |
|---|---|---|---|---|---|
| Monday | Rest | Rest | Rest | Rest | Take it easy. Don't run. If you need to exercise, I recommend a walk for no longer than 30 minutes. |
| Tuesday | 3 | 5 | E | 16:30 - 18:30 | walk/run at an easy pace. |
| Wednesday | 5 | 8 | HM | 16:30 | walk/run at your half marathon pace. |
| Thursday | 3 | 5 | M | 16:30 - 17:30 | walk/run at a medium pace. |
| Friday | Rest | Rest | Rest | Rest | Rest. |
| Saturday | 8.5 | 13.5 | S | 16:30 - 19:00 | walk/run at a slow pace. The most important piece of your long duration runs is finishing the run. |
| Sunday | Rest/CT | Rest/CT | Rest | Rest | Rest. If your body feels good, then go ahead and do some form of cross-training for 30 to 60 minutes. |

## 13.1 Beta/Test Run Optional

| Day | Dist. Mile | Dist. KM | Difficulty | Pace (Range) | Instructions |
|---|---|---|---|---|---|
| Thursday | Rest | Rest | Rest | Rest | This is a rest day – it simulates race week |
| Friday | Rest | Rest | Rest | Rest | This is a rest day – it simulates race week |
| Saturday | 13.1 | 21 | S | 15:09 | I recommend that you attempt to go the full 13.1 miles (21 km) for a half marathon test run. <u>Only walk/run the first 10 miles (16 km) then walk the last 3.1 miles (5 km).</u> If you are successful, you will have a race ghost time to compete against. It will help energize and refocus your training on beating yourself in 3 weeks at the half marathon race. Also, it allows your mind to grasp the achievement of "completing the distance of a half marathon." |

# Training - Week 10

5K Pace: **15:09**     5k Finish Time: **47 minutes**

| Day | Dist. Mile | Dist. KM | Difficulty | Pace (Range) | Instructions |
|---|---|---|---|---|---|
| Monday | Rest | Rest | Rest | Rest | Take it easy. Don't run. If you need to exercise, I recommend a walk for no longer than 30 minutes. |
| Tuesday | 3 | 5 | E | 16:30 - 18:30 | walk/run at an easy pace. |
| Wednesday | 5 | 8 | HM | 16:30 | walk/run at your half marathon pace. |
| Thursday | 3 | 5 | M | 16:30 - 17:30 | walk/run at a medium pace. |
| Friday | Rest | Rest | Rest | Rest | Rest. |
| Saturday | 11 | 18 | S | 16:30 - 19:00 | walk/run at a slow pace. The most important piece of your long duration runs is finishing the run. |
| Sunday | Rest/CT | Rest/CT | Rest | Rest | Rest. If your body feels good, then go ahead and do some form of cross-training for 30 to 60 minutes. |

# Training - Week 11

| Day | Dist. Mile | Dist. KM | Difficulty | Pace (Range) | Instructions |
|---|---|---|---|---|---|
| Monday | Rest | Rest | Rest | Rest | Take it easy. Don't run. If you need to exercise, I recommend a walk for no longer than 30 minutes. |
| Tuesday | 3 | 5 | E | 16:30 - 18:30 | walk/run at an easy pace. |
| Wednesday | 5 | 8 | HM | 16:30 | walk/run at your half marathon pace. |
| Thursday | 3 | 5 | M | 16:30 - 17:30 | walk/run at a medium pace. |
| Friday | Rest | Rest | Rest | Rest | Rest. |
| Saturday | 12 | 20 | S | 16:30 - 19:00 | walk/run at a slow pace. The most important piece of your long duration runs is finishing the run. |
| Sunday | Rest/CT | Rest/CT | Rest | Rest | Rest. If your body feels good, then go ahead and do some form of cross-training for 30 to 60 minutes. |

# Training - Week 12

5K Pace: **15:09**     5k Finish Time: **47 minutes**

| Day | Dist. Mile | Dist. KM | Difficulty | Pace (Range) | Instructions |
|---|---|---|---|---|---|
| Monday | Rest | Rest | Rest | Rest | Take it easy. Don't run. If you need to exercise, I recommend a walk for no longer than 30 minutes. |
| Tuesday | 3 | 5 | E | 16:30 - 18:30 | walk/run at an easy pace. |
| Wednesday | 2 | 1.5 | HM | 16:30 | walk/run at your half marathon pace. |
| Thursday | Rest | Rest | Rest | Rest | Rest. |
| Friday | Rest | Rest | Rest | Rest | Rest. |
| Saturday | 13.1 | 21 | HM | 16:30 | RACE DAY! |
| Sunday | Rest | Rest | Rest | Rest | DRINK A VICTORY BEER! |

## NOTE:

- Get plenty of sleep the night before your long duration run.
- Try to run your long duration run early in the morning.
- After each run, it's important to stretch out your muscles.
- This week your body needs as much rest as possible.
- Don't run past Wednesday.

Half Marathon Training Schedule for
runners with a 5K finish time of 48 minutes
and a pace of *15:29* minutes/mile.

# Predicted Half Marathon Finish Time:
# *3* hour(s) *41* minutes

# PACING TABLES

| Pace | Pace (minutes/miles) |
|---:|---|
| 5k | 15:29 |
| Half marathon | 16:52 |
| Medium | Between 16:52 - 17:52 |
| Easy | Between 16:52 - 18:52 |
| Slow | Between 16:52 - 19:22 |

| Race | Finish Times (predicted) |
|---:|---|
| 5k | 48 minutes |
| Half marathon | 3 hour(s) 41 minutes |

| Determining your pace ||
|---|---|
| Slow Pace | Extremely easy to hold a conversation. |
| Easy Pace | You can hold a conversation with someone. Your breathing might break up some of the flow of the conversation. |
| Medium | You can hold a conversation with someone, but it's broken up into smaller sentences and smaller responses. |
| Half Marathon Pace | Conversation is difficult. One and two word responses back and forth at best. |

## Definitions in the table below:

CT = Cross Training

S = Slow Pace (long run pace)

E = Easy Pace

M = Medium Pace

HM = Half Marathon Pace

# Training - Week A (Optional)

5K Pace: **15:29**   5k Finish Time: **48 minutes**

| Day | Dist. Mile | Dist. KM | Difficulty | Pace (Range) | Instructions |
|---|---|---|---|---|---|
| Monday | Rest | Rest | Rest | Rest | Take it easy. Don't run. If you need to exercise, I recommend a walk for no longer than 30 minutes. |
| Tuesday | 1 | 1.5 | E | 16:52 - 18:52 | walk/run at an easy pace. |
| Wednesday | 1 | 1.5 | HM | 16:52 | walk/run at your half marathon pace. |
| Thursday | 1 | 1.5 | M | 16:52 - 17:52 | walk/run at a medium pace. |
| Friday | Rest | Rest | Rest | Rest | Rest. |
| Saturday | 1.5 | 2.5 | S | 16:52 - 19:22 | walk/run at a slow pace. The most important piece of your long duration runs is finishing the run. |
| Sunday | Rest/CT | Rest/CT | Rest | Rest | Rest. If your body feels good, then go ahead and do some form of cross-training for 30 to 60 minutes. |

# Training - Week B (Optional)

| Day | Dist. Mile | Dist. KM | Difficulty | Pace (Range) | Instructions |
|---|---|---|---|---|---|
| Monday | Rest | Rest | Rest | Rest | Take it easy. Don't run. If you need to exercise, I recommend a walk for no longer than 30 minutes. |
| Tuesday | 1.5 | 2.5 | E | 16:52 - 18:52 | walk/run at an easy pace. |
| Wednesday | 1.5 | 2.5 | HM | 16:52 | walk/run at your half marathon pace. |
| Thursday | 1.5 | 2.5 | M | 16:52 - 17:52 | walk/run at a medium pace. |
| Friday | Rest | Rest | Rest | Rest | Rest. |
| Saturday | 2 | 3 | S | 16:52 - 19:22 | walk/run at a slow pace. The most important piece of your long duration runs is finishing the run. |
| Sunday | Rest/CT | Rest/CT | Rest | Rest | Rest. If your body feels good, then go ahead and do some form of cross-training for 30 to 60 minutes. |

# Training - Week C (Optional)

**5K Pace: 15:29**     **5k Finish Time: 48 minutes**

| Day | Dist. Mile | Dist. KM | Difficulty | Pace (Range) | Instructions |
|---|---|---|---|---|---|
| Monday | Rest | Rest | Rest | Rest | Take it easy. Don't run. If you need to exercise, I recommend a walk for no longer than 30 minutes. |
| Tuesday | 2 | 3 | E | 16:52 - 18:52 | walk/run at an easy pace. |
| Wednesday | 2 | 3 | HM | 16:52 | walk/run at your half marathon pace. |
| Thursday | 2 | 3 | M | 16:52 - 17:52 | walk/run at a medium pace. |
| Friday | Rest | Rest | Rest | Rest | Rest. |
| Saturday | 3 | 5 | S | 16:52 - 19:22 | walk/run at a slow pace. The most important piece of your long duration runs is finishing the run. |
| Sunday | Rest/CT | Rest/CT | Rest | Rest | Rest. If your body feels good, then go ahead and do some form of cross-training for 30 to 60 minutes. |

# Training - Week 1

5K Pace: **15:29**     5k Finish Time: **48 minutes**

| Day | Dist. Mile | Dist. KM | Difficulty | Pace (Range) | Instructions |
|---|---|---|---|---|---|
| Monday | Rest | Rest | Rest | Rest | Take it easy. Don't run. If you need to exercise, I recommend a walk for no longer than 30 minutes. |
| Tuesday | 3 | 5 | E | 16:52 - 18:52 | walk/run at an easy pace. |
| Wednesday | 3 | 5 | HM | 16:52 | walk/run at your half marathon pace. |
| Thursday | 3 | 5 | M | 16:52 - 17:52 | walk/run at a medium pace. |
| Friday | Rest | Rest | Rest | Rest | Rest. |
| Saturday | 4 | 6 | S | 16:52 - 19:22 | walk/run at a slow pace. The most important piece of your long duration runs is finishing the run. |
| Sunday | Rest/CT | Rest/CT | Rest | Rest | Rest. If your body feels good, then go ahead and do some form of cross-training for 30 to 60 minutes. |

# Training - Week 2

| Day | Dist. Mile | Dist. KM | Difficulty | Pace (Range) | Instructions |
|---|---|---|---|---|---|
| Monday | Rest | Rest | Rest | Rest | Take it easy. Don't run. If you need to exercise, I recommend a walk for no longer than 30 minutes. |
| Tuesday | 3 | 5 | E | 16:52 - 18:52 | walk/run at an easy pace. |
| Wednesday | 3 | 5 | HM | 16:52 | walk/run at your half marathon pace. |
| Thursday | 3 | 5 | M | 16:52 - 17:52 | walk/run at a medium pace. |
| Friday | Rest | Rest | Rest | Rest | Rest. |
| Saturday | 5 | 8 | S | 16:52 - 19:22 | walk/run at a slow pace. The most important piece of your long duration runs is finishing the run. |
| Sunday | Rest/CT | Rest/CT | Rest | Rest | Rest. If your body feels good, then go ahead and do some form of cross-training for 30 to 60 minutes. |

# Training - Week 3

5K Pace: **15:29**     5k Finish Time: **48 minutes**

| Day | Dist. Mile | Dist. KM | Difficulty | Pace (Range) | Instructions |
|---|---|---|---|---|---|
| Monday | Rest | Rest | Rest | Rest | Take it easy. Don't run. If you need to exercise, I recommend a walk for no longer than 30 minutes. |
| Tuesday | 3 | 5 | E | 16:52 - 18:52 | walk/run at an easy pace. |
| Wednesday | 4 | 6 | HM | 16:52 | walk/run at your half marathon pace. |
| Thursday | 3 | 5 | M | 16:52 - 17:52 | walk/run at a medium pace. |
| Friday | Rest | Rest | Rest | Rest | Rest. |
| Saturday | 6 | 10 | S | 16:52 - 19:22 | walk/run at a slow pace. The most important piece of your long duration runs is finishing the run. |
| Sunday | Rest/CT | Rest/CT | Rest | Rest | Rest. If your body feels good, then go ahead and do some form of cross-training for 30 to 60 minutes. |

# Training - Week 4 (5K Optional)

5K Pace: **15:29**      5k Finish Time: **48 minutes**

| Day | Dist. Mile | Dist. KM | Difficulty | Pace (Range) | Instructions |
|---|---|---|---|---|---|
| Monday | Rest | Rest | Rest | Rest | Take it easy. Don't run. If you need to exercise, I recommend a walk for no longer than 30 minutes. |
| Tuesday | 3 | 5 | E | 16:52 - 18:52 | walk/run at an easy pace. |
| Wednesday | 4 | 6 | HM | 16:52 | walk/run at your half marathon pace. |
| Thursday | 3 | 5 | M | 16:52 - 17:52 | walk/run at a medium pace. |
| Friday | Rest | Rest | Rest | Rest | Rest. |
| Saturday | 6.5 | 10.5 | S | 16:52 - 19:22 | walk/run at a slow pace. The most important piece of your long duration runs is finishing the run. |
| Sunday | Rest/CT | Rest/CT | Rest | Rest | Rest. If your body feels good, then go ahead and do some form of cross-training for 30 to 60 minutes. |

## 5K Optional

| Day | Dist. Mile | Dist. KM | Difficulty | Pace (Range) | Instructions |
|---|---|---|---|---|---|
| Saturday | 3.1 | 5 | - | 15:29 | Run a 5k race instead of your long run. This is completely your choice. I recommend running a 5k race to help you get used to running races. You should see a difference in your race time if you have kept to your training schedule. Don't try for a personal best, run the 5K at your 5K pace. |

# Training - Week 5

5K Pace: **15:29**     5k Finish Time: **48 minutes**

| Day | Dist. Mile | Dist. KM | Difficulty | Pace (Range) | Instructions |
|---|---|---|---|---|---|
| Monday | Rest | Rest | Rest | Rest | Take it easy. Don't run. If you need to exercise, I recommend a walk for no longer than 30 minutes. |
| Tuesday | 3 | 5 | E | 16:52 - 18:52 | walk/run at an easy pace. |
| Wednesday | 4 | 6 | HM | 16:52 | walk/run at your half marathon pace. |
| Thursday | 3 | 5 | M | 16:52 - 17:52 | walk/run at a medium pace. |
| Friday | Rest | Rest | Rest | Rest | Rest. |
| Saturday | 7 | 11 | S | 16:52 - 19:22 | walk/run at a slow pace. The most important piece of your long duration runs is finishing the run. |
| Sunday | Rest/CT | Rest/CT | Rest | Rest | Rest. If your body feels good, then go ahead and do some form of cross-training for 30 to 60 minutes. |

## NOTE:

- Your long duration runs will begin to become more difficult for week 5 and beyond.
- If you get tired during a long duration run, walk for 1/10 mile or 3-5 minutes.

# Training - Week 6

5K Pace: **15:29**     5k Finish Time: **48 minutes**

| Day | Dist. Mile | Dist. KM | Difficulty | Pace (Range) | Instructions |
|---|---|---|---|---|---|
| Monday | Rest | Rest | Rest | Rest | Take it easy. Don't run. If you need to exercise, I recommend a walk for no longer than 30 minutes. |
| Tuesday | 3 | 5 | E | 16:52 - 18:52 | walk/run at an easy pace. |
| Wednesday | 4 | 6 | HM | 16:52 | walk/run at your half marathon pace. |
| Thursday | 3 | 5 | M | 16:52 - 17:52 | walk/run at a medium pace. |
| Friday | Rest | Rest | Rest | Rest | Rest. |
| Saturday | 8 | 13 | S | 16:52 - 19:22 | walk/run at a slow pace. The most important piece of your long duration runs is finishing the run. |
| Sunday | Rest/CT | Rest/CT | Rest | Rest | Rest. If your body feels good, then go ahead and do some form of cross-training for 30 to 60 minutes. |

# Training - Week 7

5K Pace: **15:29**     5k Finish Time: **48 minutes**

| Day | Dist. Mile | Dist. KM | Difficulty | Pace (Range) | Instructions |
|---|---|---|---|---|---|
| Monday | Rest | Rest | Rest | Rest | Take it easy. Don't run. If you need to exercise, I recommend a walk for no longer than 30 minutes. |
| Tuesday | 3 | 5 | E | 16:52 - 18:52 | walk/run at an easy pace. |
| Wednesday | 5 | 8 | HM | 16:52 | walk/run at your half marathon pace. |
| Thursday | 3 | 5 | M | 16:52 - 17:52 | walk/run at a medium pace. |
| Friday | Rest | Rest | Rest | Rest | Rest. |
| Saturday | 8.5 | 13.5 | S | 16:52 - 19:22 | walk/run at a slow pace. The most important piece of your long duration runs is finishing the run. |
| Sunday | Rest/CT | Rest/CT | Rest | Rest | Rest. If your body feels good, then go ahead and do some form of cross-training for 30 to 60 minutes. |

## 10K Optional

| Day | Dist. Mile | Dist. KM | Difficulty | Pace (Range) | Instructions |
|---|---|---|---|---|---|
| Thursday | 2 | 3 | E | 16:52 - 18:52 | If you run the optional 10K, either completely rest today or run 2 miles (3 km). |
| Saturday | 6.2 | 10K | - | **15:29** | Run a 10k race instead of your long run. This is completely your choice. I recommend running a 10k race to help you get used to running races. You should see a difference in your race time if you have kept to your training schedule. Don't try for a personal best, run the 10K at your 5K pace. |

# Training - Week 8

5K Pace: **15:29**     5k Finish Time: **48 minutes**

| Day | Dist. Mile | Dist. KM | Difficulty | Pace (Range) | Instructions |
|---|---|---|---|---|---|
| Monday | Rest | Rest | Rest | Rest | Take it easy. Don't run. If you need to exercise, I recommend a walk for no longer than 30 minutes. |
| Tuesday | 3 | 5 | E | 16:52 - 18:52 | walk/run at an easy pace. |
| Wednesday | 5 | 8 | HM | 16:52 | walk/run at your half marathon pace. |
| Thursday | 3 | 5 | M | 16:52 - 17:52 | walk/run at a medium pace. |
| Friday | Rest | Rest | Rest | Rest | Rest. |
| Saturday | 9 | 14 | S | 16:52 - 19:22 | walk/run at a slow pace. The most important piece of your long duration runs is finishing the run. |
| Sunday | Rest/CT | Rest/CT | Rest | Rest | Rest. If your body feels good, then go ahead and do some form of cross-training for 30 to 60 minutes. |

# Training - Week 9

5K Pace: **15:29**     5k Finish Time: **48 minutes**

| Day | Dist. Mile | Dist. KM | Difficulty | Pace (Range) | Instructions |
|---|---|---|---|---|---|
| Monday | Rest | Rest | Rest | Rest | Take it easy. Don't run. If you need to exercise, I recommend a walk for no longer than 30 minutes. |
| Tuesday | 3 | 5 | E | 16:52 - 18:52 | walk/run at an easy pace. |
| Wednesday | 5 | 8 | HM | 16:52 | walk/run at your half marathon pace. |
| Thursday | 3 | 5 | M | 16:52 - 17:52 | walk/run at a medium pace. |
| Friday | Rest | Rest | Rest | Rest | Rest. |
| Saturday | 8.5 | 13.5 | S | 16:52 - 19:22 | walk/run at a slow pace. The most important piece of your long duration runs is finishing the run. |
| Sunday | Rest/CT | Rest/CT | Rest | Rest | Rest. If your body feels good, then go ahead and do some form of cross-training for 30 to 60 minutes. |

## 13.1 Beta/Test Run Optional

| Day | Dist. Mile | Dist. KM | Difficulty | Pace (Range) | Instructions |
|---|---|---|---|---|---|
| Thursday | Rest | Rest | Rest | Rest | This is a rest day – it simulates race week |
| Friday | Rest | Rest | Rest | Rest | This is a rest day – it simulates race week |
| Saturday | 13.1 | 21 | S | 15:29 | I recommend that you attempt to go the full 13.1 miles (21 km) for a half marathon test run. <u>Only walk/run the first 10 miles (16 km) then walk the last 3.1 miles (5 km).</u> If you are successful, you will have a race ghost time to compete against. It will help energize and refocus your training on beating yourself in 3 weeks at the half marathon race. Also, it allows your mind to grasp the achievement of "completing the distance of a half marathon." |

# Training - Week 10

5K Pace: **15:29**     5k Finish Time: **48 minutes**

| Day | Dist. Mile | Dist. KM | Difficulty | Pace (Range) | Instructions |
|---|---|---|---|---|---|
| Monday | Rest | Rest | Rest | Rest | Take it easy. Don't run. If you need to exercise, I recommend a walk for no longer than 30 minutes. |
| Tuesday | 3 | 5 | E | 16:52 - 18:52 | walk/run at an easy pace. |
| Wednesday | 5 | 8 | HM | 16:52 | walk/run at your half marathon pace. |
| Thursday | 3 | 5 | M | 16:52 - 17:52 | walk/run at a medium pace. |
| Friday | Rest | Rest | Rest | Rest | Rest. |
| Saturday | 11 | 18 | S | 16:52 - 19:22 | walk/run at a slow pace. The most important piece of your long duration runs is finishing the run. |
| Sunday | Rest/CT | Rest/CT | Rest | Rest | Rest. If your body feels good, then go ahead and do some form of cross-training for 30 to 60 minutes. |

# Training - Week 11

| Day | Dist. Mile | Dist. KM | Difficulty | Pace (Range) | Instructions |
|---|---|---|---|---|---|
| Monday | Rest | Rest | Rest | Rest | Take it easy. Don't run. If you need to exercise, I recommend a walk for no longer than 30 minutes. |
| Tuesday | 3 | 5 | E | 16:52 - 18:52 | walk/run at an easy pace. |
| Wednesday | 5 | 8 | HM | 16:52 | walk/run at your half marathon pace. |
| Thursday | 3 | 5 | M | 16:52 - 17:52 | walk/run at a medium pace. |
| Friday | Rest | Rest | Rest | Rest | Rest. |
| Saturday | 12 | 20 | S | 16:52 - 19:22 | walk/run at a slow pace. The most important piece of your long duration runs is finishing the run. |
| Sunday | Rest/CT | Rest/CT | Rest | Rest | Rest. If your body feels good, then go ahead and do some form of cross-training for 30 to 60 minutes. |

# Training - Week 12

5K Pace: **15:29**     5k Finish Time: **48 minutes**

| Day | Dist. Mile | Dist. KM | Difficulty | Pace (Range) | Instructions |
|---|---|---|---|---|---|
| Monday | Rest | Rest | Rest | Rest | Take it easy. Don't run. If you need to exercise, I recommend a walk for no longer than 30 minutes. |
| Tuesday | 3 | 5 | E | 16:52 - 18:52 | walk/run at an easy pace. |
| Wednesday | 2 | 1.5 | HM | 16:52 | walk/run at your half marathon pace. |
| Thursday | Rest | Rest | Rest | Rest | Rest. |
| Friday | Rest | Rest | Rest | Rest | Rest. |
| Saturday | 13.1 | 21 | HM | 16:52 | RACE DAY! |
| Sunday | Rest | Rest | Rest | Rest | DRINK A VICTORY BEER! |

## NOTE:

- Get plenty of sleep the night before your long duration run.
- Try to run your long duration run early in the morning.
- After each run, it's important to stretch out your muscles.
- This week your body needs as much rest as possible.
- Don't run past Wednesday.

# BEGINNER TO FINISHER RUNNING

Half Marathon Training Schedule for

runners with a 5K finish time of 49 minutes

and a pace of *15:48* minutes/mile.

## Predicted Half Marathon Finish Time:

### *3* hour(s) *46* minutes

# PACING TABLES

| Pace | Pace (minutes/miles) |
|---:|---|
| 5k | 15:48 |
| Half marathon | 17:15 |
| Medium | Between 17:15 - 18:15 |
| Easy | Between 17:15 - 19:15 |
| Slow | Between 17:15 - 19:45 |

| Race | Finish Times (predicted) |
|---:|---|
| 5k | 49 minutes |
| Half marathon | 3 hour(s) 46 minutes |

| Determining your pace ||
|---|---|
| Slow Pace | Extremely easy to hold a conversation. |
| Easy Pace | You can hold a conversation with someone. Your breathing might break up some of the flow of the conversation. |
| Medium | You can hold a conversation with someone, but it's broken up into smaller sentences and smaller responses. |
| Half Marathon Pace | Conversation is difficult. One and two word responses back and forth at best. |

## Definitions in the table below:

CT = Cross Training

S = Slow Pace (long run pace)

E = Easy Pace

M = Medium Pace

HM = Half Marathon Pace

## Training - Week A (Optional)

5K Pace: **15:48**    5k Finish Time: **49 minutes**

| Day | Dist. Mile | Dist. KM | Difficulty | Pace (Range) | Instructions |
|---|---|---|---|---|---|
| Monday | Rest | Rest | Rest | Rest | Take it easy. Don't run. If you need to exercise, I recommend a walk for no longer than 30 minutes. |
| Tuesday | 1 | 1.5 | E | 17:15 - 19:15 | walk/run at an easy pace. |
| Wednesday | 1 | 1.5 | HM | 17:15 | walk/run at your half marathon pace. |
| Thursday | 1 | 1.5 | M | 17:15 - 18:15 | walk/run at a medium pace. |
| Friday | Rest | Rest | Rest | Rest | Rest. |
| Saturday | 1.5 | 2.5 | S | 17:15 - 19:45 | walk/run at a slow pace. The most important piece of your long duration runs is finishing the run. |
| Sunday | Rest/CT | Rest/CT | Rest | Rest | Rest. If your body feels good, then go ahead and do some form of cross-training for 30 to 60 minutes. |

## Training - Week B (Optional)

| Day | Dist. Mile | Dist. KM | Difficulty | Pace (Range) | Instructions |
|---|---|---|---|---|---|
| Monday | Rest | Rest | Rest | Rest | Take it easy. Don't run. If you need to exercise, I recommend a walk for no longer than 30 minutes. |
| Tuesday | 1.5 | 2.5 | E | 17:15 - 19:15 | walk/run at an easy pace. |
| Wednesday | 1.5 | 2.5 | HM | 17:15 | walk/run at your half marathon pace. |
| Thursday | 1.5 | 2.5 | M | 17:15 - 18:15 | walk/run at a medium pace. |
| Friday | Rest | Rest | Rest | Rest | Rest. |
| Saturday | 2 | 3 | S | 17:15 - 19:45 | walk/run at a slow pace. The most important piece of your long duration runs is finishing the run. |
| Sunday | Rest/CT | Rest/CT | Rest | Rest | Rest. If your body feels good, then go ahead and do some form of cross-training for 30 to 60 minutes. |

# Training - Week C (Optional)

5K Pace: **15:48**  5k Finish Time: **49 minutes**

| Day | Dist. Mile | Dist. KM | Difficulty | Pace (Range) | Instructions |
|---|---|---|---|---|---|
| Monday | Rest | Rest | Rest | Rest | Take it easy. Don't run. If you need to exercise, I recommend a walk for no longer than 30 minutes. |
| Tuesday | 2 | 3 | E | 17:15 - 19:15 | walk/run at an easy pace. |
| Wednesday | 2 | 3 | HM | 17:15 | walk/run at your half marathon pace. |
| Thursday | 2 | 3 | M | 17:15 - 18:15 | walk/run at a medium pace. |
| Friday | Rest | Rest | Rest | Rest | Rest. |
| Saturday | 3 | 5 | S | 17:15 - 19:45 | walk/run at a slow pace. The most important piece of your long duration runs is finishing the run. |
| Sunday | Rest/CT | Rest/CT | Rest | Rest | Rest. If your body feels good, then go ahead and do some form of cross-training for 30 to 60 minutes. |

# Training - Week 1

5K Pace: **15:48**     5k Finish Time: **49 minutes**

| Day | Dist. Mile | Dist. KM | Difficulty | Pace (Range) | Instructions |
|---|---|---|---|---|---|
| Monday | Rest | Rest | Rest | Rest | Take it easy. Don't run. If you need to exercise, I recommend a walk for no longer than 30 minutes. |
| Tuesday | 3 | 5 | E | 17:15 - 19:15 | walk/run at an easy pace. |
| Wednesday | 3 | 5 | HM | 17:15 | walk/run at your half marathon pace. |
| Thursday | 3 | 5 | M | 17:15 - 18:15 | walk/run at a medium pace. |
| Friday | Rest | Rest | Rest | Rest | Rest. |
| Saturday | 4 | 6 | S | 17:15 - 19:45 | walk/run at a slow pace. The most important piece of your long duration runs is finishing the run. |
| Sunday | Rest/CT | Rest/CT | Rest | Rest | Rest. If your body feels good, then go ahead and do some form of cross-training for 30 to 60 minutes. |

# Training - Week 2

| Day | Dist. Mile | Dist. KM | Difficulty | Pace (Range) | Instructions |
|---|---|---|---|---|---|
| Monday | Rest | Rest | Rest | Rest | Take it easy. Don't run. If you need to exercise, I recommend a walk for no longer than 30 minutes. |
| Tuesday | 3 | 5 | E | 17:15 - 19:15 | walk/run at an easy pace. |
| Wednesday | 3 | 5 | HM | 17:15 | walk/run at your half marathon pace. |
| Thursday | 3 | 5 | M | 17:15 - 18:15 | walk/run at a medium pace. |
| Friday | Rest | Rest | Rest | Rest | Rest. |
| Saturday | 5 | 8 | S | 17:15 - 19:45 | walk/run at a slow pace. The most important piece of your long duration runs is finishing the run. |
| Sunday | Rest/CT | Rest/CT | Rest | Rest | Rest. If your body feels good, then go ahead and do some form of cross-training for 30 to 60 minutes. |

# Training - Week 3

5K Pace: **15:48**     5k Finish Time: **49 minutes**

| Day | Dist. Mile | Dist. KM | Difficulty | Pace (Range) | Instructions |
|---|---|---|---|---|---|
| Monday | Rest | Rest | Rest | Rest | Take it easy. Don't run. If you need to exercise, I recommend a walk for no longer than 30 minutes. |
| Tuesday | 3 | 5 | E | 17:15 - 19:15 | walk/run at an easy pace. |
| Wednesday | 4 | 6 | HM | 17:15 | walk/run at your half marathon pace. |
| Thursday | 3 | 5 | M | 17:15 - 18:15 | walk/run at a medium pace. |
| Friday | Rest | Rest | Rest | Rest | Rest. |
| Saturday | 6 | 10 | S | 17:15 - 19:45 | walk/run at a slow pace. The most important piece of your long duration runs is finishing the run. |
| Sunday | Rest/CT | Rest/CT | Rest | Rest | Rest. If your body feels good, then go ahead and do some form of cross-training for 30 to 60 minutes. |

# Training - Week 4 (5K Optional)

5K Pace: **15:48**     5k Finish Time: **49 minutes**

| Day | Dist. Mile | Dist. KM | Difficulty | Pace (Range) | Instructions |
|---|---|---|---|---|---|
| Monday | Rest | Rest | Rest | Rest | Take it easy. Don't run. If you need to exercise, I recommend a walk for no longer than 30 minutes. |
| Tuesday | 3 | 5 | E | 17:15 - 19:15 | walk/run at an easy pace. |
| Wednesday | 4 | 6 | HM | 17:15 | walk/run at your half marathon pace. |
| Thursday | 3 | 5 | M | 17:15 - 18:15 | walk/run at a medium pace. |
| Friday | Rest | Rest | Rest | Rest | Rest. |
| Saturday | 6.5 | 10.5 | S | 17:15 - 19:45 | walk/run at a slow pace. The most important piece of your long duration runs is finishing the run. |
| Sunday | Rest/CT | Rest/CT | Rest | Rest | Rest. If your body feels good, then go ahead and do some form of cross-training for 30 to 60 minutes. |

## 5K Optional

| Day | Dist. Mile | Dist. KM | Difficulty | Pace (Range) | Instructions |
|---|---|---|---|---|---|
| Saturday | 3.1 | 5 | - | 15:48 | Run a 5k race instead of your long run. This is completely your choice. I recommend running a 5k race to help you get used to running races. You should see a difference in your race time if you have kept to your training schedule. Don't try for a personal best, run the 5K at your 5K pace. |

# Training - Week 5

5K Pace: **15:48**     5k Finish Time: **49 minutes**

| Day | Dist. Mile | Dist. KM | Difficulty | Pace (Range) | Instructions |
|---|---|---|---|---|---|
| Monday | Rest | Rest | Rest | Rest | Take it easy. Don't run. If you need to exercise, I recommend a walk for no longer than 30 minutes. |
| Tuesday | 3 | 5 | E | 17:15 - 19:15 | walk/run at an easy pace. |
| Wednesday | 4 | 6 | HM | 17:15 | walk/run at your half marathon pace. |
| Thursday | 3 | 5 | M | 17:15 - 18:15 | walk/run at a medium pace. |
| Friday | Rest | Rest | Rest | Rest | Rest. |
| Saturday | 7 | 11 | S | 17:15 - 19:45 | walk/run at a slow pace. The most important piece of your long duration runs is finishing the run. |
| Sunday | Rest/CT | Rest/CT | Rest | Rest | Rest. If your body feels good, then go ahead and do some form of cross-training for 30 to 60 minutes. |

## NOTE:

- Your long duration runs will begin to become more difficult for week 5 and beyond.
- If you get tired during a long duration run, walk for 1/10 mile or 3-5 minutes.

# Training - Week 6

5K Pace: **15:48**     5k Finish Time: **49 minutes**

| Day | Dist. Mile | Dist. KM | Difficulty | Pace (Range) | Instructions |
|---|---|---|---|---|---|
| Monday | Rest | Rest | Rest | Rest | Take it easy. Don't run. If you need to exercise, I recommend a walk for no longer than 30 minutes. |
| Tuesday | 3 | 5 | E | 17:15 - 19:15 | walk/run at an easy pace. |
| Wednesday | 4 | 6 | HM | 17:15 | walk/run at your half marathon pace. |
| Thursday | 3 | 5 | M | 17:15 - 18:15 | walk/run at a medium pace. |
| Friday | Rest | Rest | Rest | Rest | Rest. |
| Saturday | 8 | 13 | S | 17:15 - 19:45 | walk/run at a slow pace. The most important piece of your long duration runs is finishing the run. |
| Sunday | Rest/CT | Rest/CT | Rest | Rest | Rest. If your body feels good, then go ahead and do some form of cross-training for 30 to 60 minutes. |

# Training - Week 7

5K Pace: **15:48**     5k Finish Time: **49 minutes**

| Day | Dist. Mile | Dist. KM | Difficulty | Pace (Range) | Instructions |
|---|---|---|---|---|---|
| Monday | Rest | Rest | Rest | Rest | Take it easy. Don't run. If you need to exercise, I recommend a walk for no longer than 30 minutes. |
| Tuesday | 3 | 5 | E | 17:15 - 19:15 | walk/run at an easy pace. |
| Wednesday | 5 | 8 | HM | 17:15 | walk/run at your half marathon pace. |
| Thursday | 3 | 5 | M | 17:15 - 18:15 | walk/run at a medium pace. |
| Friday | Rest | Rest | Rest | Rest | Rest. |
| Saturday | 8.5 | 13.5 | S | 17:15 - 19:45 | walk/run at a slow pace. The most important piece of your long duration runs is finishing the run. |
| Sunday | Rest/CT | Rest/CT | Rest | Rest | Rest. If your body feels good, then go ahead and do some form of cross-training for 30 to 60 minutes. |

## 10K Optional

| Day | Dist. Mile | Dist. KM | Difficulty | Pace (Range) | Instructions |
|---|---|---|---|---|---|
| Thursday | 2 | 3 | E | 17:15 - 19:15 | If you run the optional 10K, either completely rest today or run 2 miles (3 km). |
| Saturday | 6.2 | 10K | - | 15:48 | Run a 10k race instead of your long run. This is completely your choice. I recommend running a 10k race to help you get used to running races. You should see a difference in your race time if you have kept to your training schedule. Don't try for a personal best, run the 10K at your 5K pace. |

# Training - Week 8

5K Pace: **15:48**     5k Finish Time: **49 minutes**

| Day | Dist. Mile | Dist. KM | Difficulty | Pace (Range) | Instructions |
|---|---|---|---|---|---|
| Monday | Rest | Rest | Rest | Rest | Take it easy. Don't run. If you need to exercise, I recommend a walk for no longer than 30 minutes. |
| Tuesday | 3 | 5 | E | 17:15 - 19:15 | walk/run at an easy pace. |
| Wednesday | 5 | 8 | HM | 17:15 | walk/run at your half marathon pace. |
| Thursday | 3 | 5 | M | 17:15 - 18:15 | walk/run at a medium pace. |
| Friday | Rest | Rest | Rest | Rest | Rest. |
| Saturday | 9 | 14 | S | 17:15 - 19:45 | walk/run at a slow pace. The most important piece of your long duration runs is finishing the run. |
| Sunday | Rest/CT | Rest/CT | Rest | Rest | Rest. If your body feels good, then go ahead and do some form of cross-training for 30 to 60 minutes. |

# Training - Week 9

5K Pace: **15:48**     5k Finish Time: **49 minutes**

| Day | Dist. Mile | Dist. KM | Difficulty | Pace (Range) | Instructions |
|---|---|---|---|---|---|
| Monday | Rest | Rest | Rest | Rest | Take it easy. Don't run. If you need to exercise, I recommend a walk for no longer than 30 minutes. |
| Tuesday | 3 | 5 | E | 17:15 - 19:15 | walk/run at an easy pace. |
| Wednesday | 5 | 8 | HM | 17:15 | walk/run at your half marathon pace. |
| Thursday | 3 | 5 | M | 17:15 - 18:15 | walk/run at a medium pace. |
| Friday | Rest | Rest | Rest | Rest | Rest. |
| Saturday | 8.5 | 13.5 | S | 17:15 - 19:45 | walk/run at a slow pace. The most important piece of your long duration runs is finishing the run. |
| Sunday | Rest/CT | Rest/CT | Rest | Rest | Rest. If your body feels good, then go ahead and do some form of cross-training for 30 to 60 minutes. |

## 13.1 Beta/Test Run Optional

| Day | Dist. Mile | Dist. KM | Difficulty | Pace (Range) | Instructions |
|---|---|---|---|---|---|
| Thursday | Rest | Rest | Rest | Rest | This is a rest day – it simulates race week |
| Friday | Rest | Rest | Rest | Rest | This is a rest day – it simulates race week |
| Saturday | 13.1 | 21 | S | 15:48 | I recommend that you attempt to go the full 13.1 miles (21 km) for a half marathon test run. <u>Only walk/run the first 10 miles (16 km) then walk the last 3.1 miles (5 km).</u> If you are successful, you will have a race ghost time to compete against. It will help energize and refocus your training on beating yourself in 3 weeks at the half marathon race. Also, it allows your mind to grasp the achievement of "completing the distance of a half marathon." |

# Training - Week 10

5K Pace: **15:48**    5k Finish Time: **49 minutes**

| Day | Dist. Mile | Dist. KM | Difficulty | Pace (Range) | Instructions |
|---|---|---|---|---|---|
| Monday | Rest | Rest | Rest | Rest | Take it easy. Don't run. If you need to exercise, I recommend a walk for no longer than 30 minutes. |
| Tuesday | 3 | 5 | E | 17:15 - 19:15 | walk/run at an easy pace. |
| Wednesday | 5 | 8 | HM | 17:15 | walk/run at your half marathon pace. |
| Thursday | 3 | 5 | M | 17:15 - 18:15 | walk/run at a medium pace. |
| Friday | Rest | Rest | Rest | Rest | Rest. |
| Saturday | 11 | 18 | S | 17:15 - 19:45 | walk/run at a slow pace. The most important piece of your long duration runs is finishing the run. |
| Sunday | Rest/CT | Rest/CT | Rest | Rest | Rest. If your body feels good, then go ahead and do some form of cross-training for 30 to 60 minutes. |

# Training - Week 11

| Day | Dist. Mile | Dist. KM | Difficulty | Pace (Range) | Instructions |
|---|---|---|---|---|---|
| Monday | Rest | Rest | Rest | Rest | Take it easy. Don't run. If you need to exercise, I recommend a walk for no longer than 30 minutes. |
| Tuesday | 3 | 5 | E | 17:15 - 19:15 | walk/run at an easy pace. |
| Wednesday | 5 | 8 | HM | 17:15 | walk/run at your half marathon pace. |
| Thursday | 3 | 5 | M | 17:15 - 18:15 | walk/run at a medium pace. |
| Friday | Rest | Rest | Rest | Rest | Rest. |
| Saturday | 12 | 20 | S | 17:15 - 19:45 | walk/run at a slow pace. The most important piece of your long duration runs is finishing the run. |
| Sunday | Rest/CT | Rest/CT | Rest | Rest | Rest. If your body feels good, then go ahead and do some form of cross-training for 30 to 60 minutes. |

# Training - Week 12

5K Pace: **15:48**     5k Finish Time: **49 minutes**

| Day | Dist. Mile | Dist. KM | Difficulty | Pace (Range) | Instructions |
|---|---|---|---|---|---|
| Monday | Rest | Rest | Rest | Rest | Take it easy. Don't run. If you need to exercise, I recommend a walk for no longer than 30 minutes. |
| Tuesday | 3 | 5 | E | 17:15 - 19:15 | walk/run at an easy pace. |
| Wednesday | 2 | 1.5 | HM | 17:15 | walk/run at your half marathon pace. |
| Thursday | Rest | Rest | Rest | Rest | Rest. |
| Friday | Rest | Rest | Rest | Rest | Rest. |
| Saturday | 13.1 | 21 | HM | 17:15 | RACE DAY! |
| Sunday | Rest | Rest | Rest | Rest | DRINK A VICTORY BEER! |

## NOTE:

- Get plenty of sleep the night before your long duration run.
- Try to run your long duration run early in the morning.
- After each run, it's important to stretch out your muscles.
- This week your body needs as much rest as possible.
- Don't run past Wednesday.

## BEGINNER TO FINISHER RUNNING

Half Marathon Training Schedule for

runners with a 5K finish time of 50 minutes

and a pace of *16:07* minutes/mile.

# Predicted Half Marathon Finish Time:
# *3* hour(s) *50* minutes

# PACING TABLES

| Pace | Pace (minutes/miles) |
|---:|---|
| 5k | 16:07 |
| Half marathon | 17:35 |
| Medium | Between 17:35 - 18:35 |
| Easy | Between 17:35 - 19:35 |
| Slow | Between 17:35 - 20:05 |

| Race | Finish Times (predicted) |
|---:|---|
| 5k | 50 minutes |
| Half marathon | 3 hour(s) 50 minutes |

| Determining your pace | |
|---|---|
| Slow Pace | Extremely easy to hold a conversation. |
| Easy Pace | You can hold a conversation with someone. Your breathing might break up some of the flow of the conversation. |
| Medium | You can hold a conversation with someone, but it's broken up into smaller sentences and smaller responses. |
| Half Marathon Pace | Conversation is difficult. One and two word responses back and forth at best. |

## Definitions in the table below:

CT = Cross Training

S = Slow Pace (long run pace)

E = Easy Pace

M = Medium Pace

HM = Half Marathon Pace

# Training - Week A (Optional)

5K Pace: **16:07**     5k Finish Time: **50 minutes**

| Day | Dist. Mile | Dist. KM | Difficulty | Pace (Range) | Instructions |
|---|---|---|---|---|---|
| Monday | Rest | Rest | Rest | Rest | Take it easy. Don't run. If you need to exercise, I recommend a walk for no longer than 30 minutes. |
| Tuesday | 1 | 1.5 | E | 17:35 - 19:35 | walk/run at an easy pace. |
| Wednesday | 1 | 1.5 | HM | 17:35 | walk/run at your half marathon pace. |
| Thursday | 1 | 1.5 | M | 17:35 - 18:35 | walk/run at a medium pace. |
| Friday | Rest | Rest | Rest | Rest | Rest. |
| Saturday | 1.5 | 2.5 | S | 17:35 - 20:05 | walk/run at a slow pace. The most important piece of your long duration runs is finishing the run. |
| Sunday | Rest/CT | Rest/CT | Rest | Rest | Rest. If your body feels good, then go ahead and do some form of cross-training for 30 to 60 minutes. |

# Training - Week B (Optional)

| Day | Dist. Mile | Dist. KM | Difficulty | Pace (Range) | Instructions |
|---|---|---|---|---|---|
| Monday | Rest | Rest | Rest | Rest | Take it easy. Don't run. If you need to exercise, I recommend a walk for no longer than 30 minutes. |
| Tuesday | 1.5 | 2.5 | E | 17:35 - 19:35 | walk/run at an easy pace. |
| Wednesday | 1.5 | 2.5 | HM | 17:35 | walk/run at your half marathon pace. |
| Thursday | 1.5 | 2.5 | M | 17:35 - 18:35 | walk/run at a medium pace. |
| Friday | Rest | Rest | Rest | Rest | Rest. |
| Saturday | 2 | 3 | S | 17:35 - 20:05 | walk/run at a slow pace. The most important piece of your long duration runs is finishing the run. |
| Sunday | Rest/CT | Rest/CT | Rest | Rest | Rest. If your body feels good, then go ahead and do some form of cross-training for 30 to 60 minutes. |

# Training - Week C (Optional)

5K Pace: **16:07**     5k Finish Time: **50 minutes**

| Day | Dist. Mile | Dist. KM | Difficulty | Pace (Range) | Instructions |
|---|---|---|---|---|---|
| Monday | Rest | Rest | Rest | Rest | Take it easy. Don't run. If you need to exercise, I recommend a walk for no longer than 30 minutes. |
| Tuesday | 2 | 3 | E | 17:35 - 19:35 | walk/run at an easy pace. |
| Wednesday | 2 | 3 | HM | 17:35 | walk/run at your half marathon pace. |
| Thursday | 2 | 3 | M | 17:35 - 18:35 | walk/run at a medium pace. |
| Friday | Rest | Rest | Rest | Rest | Rest. |
| Saturday | 3 | 5 | S | 17:35 - 20:05 | walk/run at a slow pace. The most important piece of your long duration runs is finishing the run. |
| Sunday | Rest/CT | Rest/CT | Rest | Rest | Rest. If your body feels good, then go ahead and do some form of cross-training for 30 to 60 minutes. |

# Training - Week 1

5K Pace: **16:07**    5k Finish Time: **50 minutes**

| Day | Dist. Mile | Dist. KM | Difficulty | Pace (Range) | Instructions |
|---|---|---|---|---|---|
| Monday | Rest | Rest | Rest | Rest | Take it easy. Don't run. If you need to exercise, I recommend a walk for no longer than 30 minutes. |
| Tuesday | 3 | 5 | E | 17:35 - 19:35 | walk/run at an easy pace. |
| Wednesday | 3 | 5 | HM | 17:35 | walk/run at your half marathon pace. |
| Thursday | 3 | 5 | M | 17:35 - 18:35 | walk/run at a medium pace. |
| Friday | Rest | Rest | Rest | Rest | Rest. |
| Saturday | 4 | 6 | S | 17:35 - 20:05 | walk/run at a slow pace. The most important piece of your long duration runs is finishing the run. |
| Sunday | Rest/CT | Rest/CT | Rest | Rest | Rest. If your body feels good, then go ahead and do some form of cross-training for 30 to 60 minutes. |

# Training - Week 2

| Day | Dist. Mile | Dist. KM | Difficulty | Pace (Range) | Instructions |
|---|---|---|---|---|---|
| Monday | Rest | Rest | Rest | Rest | Take it easy. Don't run. If you need to exercise, I recommend a walk for no longer than 30 minutes. |
| Tuesday | 3 | 5 | E | 17:35 - 19:35 | walk/run at an easy pace. |
| Wednesday | 3 | 5 | HM | 17:35 | walk/run at your half marathon pace. |
| Thursday | 3 | 5 | M | 17:35 - 18:35 | walk/run at a medium pace. |
| Friday | Rest | Rest | Rest | Rest | Rest. |
| Saturday | 5 | 8 | S | 17:35 - 20:05 | walk/run at a slow pace. The most important piece of your long duration runs is finishing the run. |
| Sunday | Rest/CT | Rest/CT | Rest | Rest | Rest. If your body feels good, then go ahead and do some form of cross-training for 30 to 60 minutes. |

# Training - Week 3

5K Pace: **16:07**     5k Finish Time: **50 minutes**

| Day | Dist. Mile | Dist. KM | Difficulty | Pace (Range) | Instructions |
|---|---|---|---|---|---|
| Monday | Rest | Rest | Rest | Rest | Take it easy. Don't run. If you need to exercise, I recommend a walk for no longer than 30 minutes. |
| Tuesday | 3 | 5 | E | 17:35 - 19:35 | walk/run at an easy pace. |
| Wednesday | 4 | 6 | HM | 17:35 | walk/run at your half marathon pace. |
| Thursday | 3 | 5 | M | 17:35 - 18:35 | walk/run at a medium pace. |
| Friday | Rest | Rest | Rest | Rest | Rest. |
| Saturday | 6 | 10 | S | 17:35 - 20:05 | walk/run at a slow pace. The most important piece of your long duration runs is finishing the run. |
| Sunday | Rest/CT | Rest/CT | Rest | Rest | Rest. If your body feels good, then go ahead and do some form of cross-training for 30 to 60 minutes. |

# Training - Week 4 (5K Optional)

5K Pace: **16:07**     5k Finish Time: **50 minutes**

| Day | Dist. Mile | Dist. KM | Difficulty | Pace (Range) | Instructions |
|---|---|---|---|---|---|
| Monday | Rest | Rest | Rest | Rest | Take it easy. Don't run. If you need to exercise, I recommend a walk for no longer than 30 minutes. |
| Tuesday | 3 | 5 | E | 17:35 - 19:35 | walk/run at an easy pace. |
| Wednesday | 4 | 6 | HM | 17:35 | walk/run at your half marathon pace. |
| Thursday | 3 | 5 | M | 17:35 - 18:35 | walk/run at a medium pace. |
| Friday | Rest | Rest | Rest | Rest | Rest. |
| Saturday | 6.5 | 10.5 | S | 17:35 - 20:05 | walk/run at a slow pace. The most important piece of your long duration runs is finishing the run. |
| Sunday | Rest/CT | Rest/CT | Rest | Rest | Rest. If your body feels good, then go ahead and do some form of cross-training for 30 to 60 minutes. |

## 5K Optional

| Day | Dist. Mile | Dist. KM | Difficulty | Pace (Range) | Instructions |
|---|---|---|---|---|---|
| Saturday | 3.1 | 5 | - | **16:07** | Run a 5k race instead of your long run. This is completely your choice. I recommend running a 5k race to help you get used to running races. You should see a difference in your race time if you have kept to your training schedule. Don't try for a personal best, run the 5K at your 5K pace. |

# Training - Week 5

5K Pace: **16:07**     5k Finish Time: **50 minutes**

| Day | Dist. Mile | Dist. KM | Difficulty | Pace (Range) | Instructions |
|---|---|---|---|---|---|
| Monday | Rest | Rest | Rest | Rest | Take it easy. Don't run. If you need to exercise, I recommend a walk for no longer than 30 minutes. |
| Tuesday | 3 | 5 | E | 17:35 - 19:35 | walk/run at an easy pace. |
| Wednesday | 4 | 6 | HM | 17:35 | walk/run at your half marathon pace. |
| Thursday | 3 | 5 | M | 17:35 - 18:35 | walk/run at a medium pace. |
| Friday | Rest | Rest | Rest | Rest | Rest. |
| Saturday | 7 | 11 | S | 17:35 - 20:05 | walk/run at a slow pace. The most important piece of your long duration runs is finishing the run. |
| Sunday | Rest/CT | Rest/CT | Rest | Rest | Rest. If your body feels good, then go ahead and do some form of cross-training for 30 to 60 minutes. |

## NOTE:

- Your long duration runs will begin to become more difficult for week 5 and beyond.
- If you get tired during a long duration run, walk for 1/10 mile or 3-5 minutes.

# Training - Week 6

5K Pace: **16:07**     5k Finish Time: **50 minutes**

| Day | Dist. Mile | Dist. KM | Difficulty | Pace (Range) | Instructions |
|---|---|---|---|---|---|
| Monday | Rest | Rest | Rest | Rest | Take it easy. Don't run. If you need to exercise, I recommend a walk for no longer than 30 minutes. |
| Tuesday | 3 | 5 | E | 17:35 - 19:35 | walk/run at an easy pace. |
| Wednesday | 4 | 6 | HM | 17:35 | walk/run at your half marathon pace. |
| Thursday | 3 | 5 | M | 17:35 - 18:35 | walk/run at a medium pace. |
| Friday | Rest | Rest | Rest | Rest | Rest. |
| Saturday | 8 | 13 | S | 17:35 - 20:05 | walk/run at a slow pace. The most important piece of your long duration runs is finishing the run. |
| Sunday | Rest/CT | Rest/CT | Rest | Rest | Rest. If your body feels good, then go ahead and do some form of cross-training for 30 to 60 minutes. |

# Training - Week 7

5K Pace: **16:07**     5k Finish Time: **50 minutes**

| Day | Dist. Mile | Dist. KM | Difficulty | Pace (Range) | Instructions |
|---|---|---|---|---|---|
| Monday | Rest | Rest | Rest | Rest | Take it easy. Don't run. If you need to exercise, I recommend a walk for no longer than 30 minutes. |
| Tuesday | 3 | 5 | E | 17:35 - 19:35 | walk/run at an easy pace. |
| Wednesday | 5 | 8 | HM | 17:35 | walk/run at your half marathon pace. |
| Thursday | 3 | 5 | M | 17:35 - 18:35 | walk/run at a medium pace. |
| Friday | Rest | Rest | Rest | Rest | Rest. |
| Saturday | 8.5 | 13.5 | S | 17:35 - 20:05 | walk/run at a slow pace. The most important piece of your long duration runs is finishing the run. |
| Sunday | Rest/CT | Rest/CT | Rest | Rest | Rest. If your body feels good, then go ahead and do some form of cross-training for 30 to 60 minutes. |

## 10K Optional

| Day | Dist. Mile | Dist. KM | Difficulty | Pace (Range) | Instructions |
|---|---|---|---|---|---|
| Thursday | 2 | 3 | E | 17:35 - 19:35 | If you run the optional 10K, either completely rest today or run 2 miles (3 km). |
| Saturday | 6.2 | 10K | - | 16:07 | Run a 10k race instead of your long run. This is completely your choice. I recommend running a 10k race to help you get used to running races. You should see a difference in your race time if you have kept to your training schedule. Don't try for a personal best, run the 10K at your 5K pace. |

# Training - Week 8

5K Pace: **16:07**     5k Finish Time: **50 minutes**

| Day | Dist. Mile | Dist. KM | Difficulty | Pace (Range) | Instructions |
|---|---|---|---|---|---|
| Monday | Rest | Rest | Rest | Rest | Take it easy. Don't run. If you need to exercise, I recommend a walk for no longer than 30 minutes. |
| Tuesday | 3 | 5 | E | 17:35 - 19:35 | walk/run at an easy pace. |
| Wednesday | 5 | 8 | HM | 17:35 | walk/run at your half marathon pace. |
| Thursday | 3 | 5 | M | 17:35 - 18:35 | walk/run at a medium pace. |
| Friday | Rest | Rest | Rest | Rest | Rest. |
| Saturday | 9 | 14 | S | 17:35 - 20:05 | walk/run at a slow pace. The most important piece of your long duration runs is finishing the run. |
| Sunday | Rest/CT | Rest/CT | Rest | Rest | Rest. If your body feels good, then go ahead and do some form of cross-training for 30 to 60 minutes. |

# Training - Week 9

5K Pace: **16:07**     5k Finish Time: **50 minutes**

| Day | Dist. Mile | Dist. KM | Difficulty | Pace (Range) | Instructions |
|---|---|---|---|---|---|
| Monday | Rest | Rest | Rest | Rest | Take it easy. Don't run. If you need to exercise, I recommend a walk for no longer than 30 minutes. |
| Tuesday | 3 | 5 | E | 17:35 - 19:35 | walk/run at an easy pace. |
| Wednesday | 5 | 8 | HM | 17:35 | walk/run at your half marathon pace. |
| Thursday | 3 | 5 | M | 17:35 - 18:35 | walk/run at a medium pace. |
| Friday | Rest | Rest | Rest | Rest | Rest. |
| Saturday | 8.5 | 13.5 | S | 17:35 - 20:05 | walk/run at a slow pace. The most important piece of your long duration runs is finishing the run. |
| Sunday | Rest/CT | Rest/CT | Rest | Rest | Rest. If your body feels good, then go ahead and do some form of cross-training for 30 to 60 minutes. |

## 13.1 Beta/Test Run Optional

| Day | Dist. Mile | Dist. KM | Difficulty | Pace (Range) | Instructions |
|---|---|---|---|---|---|
| Thursday | Rest | Rest | Rest | Rest | This is a rest day – it simulates race week |
| Friday | Rest | Rest | Rest | Rest | This is a rest day – it simulates race week |
| Saturday | 13.1 | 21 | S | 16:07 | I recommend that you attempt to go the full 13.1 miles (21 km) for a half marathon test run. <u>Only walk/run the first 10 miles (16 km) then walk the last 3.1 miles (5 km).</u> If you are successful, you will have a race ghost time to compete against. It will help energize and refocus your training on beating yourself in 3 weeks at the half marathon race. Also, it allows your mind to grasp the achievement of "completing the distance of a half marathon." |

# Training - Week 10

5K Pace: **16:07**     5k Finish Time: **50 minutes**

| Day | Dist. Mile | Dist. KM | Difficulty | Pace (Range) | Instructions |
|---|---|---|---|---|---|
| Monday | Rest | Rest | Rest | Rest | Take it easy. Don't run. If you need to exercise, I recommend a walk for no longer than 30 minutes. |
| Tuesday | 3 | 5 | E | 17:35 - 19:35 | walk/run at an easy pace. |
| Wednesday | 5 | 8 | HM | 17:35 | walk/run at your half marathon pace. |
| Thursday | 3 | 5 | M | 17:35 - 18:35 | walk/run at a medium pace. |
| Friday | Rest | Rest | Rest | Rest | Rest. |
| Saturday | 11 | 18 | S | 17:35 - 20:05 | walk/run at a slow pace. The most important piece of your long duration runs is finishing the run. |
| Sunday | Rest/CT | Rest/CT | Rest | Rest | Rest. If your body feels good, then go ahead and do some form of cross-training for 30 to 60 minutes. |

# Training - Week 11

| Day | Dist. Mile | Dist. KM | Difficulty | Pace (Range) | Instructions |
|---|---|---|---|---|---|
| Monday | Rest | Rest | Rest | Rest | Take it easy. Don't run. If you need to exercise, I recommend a walk for no longer than 30 minutes. |
| Tuesday | 3 | 5 | E | 17:35 - 19:35 | walk/run at an easy pace. |
| Wednesday | 5 | 8 | HM | 17:35 | walk/run at your half marathon pace. |
| Thursday | 3 | 5 | M | 17:35 - 18:35 | walk/run at a medium pace. |
| Friday | Rest | Rest | Rest | Rest | Rest. |
| Saturday | 12 | 20 | S | 17:35 - 20:05 | walk/run at a slow pace. The most important piece of your long duration runs is finishing the run. |
| Sunday | Rest/CT | Rest/CT | Rest | Rest | Rest. If your body feels good, then go ahead and do some form of cross-training for 30 to 60 minutes. |

# Training - Week 12

5K Pace: **16:07**     5k Finish Time: **50 minutes**

| Day | Dist. Mile | Dist. KM | Difficulty | Pace (Range) | Instructions |
|---|---|---|---|---|---|
| Monday | Rest | Rest | Rest | Rest | Take it easy. Don't run. If you need to exercise, I recommend a walk for no longer than 30 minutes. |
| Tuesday | 3 | 5 | E | 17:35 - 19:35 | walk/run at an easy pace. |
| Wednesday | 2 | 1.5 | HM | 17:35 | walk/run at your half marathon pace. |
| Thursday | Rest | Rest | Rest | Rest | Rest. |
| Friday | Rest | Rest | Rest | Rest | Rest. |
| Saturday | 13.1 | 21 | HM | 17:35 | RACE DAY! |
| Sunday | Rest | Rest | Rest | Rest | DRINK A VICTORY BEER! |

## NOTE:

- Get plenty of sleep the night before your long duration run.
- Try to run your long duration run early in the morning.
- After each run, it's important to stretch out your muscles.
- This week your body needs as much rest as possible.
- Don't run past Wednesday.

Half Marathon Training Schedule for

runners with a 5K finish time of 51 minutes

and a pace of *16:27* minutes/mile.

# Predicted Half Marathon Finish Time:

## *3* hour(s) *55* minutes

# PACING TABLES

| Pace | Pace (minutes/miles) |
|---:|---|
| 5k | 16:27 |
| Half marathon | 17:55 |
| Medium | Between 17:55 - 18:55 |
| Easy | Between 17:55 - 19:55 |
| Slow | Between 17:55 - 20:25 |

| Race | Finish Times (predicted) |
|---:|---|
| 5k | 51 minutes |
| Half marathon | 3 hour(s) 55 minutes |

| Determining your pace ||
|---|---|
| Slow Pace | Extremely easy to hold a conversation. |
| Easy Pace | You can hold a conversation with someone. Your breathing might break up some of the flow of the conversation. |
| Medium | You can hold a conversation with someone, but it's broken up into smaller sentences and smaller responses. |
| Half Marathon Pace | Conversation is difficult. One and two word responses back and forth at best. |

## Definitions in the table below:

CT = Cross Training

S = Slow Pace (long run pace)

E = Easy Pace

M = Medium Pace

HM = Half Marathon Pace

## Training - Week A (Optional)

5K Pace: **16:27**      5k Finish Time: **51 minutes**

| Day | Dist. Mile | Dist. KM | Difficulty | Pace (Range) | Instructions |
|---|---|---|---|---|---|
| Monday | Rest | Rest | Rest | Rest | Take it easy. Don't run. If you need to exercise, I recommend a walk for no longer than 30 minutes. |
| Tuesday | 1 | 1.5 | E | 17:55 - 19:55 | walk/run at an easy pace. |
| Wednesday | 1 | 1.5 | HM | 17:55 | walk/run at your half marathon pace. |
| Thursday | 1 | 1.5 | M | 17:55 - 18:55 | walk/run at a medium pace. |
| Friday | Rest | Rest | Rest | Rest | Rest. |
| Saturday | 1.5 | 2.5 | S | 17:55 - 20:25 | walk/run at a slow pace. The most important piece of your long duration runs is finishing the run. |
| Sunday | Rest/CT | Rest/CT | Rest | Rest | Rest. If your body feels good, then go ahead and do some form of cross-training for 30 to 60 minutes. |

## Training - Week B (Optional)

| Day | Dist. Mile | Dist. KM | Difficulty | Pace (Range) | Instructions |
|---|---|---|---|---|---|
| Monday | Rest | Rest | Rest | Rest | Take it easy. Don't run. If you need to exercise, I recommend a walk for no longer than 30 minutes. |
| Tuesday | 1.5 | 2.5 | E | 17:55 - 19:55 | walk/run at an easy pace. |
| Wednesday | 1.5 | 2.5 | HM | 17:55 | walk/run at your half marathon pace. |
| Thursday | 1.5 | 2.5 | M | 17:55 - 18:55 | walk/run at a medium pace. |
| Friday | Rest | Rest | Rest | Rest | Rest. |
| Saturday | 2 | 3 | S | 17:55 - 20:25 | walk/run at a slow pace. The most important piece of your long duration runs is finishing the run. |
| Sunday | Rest/CT | Rest/CT | Rest | Rest | Rest. If your body feels good, then go ahead and do some form of cross-training for 30 to 60 minutes. |

# Training - Week C (Optional)

5K Pace: **16:27**     5k Finish Time: **51 minutes**

| Day | Dist. Mile | Dist. KM | Difficulty | Pace (Range) | Instructions |
|---|---|---|---|---|---|
| Monday | Rest | Rest | Rest | Rest | Take it easy. Don't run. If you need to exercise, I recommend a walk for no longer than 30 minutes. |
| Tuesday | 2 | 3 | E | 17:55 - 19:55 | walk/run at an easy pace. |
| Wednesday | 2 | 3 | HM | 17:55 | walk/run at your half marathon pace. |
| Thursday | 2 | 3 | M | 17:55 - 18:55 | walk/run at a medium pace. |
| Friday | Rest | Rest | Rest | Rest | Rest. |
| Saturday | 3 | 5 | S | 17:55 - 20:25 | walk/run at a slow pace. The most important piece of your long duration runs is finishing the run. |
| Sunday | Rest/CT | Rest/CT | Rest | Rest | Rest. If your body feels good, then go ahead and do some form of cross-training for 30 to 60 minutes. |

# Training - Week 1

5K Pace: **16:27**     5k Finish Time: **51 minutes**

| Day | Dist. Mile | Dist. KM | Difficulty | Pace (Range) | Instructions |
|---|---|---|---|---|---|
| Monday | Rest | Rest | Rest | Rest | Take it easy. Don't run. If you need to exercise, I recommend a walk for no longer than 30 minutes. |
| Tuesday | 3 | 5 | E | 17:55 - 19:55 | walk/run at an easy pace. |
| Wednesday | 3 | 5 | HM | 17:55 | walk/run at your half marathon pace. |
| Thursday | 3 | 5 | M | 17:55 - 18:55 | walk/run at a medium pace. |
| Friday | Rest | Rest | Rest | Rest | Rest. |
| Saturday | 4 | 6 | S | 17:55 - 20:25 | walk/run at a slow pace. The most important piece of your long duration runs is finishing the run. |
| Sunday | Rest/CT | Rest/CT | Rest | Rest | Rest. If your body feels good, then go ahead and do some form of cross-training for 30 to 60 minutes. |

# Training - Week 2

| Day | Dist. Mile | Dist. KM | Difficulty | Pace (Range) | Instructions |
|---|---|---|---|---|---|
| Monday | Rest | Rest | Rest | Rest | Take it easy. Don't run. If you need to exercise, I recommend a walk for no longer than 30 minutes. |
| Tuesday | 3 | 5 | E | 17:55 - 19:55 | walk/run at an easy pace. |
| Wednesday | 3 | 5 | HM | 17:55 | walk/run at your half marathon pace. |
| Thursday | 3 | 5 | M | 17:55 - 18:55 | walk/run at a medium pace. |
| Friday | Rest | Rest | Rest | Rest | Rest. |
| Saturday | 5 | 8 | S | 17:55 - 20:25 | walk/run at a slow pace. The most important piece of your long duration runs is finishing the run. |
| Sunday | Rest/CT | Rest/CT | Rest | Rest | Rest. If your body feels good, then go ahead and do some form of cross-training for 30 to 60 minutes. |

# Training - Week 3

5K Pace: **16:27**     5k Finish Time: **51 minutes**

| Day | Dist. Mile | Dist. KM | Difficulty | Pace (Range) | Instructions |
|---|---|---|---|---|---|
| Monday | Rest | Rest | Rest | Rest | Take it easy. Don't run. If you need to exercise, I recommend a walk for no longer than 30 minutes. |
| Tuesday | 3 | 5 | E | 17:55 - 19:55 | walk/run at an easy pace. |
| Wednesday | 4 | 6 | HM | 17:55 | walk/run at your half marathon pace. |
| Thursday | 3 | 5 | M | 17:55 - 18:55 | walk/run at a medium pace. |
| Friday | Rest | Rest | Rest | Rest | Rest. |
| Saturday | 6 | 10 | S | 17:55 - 20:25 | walk/run at a slow pace. The most important piece of your long duration runs is finishing the run. |
| Sunday | Rest/CT | Rest/CT | Rest | Rest | Rest. If your body feels good, then go ahead and do some form of cross-training for 30 to 60 minutes. |

# Training - Week 4 (5K Optional)

5K Pace: **16:27**     5k Finish Time: **51 minutes**

| Day | Dist. Mile | Dist. KM | Difficulty | Pace (Range) | Instructions |
|---|---|---|---|---|---|
| Monday | Rest | Rest | Rest | Rest | Take it easy. Don't run. If you need to exercise, I recommend a walk for no longer than 30 minutes. |
| Tuesday | 3 | 5 | E | 17:55 - 19:55 | walk/run at an easy pace. |
| Wednesday | 4 | 6 | HM | 17:55 | walk/run at your half marathon pace. |
| Thursday | 3 | 5 | M | 17:55 - 18:55 | walk/run at a medium pace. |
| Friday | Rest | Rest | Rest | Rest | Rest. |
| Saturday | 6.5 | 10.5 | S | 17:55 - 20:25 | walk/run at a slow pace. The most important piece of your long duration runs is finishing the run. |
| Sunday | Rest/CT | Rest/CT | Rest | Rest | Rest. If your body feels good, then go ahead and do some form of cross-training for 30 to 60 minutes. |

## 5K Optional

| Day | Dist. Mile | Dist. KM | Difficulty | Pace (Range) | Instructions |
|---|---|---|---|---|---|
| Saturday | 3.1 | 5 | - | **16:27** | Run a 5k race instead of your long run. This is completely your choice. I recommend running a 5k race to help you get used to running races. You should see a difference in your race time if you have kept to your training schedule. Don't try for a personal best, run the 5K at your 5K pace. |

# Training - Week 5

5K Pace: **16:27**     5k Finish Time: **51 minutes**

| Day | Dist. Mile | Dist. KM | Difficulty | Pace (Range) | Instructions |
|---|---|---|---|---|---|
| Monday | Rest | Rest | Rest | Rest | Take it easy. Don't run. If you need to exercise, I recommend a walk for no longer than 30 minutes. |
| Tuesday | 3 | 5 | E | 17:55 - 19:55 | walk/run at an easy pace. |
| Wednesday | 4 | 6 | HM | 17:55 | walk/run at your half marathon pace. |
| Thursday | 3 | 5 | M | 17:55 - 18:55 | walk/run at a medium pace. |
| Friday | Rest | Rest | Rest | Rest | Rest. |
| Saturday | 7 | 11 | S | 17:55 - 20:25 | walk/run at a slow pace. The most important piece of your long duration runs is finishing the run. |
| Sunday | Rest/CT | Rest/CT | Rest | Rest | Rest. If your body feels good, then go ahead and do some form of cross-training for 30 to 60 minutes. |

## NOTE:

- Your long duration runs will begin to become more difficult for week 5 and beyond.
- If you get tired during a long duration run, walk for 1/10 mile or 3-5 minutes.

# Training - Week 6

5K Pace: **16:27**     5k Finish Time: **51 minutes**

| Day | Dist. Mile | Dist. KM | Difficulty | Pace (Range) | Instructions |
|---|---|---|---|---|---|
| Monday | Rest | Rest | Rest | Rest | Take it easy. Don't run. If you need to exercise, I recommend a walk for no longer than 30 minutes. |
| Tuesday | 3 | 5 | E | 17:55 - 19:55 | walk/run at an easy pace. |
| Wednesday | 4 | 6 | HM | 17:55 | walk/run at your half marathon pace. |
| Thursday | 3 | 5 | M | 17:55 - 18:55 | walk/run at a medium pace. |
| Friday | Rest | Rest | Rest | Rest | Rest. |
| Saturday | 8 | 13 | S | 17:55 - 20:25 | walk/run at a slow pace. The most important piece of your long duration runs is finishing the run. |
| Sunday | Rest/CT | Rest/CT | Rest | Rest | Rest. If your body feels good, then go ahead and do some form of cross-training for 30 to 60 minutes. |

# Training - Week 7

5K Pace: **16:27**     5k Finish Time: **51 minutes**

| Day | Dist. Mile | Dist. KM | Difficulty | Pace (Range) | Instructions |
|---|---|---|---|---|---|
| Monday | Rest | Rest | Rest | Rest | Take it easy. Don't run. If you need to exercise, I recommend a walk for no longer than 30 minutes. |
| Tuesday | 3 | 5 | E | 17:55 - 19:55 | walk/run at an easy pace. |
| Wednesday | 5 | 8 | HM | 17:55 | walk/run at your half marathon pace. |
| Thursday | 3 | 5 | M | 17:55 - 18:55 | walk/run at a medium pace. |
| Friday | Rest | Rest | Rest | Rest | Rest. |
| Saturday | 8.5 | 13.5 | S | 17:55 - 20:25 | walk/run at a slow pace. The most important piece of your long duration runs is finishing the run. |
| Sunday | Rest/CT | Rest/CT | Rest | Rest | Rest. If your body feels good, then go ahead and do some form of cross-training for 30 to 60 minutes. |

## 10K Optional

| Day | Dist. Mile | Dist. KM | Difficulty | Pace (Range) | Instructions |
|---|---|---|---|---|---|
| Thursday | 2 | 3 | E | 17:55 - 19:55 | If you run the optional 10K, either completely rest today or run 2 miles (3 km). |
| Saturday | 6.2 | 10K | - | 16:27 | Run a 10k race instead of your long run. This is completely your choice. I recommend running a 10k race to help you get used to running races. You should see a difference in your race time if you have kept to your training schedule. Don't try for a personal best, run the 10K at your 5K pace. |

# Training - Week 8

5K Pace: **16:27**     5k Finish Time: **51 minutes**

| Day | Dist. Mile | Dist. KM | Difficulty | Pace (Range) | Instructions |
|---|---|---|---|---|---|
| Monday | Rest | Rest | Rest | Rest | Take it easy. Don't run. If you need to exercise, I recommend a walk for no longer than 30 minutes. |
| Tuesday | 3 | 5 | E | 17:55 - 19:55 | walk/run at an easy pace. |
| Wednesday | 5 | 8 | HM | 17:55 | walk/run at your half marathon pace. |
| Thursday | 3 | 5 | M | 17:55 - 18:55 | walk/run at a medium pace. |
| Friday | Rest | Rest | Rest | Rest | Rest. |
| Saturday | 9 | 14 | S | 17:55 - 20:25 | walk/run at a slow pace. The most important piece of your long duration runs is finishing the run. |
| Sunday | Rest/CT | Rest/CT | Rest | Rest | Rest. If your body feels good, then go ahead and do some form of cross-training for 30 to 60 minutes. |

# Training - Week 9

5K Pace: **16:27**     5k Finish Time: **51 minutes**

| Day | Dist. Mile | Dist. KM | Difficulty | Pace (Range) | Instructions |
|---|---|---|---|---|---|
| Monday | Rest | Rest | Rest | Rest | Take it easy. Don't run. If you need to exercise, I recommend a walk for no longer than 30 minutes. |
| Tuesday | 3 | 5 | E | 17:55 - 19:55 | walk/run at an easy pace. |
| Wednesday | 5 | 8 | HM | 17:55 | walk/run at your half marathon pace. |
| Thursday | 3 | 5 | M | 17:55 - 18:55 | walk/run at a medium pace. |
| Friday | Rest | Rest | Rest | Rest | Rest. |
| Saturday | 8.5 | 13.5 | S | 17:55 - 20:25 | walk/run at a slow pace. The most important piece of your long duration runs is finishing the run. |
| Sunday | Rest/CT | Rest/CT | Rest | Rest | Rest. If your body feels good, then go ahead and do some form of cross-training for 30 to 60 minutes. |

## 13.1 Beta/Test Run Optional

| Day | Dist. Mile | Dist. KM | Difficulty | Pace (Range) | Instructions |
|---|---|---|---|---|---|
| Thursday | Rest | Rest | Rest | Rest | This is a rest day – it simulates race week |
| Friday | Rest | Rest | Rest | Rest | This is a rest day – it simulates race week |
| Saturday | 13.1 | 21 | S | 16:27 | I recommend that you attempt to go the full 13.1 miles (21 km) for a half marathon test run. <u>Only walk/run the first 10 miles (16 km) then walk the last 3.1 miles (5 km)</u>. If you are successful, you will have a race ghost time to compete against. It will help energize and refocus your training on beating yourself in 3 weeks at the half marathon race. Also, it allows your mind to grasp the achievement of "completing the distance of a half marathon." |

# Training - Week 10

5K Pace: **16:27**     5k Finish Time: **51 minutes**

| Day | Dist. Mile | Dist. KM | Difficulty | Pace (Range) | Instructions |
|---|---|---|---|---|---|
| Monday | Rest | Rest | Rest | Rest | Take it easy. Don't run. If you need to exercise, I recommend a walk for no longer than 30 minutes. |
| Tuesday | 3 | 5 | E | 17:55 - 19:55 | walk/run at an easy pace. |
| Wednesday | 5 | 8 | HM | 17:55 | walk/run at your half marathon pace. |
| Thursday | 3 | 5 | M | 17:55 - 18:55 | walk/run at a medium pace. |
| Friday | Rest | Rest | Rest | Rest | Rest. |
| Saturday | 11 | 18 | S | 17:55 - 20:25 | walk/run at a slow pace. The most important piece of your long duration runs is finishing the run. |
| Sunday | Rest/CT | Rest/CT | Rest | Rest | Rest. If your body feels good, then go ahead and do some form of cross-training for 30 to 60 minutes. |

# Training - Week 11

| Day | Dist. Mile | Dist. KM | Difficulty | Pace (Range) | Instructions |
|---|---|---|---|---|---|
| Monday | Rest | Rest | Rest | Rest | Take it easy. Don't run. If you need to exercise, I recommend a walk for no longer than 30 minutes. |
| Tuesday | 3 | 5 | E | 17:55 - 19:55 | walk/run at an easy pace. |
| Wednesday | 5 | 8 | HM | 17:55 | walk/run at your half marathon pace. |
| Thursday | 3 | 5 | M | 17:55 - 18:55 | walk/run at a medium pace. |
| Friday | Rest | Rest | Rest | Rest | Rest. |
| Saturday | 12 | 20 | S | 17:55 - 20:25 | walk/run at a slow pace. The most important piece of your long duration runs is finishing the run. |
| Sunday | Rest/CT | Rest/CT | Rest | Rest | Rest. If your body feels good, then go ahead and do some form of cross-training for 30 to 60 minutes. |

# Training - Week 12

5K Pace: **16:27**     5k Finish Time: **51 minutes**

| Day | Dist. Mile | Dist. KM | Difficulty | Pace (Range) | Instructions |
|---|---|---|---|---|---|
| Monday | Rest | Rest | Rest | Rest | Take it easy. Don't run. If you need to exercise, I recommend a walk for no longer than 30 minutes. |
| Tuesday | 3 | 5 | E | 17:55 - 19:55 | walk/run at an easy pace. |
| Wednesday | 2 | 1.5 | HM | 17:55 | walk/run at your half marathon pace. |
| Thursday | Rest | Rest | Rest | Rest | Rest. |
| Friday | Rest | Rest | Rest | Rest | Rest. |
| Saturday | 13.1 | 21 | HM | 17:55 | RACE DAY! |
| Sunday | Rest | Rest | Rest | Rest | DRINK A VICTORY BEER! |

## NOTE:

- Get plenty of sleep the night before your long duration run.
- Try to run your long duration run early in the morning.
- After each run, it's important to stretch out your muscles.
- This week your body needs as much rest as possible.
- Don't run past Wednesday.

# Beginner to Finisher Running

Half Marathon Training Schedule for

runners with a 5K finish time of 52 minutes

and a pace of *16:46* minutes/mile.

## Predicted Half Marathon Finish Time:
## *3* hour(s) *59* minutes

# PACING TABLES

| Pace | Pace (minutes/miles) |
|---:|:---|
| 5k | 16:46 |
| Half marathon | 18:15 |
| Medium | Between 18:15 - 19:15 |
| Easy | Between 18:15 - 20:15 |
| Slow | Between 18:15 - 20:45 |

| Race | Finish Times (predicted) |
|---:|:---|
| 5k | 52 minutes |
| Half marathon | 3 hour(s) 59 minutes |

| Determining your pace | |
|:---:|:---|
| Slow Pace | Extremely easy to hold a conversation. |
| Easy Pace | You can hold a conversation with someone. Your breathing might break up some of the flow of the conversation. |
| Medium | You can hold a conversation with someone, but it's broken up into smaller sentences and smaller responses. |
| Half Marathon Pace | Conversation is difficult. One and two word responses back and forth at best. |

## Definitions in the table below:

CT = Cross Training

S = Slow Pace (long run pace)

E = Easy Pace

M = Medium Pace

HM = Half Marathon Pace

## Training - Week A (Optional)

5K Pace: **16:46**     5k Finish Time: **52 minutes**

| Day | Dist. Mile | Dist. KM | Difficulty | Pace (Range) | Instructions |
|---|---|---|---|---|---|
| Monday | Rest | Rest | Rest | Rest | Take it easy. Don't run. If you need to exercise, I recommend a walk for no longer than 30 minutes. |
| Tuesday | 1 | 1.5 | E | 18:15 - 20:15 | walk/run at an easy pace. |
| Wednesday | 1 | 1.5 | HM | 18:15 | walk/run at your half marathon pace. |
| Thursday | 1 | 1.5 | M | 18:15 - 19:15 | walk/run at a medium pace. |
| Friday | Rest | Rest | Rest | Rest | Rest. |
| Saturday | 1.5 | 2.5 | S | 18:15 - 20:45 | walk/run at a slow pace. The most important piece of your long duration runs is finishing the run. |
| Sunday | Rest/CT | Rest/CT | Rest | Rest | Rest. If your body feels good, then go ahead and do some form of cross-training for 30 to 60 minutes. |

## Training - Week B (Optional)

| Day | Dist. Mile | Dist. KM | Difficulty | Pace (Range) | Instructions |
|---|---|---|---|---|---|
| Monday | Rest | Rest | Rest | Rest | Take it easy. Don't run. If you need to exercise, I recommend a walk for no longer than 30 minutes. |
| Tuesday | 1.5 | 2.5 | E | 18:15 - 20:15 | walk/run at an easy pace. |
| Wednesday | 1.5 | 2.5 | HM | 18:15 | walk/run at your half marathon pace. |
| Thursday | 1.5 | 2.5 | M | 18:15 - 19:15 | walk/run at a medium pace. |
| Friday | Rest | Rest | Rest | Rest | Rest. |
| Saturday | 2 | 3 | S | 18:15 - 20:45 | walk/run at a slow pace. The most important piece of your long duration runs is finishing the run. |
| Sunday | Rest/CT | Rest/CT | Rest | Rest | Rest. If your body feels good, then go ahead and do some form of cross-training for 30 to 60 minutes. |

# Training - Week C (Optional)

5K Pace: **16:46**     5k Finish Time: **52 minutes**

| Day | Dist. Mile | Dist. KM | Difficulty | Pace (Range) | Instructions |
|---|---|---|---|---|---|
| Monday | Rest | Rest | Rest | Rest | Take it easy. Don't run. If you need to exercise, I recommend a walk for no longer than 30 minutes. |
| Tuesday | 2 | 3 | E | 18:15 - 20:15 | walk/run at an easy pace. |
| Wednesday | 2 | 3 | HM | 18:15 | walk/run at your half marathon pace. |
| Thursday | 2 | 3 | M | 18:15 - 19:15 | walk/run at a medium pace. |
| Friday | Rest | Rest | Rest | Rest | Rest. |
| Saturday | 3 | 5 | S | 18:15 - 20:45 | walk/run at a slow pace. The most important piece of your long duration runs is finishing the run. |
| Sunday | Rest/CT | Rest/CT | Rest | Rest | Rest. If your body feels good, then go ahead and do some form of cross-training for 30 to 60 minutes. |

# Training - Week 1

5K Pace: **16:46**     5k Finish Time: **52 minutes**

| Day | Dist. Mile | Dist. KM | Difficulty | Pace (Range) | Instructions |
|---|---|---|---|---|---|
| Monday | Rest | Rest | Rest | Rest | Take it easy. Don't run. If you need to exercise, I recommend a walk for no longer than 30 minutes. |
| Tuesday | 3 | 5 | E | 18:15 - 20:15 | walk/run at an easy pace. |
| Wednesday | 3 | 5 | HM | 18:15 | walk/run at your half marathon pace. |
| Thursday | 3 | 5 | M | 18:15 - 19:15 | walk/run at a medium pace. |
| Friday | Rest | Rest | Rest | Rest | Rest. |
| Saturday | 4 | 6 | S | 18:15 - 20:45 | walk/run at a slow pace. The most important piece of your long duration runs is finishing the run. |
| Sunday | Rest/CT | Rest/CT | Rest | Rest | Rest. If your body feels good, then go ahead and do some form of cross-training for 30 to 60 minutes. |

# Training - Week 2

| Day | Dist. Mile | Dist. KM | Difficulty | Pace (Range) | Instructions |
|---|---|---|---|---|---|
| Monday | Rest | Rest | Rest | Rest | Take it easy. Don't run. If you need to exercise, I recommend a walk for no longer than 30 minutes. |
| Tuesday | 3 | 5 | E | 18:15 - 20:15 | walk/run at an easy pace. |
| Wednesday | 3 | 5 | HM | 18:15 | walk/run at your half marathon pace. |
| Thursday | 3 | 5 | M | 18:15 - 19:15 | walk/run at a medium pace. |
| Friday | Rest | Rest | Rest | Rest | Rest. |
| Saturday | 5 | 8 | S | 18:15 - 20:45 | walk/run at a slow pace. The most important piece of your long duration runs is finishing the run. |
| Sunday | Rest/CT | Rest/CT | Rest | Rest | Rest. If your body feels good, then go ahead and do some form of cross-training for 30 to 60 minutes. |

# Training - Week 3

5K Pace: **16:46**     5k Finish Time: **52 minutes**

| Day | Dist. Mile | Dist. KM | Difficulty | Pace (Range) | Instructions |
|---|---|---|---|---|---|
| Monday | Rest | Rest | Rest | Rest | Take it easy. Don't run. If you need to exercise, I recommend a walk for no longer than 30 minutes. |
| Tuesday | 3 | 5 | E | 18:15 - 20:15 | walk/run at an easy pace. |
| Wednesday | 4 | 6 | HM | 18:15 | walk/run at your half marathon pace. |
| Thursday | 3 | 5 | M | 18:15 - 19:15 | walk/run at a medium pace. |
| Friday | Rest | Rest | Rest | Rest | Rest. |
| Saturday | 6 | 10 | S | 18:15 - 20:45 | walk/run at a slow pace. The most important piece of your long duration runs is finishing the run. |
| Sunday | Rest/CT | Rest/CT | Rest | Rest | Rest. If your body feels good, then go ahead and do some form of cross-training for 30 to 60 minutes. |

# Training - Week 4 (5K Optional)

5K Pace: **16:46**     5k Finish Time: **52 minutes**

| Day | Dist. Mile | Dist. KM | Difficulty | Pace (Range) | Instructions |
|---|---|---|---|---|---|
| Monday | Rest | Rest | Rest | Rest | Take it easy. Don't run. If you need to exercise, I recommend a walk for no longer than 30 minutes. |
| Tuesday | 3 | 5 | E | 18:15 - 20:15 | walk/run at an easy pace. |
| Wednesday | 4 | 6 | HM | 18:15 | walk/run at your half marathon pace. |
| Thursday | 3 | 5 | M | 18:15 - 19:15 | walk/run at a medium pace. |
| Friday | Rest | Rest | Rest | Rest | Rest. |
| Saturday | 6.5 | 10.5 | S | 18:15 - 20:45 | walk/run at a slow pace. The most important piece of your long duration runs is finishing the run. |
| Sunday | Rest/CT | Rest/CT | Rest | Rest | Rest. If your body feels good, then go ahead and do some form of cross-training for 30 to 60 minutes. |

## 5K Optional

| Day | Dist. Mile | Dist. KM | Difficulty | Pace (Range) | Instructions |
|---|---|---|---|---|---|
| Saturday | 3.1 | 5 | - | 16:46 | Run a 5k race instead of your long run. This is completely your choice. I recommend running a 5k race to help you get used to running races. You should see a difference in your race time if you have kept to your training schedule. Don't try for a personal best, run the 5K at your 5K pace. |

# Training - Week 5

5K Pace: **16:46**     5k Finish Time: **52 minutes**

| Day | Dist. Mile | Dist. KM | Difficulty | Pace (Range) | Instructions |
|---|---|---|---|---|---|
| Monday | Rest | Rest | Rest | Rest | Take it easy. Don't run. If you need to exercise, I recommend a walk for no longer than 30 minutes. |
| Tuesday | 3 | 5 | E | 18:15 - 20:15 | walk/run at an easy pace. |
| Wednesday | 4 | 6 | HM | 18:15 | walk/run at your half marathon pace. |
| Thursday | 3 | 5 | M | 18:15 - 19:15 | walk/run at a medium pace. |
| Friday | Rest | Rest | Rest | Rest | Rest. |
| Saturday | 7 | 11 | S | 18:15 - 20:45 | walk/run at a slow pace. The most important piece of your long duration runs is finishing the run. |
| Sunday | Rest/CT | Rest/CT | Rest | Rest | Rest. If your body feels good, then go ahead and do some form of cross-training for 30 to 60 minutes. |

## NOTE:

- Your long duration runs will begin to become more difficult for week 5 and beyond.
- If you get tired during a long duration run, walk for 1/10 mile or 3-5 minutes.

# Training - Week 6

5K Pace: **16:46**     5k Finish Time: **52 minutes**

| Day | Dist. Mile | Dist. KM | Difficulty | Pace (Range) | Instructions |
|---|---|---|---|---|---|
| Monday | Rest | Rest | Rest | Rest | Take it easy. Don't run. If you need to exercise, I recommend a walk for no longer than 30 minutes. |
| Tuesday | 3 | 5 | E | 18:15 - 20:15 | walk/run at an easy pace. |
| Wednesday | 4 | 6 | HM | 18:15 | walk/run at your half marathon pace. |
| Thursday | 3 | 5 | M | 18:15 - 19:15 | walk/run at a medium pace. |
| Friday | Rest | Rest | Rest | Rest | Rest. |
| Saturday | 8 | 13 | S | 18:15 - 20:45 | walk/run at a slow pace. The most important piece of your long duration runs is finishing the run. |
| Sunday | Rest/CT | Rest/CT | Rest | Rest | Rest. If your body feels good, then go ahead and do some form of cross-training for 30 to 60 minutes. |

# Training - Week 7

5K Pace: **16:46**     5k Finish Time: **52 minutes**

| Day | Dist. Mile | Dist. KM | Difficulty | Pace (Range) | Instructions |
|---|---|---|---|---|---|
| Monday | Rest | Rest | Rest | Rest | Take it easy. Don't run. If you need to exercise, I recommend a walk for no longer than 30 minutes. |
| Tuesday | 3 | 5 | E | 18:15 - 20:15 | walk/run at an easy pace. |
| Wednesday | 5 | 8 | HM | 18:15 | walk/run at your half marathon pace. |
| Thursday | 3 | 5 | M | 18:15 - 19:15 | walk/run at a medium pace. |
| Friday | Rest | Rest | Rest | Rest | Rest. |
| Saturday | 8.5 | 13.5 | S | 18:15 - 20:45 | walk/run at a slow pace. The most important piece of your long duration runs is finishing the run. |
| Sunday | Rest/CT | Rest/CT | Rest | Rest | Rest. If your body feels good, then go ahead and do some form of cross-training for 30 to 60 minutes. |

## 10K Optional

| Day | Dist. Mile | Dist. KM | Difficulty | Pace (Range) | Instructions |
|---|---|---|---|---|---|
| Thursday | 2 | 3 | E | 18:15 - 20:15 | If you run the optional 10K, either completely rest today or run 2 miles (3 km). |
| Saturday | 6.2 | 10K | - | 16:46 | Run a 10k race instead of your long run. This is completely your choice. I recommend running a 10k race to help you get used to running races. You should see a difference in your race time if you have kept to your training schedule. Don't try for a personal best, run the 10K at your 5K pace. |

# Training - Week 8

5K Pace: **16:46**     5k Finish Time: **52 minutes**

| Day | Dist. Mile | Dist. KM | Difficulty | Pace (Range) | Instructions |
|---|---|---|---|---|---|
| Monday | Rest | Rest | Rest | Rest | Take it easy. Don't run. If you need to exercise, I recommend a walk for no longer than 30 minutes. |
| Tuesday | 3 | 5 | E | 18:15 - 20:15 | walk/run at an easy pace. |
| Wednesday | 5 | 8 | HM | 18:15 | walk/run at your half marathon pace. |
| Thursday | 3 | 5 | M | 18:15 - 19:15 | walk/run at a medium pace. |
| Friday | Rest | Rest | Rest | Rest | Rest. |
| Saturday | 9 | 14 | S | 18:15 - 20:45 | walk/run at a slow pace. The most important piece of your long duration runs is finishing the run. |
| Sunday | Rest/CT | Rest/CT | Rest | Rest | Rest. If your body feels good, then go ahead and do some form of cross-training for 30 to 60 minutes. |

# Training - Week 9

5K Pace: **16:46**    5k Finish Time: **52 minutes**

| Day | Dist. Mile | Dist. KM | Difficulty | Pace (Range) | Instructions |
|---|---|---|---|---|---|
| Monday | Rest | Rest | Rest | Rest | Take it easy. Don't run. If you need to exercise, I recommend a walk for no longer than 30 minutes. |
| Tuesday | 3 | 5 | E | 18:15 - 20:15 | walk/run at an easy pace. |
| Wednesday | 5 | 8 | HM | 18:15 | walk/run at your half marathon pace. |
| Thursday | 3 | 5 | M | 18:15 - 19:15 | walk/run at a medium pace. |
| Friday | Rest | Rest | Rest | Rest | Rest. |
| Saturday | 8.5 | 13.5 | S | 18:15 - 20:45 | walk/run at a slow pace. The most important piece of your long duration runs is finishing the run. |
| Sunday | Rest/CT | Rest/CT | Rest | Rest | Rest. If your body feels good, then go ahead and do some form of cross-training for 30 to 60 minutes. |

## 13.1 Beta/Test Run Optional

| Day | Dist. Mile | Dist. KM | Difficulty | Pace (Range) | Instructions |
|---|---|---|---|---|---|
| Thursday | Rest | Rest | Rest | Rest | This is a rest day – it simulates race week |
| Friday | Rest | Rest | Rest | Rest | This is a rest day – it simulates race week |
| Saturday | 13.1 | 21 | S | 16:46 | I recommend that you attempt to go the full 13.1 miles (21 km) for a half marathon test run. <u>Only walk/run the first 10 miles (16 km) then walk the last 3.1 miles (5 km)</u>. If you are successful, you will have a race ghost time to compete against. It will help energize and refocus your training on beating yourself in 3 weeks at the half marathon race. Also, it allows your mind to grasp the achievement of "completing the distance of a half marathon." |

# Training - Week 10

5K Pace: **16:46**     5k Finish Time: **52 minutes**

| Day | Dist. Mile | Dist. KM | Difficulty | Pace (Range) | Instructions |
|---|---|---|---|---|---|
| Monday | Rest | Rest | Rest | Rest | Take it easy. Don't run. If you need to exercise, I recommend a walk for no longer than 30 minutes. |
| Tuesday | 3 | 5 | E | 18:15 - 20:15 | walk/run at an easy pace. |
| Wednesday | 5 | 8 | HM | 18:15 | walk/run at your half marathon pace. |
| Thursday | 3 | 5 | M | 18:15 - 19:15 | walk/run at a medium pace. |
| Friday | Rest | Rest | Rest | Rest | Rest. |
| Saturday | 11 | 18 | S | 18:15 - 20:45 | walk/run at a slow pace. The most important piece of your long duration runs is finishing the run. |
| Sunday | Rest/CT | Rest/CT | Rest | Rest | Rest. If your body feels good, then go ahead and do some form of cross-training for 30 to 60 minutes. |

# Training - Week 11

| Day | Dist. Mile | Dist. KM | Difficulty | Pace (Range) | Instructions |
|---|---|---|---|---|---|
| Monday | Rest | Rest | Rest | Rest | Take it easy. Don't run. If you need to exercise, I recommend a walk for no longer than 30 minutes. |
| Tuesday | 3 | 5 | E | 18:15 - 20:15 | walk/run at an easy pace. |
| Wednesday | 5 | 8 | HM | 18:15 | walk/run at your half marathon pace. |
| Thursday | 3 | 5 | M | 18:15 - 19:15 | walk/run at a medium pace. |
| Friday | Rest | Rest | Rest | Rest | Rest. |
| Saturday | 12 | 20 | S | 18:15 - 20:45 | walk/run at a slow pace. The most important piece of your long duration runs is finishing the run. |
| Sunday | Rest/CT | Rest/CT | Rest | Rest | Rest. If your body feels good, then go ahead and do some form of cross-training for 30 to 60 minutes. |

# Training - Week 12

5K Pace: **16:46**     5k Finish Time: **52 minutes**

| Day | Dist. Mile | Dist. KM | Difficulty | Pace (Range) | Instructions |
|---|---|---|---|---|---|
| Monday | Rest | Rest | Rest | Rest | Take it easy. Don't run. If you need to exercise, I recommend a walk for no longer than 30 minutes. |
| Tuesday | 3 | 5 | E | 18:15 - 20:15 | walk/run at an easy pace. |
| Wednesday | 2 | 1.5 | HM | 18:15 | walk/run at your half marathon pace. |
| Thursday | Rest | Rest | Rest | Rest | Rest. |
| Friday | Rest | Rest | Rest | Rest | Rest. |
| Saturday | 13.1 | 21 | HM | 18:15 | RACE DAY! |
| Sunday | Rest | Rest | Rest | Rest | DRINK A VICTORY BEER! |

## NOTE:

- Get plenty of sleep the night before your long duration run.
- Try to run your long duration run early in the morning.
- After each run, it's important to stretch out your muscles.
- This week your body needs as much rest as possible.
- Don't run past Wednesday.

Half Marathon Training Schedule for

<u>runners with a 5K finish time of 53 minutes</u>

and a pace of *17:05* minutes/mile.

## Predicted Half Marathon Finish Time:

<u>*4* hour(s) *4* minutes</u>

# PACING TABLES

| Pace | Pace (minutes/miles) |
|---:|---|
| 5k | 17:05 |
| Half marathon | 18:36 |
| Medium | Between 18:36 - 19:36 |
| Easy | Between 18:36 - 20:36 |
| Slow | Between 18:36 - 21:06 |

| Race | Finish Times (predicted) |
|---:|---|
| 5k | 53 minutes |
| Half marathon | 4 hour(s) 4 minutes |

| Determining your pace ||
|---|---|
| Slow Pace | Extremely easy to hold a conversation. |
| Easy Pace | You can hold a conversation with someone. Your breathing might break up some of the flow of the conversation. |
| Medium | You can hold a conversation with someone, but it's broken up into smaller sentences and smaller responses. |
| Half Marathon Pace | Conversation is difficult. One and two word responses back and forth at best. |

## Definitions in the table below:

CT = Cross Training

S = Slow Pace (long run pace)

E = Easy Pace

M = Medium Pace

HM = Half Marathon Pace

## Training - Week A (Optional)

5K Pace: **17:05**     5k Finish Time: **53 minutes**

| Day | Dist. Mile | Dist. KM | Difficulty | Pace (Range) | Instructions |
|---|---|---|---|---|---|
| Monday | Rest | Rest | Rest | Rest | Take it easy. Don't run. If you need to exercise, I recommend a walk for no longer than 30 minutes. |
| Tuesday | 1 | 1.5 | E | 18:36 - 20:36 | walk/run at an easy pace. |
| Wednesday | 1 | 1.5 | HM | 18:36 | walk/run at your half marathon pace. |
| Thursday | 1 | 1.5 | M | 18:36 - 19:36 | walk/run at a medium pace. |
| Friday | Rest | Rest | Rest | Rest | Rest. |
| Saturday | 1.5 | 2.5 | S | 18:36 - 21:06 | walk/run at a slow pace. The most important piece of your long duration runs is finishing the run. |
| Sunday | Rest/CT | Rest/CT | Rest | Rest | Rest. If your body feels good, then go ahead and do some form of cross-training for 30 to 60 minutes. |

## Training - Week B (Optional)

| Day | Dist. Mile | Dist. KM | Difficulty | Pace (Range) | Instructions |
|---|---|---|---|---|---|
| Monday | Rest | Rest | Rest | Rest | Take it easy. Don't run. If you need to exercise, I recommend a walk for no longer than 30 minutes. |
| Tuesday | 1.5 | 2.5 | E | 18:36 - 20:36 | walk/run at an easy pace. |
| Wednesday | 1.5 | 2.5 | HM | 18:36 | walk/run at your half marathon pace. |
| Thursday | 1.5 | 2.5 | M | 18:36 - 19:36 | walk/run at a medium pace. |
| Friday | Rest | Rest | Rest | Rest | Rest. |
| Saturday | 2 | 3 | S | 18:36 - 21:06 | walk/run at a slow pace. The most important piece of your long duration runs is finishing the run. |
| Sunday | Rest/CT | Rest/CT | Rest | Rest | Rest. If your body feels good, then go ahead and do some form of cross-training for 30 to 60 minutes. |

# Training - Week C (Optional)

5K Pace: **17:05**     5k Finish Time: **53 minutes**

| Day | Dist. Mile | Dist. KM | Difficulty | Pace (Range) | Instructions |
|---|---|---|---|---|---|
| Monday | Rest | Rest | Rest | Rest | Take it easy. Don't run. If you need to exercise, I recommend a walk for no longer than 30 minutes. |
| Tuesday | 2 | 3 | E | 18:36 - 20:36 | walk/run at an easy pace. |
| Wednesday | 2 | 3 | HM | 18:36 | walk/run at your half marathon pace. |
| Thursday | 2 | 3 | M | 18:36 - 19:36 | walk/run at a medium pace. |
| Friday | Rest | Rest | Rest | Rest | Rest. |
| Saturday | 3 | 5 | S | 18:36 - 21:06 | walk/run at a slow pace. The most important piece of your long duration runs is finishing the run. |
| Sunday | Rest/CT | Rest/CT | Rest | Rest | Rest. If your body feels good, then go ahead and do some form of cross-training for 30 to 60 minutes. |

# Training - Week 1

5K Pace: **17:05**     5k Finish Time: **53 minutes**

| Day | Dist. Mile | Dist. KM | Difficulty | Pace (Range) | Instructions |
|---|---|---|---|---|---|
| Monday | Rest | Rest | Rest | Rest | Take it easy. Don't run. If you need to exercise, I recommend a walk for no longer than 30 minutes. |
| Tuesday | 3 | 5 | E | 18:36 - 20:36 | walk/run at an easy pace. |
| Wednesday | 3 | 5 | HM | 18:36 | walk/run at your half marathon pace. |
| Thursday | 3 | 5 | M | 18:36 - 19:36 | walk/run at a medium pace. |
| Friday | Rest | Rest | Rest | Rest | Rest. |
| Saturday | 4 | 6 | S | 18:36 - 21:06 | walk/run at a slow pace. The most important piece of your long duration runs is finishing the run. |
| Sunday | Rest/CT | Rest/CT | Rest | Rest | Rest. If your body feels good, then go ahead and do some form of cross-training for 30 to 60 minutes. |

# Training - Week 2

| Day | Dist. Mile | Dist. KM | Difficulty | Pace (Range) | Instructions |
|---|---|---|---|---|---|
| Monday | Rest | Rest | Rest | Rest | Take it easy. Don't run. If you need to exercise, I recommend a walk for no longer than 30 minutes. |
| Tuesday | 3 | 5 | E | 18:36 - 20:36 | walk/run at an easy pace. |
| Wednesday | 3 | 5 | HM | 18:36 | walk/run at your half marathon pace. |
| Thursday | 3 | 5 | M | 18:36 - 19:36 | walk/run at a medium pace. |
| Friday | Rest | Rest | Rest | Rest | Rest. |
| Saturday | 5 | 8 | S | 18:36 - 21:06 | walk/run at a slow pace. The most important piece of your long duration runs is finishing the run. |
| Sunday | Rest/CT | Rest/CT | Rest | Rest | Rest. If your body feels good, then go ahead and do some form of cross-training for 30 to 60 minutes. |

# Training - Week 3

5K Pace: **17:05**    5k Finish Time: **53 minutes**

| Day | Dist. Mile | Dist. KM | Difficulty | Pace (Range) | Instructions |
|---|---|---|---|---|---|
| Monday | Rest | Rest | Rest | Rest | Take it easy. Don't run. If you need to exercise, I recommend a walk for no longer than 30 minutes. |
| Tuesday | 3 | 5 | E | 18:36 - 20:36 | walk/run at an easy pace. |
| Wednesday | 4 | 6 | HM | 18:36 | walk/run at your half marathon pace. |
| Thursday | 3 | 5 | M | 18:36 - 19:36 | walk/run at a medium pace. |
| Friday | Rest | Rest | Rest | Rest | Rest. |
| Saturday | 6 | 10 | S | 18:36 - 21:06 | walk/run at a slow pace. The most important piece of your long duration runs is finishing the run. |
| Sunday | Rest/CT | Rest/CT | Rest | Rest | Rest. If your body feels good, then go ahead and do some form of cross-training for 30 to 60 minutes. |

# Training - Week 4 (5K Optional)

5K Pace: **17:05**    5k Finish Time: **53 minutes**

| Day | Dist. Mile | Dist. KM | Difficulty | Pace (Range) | Instructions |
|---|---|---|---|---|---|
| Monday | Rest | Rest | Rest | Rest | Take it easy. Don't run. If you need to exercise, I recommend a walk for no longer than 30 minutes. |
| Tuesday | 3 | 5 | E | 18:36 - 20:36 | walk/run at an easy pace. |
| Wednesday | 4 | 6 | HM | 18:36 | walk/run at your half marathon pace. |
| Thursday | 3 | 5 | M | 18:36 - 19:36 | walk/run at a medium pace. |
| Friday | Rest | Rest | Rest | Rest | Rest. |
| Saturday | 6.5 | 10.5 | S | 18:36 - 21:06 | walk/run at a slow pace. The most important piece of your long duration runs is finishing the run. |
| Sunday | Rest/CT | Rest/CT | Rest | Rest | Rest. If your body feels good, then go ahead and do some form of cross-training for 30 to 60 minutes. |

## 5K Optional

| Day | Dist. Mile | Dist. KM | Difficulty | Pace (Range) | Instructions |
|---|---|---|---|---|---|
| Saturday | 3.1 | 5 | - | 17:05 | Run a 5k race instead of your long run. This is completely your choice. I recommend running a 5k race to help you get used to running races. You should see a difference in your race time if you have kept to your training schedule. Don't try for a personal best, run the 5K at your 5K pace. |

# Training - Week 5

5K Pace: **17:05**     5k Finish Time: **53 minutes**

| Day | Dist. Mile | Dist. KM | Difficulty | Pace (Range) | Instructions |
|---|---|---|---|---|---|
| Monday | Rest | Rest | Rest | Rest | Take it easy. Don't run. If you need to exercise, I recommend a walk for no longer than 30 minutes. |
| Tuesday | 3 | 5 | E | 18:36 - 20:36 | walk/run at an easy pace. |
| Wednesday | 4 | 6 | HM | 18:36 | walk/run at your half marathon pace. |
| Thursday | 3 | 5 | M | 18:36 - 19:36 | walk/run at a medium pace. |
| Friday | Rest | Rest | Rest | Rest | Rest. |
| Saturday | 7 | 11 | S | 18:36 - 21:06 | walk/run at a slow pace. The most important piece of your long duration runs is finishing the run. |
| Sunday | Rest/CT | Rest/CT | Rest | Rest | Rest. If your body feels good, then go ahead and do some form of cross-training for 30 to 60 minutes. |

## NOTE:

- Your long duration runs will begin to become more difficult for week 5 and beyond.
- If you get tired during a long duration run, walk for 1/10 mile or 3-5 minutes.

# Training - Week 6

5K Pace: **17:05**    5k Finish Time: **53 minutes**

| Day | Dist. Mile | Dist. KM | Difficulty | Pace (Range) | Instructions |
|---|---|---|---|---|---|
| Monday | Rest | Rest | Rest | Rest | Take it easy. Don't run. If you need to exercise, I recommend a walk for no longer than 30 minutes. |
| Tuesday | 3 | 5 | E | 18:36 - 20:36 | walk/run at an easy pace. |
| Wednesday | 4 | 6 | HM | 18:36 | walk/run at your half marathon pace. |
| Thursday | 3 | 5 | M | 18:36 - 19:36 | walk/run at a medium pace. |
| Friday | Rest | Rest | Rest | Rest | Rest. |
| Saturday | 8 | 13 | S | 18:36 - 21:06 | walk/run at a slow pace. The most important piece of your long duration runs is finishing the run. |
| Sunday | Rest/CT | Rest/CT | Rest | Rest | Rest. If your body feels good, then go ahead and do some form of cross-training for 30 to 60 minutes. |

# Training - Week 7

5K Pace: **17:05**   5k Finish Time: **53 minutes**

| Day | Dist. Mile | Dist. KM | Difficulty | Pace (Range) | Instructions |
|---|---|---|---|---|---|
| Monday | Rest | Rest | Rest | Rest | Take it easy. Don't run. If you need to exercise, I recommend a walk for no longer than 30 minutes. |
| Tuesday | 3 | 5 | E | 18:36 - 20:36 | walk/run at an easy pace. |
| Wednesday | 5 | 8 | HM | 18:36 | walk/run at your half marathon pace. |
| Thursday | 3 | 5 | M | 18:36 - 19:36 | walk/run at a medium pace. |
| Friday | Rest | Rest | Rest | Rest | Rest. |
| Saturday | 8.5 | 13.5 | S | 18:36 - 21:06 | walk/run at a slow pace. The most important piece of your long duration runs is finishing the run. |
| Sunday | Rest/CT | Rest/CT | Rest | Rest | Rest. If your body feels good, then go ahead and do some form of cross-training for 30 to 60 minutes. |

## 10K Optional

| Day | Dist. Mile | Dist. KM | Difficulty | Pace (Range) | Instructions |
|---|---|---|---|---|---|
| Thursday | 2 | 3 | E | 18:36 - 20:36 | If you run the optional 10K, either completely rest today or run 2 miles (3 km). |
| Saturday | 6.2 | 10K | - | **17:05** | Run a 10k race instead of your long run. This is completely your choice. I recommend running a 10k race to help you get used to running races. You should see a difference in your race time if you have kept to your training schedule. Don't try for a personal best, run the 10K at your 5K pace. |

# Training - Week 8

5K Pace: **17:05**     5k Finish Time: **53 minutes**

| Day | Dist. Mile | Dist. KM | Difficulty | Pace (Range) | Instructions |
|---|---|---|---|---|---|
| Monday | Rest | Rest | Rest | Rest | Take it easy. Don't run. If you need to exercise, I recommend a walk for no longer than 30 minutes. |
| Tuesday | 3 | 5 | E | 18:36 - 20:36 | walk/run at an easy pace. |
| Wednesday | 5 | 8 | HM | 18:36 | walk/run at your half marathon pace. |
| Thursday | 3 | 5 | M | 18:36 - 19:36 | walk/run at a medium pace. |
| Friday | Rest | Rest | Rest | Rest | Rest. |
| Saturday | 9 | 14 | S | 18:36 - 21:06 | walk/run at a slow pace. The most important piece of your long duration runs is finishing the run. |
| Sunday | Rest/CT | Rest/CT | Rest | Rest | Rest. If your body feels good, then go ahead and do some form of cross-training for 30 to 60 minutes. |

# Training - Week 9

5K Pace: **17:05**    5k Finish Time: **53 minutes**

| Day | Dist. Mile | Dist. KM | Difficulty | Pace (Range) | Instructions |
|---|---|---|---|---|---|
| Monday | Rest | Rest | Rest | Rest | Take it easy. Don't run. If you need to exercise, I recommend a walk for no longer than 30 minutes. |
| Tuesday | 3 | 5 | E | 18:36 - 20:36 | walk/run at an easy pace. |
| Wednesday | 5 | 8 | HM | 18:36 | walk/run at your half marathon pace. |
| Thursday | 3 | 5 | M | 18:36 - 19:36 | walk/run at a medium pace. |
| Friday | Rest | Rest | Rest | Rest | Rest. |
| Saturday | 8.5 | 13.5 | S | 18:36 - 21:06 | walk/run at a slow pace. The most important piece of your long duration runs is finishing the run. |
| Sunday | Rest/CT | Rest/CT | Rest | Rest | Rest. If your body feels good, then go ahead and do some form of cross-training for 30 to 60 minutes. |

## 13.1 Beta/Test Run Optional

| Day | Dist. Mile | Dist. KM | Difficulty | Pace (Range) | Instructions |
|---|---|---|---|---|---|
| Thursday | Rest | Rest | Rest | Rest | This is a rest day – it simulates race week |
| Friday | Rest | Rest | Rest | Rest | This is a rest day – it simulates race week |
| Saturday | 13.1 | 21 | S | 17:05 | I recommend that you attempt to go the full 13.1 miles (21 km) for a half marathon test run. <u>Only walk/run the first 10 miles (16 km) then walk the last 3.1 miles (5 km).</u> If you are successful, you will have a race ghost time to compete against. It will help energize and refocus your training on beating yourself in 3 weeks at the half marathon race. Also, it allows your mind to grasp the achievement of "completing the distance of a half marathon." |

# Training - Week 10

5K Pace: **17:05**     5k Finish Time: **53 minutes**

| Day | Dist. Mile | Dist. KM | Difficulty | Pace (Range) | Instructions |
|---|---|---|---|---|---|
| Monday | Rest | Rest | Rest | Rest | Take it easy. Don't run. If you need to exercise, I recommend a walk for no longer than 30 minutes. |
| Tuesday | 3 | 5 | E | 18:36 - 20:36 | walk/run at an easy pace. |
| Wednesday | 5 | 8 | HM | 18:36 | walk/run at your half marathon pace. |
| Thursday | 3 | 5 | M | 18:36 - 19:36 | walk/run at a medium pace. |
| Friday | Rest | Rest | Rest | Rest | Rest. |
| Saturday | 11 | 18 | S | 18:36 - 21:06 | walk/run at a slow pace. The most important piece of your long duration runs is finishing the run. |
| Sunday | Rest/CT | Rest/CT | Rest | Rest | Rest. If your body feels good, then go ahead and do some form of cross-training for 30 to 60 minutes. |

# Training - Week 11

| Day | Dist. Mile | Dist. KM | Difficulty | Pace (Range) | Instructions |
|---|---|---|---|---|---|
| Monday | Rest | Rest | Rest | Rest | Take it easy. Don't run. If you need to exercise, I recommend a walk for no longer than 30 minutes. |
| Tuesday | 3 | 5 | E | 18:36 - 20:36 | walk/run at an easy pace. |
| Wednesday | 5 | 8 | HM | 18:36 | walk/run at your half marathon pace. |
| Thursday | 3 | 5 | M | 18:36 - 19:36 | walk/run at a medium pace. |
| Friday | Rest | Rest | Rest | Rest | Rest. |
| Saturday | 12 | 20 | S | 18:36 - 21:06 | walk/run at a slow pace. The most important piece of your long duration runs is finishing the run. |
| Sunday | Rest/CT | Rest/CT | Rest | Rest | Rest. If your body feels good, then go ahead and do some form of cross-training for 30 to 60 minutes. |

# Training - Week 12

5K Pace: **17:05**     5k Finish Time: **53 minutes**

| Day | Dist. Mile | Dist. KM | Difficulty | Pace (Range) | Instructions |
|---|---|---|---|---|---|
| Monday | Rest | Rest | Rest | Rest | Take it easy. Don't run. If you need to exercise, I recommend a walk for no longer than 30 minutes. |
| Tuesday | 3 | 5 | E | 18:36 - 20:36 | walk/run at an easy pace. |
| Wednesday | 2 | 1.5 | HM | 18:36 | walk/run at your half marathon pace. |
| Thursday | Rest | Rest | Rest | Rest | Rest. |
| Friday | Rest | Rest | Rest | Rest | Rest. |
| Saturday | 13.1 | 21 | HM | 18:36 | RACE DAY! |
| Sunday | Rest | Rest | Rest | Rest | DRINK A VICTORY BEER! |

## NOTE:

- Get plenty of sleep the night before your long duration run.
- Try to run your long duration run early in the morning.
- After each run, it's important to stretch out your muscles.
- This week your body needs as much rest as possible.
- Don't run past Wednesday.

# How to use the following training log:

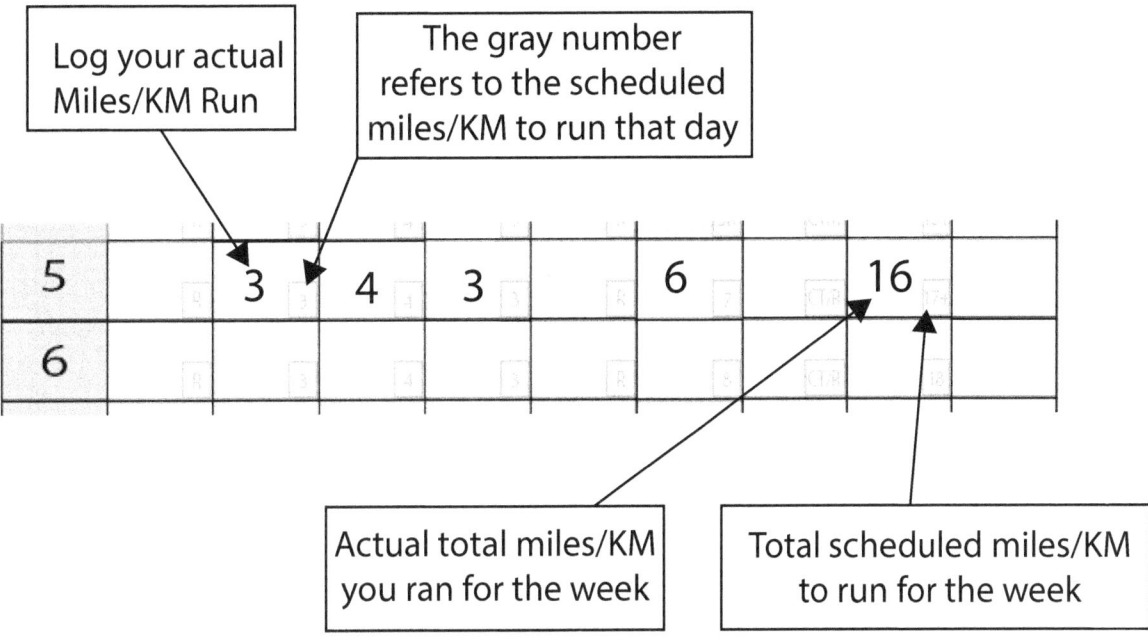

# How to use the following Long Run Fueling log:

| Week # | BEGINNER TO FINISHER RUNNING - LONG RUN FUELING LOG | | | HOW DO YOU FEEL? | NOTES |
| --- | --- | --- | --- | --- | --- |
| | PRE-RUN | FUEL DURING RUN | POST-RUN | | |
| 10 | 2 eggs, 1 cup oatmeal, 2 pieces cinn. bread | 4 x GU gels every 30 min | 1 banana<br>1 apple | ☹ 😕 😐 🙂 😊 | |

## BEGINNER TO FINISHER RUNNING - BEGINNER HALF MARATHON TRAINING SCHEDULE (MILES)

| Week # | Monday | Tuesday | Wednesday | Thursday | Friday | Saturday | Sunday | Weekly Totals | Notes |
|---|---|---|---|---|---|---|---|---|---|
| 1 | R | 3 | 3 | 3 | R | 4 | CT/R | 13 | |
| 2 | R | 3 | 3 | 3 | R | 5 | CT/R | 14 | |
| 3 | R | 3 | 4 | 3 | R | 6 | CT/R | 16 | |
| 4 | R | 3 | 4 | 3 | R | 5K | CT/R | 13+ | |
| 5 | R | 3 | 4 | 3 | R | 7 | CT/R | 17+ | |
| 6 | R | 3 | 4 | 3 | R | 8 | CT/R | 18 | |
| 7 | R | 3 | 5 | 3 | R | 10K | CT/R | 17 | |
| 8 | R | 3 | 5 | 3 | R | 9 | CT/R | 20 | |
| 9 | R | 3 | 5 | R | R | 13.1 | CT/R | 18+ | |
| 10 | R | 3 | 5 | 3 | R | 11 | CT/R | 22 | |
| 11 | R | 3 | 5 | 3 | R | 12 | CT/R | 23 | |
| 12 | R | 3 | 2 | R | R | HM | CT/R | 18 | |

## BEGINNER TO FINISHER RUNNING - BEGINNER HALF MARATHON TRAINING SCHEDULE (KILOMETERS)

| Week # | Monday | Tuesday | Wednesday | Thursday | Friday | Saturday | Sunday | Weekly Totals | Notes |
|---|---|---|---|---|---|---|---|---|---|
| 1 | R | 5 | 5 | 5 | R | 6 | CT/R | 21 | |
| 2 | R | 5 | 5 | 5 | R | 8 | CT/R | 23 | |
| 3 | R | 5 | 6 | 5 | R | 10 | CT/R | 26 | |
| 4 | R | 5 | 6 | 5 | R | 5K | CT/R | 21 | |
| 5 | R | 5 | 6 | 5 | R | 11 | CT/R | 27 | |
| 6 | R | 5 | 6 | 5 | R | 13 | CT/R | 29 | |
| 7 | R | 5 | 8 | 5 | R | 10K | CT/R | 28 | |
| 8 | R | 5 | 8 | 5 | R | 14 | CT/R | 30 | |
| 9 | R | 5 | 8 | R | R | 21 | CT/R | 33 | |
| 10 | R | 5 | 8 | 5 | R | 18 | CT/R | 36 | |
| 11 | R | 5 | 8 | 5 | R | 20 | CT/R | 38 | |
| 12 | R | 5 | 2 | R | R | HM | CT/R | 28 | |

## BEGINNER TO FINISHER RUNNING - BEGINNER HALF MARATHON TRAINING SCHEDULE

| Week # | Monday | Tuesday | Wednesday | Thursday | Friday | Saturday | Sunday | Weekly Totals | Notes |
|---|---|---|---|---|---|---|---|---|---|
| | | | | | | | | | |
| | | | | | | | | | |
| | | | | | | | | | |
| | | | | | | | | | |
| | | | | | | | | | |
| | | | | | | | | | |
| | | | | | | | | | |
| | | | | | | | | | |
| | | | | | | | | | |
| | | | | | | | | | |
| | | | | | | | | | |
| | | | | | | | | | |

## BEGINNER TO FINISHER RUNNING - LONG RUN FUELING LOG

| Week # | PRE-RUN | FUEL DURING RUN | POST-RUN | HOW DO YOU FEEL? | NOTES |
|---|---|---|---|---|---|
| 1 | | | | :) :) :\| :( :( | |
| 2 | | | | :) :) :\| :( :( | |
| 3 | | | | :) :) :\| :( :( | |
| 4 | | | | :) :) :\| :( :( | |
| 5 | | | | :) :) :\| :( :( | |
| 6 | | | | :) :) :\| :( :( | |
| 7 | | | | :) :) :\| :( :( | |
| 8 | | | | :) :) :\| :( :( | |
| 9 | | | | :) :) :\| :( :( | |
| 10 | | | | :) :) :\| :( :( | |
| 11 | | | | :) :) :\| :( :( | |
| 12 | | | | :) :) :\| :( :( | |

## Standard Training Schedule (12 weeks)

| Week # | Mon. | Tues. (EP) | Wed. (HMP) | Thur. (MP) | Fri. | Sat. (LD) | Sun. |
|---|---|---|---|---|---|---|---|
| 1 | Rest | 3 mi | 3 mi | 3 mi | Rest | 4 mi | Rest/CT |
| 2 | Rest | 3 mi | 3 mi | 3 mi | Rest | 5 mi | Rest/CT |
| 3 | Rest | 3 mi | 4 mi | 3 mi | Rest | 6 mi | Rest/CT |
| 4 | Rest | 3 mi | 4 mi | 3 mi | Rest | 5k | Rest/CT |
| 5 | Rest | 3 mi | 4 mi | 3 mi | Rest | 7 mi | Rest/CT |
| 6 | Rest | 3 mi | 4 mi | 3 mi | Rest | 8 mi | Rest/CT |
| 7 | Rest | 3 mi | 5 mi | 3 mi | Rest | 10K | Rest/CT |
| 8 | Rest | 3 mi | 5 mi | 3 mi | Rest | 9 mi | Rest/CT |
| 9 | Rest | 3 mi | 5 mi | Rest | Rest | Beta 13.1 | Rest/CT |
| 10 | Rest | 3 mi | 5 mi | 3 mi | Rest | 11 mi | Rest/CT |
| 11 | Rest | 3 mi | 5 mi | 3 mi | Rest | 12 mi | Rest/CT |
| 12 | Rest | 3 mi | 2 mi | Rest | Rest | HM | Rest/CT |

```
EP=Easy Pace, HMP=Half Marathon Pace,
MP=Medium Pace, LD=Long Duration, CT=Cross Train
```

## Compact

| | M | T | W | T | F | Sa | S |
|---|---|---|---|---|---|---|---|
| 1 | R | 3 | 3 | 3 | R | 4 | R/CT |
| 2 | R | 3 | 3 | 3 | R | 5 | R/CT |
| 3 | R | 3 | 4 | 3 | R | 6 | R/CT |
| 4 | R | 3 | 4 | 3 | R | 5k | R/CT |
| 5 | R | 3 | R | 3 | R | 7 | R/CT |
| 6 | R | 3 | 4 | 3 | R | 8 | R/CT |
| 7 | R | 3 | 5 | 3 | R | 10K | R/CT |
| 8 | R | 3 | 5 | 3 | R | 9 | R/CT |
| 9 | R | 3 | 5 | R | R | B13.1 | R/CT |
| 10 | R | 3 | 5 | 3 | R | 11 | R/CT |
| 11 | R | 3 | 5 | 3 | R | 12 | R/CT |
| 12 | R | 3 | 2 | R | R | HM | R/CT |

```
R=Rest, CT=Cross Train
```

## Beginner Training Schedule (15 weeks)

| Week # | Mon. | Tues. (EP) | Wed. (HMP) | Thur. (MP) | Fri. | Sat. (LD) | Sun. |
|---|---|---|---|---|---|---|---|
| A | Rest | 1 mi | 1 mi | 1 mi | Rest | 1.5 mi | Rest/CT |
| B | Rest | 1.5 mi | 1.5 mi | 1.5 mi | Rest | 2 mi | Rest/CT |
| C | Rest | 2 mi | 2 mi | 2 mi | Rest | 3 mi | Rest/CT |
| 1 | Rest | 3 mi | 3 mi | 3 mi | Rest | 4 mi | Rest/CT |
| 2 | Rest | 3 mi | 3 mi | 3 mi | Rest | 5 mi | Rest/CT |
| 3 | Rest | 3 mi | 4 mi | 3 mi | Rest | 6 mi | Rest/CT |
| 4 | Rest | 3 mi | 4 mi | 3 mi | Rest | 5k | Rest/CT |
| 5 | Rest | 3 mi | 4 mi | 3 mi | Rest | 7 mi | Rest/CT |
| 6 | Rest | 3 mi | 4 mi | 3 mi | Rest | 8 mi | Rest/CT |
| 7 | Rest | 3 mi | 5 mi | 3 mi | Rest | 10K | Rest/CT |
| 8 | Rest | 3 mi | 5 mi | 3 mi | Rest | 9 mi | Rest/CT |
| 9 | Rest | 3 mi | 5 mi | Rest | Rest | Beta 13.1 | Rest/CT |
| 10 | Rest | 3 mi | 5 mi | 3 mi | Rest | 11 mi | Rest/CT |
| 11 | Rest | 3 mi | 5 mi | 3 mi | Rest | 12 mi | Rest/CT |
| 12 | Rest | 3 mi | 2 mi | Rest | Rest | HM | Rest/CT |

EP=Easy Pace, HMP=Half Marathon Pace, MP=Medium Pace, LD=Long Duration, CT=Cross Train

## Compact

| | M | T | W | T | F | Sa | S |
|---|---|---|---|---|---|---|---|
| A | R | 1 | 1 | 1 | R | 1.5 | R/CT |
| B | R | 1.5 | 1.5 | 1.5 | R | 2 | R/CT |
| C | R | 2 | 2 | 2 | R | 3 | R/CT |
| 1 | R | 3 | 3 | 3 | R | 4 | R/CT |
| 2 | R | 3 | 3 | 3 | R | 5 | R/CT |
| 3 | R | 3 | 4 | 3 | R | 6 | R/CT |
| 4 | R | 3 | 4 | 3 | R | 5k | R/CT |
| 5 | R | 3 | R | 3 | R | 7 | R/CT |
| 6 | R | 3 | 4 | 3 | R | 8 | R/CT |
| 7 | R | 3 | 5 | 3 | R | 10K | R/CT |
| 8 | R | 3 | 5 | 3 | R | 9 | R/CT |
| 9 | R | 3 | 5 | R | R | B13.1 | R/CT |
| 10 | R | 3 | 5 | 3 | R | 11 | R/CT |
| 11 | R | 3 | 5 | 3 | R | 12 | R/CT |
| 12 | R | 3 | 2 | R | R | HM | R/CT |

R=Rest, CT=Cross Train

# Beginner's Guide to Half Marathons: A Simple Step-by-step solution to get you to the finish line in 12 weeks!

### Standard (Kilometers)

| Week | Mon | Tue | Wed | Thur | Fri | Sat | Sun |
|---|---|---|---|---|---|---|---|
| 1 | Rest | 5 | 5 | 5 | Rest | 6 | CT/Rest |
| 2 | Rest | 5 | 5 | 5 | Rest | 8 | CT/Rest |
| 3 | Rest | 5 | 6 | 5 | Rest | 10 | CT/Rest |
| 4 | Rest | 5 | 6 | 5 | Rest | 5K Race | CT/Rest |
| 5 | Rest | 5 | 6 | 5 | Rest | 11 | CT/Rest |
| 6 | Rest | 5 | 6 | 5 | Rest | 13 | CT/Rest |
| 7 | Rest | 5 | 8 | 5 | Rest | 10K Race | CT/Rest |
| 8 | Rest | 5 | 8 | 5 | Rest | 14 | CT/Rest |
| 9 | Rest | 5 | 8 | Rest | Rest | 21 Beta | CT/Rest |
| 10 | Rest | 5 | 8 | 5 | Rest | 18 | CT/Rest |
| 11 | Rest | 5 | 8 | 5 | Rest | 20 | CT/Rest |
| 12 | Rest | 5 | 2 | Rest | Rest | Half Marathon | CT/Rest |

**CT**=Cross Training (30 minutes of biking, walking, yoga, or weight lifting, if you have the energy. If not then simply rest).
**21 Beta**=A half marathon test run. Run 16 km and then walk the remaining 5 kms.

### Beginner (Kilometers)

| Week | Mon | Tue | Wed | Thur | Fri | Sat | Sun |
|---|---|---|---|---|---|---|---|
| A | Rest | 1.5 | 1.5 | 1.5 | Rest | 2.5 | CT/Rest |
| B | Rest | 2.5 | 2.5 | 2.5 | Rest | 3 | CT/Rest |
| C | Rest | 3 | 3 | 3 | Rest | 5 | CT/Rest |
| 1 | Rest | 5 | 5 | 5 | Rest | 6 | CT/Rest |
| 2 | Rest | 5 | 5 | 5 | Rest | 8 | CT/Rest |
| 3 | Rest | 5 | 6 | 5 | Rest | 10 | CT/Rest |
| 4 | Rest | 5 | 6 | 5 | Rest | 5K Race | CT/Rest |
| 5 | Rest | 5 | 6 | 5 | Rest | 11 | CT/Rest |
| 6 | Rest | 5 | 6 | 5 | Rest | 13 | CT/Rest |
| 7 | Rest | 5 | 8 | 5 | Rest | 10K Race | CT/Rest |
| 8 | Rest | 5 | 8 | 5 | Rest | 14 | CT/Rest |
| 9 | Rest | 5 | 8 | Rest | Rest | 21 Beta | CT/Rest |
| 10 | Rest | 5 | 8 | 5 | Rest | 18 | CT/Rest |
| 11 | Rest | 5 | 8 | 5 | Rest | 20 | CT/Rest |
| 12 | Rest | 5 | 2 | Rest | Rest | Half Marathon | CT/Rest |

**CT**=Cross Training (30 minutes of biking, walking, yoga, or weight lifting, if you have the energy. If not then simply rest).
**21 Beta**=A half marathon test run. Run 16 km and then walk the remaining 5 kms.

LERK
Publishing

© 2017 - All rights reserved

# About the Author

I played sports throughout my youth and even into my adult years. I ran my first 5k at the age of 37 in March of 2008 without any training at all. I finished third place, although my leg muscles felt like I deserved first place. My legs were sore for six days after the race. My next 5k attempt was in 2015 at the age of 42 in my local hometown. I had no intention of placing at all. I ended up running worse than my first 5k by almost two minutes. I placed second with no training at all. I thought I would have learned a lesson by now - nope.

In May 2016, I was flying to Las Vegas for our yearly guys' trip. I was reading a *Sky Mall* magazine, and I came across an article called "Top 100 things to do in Las Vegas." Number eight on the list was run a race through the streets of Las Vegas. During the race, the city blocks off sections of the strip. I was hooked. They offered a 5k, 10k, half marathon and marathon. I liked walking a lot; in fact, one of my favorite things to do in Las Vegas was to see how many steps I could get in a day (my record to date is 42,000). The Rock-and-Roll Half Marathon/Marathon would be taking place in November 2016. I scoured the Internet for any information related to training for a half marathon.

My wife asked me, "Why in the world do you want to run a half marathon?" I told her because I was physically able to. She said, "You just want to put one of those 13.1 stickers on the back of your car." But truthfully the real reason was much deeper than that. Whenever I catch a fresh dump of powder on my snowboard, there is no other experience like it. I feel like a kid again, and I feel alive. The real reason I wanted to run was because I wanted to feel the accomplishment, feel the pain and feel the glory of crossing the finish line all the while feeling alive. Running allows me to unleash that competitive kid inside me who yearns to feel alive.

# Help an Author Out

Thanks for reading! If you've enjoyed this book, please leave me a short, gleaming review on Amazon. I take the time to read every review so that I can change and update this book based on reviewer feedback.

## http://geni.us/ZzGBs

If you've just finished your first half marathon race and you want someone to tell, send me an email. I would be delighted to hear from you.

**Follow me on Facebook and Twitter:**

Twitter: @BeginR2FinishR

Facebook: facebook.com/BeginnerToFinisher/

Website: www.halfmarathonforbeginners.com

Email: scottmorton@halfmarathonforbeginners.com

# Other Books by Scott O. Morton

## Beginner to Finisher Series:

**Book 1:** *Why New Runners Fail: 26 Ultimate Tips You Should Know Before You Start Running!*

**Book 2**: *5K Fury: 10 Proven Steps to Get You to the Finish Line in 9 weeks or less!*

**Book 3:** *10K Titan: Push Beyond the 5K in 6 Weeks or Less!*

**Book 4:** *Beginner's Guide to Half Marathons: A Simple Step-By-Step Solution to Get You to the Finish Line in 12 Weeks!*

**Book 5:** *Long Run Hacks: 20 Ultimate Tips to Help You Push Through Hard Runs!*

**Book 6:** *How to Avoid a Half Marathon Meltdown: 10 Things You Need to Know to Make Sure Your First Half Marathon Isn't Your Last!*

**Book 7:** *Marathon Machine - Breakthrough Your Running Barrier in 18 weeks and Conquer Your Dream! (COMING SOON)*

## Supercharge Your Walking Life:

**Book 1:** *42,000 Steps: 100 simple ways to maximize your daily step count!*

**Book 2:** *Supercharged Walking: 20 Simple Methods to Help You Level Up Your Stride!*

**Book 3:** *Walkathon - The Ultimate Guide to Walking a 5K, 10K, Half Marathon, or Marathon!*

www.ingramcontent.com/pod-product-compliance
Lightning Source LLC
Chambersburg PA
CBHW080405230426
43662CB00016B/2323